WHITHER GOD BRINGS US

Cambridge and the Reformation Martyrs

DAVID LLEWELLYN JENKINS

CHARENTON REFORMED PUBLISHING
2018

Typeset in Bembo Mt Pro 12 on 14 point
by Quinta Press, Weston Rhyn, Oswestry, Shropshire

Printed and bound in Great Britain by Lightning Source

British Library Cataloguing in Publication Data.

A catalogue record for this book is available from the British Library.

Cover concept: A.C. Clifford, formatting by Barkers Print & Design, Attleborough, Norfolk

Image: In 1538 Thomas Cromwell ordered that a copy of the Great Bible—the first authorized edition of the Bible in English—be stationed in every parish church, thus underlining the move to a new Christianity. An illustration from a popular abridgement of Foxe's *Acts and Monuments* (London: Adams, 1873).

To my parents

PREFACE

This book may lay claim to being new in the sense that it attempts to do something that has not been done before, at least not in modern times: to examine, in a single volume, the lives of the twenty-two Cambridge scholars martyred in England and Wales in the reigns of Henry VIII and Mary Tudor. Marcus Loane, in his exemplary *The Masters of the English Reformation*, fixed his attention on the three leading lights of the period 1547 to 1556—Thomas Cranmer, Hugh Latimer and Nicholas Ridley—along with William Tyndale and Thomas Bilney from the first wave of reform. D'Aubigné's classic *The Reformation in England* captures and conveys all the excitement and thrill of the making of English Protestantism, but closes with the death of Henry VIII. With the exception of Tyndale—who, research has shown, was almost certainly not at Cambridge—the present volume has chapters on each of the luminaries mentioned above. The motive and centre of the book, however, is to accord full lives to eighteen lesser-known figures, to penetrate their ideas, and in many cases to rescue them from undeserved oblivion. I wanted to deal with them on their own terms, not ours: to understand the doctrine to which they cleaved and illustrate its bearing on their labours and suffering. A corollary aim is to explicate the teaching of Martin Bucer (1491–1551) and suggest how his two-year exile in Cambridge might have shaped the personal theologies of pupils such as John Bradford. The decisive part played by the university in the rediscovery of the Gospel is appraised, as is the relationship between humanism and evangelical theology.

One issue should be clarified at the outset: this is no impartial study. I stand outside of an intellectual climate which affords little scope for Bible-based enquiry, as well as little readiness to allow for the workings of the Spirit of God in the lives of individual men and women. I have no interest in reconciling secular deliberations on the Christian life. I believe that the truth of God is immortal, not one of a number of relative, competing narratives. My priority here is to record, as far as I am able, how the actions of the martyrs of the English Reformation were dictated by what God says through His Word: how they cast aside pride and self-sufficiency and were enabled to 'continue in one spirit, and in one mind, fighting together through the faith of the Gospel' (Philippians 1:27).

My desire to keep as accurate a record as possible of my obligations to others explains the copious footnotes throughout the book. These are mainly concerned with direct quotations, or areas where I relied heavily on someone else's work. Some of the spelling and punctuation has been modernized, usually for fluency's sake. The Select Bibliography represents a fair selection of the studies I have found most useful. The foundation of the book as a whole is John Foxe's *Acts and Monuments*, an inescapable—and, as J.F. Mozley has established—wholly reliable text for anyone sailing these waters. Unless otherwise indicated, Scripture is taken from the 1599 Geneva Bible. Scholars of a previous generation invariably refer to the twenty-five martyrs of Cambridge University. We must now exclude Tyndale from that list; nor can we include, I think, William Roye. Roye matriculated at Wittenberg University—as 'Guilhelmus Roy ex Londino'—in 1525, but any evidence that he was at Cambridge is elusive. George Wishart certainly *was* at Cambridge. He entered Corpus Christi College by 1542 and was burnt on 1 March 1545/6 in St Andrews. His story, however, properly belongs to that of the Scottish Reformation, and I have not included it here. One short detour—into the martyrdom of Anne Askew—was taken in order to demonstrate the cohesiveness of the reform movement outside the university towns.

Without Mr Heber Martin and the Farthing Trust this book would not exist. Heber brought the idea of a book about the martyrs of Cambridge University to me seven years ago. He has given unstinting help and encouragement ever since, including early financial support, while allowing me to get on with the project uninterrupted. I can never adequately repay my debt to him; I only hope he considers the book worthy of his trust.

It is a pleasure as well as an obligation to thank the librarians and archivists whose co-operation has lightened my labour in the following locations: British Library, Cambridge University Library, Corpus Christi College Cambridge, Eton College, King's College Cambridge, National Archives, National Library of Wales, Norfolk Record Office, Dr Williams's Library and York Minster Library. I am especially beholden to Jayne Ringrose, Deputy Keeper of Manuscripts at Cambridge University Library, and to Peter Meadows,

Keeper of the Ely Diocesan Records; to Susan Maddock, Principal Archivist of Norfolk Record Office, and to Sophie Cabot of Norwich Heritage Economic and Regeneration Trust, for sharpening my analysis of the trial and execution of Thomas Bilney. Zoe Stansell of the British Library's Maps and Manuscripts Service helped with important spadework in fields adjacent to the story of Thomas Dusgate. I must also acknowledge the generous help I have received from a host of specialists, not least from Richard Rex, Reader in Reformation History at Cambridge University. Although our approaches to the theology of the Reformation are poles apart, every enquiry directed to Dr Rex was answered with promptness and courtesy.

In Aberystwyth debts of a more personal nature are owed to Professor R.M. (Bobi) Jones and to Dr Geoffrey Thomas for boosting my morale and making it clear they believed in the usefulness of the book. In Norwich Dr Alan Clifford and his wife Marian showed limitless faith in the enterprise; their kindliness and generosity to me over many years never ceases to earn my gratitude. Dr Clifford has been throughout a staunch friend and peerless advisor, but the responsibility for the final form of the volume, and for any infelicities or errors it may contain, remains with the author alone. Len Smeath and Stephen Quinton gave timely support; Pru Bell and Sally Wilde entered fully into the spirit and purpose of my work. Meadow Lyons kept me going through an aggregation of difficulties; Lucy Kemp was a precious friend and an inspiration. By her Christian example, Rosemary Quinton was more important to the writing of this book than she will ever realize. She and her late husband Mike read the first drafts of most of the chapters, and gave the kind of uncomplicated approval an author clings to in the early stages of a book. Finally, and always, my greatest personal debt is to my parents, David and Megan, for their unconditional love at every turn of my life.

Wortwell and Aberystwyth
November 2017
D. Ll. J.

CONTENTS

I

ROBERT BARNES,

Richard Bayfield, Thomas Garrard, William Jerome

The church of St Edward King and Martyr, adjacent to the Arts Theatre and skirted by alleys and a pedestrianized street, sits on the crest of Peas Hill, Cambridge. A sandstone tower is rugged, unbroken and bright. Iron railings support pushbikes and a flock of fly-posters. Along the south chancel wall are heaped the chilled leaves of winter; inside the mood is dictated by a Perpendicular nave, two side chapels and a window by Sir Gilbert Scott. A notice introduces St Edward's as 'a centre for meditative Christianity'; a relentlessly inclusive line-up of events includes a 'Goth Eucharist'. Look elsewhere, and most of what you see would be comfortably familiar to past generations. Just to sit in a church in Cambridge, whose streets are defined by its colleges and churches, is to invite feelings of bygone days. But for someone on the trail of Reformation history, St Edward's offers something else, something that cannot be effaced by outward tokens of our sad, distracted age.

Dusk falls. Spots of rain are blown on a gusty wind; lights come on in the Arts Theatre and in shop windows. It all makes the church seem emptier, the evening more raw. On the brink of darkness, in the airless quiet, as rain patters against stained-glass, a shaft of ghost-light hits the base of the pulpit. Thoughts and imaginings shoot to and fro, from past to present, in a single moment, and it seems apt to trace the linenfold woodwork of the pulpit, to glance above the lofty chancel arch, and to conjure, in one's mind's eye, the evening of Christmas Eve 1525. On that date, and from this pulpit, a Lutheran scholar was to recast the shape of the English church.

Robert Barnes was born in King's Lynn in 1495. On the eve of his tenth birthday he was admitted to the house of Austin friars in Cambridge. A gifted pupil, he was granted the means, in 1517 or thereabouts, to pursue his education at Louvain, the university town in the Brabant province of present-day Belgium. It is entirely possible that he studied under Erasmus. Upon his return to England in 1521 Barnes began to teach, and was nominated prior of his house. Under his tutelage the eyes of young Augustinians were opened to the works of Cicero, Terence and Plautus. The letters of Paul were also accorded a place of honour. By 1523 Barnes had proceeded BTh and DTh at the university, and hundreds of students were thronging to the Augustine lecture hall to hear 'the restorer of letters', as his admirers styled him, discussing classical literature. An excitement clung to his name. To the horror of the conservatively-minded, he also joined George Stafford in expounding Scripture from Greek and Hebrew sources. Unlike Stafford, however, Robert Barnes had yet to acknowledge that *faith is by hearing, and hearing by the Word of God* (Romans 10:17). His fearlessness and ability to draw a crowd, not to mention the élan with which he outflanked opponents, had alerted the university authorities to a potential enemy in their midst. But Barnes was emotionally removed from the ideas he expounded. All this changed when he was introduced to Thomas Bilney. Also responsible for the conversions of Hugh Latimer and John Lambert (both q.v.), 'Little Bilney' was certain the brilliant Augustinian might be purged of 'his inward and outward idolatry'.[1] As a pre-eminent humanist, and proven popularizer, Barnes mattered. The efforts of Bilney, directed by simple confidence in the grace of God, quickly bore fruit. Foxe reports that 'before [Bilney's] last preaching in London, he, with Master Arthur, Master Stafford, and Master Thistel of Pembroke-hall, converted Dr Barnes to the gospel of Jesus Christ our Saviour'.[2]

Barnes began to attend the meetings held at the White Horse tavern, dubbed 'Little Germany' by the Catholic affinity. The White Horse was located across the road from Corpus Christi, on King's Lane, just west of King's Parade. A tiny door opening onto Milne Street allowed more cautious souls to slip in incognito. Bilney and Barnes, Crome and Shaxton, Parker and Lambert, Stafford and Arthur, and perhaps a dozen others, would begin to assemble in the early evening, moving off in twos and threes along King's Parade. En route they would be subjected to jeers and catcalls. 'There are the Germans' was the usual cry, 'going to Germany!' Once inside, the ideas

---

1 John Foxe, *Acts & Monuments* (London, 1838), v. 415
2 Foxe (London, 1837), iv. 620.

of Luther and the deficiencies of the old order would be sifted and weighed until dawn. Some would drop out, temporarily befuddled, only to return later, text in hand. It was an exhilarating time. A dangerous time.

Barnes made his presence felt. He is referred to in one record as 'the usual chairman' of the meetings. Another denizen of the White Horse, reflecting on the immutability of the Word and the fleetingness of youth, wrote that 'So oft as I was in the company of these brethren, me thought I was quietly placed in the new glorious Jerusalem'.[1]

On Christmas Eve 1525, at the church of St Edward King and Martyr, Barnes preached what has been called the first evangelical sermon of the English church. Though his most scathing remarks were aimed at Thomas Wolsey—the luxury of Hampton Court was contrasted with the stable in Bethlehem—Barnes tore into every corruption of doctrine supported and maintained 'in the present day by papists'. The holy church, he held, 'is the congregation of faithful men wherever they are in the world. Neither the pope nor yet his cardinals are more this church or of this church than the poorest men on earth'.[2] In *A Supplication*, a treatise printed by Simon Cock in Antwerp in 1531 (a revised edition appeared in London in 1534) Barnes expands upon the contents of his Christmas Eve sermon. One of the defining texts of the English Reformation, *A Supplication* upholds Christ as the substance of our justification, and the Word as the foundation of all true religion. It has been described by Carl Trueman as 'the nearest thing to a work of systematic theology that the Henrician Reformers produced'.[3] The moving force and bracing polemic that infuse *A Supplication* have led some to conclude that outside of Tyndale, Barnes stands as the most important English Reformer of the 1520s and early 1530s. Others take issue with that opinion, inclining towards Frith, or even Bilney. What seems inarguable, however, is that Barnes' contribution to the shaping of an English Protestant identity has been undervalued.

Among the more attentive listeners to Barnes' sermon were two fellows of King's College, Robert Ridley and Walter Preston. Both were related to Cuthbert Tunstall, bishop of Durham. Both were there for no other purpose than to report back to Tunstall any injudicious remarks the Augustine might

---

1   Becon, ii. 426 (Cambridge, 1843–4)
2   *A Critical Edition of Barnes' Supplication,* ed. Douglas H. Parker (Toronto, 2008), 560.
3   *Luther's Legacy, Salvation and the English Reformers, 1525–1556* (Oxford, 1994), 3.

make. At the end of the service, as Barnes headed off into the night, and
students, wide-eyed with conjecture, drifted back to their colleges, Ridley
and Preston remained, comparing notes and devising stratagems. In the
morning the whole of Cambridge was a-buzz with Barnes' sermon; to some
it seemed that the axis of the church had shifted overnight. With the help
of one Dr Nottoris, a 'rank enemy to Christ',[1] Ridley and Preston raised
twenty-five articles against Barnes. When the articles were handed over to
the authorities, Barnes wrote that the matter was handled 'secretly in the
common schools, the doors locked, and in the vice-chancellor's chamber, for
they knew well that all men of learning were against them'.[2] He remained
spiritedly unrepentant, knowing that 'no man among them ... could ever
say of his conscience but that these things that I had spoken against the
bishops were true'.[3]

But the truth, to frightened men, was expendable. The dignity of the
church was not. Barnes was granted eight days to reflect upon his offending
behaviour. A message was sent to Wolsey that heresy was rife in Cambridge.
Increasingly frustrated at the failure of his own campaign to staunch the flow
of 'pestilent books' being smuggled into London and the university towns,
and incensed at the personal nature of Barnes' attack, the ruler of the English
church decided that a decisive strike against Lutheran heresy was overdue.

On 5 February 1526, at the convocation house in Cambridge, Barnes was
arrested in the presence of his friends by Master Gibson, Wolsey's sergeant-
at-arms. Gibson had come hotfoot from St Thomas Apostle's in London.
Flanked by Wolsey's chaplain and a bodyguard, he broadcast his intention
to search the rooms of all those suspected of owning illicit texts. This was
no speculative venture; the Bible-men had been infiltrated by informers.
The sergeant-at-arms brandished a list of thirty men he expected to arrest,
including Bilney, Latimer, Stafford and Arthur. But in the hiatus between
Barnes' arrest and the search beginning, Dr Farman of Queen's College
sent runners to all parts of the university to signal danger. A burst of almost
comically frenzied activity ensued, with banned books flying out of windows,
being lobbed across roofs and stuffed into a variety of hiding-places. By the
time Gibson began his search the cupboard, so to speak, was bare. He burst

---

1   Foxe, v. 415.
2   Parker, 512.
3   Ibid. 512–513.

into a succession of rooms whose occupants, while appearing slightly out of breath, imparted little concern. But the main prize, from Gibson's point of view, had already been secured. The next morning Barnes was taken as a prisoner to London. Touchingly, he was followed by three of his students, none knowing the fate that awaited their hero, but each resolved that he would not face it alone. One of these was Miles Coverdale, the future Bible translator.

On Thursday 8th February, at the end of a day spent in solemn contemplation and fervent prayer, Barnes was ushered into Wolsey's private chamber. Alongside the seated lord chancellor were Stephen Gardiner, Wolsey's secretary, and Edward Foxe, master of the Wards and future architect of the king's divorce. Gardiner is synonymous with the worst excesses of the Marian regime. But in 1526, a fresh-faced man still in his twenties, he was not yet the embittered operator he was to become. He had known Barnes at Cambridge. Happy days spent in amateur theatricals and in debates at the White Horse tavern were still fresh in his memory. 'Barnes', wrote Gardiner in 1545, five years after the Lutheran's death, 'whom I knew first at Cambridge, was a trim minion Augustine, one of a merry scoffing wit, friarlike, and as a good fellow in company was beloved by many'.[1] In Barnes' interview with Wolsey, Gardiner adopted a quasi-defence counsel role, assuring the cardinal at the outset that 'we trust you will find him reformable, for he is both well-learned and wise'.[2]

Wolsey was unmoved. A man of Barnes' stamp would always be troubling to someone as fluid in his opinions and contradictory in his nature as Wolsey. He had given Henry's tumultuous reign its face: or, rather, a dozen faces. The cardinal leant forward, flexing his cramped, pudgy fingers, his tone at once solemn and gently mocking:

What!—master doctor, had you not sufficient scope in the Scriptures to teach to the people, but that my golden shoes, my pole-axes, my pillars, my golden cushions, my crosses did sore offend you, that you must make us ridiculous among the people? We were jollily that day laughed to scorn. Verily it was a sermon more fit to be preached on a stage than in

---

1   Parker, 102.
2   Foxe, v. 416.

a pulpit; for at the last you said I wear a pair of red gloves—to quote you 'bloody gloves'—that I should not be cold in the midst of my ceremonies.[1]

To which Barnes answered that he 'spake nothing but the truth out of the Scriptures, according to my conscience, and according to the old doctors'.[2] God was with him indeed, and he was with God. To address such remarks to the most powerful churchman in English history is a breath-catching lesson in Christian obedience. But Barnes was not finished: in fact, he had scarcely begun. Under the horrified gaze of Gardiner and Foxe, he held up a sheaf of papers which, he claimed, substantiated all he had said. The carnal cardinal snatched up a page. Did Barnes really think he ought to gather up the symbols of his office, sell them, and give the proceeds to the poor?—the *poor*, repeated Wolsey, almost choking on the word, 'who shortly will cast it against the wall?'[3] Barnes didn't bat an eyelid. 'I think it necessary', he said. 'For this is not comely for your calling, nor is the king's majesty maintained by your pomp and pole-axes; but by God who saith "Kings and their majesties reign and stand by me"'.[4] It is easy to imagine the muscles in Wolsey's fleshy face sagging. As Gardiner and Foxe sank to their knees, wailing 'he will be reformable', Wolsey turned malignantly upon the Augustine: 'How say you, Master Doctor; do you not know that I am *Legatus de latere*[5] and that I am able to dispense in all matters of religion within this realm, as much as the pope may?' Barnes agreed that this was so. 'Will you then be ruled by us, and we will do all things for your honesty, and for the honesty of the university?'[6] Barnes gazed steadfastly back. 'I will stick to the holy Scripture and to God's book', he replied, 'according to the simple talent that God hath lent me'.[7] The interview was over. Gardiner and Foxe half-steered, half-pulled Barnes out of the legatine presence.

Barnes, reports Foxe, 'should have gone to the Tower, but that Gardiner and Foxe became his sureties that night'.[8] Instead he was returned to the home of one Master Parnell, where, in the company of the three students

---

1   Ibid.
2   Ibid.
3   Ibid. 417.
4   Ibid.
5   The highest order of papal legate.
6   Foxe, v. 417.
7   Ibid.
8   Ibid.

who had followed him from Cambridge, he 'fell to writing again and slept not'.[1] Further interviews saw him committed to the Fleet prison. In a letter to the king, Barnes wrote that 'there are certain men like conditioned to dogs; if there be any man that is not their countryman, or that they love not, or know not, say anything against them, then cry they: an heretic, an heretic, to the fire, to the fire! These be the dogs that fear true preachers'. On the 11 February 1526 Barnes was taken from his cell and conducted to St Paul's. There he was forced to carry a faggot of wood under the eyes of Wolsey ('enthronised ... like a bloody antichrist')[2] and thirty-six abbots, friars and bishops, arrayed like peacocks in their damask and satin gowns, seated upon a stand specially constructed for the occasion. Alongside four Steelyard Lutherans,[3] all convicted of smuggling Tyndale's New Testament into London, Barnes knelt before John Fisher, the bishop of Rochester,[4] while he inveighed against the person and teaching of Luther. Baskets of 'pestylent bokes' were carried outside and added to an already raging bonfire. Barnes was walked three times around the perimeter; at the end he tossed his faggot into the flames. He was then granted absolution and placed under house arrest at the Austin Friary in London: his home for the next two years. He was forbidden to return to Cambridge.

The ritual at Paul's Cross steeled Barnes' resolve to establish the Word as the source of all authority, civil and religious. Those who would keep the nation stupefied and spiritually disenfranchised had to be bested. To that end he forged links with the Lollard underground, and established the house of Austin friars as a centre for the circulation of Tyndale's New Testament. The Latin Text was compared to 'a cymbal tinkling, and brass sounding'.[5] With Thomas More's agents crawling all over the London docks, it is likely that Barnes drew on ties with his birthplace, the port of King's Lynn, to smuggle in books from Antwerp, Worms and Cologne. In October 1526, two Lollards, John Tyball and Thomas Hilles, each purchased a New Testament from Barnes at a combined cost of three shillings. They also prompted Barnes to enter into correspondence with Richard Fox, a Lollard leader who doubled as curate of Steeple Bumstead. The notorious Joan Bocher, also known as

---

1   Ibid.
2   Ibid. 418.
3   Merchants of the Steelyard, the London counter of the Hanseatic League.
4   Fisher was also chancellor of Cambridge University.
5   Strype, *Ecclesiastical Memorials,* 3 vols. in 6 (Oxford, 1822), 1–2.55 (*LP*, 4/2.4218).

Joan of Kent, was an associate of Fox.[1] In 1528 Tyball and Hilles, betrayed by 'caterpillars and bloody beasts'[2] within the Austin House, fell into the hands of bishop Tunstall. Their confession led to Barnes' arrest and removal to the Austin priory in Northampton, to await examination and burning.

Though what happens next might appear to belong to a work of fiction, it demonstrates, as much as anything else, how contingent life was in this period: how at any moment a disaster might strike, or an opportunity present itself. Barnes was seen looking disconsolate. He was overheard talking about suicide. He gave every indication of being a broken man. And when, one thundery dawn, a boy brought word that a pile of clothes had been found on a river bank, the news was greeted with irritation more than surprise. A suicide note was found, addressed to Wolsey. In a letter to the mayor of Northampton, Barnes claimed that another message for Wolsey, encased in wax, was tied around his neck. The agitated authorities spent seven days dragging the river. But Barnes, bursting with vigour and dressed in 'a poor man's apparel'[3] had fled to London, where the Lollards smuggled him on board a ship bound for the Continent. When the deception was uncovered, the church hierarchy was apoplectic. 'The cardinal will catch him even now', raged Tunstall, 'whatever amount of money it may cost him'.[4] To the world at large Barnes was a desperate figure, cast adrift from his friends and from all he had known and held dear. But his spiritual posture had never been more upright. 'I am a poor and simple wretch,' wrote he, 'not worth the tenth penny they will gain for me. Besides, if they burn me, what will they gain by it? The sun and moon, fire and water, the stars and the elements, yea, and also the stones shall defend this cause against them rather than the truth shall perish'.[5] Under the shield of his Saviour's mercy, he sailed first to Antwerp before travelling on to eastern Germany: to Wittenberg, the capital of what we now call Saxony-Anhalt.

Originally a 12th century settlement on the northern shore of the Elbe river, Wittenberg had nearly three thousand inhabitants by the time of Barnes' arrival. Due to the vision of its elector, Frederick the Wise, Wittenberg

---

1 In 1550 Bocher was arrested for preaching that Christ was not incarnate of Mary. She was condemned as an anabaptist and burned at Smithfield.

2 Foxe, v. 419.

3 Ibid.

4 Quoted in J. H. Merle d'Aubigné, *The Reformation in England* (London, 1962), i. 274.

5 Ibid.

boasted a Renaissance castle, an elegant castle church, and painting workshops under the supervision of Lucas Cranach the elder. But the Wittenbergers' greatest source of civic pride was their university. Luther's assumption in 1512 of the professorial chair in Bible, and the election of Philipp Melanchthon as professor of Greek, had ushered in a new epoch. Students from all over Europe flocked to Wittenberg in unprecedented numbers. Barnes kept no record of his years in exile. But we know from other sources that he enrolled at the university under the name of Antonius Anglus. The adoption of an assumed name by a refugee was an established means of avoiding exposure and arrest; William Tyndale is thought to have studied at Wittenberg in 1524 under the pseudonym of 'Daltici', a slightly misspelt anagram of his real name. And John Frith, known to Barnes from his Cambridge days, published a book in Antwerp in 1529 as 'Richard Brightwell'.

Barnes was a frequent houseguest of Luther and Melanchthon. Luther called him 'mi Antoni', and praised him as one of those 'saints who have eaten with us, drunk with us (as the apostles say of Christ, *Acts 4*), and joined in our happiness'.[1] In 1530, by which time he was living with the Reformer Johannes Buganhagen, he took advantage of Wittenberg's network of printing houses to publish his first extended work, usually called *The Sentences* in English.[2] It was printed by Johannes Klug, with Buganhagen providing a preface. As a no-nonsense debating manual for ordinary Protestants, *The Sentences* is hard to fault. Nineteen points are affirmed, including that we are justified by faith, that we are morally impotent outside of Christ, and that priests may take wives in marriage. Saints should not be called on as mediators. Monks are no more holy than laymen. Nor does papal excommunication harm the excommunicated. *The Sentences* proved wildly popular. Two editions were published in 1531 alone. Only two years after his dramatic flight from Northampton, the 'stormy petrel of English Lutheranism'[3] had established a Europe-wide reputation.

It was in Wittenberg that Barnes developed an understanding of the Lord's Supper that would set him apart from other key figures in the English Reformation. It cannot be regarded as immaterial that Barnes was in Germany at the time of the Marburg Colloquy, convened by Landgrave Philipp of Hesse

---

1   *D. Martin Luther's Werke, Kritische Gesamtausgabe, Schriften*, 62 vols. (Weimar, 1883–1986).
2   *Sentenciae ex doctoribus collectae, quas papistae valde impudenter hodie damnant.*
3   Diarmaid MacCulloch, *Thomas Cranmer* (New Haven, 1996), 216.

to settle disputes between Lutherans and Zwinglians. Barnes rejected the
doctrine of transubstantiation; the bread and wine of the eucharist, he said,
do not cease to be bread and wine at any stage. But he was equally dismissive
of the Christ-absence view of the Swiss. Like most Lutherans, Barnes held a
view akin, though not identical, to consubstantiation.[1] He wholeheartedly
preached recognition of the risen Lord through the breaking of bread. But
whereas Roman Catholics identified the sign (the bread) with the thing
signified (the body of Christ), and the Swiss divorced them, Barnes saw, in
the sacramental act of eating and drinking, a union between the two. So in
Barnes'—more properly Luther's—scheme of things, the actual body of our
Lord can be said to be *with* the bread, rather than in it. The Supper is the
sacrament of Christ's body: 'the words by which the body is made', wrote
Barnes, 'were given by the Lord Himself'.[2] This conception, says Korey
Maas, 'not only distances Barnes from those who hold a symbolic view of
the elements; it also distinguishes him from those who argue that the body
of Christ is present virtually and only on account of the communicant's
faith'.[3] The latter group would include John Calvin, Martin Bucer and
Peter Martyr Vermigli.

Barnes' ties to German Lutheranism, and espousal of its traditional doctrine,
explains to a large extent the lack of generosity that attaches itself to discussions
of his legacy. His memory was not, says Clebsch, 'resurrected by English
romantic historical scholarship in the nineteenth century as was that of
Tyndale and, to a lesser degree, that of Frith'.[4] J.A. Wylie, in *The History of
Protestantism*, a fixture on Christian shelves since 1878, avoids mentioning
Barnes at all. Others place the least complimentary construction upon his
motives. Thus he was 'somewhat imprudent'[5] in his pursuit of truth. To

---

1   A.G. Voight, in his *Biblical Dogmatics* (Columbia, 1917), 214–15, expertly navigates this
terminological barrier reef: 'In the Lord's Supper there is an earthly material, bread and wine, and a
celestial material, the body and blood of Christ. The doctrine of transubstantiation identifies these.
That of consubstantiation confuses and mingles them. The symbolic doctrine separates them. The
Lutheran doctrine of the real presence unites them. The Lutheran church holds to a sacramental
union, unique in its nature, of the terrestrial and the celestial, but only in the sacramental act of
eating and drinking'.

2   *Sentenciae*, sig. K5r. See Maas, 52.

3   Maas, 54.

4   Clebsch, 57.

5   D'Aubigné, i. 235.

attack Wolsey's avarice was 'a foolish action'.[1] His advice to the king was both 'presumptuous' and 'impertinent'.[2] His seminal action at St Edward's was 'more marked by hot language than by honest proclamation of the Gospel'.[3] His fears are represented as cowardice ('he trembled like a leaf').[4] And his daunting intellect apparently disguised 'something undecided in his character'.[5] In any impartial appraisal of Barnes' remarkable life a very different kind of individual emerges: one who promised himself safety in God, and in nothing else. One who believed that wholehearted work in the Gospel cause could never fail. Amidst darkness and chaos and the threat of violent death he did his best and he did his utmost.

Much to the consternation of opponents at home—chief among them Thomas More, the lord chancellor, whose hatred of Barnes was said to eclipse even his hatred of Tyndale—in the summer of 1531 Barnes' career sprouted a tentative branch in another direction. He was asked, in all likelihood by Thomas Cromwell, to elicit Luther's opinion on Henry VIII's 'Great Matter': his proposed divorce from Catherine of Aragon. Given its less-than-respectful tone, claims that *A Supplication* made Barnes' commission possible seem undercooked. More likely, it was a move born of Henry's growing desperation. Barnes' diplomatic status ensured his safe, though temporary, return to England. He met with supporters, some of whom had subsidised his European mission. He debated with senior clerics. Thomas More was furious, ranting that Barnes was an enemy of civilised order and '[had] clearly broken and forfeited his safe conduct, and lawfully might be burned for his heresies'.[6] More was in error. John Frith scrutinized Barnes' accreditation and confirmed that there were no conditions attached, other than that Barnes should land in England by Christmas 1531. Frith then wrote to More, alleging that 'notwithstanding his safe conduct you were minded to murder him'.[7]

A Supplication had created more of a stir than Barnes could ever have imagined. Thomas More read it and said that of all the books so far arrived from the Continent 'there was none yet so bad, so foolish, nor so false

1   Parker, 4.
2   Parker, 28.
3   Marcus Loane, *Masters of the English Reformation* (London, rep. 1956), 16.
4   D'Aubigné, i. 263.
5   Ibid. 235.
6   Quoted in Brian Moynahan, *If God Spare my Life* (London, 2002), 344.
7   Quoted in *John Frith, Scholar and Martyr* (Sevenoaks, 2000), 99.

as this'.[1] In a counterblast he described Lutheranism as a 'mad poisoned process', and Barnes' restatement of it as 'Bible babble'. A torrent of abuse is spewed out upon the heretic with a 'gargoyle face'[2] who had surpassed Tyndale 'in witless eloquence'.[3] But Stephen Vaughan, Cromwell's agent in the Low Countries, bid his master to 'Look well upon Dr Barnes' book. It is such a piece of work as I have not yet seen any like it. I think he shall seal it with his blood'.[4] In fact, as we have learnt, Barnes' value to the king had, for the time being, put him beyond the reach of his enemies. More, says Foxe, 'would fain have entrapped him, but the king would not let him, for Cromwell was his great friend'.[5] But More was biding his time. 'Let him go this once', he wrote chillingly, 'for God shall find his time full well'.[6] Besides, an opportunity for More to exercise his pathology of vengeance had arrived in the form of Richard Bayfield, another in our company of Cambridge martyrs, and one of Barnes' most highly-regarded protégés.

In the early 1520s Barnes rode to the abbey of Bury St Edmunds to call on Edmund Rougham, a friend from his student days at Louvain. Since the early Middle Ages the abbey had been one of the richest and most venerated of all the Benedictine monasteries. By 1535 the prior was reporting an income of £2,336 16s 11d: a quite staggering sum for the day. Every year £400 was given to the poor; the monks also distributed 'broken meat' among the sick and bedridden. In the course of his visit Barnes was introduced to Richard Bayfield, the chamberlain of the abbey. Although Hadleigh in Suffolk is generally given as Bayfield's birthplace, one of his aliases—thought to have been a locative name—suggests a link with Somersham, a few miles north-east of Hadleigh. Barnes, we are told, was sufficiently taken with Bayfield to gift him an edition of Erasmus' Latin New Testament. Also visiting the abbey that day were two of Barnes' Lollard friends: Laurence Maxwell and John Stacey. These working men, wardens of the company of brickmakers, being 'well grafted in the doctrine of Christ',[7] won Bayfield's heart by their quiet decency. Before leaving they too presented him with books: Tyndale's

---

1   Quoted in Neelak S. Tjernagel, *The Reformation Essays of Dr Robert Barnes* (London, 1963), 7.
2   Ibid.
3   Ibid. 67.
4   Ibid. 7.
5   Foxe, v. 419.
6   *Complete Works of Thomas More* (New Haven & London, 1973), 11.
7   Foxe, iv. 681.

New Testament, *The Parable of the Wicked Mammon* and *The Obedience of a Christian Man*. Bayfield's life was changed forever. In the days and nights ahead he was gripped by a holy compulsion to resist Roman ritual and cleave instead to the Word of God, to which faith itself cleaves. His dreams were feverishly agitated; their unbalanced mood lingered until dawn. On his knees, at his bedside, he offered God the sacrifice of a contrite heart. 'Wherein', writes Foxe, 'he prospered so mightily in two years' space, that he was cast into the prison of his house, there sore whipped, with a gag in his mouth, and then stocked; and so continued in the same torment three quarters of a year before Dr Barnes could get him out'.[1]

Barnes took him to Cambridge, where he came under the influence of Thomas Bilney. 'By the time he had been there a good while', says Foxe, 'he tasted so well of good letters, that he never returned home again to his abbey'.[2] He is thought to have been admitted to Corpus Christi College, but this has proved impossible to verify. Given his closeness to Barnes, it seems likely that Bayfield would have heard the famous sermon at St Edward's on Christmas Eve 1525. Upon his mentor's arrest, and fearing for his own safety, Bayfield fled to London and sought the protection of his Lollard friends, Maxwell and Stacy.

One day, weary of his hiding place, Bayfield ventured out and was spotted crossing Lombard Street by two former friends. 'You must depart forthwith',[3] urged Maxwell, and bundled him down to the docks to find a ship bound for Antwerp. In the years ahead, as a trusted confidant of Tyndale and Frith, Bayfield replaced Thomas Garrard (q.v.) as the main supplier of prohibited books to the English market. He was quite fearless. On his first trip he narrowly escaped detection after landing on the Norfolk coast. On another occasion he shipped a cargo of books to St Katherine's dock, a stone's throw from the Tower itself. Eventually he was betrayed by the infamous George Constantine. A Cambridge canon lawyer, Constantine had decamped to the Low Countries in 1528. Having met Tyndale in Antwerp, he sailed to England in 1531 with a consignment of illegal Testaments. More's men were waiting. Constantine was arrested and personally examined by More in the porter's lodge of his house in Chelsea. He immediately turned king's evidence,

---

1   Ibid.
2   Ibid.
3   Quoted in D'Aubigné, i. 268.

babbling out the names of confederates and revealing details of their plans. He was then allowed to escape; the lord chancellor joking with his porter that they should secure the house 'lest the prisoner try to steal back in'.[1]

Many years later, as diocesan registrar of St David's in Wales, Constantine would plot the downfall of bishop Robert Ferrar (q.v.). But in October 1531, his duplicity resulted in Richard Bayfield's arrest at a bookbinders' shop in Mark Lane. Bayfield was taken to the Tower and shackled to the wall of the coal-house 'by the neck, middle and legs'.[2] More took charge of his interrogation. No candle burned in the coal-house; Bayfield stood in darkness throughout his ordeal. Each day, shivering with cold, he was shaken out of befuddled sleep to be threatened, cajoled and pressed for the names of his customers. He 'accused none, however, but stood to his religion and confession of his faith, unto the very end'.[3] It is hard to believe that More's treatment of Bayfield was not driven, at least in part, by his paranoid animus towards Barnes. Not for the first time, the lord chancellor betrayed his sordid obsession with married clerics. He accused the former monk of having 'two wives, one in Brabant, another in England',[4] an allegation entirely rooted in fantasy, wholly exhibitive of the inner life of a man whose sexuality, in the words of his biographer, 'was easily aroused'.[5] More was a sadomasochist. Every day he wore a rough and knotted hair shirt to chafe his skin. And he enjoyed being flogged by his favourite daughter, Margaret, as much as he enjoyed flogging heretics in his garden at Chelsea.

In the course of Bayfield's appearance at a hastily convened episcopal court, John Stokesley, bishop of London, demanded that he explain his motives in bringing the 'errors of Luther ... and others of that damnable sect'[6] into England. Bayfield replied, 'To make the Gospel known and to glorify God before the people'.[7] At the hearing a list of the books Bayfield was responsible for importing was read out. The quantity of books trafficked, as well as their diversity and difficulty, staggers the mind. Luther, Oecolampadius and Melanchthon provide several titles apiece; Wolfgang Capito is well represented,

1   Quoted in Moynahan, 256.
2   Foxe, iv. 681.
3   Ibid.
4   Quoted in Moynahan, 259.
5   Peter Ackroyd, *The Life of Thomas More* (London, rep. 1999), 100.
6   Quoted in D'Aubigné, ii. 76–77.
7   Ibid. 77.

as is Bucer, as is Frith, whose *A Disputation of Purgatory* Bayfield read 'to himself alone'.[1] Tyndale's *The Parable of the Wicked Mammon* was widely-used; *The Obedience of the Christian Man*, with its descriptions of idle princes being manipulated by venal clerics, even more so. Bayfield's condemnation was assured. At his ritual degrading, Stokesley struck Bayfield so savage a blow with his crozier that the Reformer fell to the ground. He momentarily lost consciousness. But in the blood that filled his mouth he tasted the sweetness of divine closeness; soon, he whispered, his heart would be purged of its impiety and he would 'be in heaven with Jesus Christ, and the church triumphant forever'.[2] His head clearing, Bayfield struggled to his feet, praising God for his deliverance from the hands of antichrist.

On 4 December 1531, Richard Bayfield was led to the stake in Smithfield. Due to the dampness of the day, and the greenness of the wood, the Benedictine stood among the flames for over three-quarters of an hour. Foxe reports that 'when the left arm was on fire and burned, he rubbed it with his right hand, and it fell from his body, and he continued in prayer to the end without moving'.[3] Thomas More, with conspicuous smugness, wrote that Bayfield, 'the monk and apostata', was 'well and worthely burned in Smythfelde'.[4] Shortly afterwards a leather merchant named John Tewkesbury, another of Constantine's victims, endured his own examination at the hand of 'Saint' Thomas. In the lord chancellor's garden he was tied to a tree, 'whipped, and also twisted in his brows with small ropes, so that blood started in his eyes'.[5] Like Bayfield before him, a beautiful spirit of truth allowed him to rise above these earthly terrors. After being sent to the Tower, Tewkesbury was racked until he was lame before being burnt at Smithfield.

That so ardent an advocate of reform as Robert Barnes, whom Henry had always disliked and distrusted, was nevertheless in royal service until the last year of his life shows the degree to which his fortunes were linked to those of Cromwell. The king's chief minister, already entrusted with the nation's domestic and foreign policy, would, in the period 1535/6, be appointed vicar-general and vicegerent. Geoffrey Elton has shown that 'so far from confining himself to a non-religious secularism, [Cromwell] quite

---

1 Foxe, iv. 683.
2 Ibid. 688.
3 Ibid.
4 Quoted in Ackroyd, 297.
5 Foxe, iv. 689.

consciously undertook to introduce the religious Reformation into England'.[1] While his star remained in the ascendant, Barnes was safe. Safer, certainly, than Thomas More, who by the time of Barnes' next visit to England, in the summer of 1534, was imprisoned in the Tower for his views on the king's divorce. The promptness of Barnes' compassion is striking. 'Truly, as God shall judge me, I am sorry for his trouble', he said. 'If I could help him with any lawful means, I would do my best'.[2] His tender feeling was not reciprocated. Even in the Tower, the former lord chancellor gave vent to the blind lust of fury that toiled darkly within him: 'The air longs to blow noxious vapours against [Barnes]', he wrote. 'The sea longs to overwhelm him in its waves, the mountains to fall upon him, the valleys to rise up to him, the earth to split open beneath him, hell to swallow him up after his headlong fall, the demons to plunge him into gulfs of ever-burning flames'.[3] Weeks away from his own execution, More was still scheming against Barnes. In April 1535, in the same plot that resulted in the capture of Tyndale, Barnes narrowly avoided arrest in Antwerp. Thomas More was beheaded on 6 July 1535, a fortnight after John Fisher. He died bravely, his beliefs intact, his good death being used ever since to sanctify a bad cause.

Barnes' diplomatic portfolio embraced efforts to bring Melanchthon to England and to persuade Cochlaeus[4] to debate the royal supremacy. He also used his contacts to arrange a meeting with Johann Friedrich, elector of Saxony, to prepare the ground for an embassy under the joint leadership of Edward Foxe, now bishop of Hereford, and Nicholas Heath, archbishop of York. He never ceased writing. Early in 1536 he published his *Lives of the Popes*[5] in Wittenberg. A typically polemical work, with a preface by Luther, its aim was to expose the corruption of the papacy across the ages. He drew upon a variety of sources, from Melanchthon to the eleventh-century cardinal Benno, from the popes Gregory VII and Pius II to Martin of Troppau, in order to describe 'how horrible mendacity, idolatry, and all kinds of abomination devastate the church, and how so many millions of souls are led to fill up

1   *The Oxford Encyclopedia of the Reformation*, ed. Hillerbrand (New York, 1996), i. 454. Elton also points out that in 1517 Cromwell learnt the New Testament by heart, using Erasmus' Latin edition.

2   Quoted in Moynahan, 345.

3   Ibid. 324.

4   Johannes Cochlaeus (1479–1552), the first Catholic biographer of Luther.

5   *Vitae Romanorum pontificum, quos papas vocamus, diligenter et fideliter collectae per Doctorem R. Barnes* (Wittenberg, 1536).

the insatiable inferno'.[1] A revised edition of *A Supplication* had appeared in 1534. The additions included Barnes' dualistic, and recognizably Calvinistic, conception of the divine will:

First must we consider that there are two manner of wills in God. One is called his godly will, or his secret and inscrutable will, whereby that all things be made, and ordered, and all things be done. Of this will no creature hath knowledge what he ought thereby to do, or not to do, for as Paul saith, it is inscrutable, and therefore it is sufficient for us to know alonely that there is an inscrutable will. The other will in God is called a declared and manifested will, the which is declared and given to us in Holy Scriptures. This will was showed unto us by our Master Christ, the Son of God, and therefore it is lawful, and also men are bound to search, to know this will, and for that consideration, was it manifested unto us. This will doth declare what every man is bound to do, and what every man is bound to flee.[2]

The arrest of the Reform-minded Anne Boleyn in May 1536 gave a considerable boost to the conservatives at court. Barnes reacted by making sure that, if anything, his words cut with a sharper edge. This honesty of purpose saw him confined to the Tower. Much to the disgust of Thomas Howard, the duke of Norfolk, Cromwell managed to secure his early release. Nor did the chief minister hesitate to approve Barnes' appointment to a commission investigating anabaptists: in the words of Eric Ives 'that inchoate religious self-help minority'.[3] Though 'anabaptist' became a blanket title of opprobrium for any holder of radical beliefs, the chief tenet of the original sect, traceable to Zürich in 1525, was that infant baptism was wrong: therefore adults had to be rebaptized (*ana-* being Greek for 'again'). As the decade wore on, however, groups in Germany and elsewhere sought the separation of church and state, rejected the corporeal birth of Christ, and developed a fleshly reliance on the work of the Spirit. Calvin and Bucer were at the forefront of efforts to shake these 'giddy men'[4] from the coat-tails of the godly Reformation. 'Through our misguided leniency', wrote Bucer, 'they have gained such strength that this evil can be neither done away with nor

---

1   *Vitae*, sig. A6v. Quoted in Maas, 136.

2   Parker, 274.

3   *The Life and Death of Anne Boleyn* (Malden, 2004), 267.

4   *Institutes*, I. ix. 1.

properly remedied'.[1] In Münster, anabaptists declared polygamy mandatory, along with the common ownership of property. In Strasbourg the situation grew so grave the pastors urged the death penalty for militants and deportation for the rest.

In September 1538 the Landgraf Philipp of Hesse and the duke of Saxony issued a joint letter, calling on Cranmer to crack down on sectarian disorder. In October a royal commission was established; in November all anabaptists active in England were given twelve days to depart the realm. As an intermediary between England and Lutheran Germany, Barnes was indispensable. For a decade or more he was the very model of a pan-European Reformer. His role in underpinning English evangelicalism at various junctures, and giving it a European face, is ripe for reappraisal. But his diplomatic work for the Crown always took second place to his mission to restore religion to its purest state. He united his preaching inseparably to Scripture. Hugh Latimer once said of Barnes: 'I pray God continue with him, for then I know no one man shall do more good'. Latimer was widely regarded as the finest preacher in England. But having sat under Barnes' ministry in the winter of 1536, Latimer wrote: 'Surely he is alone in handling a piece of Scripture, and in setting forth of Christ he hath no fellow'.[2]

In the spring and summer of 1538, Barnes was in south-west Wales, staying with bishop William Barlow of St David's.[3] This Welsh connection was formalized the following summer, when on the advice of Barlow—who deemed him 'not the unfaithfullest'[4] of Cromwell's men—Barnes was awarded the living of Llanboidy. In the autumn of 1538 he and Cranmer co-ordinated a crackdown on 'sacramentaries': those who denied Christ's actual presence in the consecrated bread and wine of the Lord's Supper. In November John Lambert went to the stake in Smithfield. A measure of responsibility for this must be laid at Barnes' door, as at Cranmer's.

In the Reformation period we see the advance of the Word of God and of the church which is built upon it. But we are reminded constantly that there is no perfect stability in human affairs, only shadows and approximations. In 1539, at the bidding of Henry VIII, the Act of Six Articles, reaffirming Catholic orthodoxy on key doctrinal issues, was passed by Parliament. A

---

1   Quoted in Martin Greschat, *Martin Bucer: A Reformer and His Times* (Louisville, 2004), 119.
2   Quoted in Loane, 113.
3   Maas, 34.
4   Ibid. 37.

mood of reaction was seeping into the body politic. Hugh Latimer examined his conscience and resigned his see; Cranmer, who had concealed his wife's existence since 1532, returned her to Germany. Foxe tells us that many and various 'vexations ensued after the setting forth of the said articles, through the whole realm of England, especially among the godly sort'.[1] The Catholic affinity, led by Stephen Gardiner, bishop of Winchester, and Thomas Howard, duke of Norfolk, had all it needed to rebuild the institutional edifice of priestcraft.

In a move calculated to bring his diplomatic isolation to an end, the king also sought a new wife. To this end, Robert Barnes was sent to assist the negotiations surrounding Henry's ill-starred marriage to Anne of Cleves: 'a circumstance', we are told, 'which did not greatly recommend him to the king'.[2] Gardiner, sensing that Cromwell's promotion of radical clergy left him vulnerable, launched a splenetic attack upon the chief minister for involving Barnes, 'a known heretic', in the king's business. He also sought, in Foxe's words, 'by all subtle means, how to entangle and entrap Barnes in further danger'.[3] God's power to sustain His own was exemplified in Barnes' refusal to return to his friends in Germany. He began to court the flame.

In February 1540, along with William Jerome and Thomas Garrard, Barnes was appointed a Lenten preacher at Paul's Cross. Edmund Bonner, who had moved from a more-or-less Erasmian to a furiously anti-Lutheran position, was the new bishop of London. Knowing that grievances against Barnes had been aired in the presence of the king, Bonner, in consultation with Gardiner, was happy to grant him a platform that would, in all likelihood, expose him to mortal danger. Barnes was the chief object of their plotting. But his Cambridge friends Garrard and Jerome had also taken strong stands for the inscripturated Word of God.

Since the rip-roaring days of his book smuggling, Garrard had risen to become Latimer's chaplain and the rector of Hartelbury, near Kidderminster. As well as defending Latimer as best he could, for the power of the Reformers was ebbing away, this clever, active man was always (Foxe's words) 'flying from place to place'.[4] At Rye in 1537 his preaching brought at least twenty men to Christ. In Kidderminster he was denounced by one heckler as 'a

---

1   Foxe, v. 440.
2   D'Aubigné, ii. 403.
3   Foxe, v. 420.
4   Ibid. 428.

foolish knave priest come to preach the new learning'. By 1539 he was a chaplain to Cranmer, who had sufficient confidence in his abilities to dispatch him to Calais, at the time an English outpost. The citizens of the seaport, according to Cranmer, were 'altogether wrapped' in 'hypocrisy, false faith, and blindness of God and His Word'.[1] Garrard's vitality and intellect gave him the capacity to overcome even the most hostile opposition.

William Jerome was vicar of Stepney, Cromwell's parish. He was 'a diligent preacher of God's Word, for the comfort and edification of the people'. As such, he had provoked 'much hatred against him amongst the adversaries of Christ's Gospel'.[2] Jerome's early life was spent in a Benedictine monastery in Canterbury. Later he served as chaplain to Sir Francis Bigod. A ward of Thomas Wolsey from the age of eight, Bigod worked in the cardinal's interest from 1527 to 1530. He also became a Member of Parliament. Always on the brink of personal crisis, and hounded by creditors, he opposed the break with Rome on economic grounds. He also joined the Pilgrimage of Grace, a popular rising in northern England between October and December 1536. The following year he incited 'pilgrims' to attack Hull and Scarborough; a mob later beseiged Carlisle Castle. Bigod was executed at Tyburn. We cannot be sure of when Jerome left his employ, but he was presented to the vicarage of Stepney in 1537.

On the first Sunday of the Lenten season, at Paul's Cross, Stephen Gardiner preached the obligatory nostrums of the Church. 'There is no forward in the new teaching', he fumed, 'but all backward. Now the devil teacheth, come back from fasting, come back from praying, come back from confession, insomuch that men must now learn to say their paternoster backward'.[3] A fortnight later a punning Barnes rebuked this 'Gardener' who had derided the Almighty and 'planted such evil herbs in the garden of Holy Scripture'.[4] With calmness and logic, although at risk of his life, he urged his hearers to resist any doctrine that rested on the traditions of men. The same theme was picked up in succeeding weeks by Jerome and Garrard.

William Jerome was the humblest agent of God's mission. But on the fourth Sunday in Lent, taking his text from Galatians, he was a lion: the voice of Reformation by the power of the Word preached. Following Luther's

---

1   Quoted in MacCulloch, 142.
2   Foxe, v. 429.
3   Ibid. 430.
4   Ibid. 431.

example, his model for allegory was Paul's figure of Sarah and Hagar. Those under the law are akin to the son Abraham had by Hagar, but Christians *are after the manner of Isaac, children of the promise* (Galatians 4:28). Who could say this wasn't 'consonant to sound doctrine, and the vein of the Gospel?'[1] Wasn't Christ the sum and substance of the Old Testament? Didn't every part of the Bible teach us about Him? What the Bible says He says: mysticism was out, typology was in. It was an audacious message. Today, for many who self-identify as Christian, theology is irrelevant to the practical issues of daily life. But it is impossible to honour the martyrs without honouring their doctrine. Their hope, after all, was not in some vague, happy destiny that lay just over the hill. They believed what the Bible told them. One thing is for sure: if they'd confined themselves to fuzzy but creditable discussions about God's love, they would not have been killed. But as Calvin reminds us: 'Nothing is more to be dreaded, than that the Lord should extinguish the light of sound doctrine, and suffer us to go astray in darkness'.[2] Furthermore: 'As soon as falsehood has made a breach in the fundamentals of religion, and the system of necessary doctrine is subverted … the certain consequence is the ruin of the church'.[3]

Jerome's exposition of God's Word resulted in him being 'charged and convented before the king at Westminster, and there accused for erroneous doctrine'.[4] Gardiner told Henry that 'if you allow Barnes to preach much, all the nation will be lost, and the people will become such heretics that they will not recognize either God or your Majesty'.[5] Nor had he forgotten how he—'the Gardener'—had been 'handled and reviled at Paul's Cross'.[6] Despite sundry expressions of regret (though for what is not clear) and his genuine desire to please his king, Barnes upon release persisted in preaching that 'the Holy Word is the very true key to heaven, for by it heaven is opened or shut'.[7] This saw him further admonished, and along with Jerome and Garrard told to preach sermons of public recantation on the first three days of Easter week. Gardiner also maintained, in a furious report on Jerome's

---

1 Ibid. 429.
2 Quoted in Graham Millar, *Calvin's Wisdom* (Edinburgh, 1992), 82.
3 Ibid. 85.
4 Foxe, v. 429.
5 *Chronicle of Henry VIII of England*, ed./tr. Hume. See Maas, 38.
6 Foxe, v. 431.
7 Quoted in Tjernagel, 58.

sermon, 'that both Jerome and Barnes denied that one's conscience could be bound by human laws'.[1]

On Tuesday 30 March, at the preaching Cross of St Mary Spital, Barnes offered up a form of words that might have been a recantation. And then he withdrew it. According to Gardiner he began 'plainly and directly to preach the contrary of that he had recanted'.[2] Jerome and Garrard mouthed formal retractions, but by gesture, by intonation, reinforced the substance of their Lenten sermons. One observer was led to remark 'how gaily they had all handled the matter'.[3] The authorities, religious and civil, called time. The Privy Council ordered that Barnes, Jerome and Garrard be confined in the Tower on a portmanteau charge of heresy. The glad morning of the Reformation would break without Barnes. Without Cromwell too. On 10 June 1540 he was arrested in the council chamber, just before the midday meal. As Cromwell was about to take his seat, he was approached by the duke of Norfolk. 'It is not meet', bellowed Norfolk, 'that traitors should sit among loyal gentlemen'. Cromwell was seized by the captain of the guard and taken to the water-gate at Westminster. From there he was rowed swiftly down the Thames to the Tower, where he landed at Traitors' Gate. No matter what crimes were later ascribed to him, d'Aubigné has put down the main motives for his arrest:

> It was alleged that he had adopted heretical (that is to say, evangelical) opinions; that he had promoted the circulation of heretical works; that he had settled in the realm many heretical ministers; and that he had caused men accused of heresy to be set at liberty. That when anyone went to him to make complaint of detestable errors, he defended the heretics and severely censured the informers; and that in March last, persons having complained to him of the new preachers, he answered that 'their preaching was good'.[4]

Even though he was confined to the Tower on what Elton calls 'totally trumped up charges of treason and totally misconceived charges of heresy',[5] Cromwell still had the ability to terrify his enemies. Unwilling to face him

---

1   Quoted in Maas, 38.
2   Ibid. 39.
3   Foxe, v. 433.
4   D'Aubigné, ii. 414.
5   *The Oxford Encyclopedia of the Reformation*, I., ed. Hillerbrand (New York, 1996), 455.

in open court, they spared no effort in pushing through a bill of attainder. Condemned without trial in late June, on the 28 July he was led to Tower Hill to be executed. And there, suddenly quiet and calm, freed of the great affairs of state, he knelt down and committed his soul into the hands of God, praying: 'Grant me, merciful Saviour! That when death hath shut up the eyes of my body, yet the eyes of my soul may still behold and look upon Thee; and when death hath taken away the use of my tongue, yet my heart may cry and say unto Thee, "Lord! Into Thy hands I commend my soul; Lord Jesu! Receive my spirit!" Amen'.[1]

This singular man, so detested by Rome and its apologists, so watchful of Reformed interests, then 'suffered the stroke of the axe, by a ragged and butcherly miser, which very ungoodly performed the office'.[2] The act of attainder that denied Cromwell the chance to defend himself also condemned Barnes, Garrard and Jerome. On the 22 July they were attainted as heretics and sentenced to burn at Smithfield.

On 30 July 1540, two days after the death of their patron Cromwell, Robert Barnes, William Jerome and Thomas Garrard were themselves taken from the Tower to be lain on hurdles (wooden frames on which traitors and heretics were brought to execution) and dragged through the streets as far as Smithfield. Foxe indicates that religious courage was embodied that day; that God blessed his faithful servants and made them a blessing to others. Each had come to terms, as we may all pray to do, with the approach of death. Each man addressed the crowd from the stake. Jerome implored his fellow sinners to 'put no trust nor confidence in their works, but in the blood of Christ, to whom I commit my soul to guide, beseeching you all to pray to God for me, and for my brethren here present with me, that our souls, leaving these wretched carcasses, may constantly depart in the true faith of Christ'.[3] Garrard, tranquilly sure of himself, because sure of Christ, declared that he 'never preached wittingly or willingly anything against God's holy Word, or contrary to the true faith, to the maintenance of errors, heresies, or vicious living, but have always, for my little learning and wit, set forth the honour of God, and the right obedience to His laws, and also the king's accordingly: and if I could have done better, I would'.[4] But it was the Barnes' confession,

---

1   Foxe, v. 403.
2   *Henry VIII (Hall's Chronicle)* ed. Whibley, ii. 306–7.
3   Foxe, v. 437.
4   Ibid.

full of grit and depth, that silenced the crowd, and led many into the hands
and tuition of Christ. 'I believe,' said Barnes, 'that through His death He
overcame sin, death, and hell; and that there is none other satisfaction unto
the Father, but this His death and passion only; and that no work of man did
deserve anything of God, but only His passion, as touching our justification:
for I know the best work that ever I did is impure and imperfect'.[1] Luther,
visibly shaken by news of Barnes' execution,[2] discerned the fabric of heaven
in his friend's words. The last part of the confession was addressed directly
to the king:

> Master Sheriff, I require you, on God's behalf, to have me commended
> unto the king's grace, and to show him that I require of his grace these
> five requests: *first*, that whereas his grace hath received into his hands all
> the goods and substance of the abbeys ... would to God it might please
> his grace to bestow the said goods, or some of them, to the comfort of
> his poor subjects, who surely have great need of them. The *second* that
> I desire his grace is, that he will see that matrimony be had in more
> reverence than it is; and that men, for every light cause invented, cast
> not off their wives, and live in adultery and fornication; and those that
> be not married should not abominably live in whoredom, following
> the filthy lusts of the flesh. And *third*, that the abominable swearers may
> be punished and straightly looked upon; for the vengeance of God will
> come on them for their mischievous oaths. The *fourth* request, that his
> grace would set forth Christ's true religion, and seeing he hath begun, go
> forward, and make an end; for many things have been done, but much
> more is to do. And that it would please his grace to look on God's Word
> himself, for that it hath been obscured with many traditions invented
> of our own brains.[3]

His energy sapped by months of imprisonment, Barnes paused for a
moment to steady himself. 'Now', he called out to the crowd, 'how many
petitions have I spoken of?' 'Four!' they roared back. 'Well', he reflected
ruefully, 'even these four be sufficient, which I desire you, that the king's
grace may be certified of; and say, that I most humbly desire him to look

---

1   Ibid. 434.
2   Luther published Barnes' confession, with a preface of his own, as *Bekenntnis des Glaubens* (1540).
3   Foxe, v. 434–436.

earnestly upon them; and that his grace take heed that he be not deceived with false preachers and teachers, and evil counsel; for Christ saith, that false prophets shall come in lambs' skins'. He then asked the crowd to bear witness that he 'died in the faith of Jesu Christ, by whom he doubted not but to be saved'. And with these words, records Foxe, 'he desired them all to pray for him, and then he turned about, and put off his clothes, making him ready to the fire'.[1] The three Reformers now joined hands, and 'kissing one another, quietly and humbly offered themselves into the hands of their tormentors'.[2]

Richard Hilles, a young evangelical, wrote to Heinrich Bullinger, the Swiss theologian, that the three men 'remained in the fire without crying out, but were as quiet and patient as though they felt no pain'.[3]

1   Ibid. 436.
2   Ibid. 437–438.
3   *Original Letters,* ed. Hastings Robinson (Cambridge, 1847), i. 209.

II

THOMAS DUSGATE,
John Cardmaker

In the early Tudor period the city of Exeter and its environs comprised one of the wealthiest civic communities in England. This prosperity was based on the Devon woollen industry; cloth was woven in the rural areas, dyed and finished in the city, and exported to France, Spain and the Low Countries. As a result Exeter avoided becoming a narrow aristocratic city of lords and dependents. Among its middle-class of merchants, skilled artisans and attendant guilds were many literate, pious, yet anti-clerical individuals. A responsiveness to social and religious change was, in a sense, inbuilt. At the same time the renowned cathedral church provided a sense of stability and purpose; it lent theological support to the existing social order and directed believers to the outward aspects of faith. Like any other great cathedral, it also generated a considerable income and provided occupation, opportunity and emoluments for the multi-tiered ecclesiastical class.

In the reign of Henry VII, Exeter played a vital part in the attempt by a Flemish pretender, Perkin Warbeck (Pierrechon Werbecque), to seize the English throne. On 17 September 1497, with French and Scottish backing, Warbeck raised a force of 8,000 in Cornwall and marched on Exeter. The citizenry shut its gates and armed its walls. Warbeck's raggle-taggle army, including a contingent from Bodmin 'whereof the most part were naked',[1] laid siege for two days before retreating to Taunton. There Warbeck surrendered to Henry's advanced guard and admitted his imposture. He was hanged at Tyburn in 1499. In the aftermath of the rebellion, the monarch visited Exeter to thank the city for its loyalty to the crown. Thirty years later that loyalty was still active, and directed towards Henry VIII. But for many of

---

1 Quoted in Susan Doran, *The Tudor Chronicles 1485–1603* (London, 2008), 48.

the merchant class the cultural life of the nation had been joined to a new religious motivation, one which pitted the Word of God, unadulterated and unabbreviated, against the customs and decrees of the medieval church. When, in 1531, a series of bills was nailed to the doors of the cathedral, Exeter was plunged into religious turmoil. One of the bills read: 'The pope is antichrist; and we ought to worship God only, and no saints'.[1]

The career of John Vesey, bishop of Exeter, might serve as an object lesson in how to survive the vicissitudes of ecclesiastical life in the Tudor age. It also points up the numerous collateral advantages of a friendship with Thomas Wolsey, de facto ruler of the English church until his downfall in 1529. A canon of the cathedral since 1509, Vesey was elevated to the bishopric of Exeter in 1519. Wolsey also awarded him the temporalities of the diocese: its secular properties and possessions. Through the issue of leases and collection of rents, and with a cluster of benefices under his stewardship, Vesey was soon mopping up an income exceeding £1,500 a year. He was no more receptive to social reform than to religious'. One of his specialities was the fencing in of common pasture. This over-rode the ancestral rights of farm tenants: a point raised vociferously by Hugh Latimer, the son of a yeoman, in Exeter in 1534. Latimer was dismissed as a 'heretick knave'. In 1527 Vesey applied for, and was granted, permission to carve out a substantial plot of land near his birthplace in Sutton Coldfield. On this he built a grand country house, crafted along Renaissance lines. He lived out the remainder of his days in opulent seclusion. Along with certain others on the church's papalist wing, Vesey had written against Henry VIII's attempts to divest himself of Catherine of Aragon. But the claims of conscience were no more than a whisper in his ear. He conformed 'without demur'[2] to the royal supremacy, going on to officiate at the consecration of the first Reformist archbishop, Thomas Cranmer. His tacit consent to Cromwell's promotion of a vernacular liturgy saw Vesey extend his episcopate to thirty-two years. By 1550, under Edward VI, he was cutting a deal to allow Miles Coverdale to serve as bishop. But, says MacCulloch, 'it took a whole year more before the wily old survivor was satisfied with the terms of his retirement':[3] a pension of £485 a year.

---

1   John Foxe, *Acts & Monuments* (London, 1838), v. 19.
2   Richard Rex, *The Theology of John Fisher* (Cambridge, 2003), 170.
3   Diarmaid MacCulloch, *Thomas Cranmer* (New Haven, 1996), 459.

Even then Vesey had the last laugh. He was restored to the see under Mary I. He died in 1554.

By 1531 Wolsey was gone. Henry was accepted as supreme head of the church 'as far as the law of Christ allows'.[1] But the formularies of Catholic belief were still entrenched. 'Our king has destroyed the pope', said John Hooper, 'but not popery'. In August, eight or nine weeks before the bills were nailed to the door of Exeter cathedral, Thomas Bilney was burned at the stake in Norwich. He had preached against devotion to images, pilgrimages, and prayers to saints, and distributed forbidden works by Tyndale. In the same year, Richard Bayfield (q.v.), a former Benedictine monk, was executed in Smithfield. 'Just as the sun appeared to be rising on the Reformation' writes d'Aubigné, with ineffable sadness, 'the storm burst forth'.[2]

Once the bills ('awful blasphemies') were discovered, the mayor of Exeter moved swiftly to secure an arrest. The lodgings of Exeter's evangelical community were scoured for *seditiosa dogmata*;[3] Vesey and his cathedral chapter, meanwhile, 'hot as coals, and enkindled as though they had been stung with a sort of wasps',[4] ran into the pulpit to defend sacerdotalism, antiquarianism and ritualism against the idea that an individual soul might have direct access to God. The following Sunday, in the midst of one of these sermons, one self-appointed heretic-hunter turned to another. He motioned towards a stranger sitting nearby, reading. In a climate of moral panic men walked in fear. A measure of suspicion might fall on anyone who wasn't visibly or volubly Catholic. Might this man be of the 'new false sect'? Might he even be the one all authority, both civil and religious, was seeking? But observing his casual demeanour, and absorption in his book, their attention soon drifted back to the priest. No one gave any thought to the book itself. It was Erasmus's *Novum instrumentum*, a Latin edition of the New Testament. This was still dynamite in 1531. His reading of the *Novum instrumentum* had caused the martyred Bilney to write: 'at last I heard speak of Jesus'.[5] Despite its many defects, for the early Reformers Erasmus' work was the means by which the light of Scripture first illumined their souls. And here it was, in the cathedral church of Exeter, being read under the noses of the city's Catholic

1 A limiting clause introduced by William Warham, then Archbishop of Canterbury.
2 J. H. Merle d'Aubigné, *The Reformation in England* (London, rep. 1962), i. 459.
3 Seditious doctrine.
4 Foxe, v. 9.
5 Foxe, iv. 635.

élite. The reckless reader was Thomas Dusgate, known as Benet, formerly of Cambridge University. Three months after this narrow escape Dusgate would be burned to death two miles outside the city walls. He had looked well on Christ's holy will and testament. He comprehended not only that we should believe in Christ, but that we should suffer for His sake.

Outside of the fact that he was born in Cambridge, nothing is known about Dusgate's early years. He was a scholar of Christ's College and appears to have graduated BA in 1522. In 1523 he became a fellow of Corpus Christi. According to Foxe he was also incepted MA, but I have found no record of this. What is certain is that he joined the circle around Bilney and Thomas Arthur, and under their guidance was born again by true faith. He thirsted for God: for His love, for His truth, for His Word. Fellows of the college, in this period, were ordained as priests. This gave Dusgate a major problem, especially as he was expected to serve St Bene't's, the college chapel. At a time when virginity was exalted, and celibacy was a prerequisite for the priesthood, Dusgate struggled to rein in his own sexual appetites. According to the frank account by his friend Ralph Morice, later secretary to Thomas Cranmer, Dusgate was 'very much combered with the concupissence of the fleshe, and stryvying gretely to suppresse the same, felt hymself to wek to overcome it'.[1] The degree of Dusgate's torment can be gauged by the singularity of his response to it. After a night of feverish agitation he packed a bag, journeyed to London and eventually found a ship bound for the Continent. He was off to Wittenberg to speak *ad libitum* with Martin Luther, the spearhead of the Reformation and the most famous man in Europe.

Luther had been outlining his views on clerical celibacy for at least two years before his meeting with Dusgate. Having searched the Scriptures, he branded the church's proscription of sexual activity extra-biblical. Ever-practical, he pointed out that as priests required housekeepers 'put[ting] man and woman thus together is like bringing fire to straw and expecting nothing to happen'.[2] The sons of God must be free to marry. 'Marriage is good', he wrote in a treatise called *On Monastic Vows* (1521), 'virginity is better, but liberty is best'.[3] There was no place in Luther's mental compass for sentiment. To condemn a natural impulse was to prefer concubinage and other types of

---

1   BL, Harley 419, folio 125 r+v.
2   Quoted in Roland Bainton, *Here I Stand: Martin Luther* (Tring, 1983), 200.
3   Ibid. 201.

nonmarital sexual activity to wedlock. Up to 1525, before his own marriage to Katherina von Bora, Luther routinely presented matrimony as a remedy for sin alone. After his marriage, according to Roland Bainton, he began to talk of it as 'a school for character'.[1] But his message to Thomas Dusgate in 1523 was plain. Without a wife the Englishman would live in torment; he should abandon the priesthood and marry. That he did. In 1524 Dusgate left Cambridge and settled in Torrington, a small market town on the banks of the river Torridge in north Devon. As if to mark the casting away of one life, and the adoption of another, he styled himself 'Benet': after, one assumes, his old college chapel. His immediate concern was to earn a livelihood. A timid soul with a keen intellect, artless with men and suited to the company of the young, Dusgate began to tutor children in Latin and Greek. After a year or so, he and his new wife moved to Exeter—to Butcher Row, Smithen Street—and opened a school.

The Reformed of Exeter welcomed Dusgate with open arms. Here, after all, was a Cambridge scholar, an associate of Bilney and an acquaintance of Luther, who had proclaimed the emptiness of the religion he had been trained to observe. For his part Dusgate was pleased to sit in fellowship with those obedient to the Word of God, and guided by it. His horror of papistry had spun him far from the hub of the new doctrine. But he was not seeking a refuge from the world: far from it. His chief ground of gladness was to initiate others into the knowledge of Christ. In the provinces, no less than in London and the university towns, the Reformed expected to suffer so that the Gospel might grow. In defiance of tradition, persuaded of the certainty of their own conversion, they would take the message of new life into the streets and taverns, to the docks and market square. That the meaning of the Bible was quite clear, if read by the guidance of the Holy Spirit in faith and love, they had no doubt. It is almost impossible for us, in an age where all truth is relative, and where God has been reduced to, at best, a sustaining influence on people's lives, to grasp how subversive an idea this was in the sixteenth century. In the Exeter of 1531 his love of the Gospel was sufficient to have one William Strowde committed to the bishop's gaol. Strowde's contempt for priestcraft had made him, in the eyes of Vesey and the canons, a danger to society. He was a heretic, an emissary of Satan, a rotten bough to be cut off. Dusgate was not personally acquainted with

---

1   Bainton, 300.

Strowde. But he was uncommonly aware that 'a holy unity exists among us, when, consenting in pure doctrine, we are united in Christ alone'.[1] His letters to his fellow Gospeller are wholeheartedly supportive, self-identifying affairs, aflame for God's Word, unsparingly personal. 'Because I would not be a whoremonger', he wrote, 'or an unclean person, therefore I married a wife, with whom I have hidden myself in Devonshire, from the tyranny of the antichristians, these six years'.[2]

'As every tree and herb has its due time to bring forth its fruit', writes Foxe, 'so it was with this man'.[3] His correspondence with Strowde, and the clarity it brought to heart and mind, was the catalyst for all that followed in the dramatic life of Thomas Dusgate. His sights were set on trying his faith; he had been silent too long. He burned with a holy indignation. All around him the virtue of Christ was being disfigured by the craft and cruelty of 'that most false usurped power of the bishop of Rome'.[4] 'Priest' was a byword for concupiscence, cynicism, and greed. An intense sense of purpose, an utter self-confidence arising from an assurance that God would direct his steps, compelled Dusgate to 'yield himself most patiently (as near as God would give him grace) to die and shed his blood therein; alleging that his death should be more profitable to the church of God, and for the edifying of His people, than his life should be'.[5] To these ends, at various times, he left his lodgings in the dead of night to post explicit summaries of Reformed doctrine on the doors of Exeter cathedral. As a new day dawned, townsfolk would cluster around the notices open-mouthed, some reading, others hearing, that the pope was antichrist and Catholicism a chaos of errors. It isn't difficult to imagine Dusgate on the edge of these gatherings, ears pricked, listening carefully, but not too carefully, lest he betray himself.

With every effort by Vesey and the mayor to flush out the heretic having failed, the priests resorted to cursing by 'bell, book and candle': a ceremony, or pageant, that had its genesis in the ninth century. Despite, or because of, its histrionic character, it was always a crowd-puller. In the autumn of 1531, in a hushed cathedral, dimly-lit and misty with incense, the Franciscan and Dominican monks of Exeter fussed and fretted around a great cross, sticking

---

1   *Calvin's Wisdom*, ed. Graham Miller (Edinburgh, 1992), 369.
2   Foxe, v. 19.
3   Ibid.
4   Ibid.
5   Ibid.

dozens of tapers upon the patibulum: its horizontal section. While this was going on, one of the canons, resplendent in white, preached on certain verses from the book of Joshua, laying especial stress upon *There is an execrable thing among you, O Israel.*[1] Finally, Vesey himself arose from his high throne, flanked by a contingent of candle-wielding canons, to pronounce the curse:

By the authority of God the Father Almighty, and of the blessed Virgin Mary, of Saint Peter and Paul, and of the holy saints, we excommunicate, we utterly curse and ban, commit and deliver to the devil of hell, him that hath ... in spite of our most holy father the pope, God's vicar here on earth ... fixed up with wax such cursed and heretical bills, full of blasphemy, upon the doors of this and other holy churches within this city. [We] give them over utterly to the power of the fiend: and let us quench their souls, if they be dead, this night in the pains of hell-fire, as this candle is now quenched and put out, and let us pray to God that their eyes might be put out, as this candle light is. And let us pray to God that all the senses of their body might fail them, and that they may have no feeling, as now the light of the candle is gone, except they come openly now and confess their blasphemy.[2]

This nerve-shredding piece of Grand Guignol also featured the ringing of a bell (to evoke a death toll), the closing of the holy book (to symbolize the heretic's separation from the church) and much snuffing out and throwing down of candles (to represent his soul being extinguished). As the ceremony approached its climax, Vesey ordered the sharp removal of the patibulum, allowing the vertical (and very heavy) part of the cross to fall to the ground. The crash echoed around the vaulted ceiling and fell like cannon shot upon the multitude. Hands flew to mouths; cries caught in throats. Heads were buried in cloaks and shawls, as the gullible and the forlorn sought shelter from the power of the divine curse. The stage was set for the heretic to reveal himself. The eyes of the priests glittered hawkishly. No one stepped forward. Remarkably, however, percolating above the pious silence came the sound, the quite unmistakeable sound, of guffawing. Thomas Dusgate had failed to stifle the mirth welling up inside him. There were gasps of indignation. 'What are you laughing at?' demanded one man. 'My friends', said Dusgate,

---

1   Joshua 7:13.
2   Foxe, v. 21.

'who could help themselves, watching such merry conceits and games played by the priests?' A sea of heads turned in his direction. 'Here is the heretic!' cried one. 'Hold him fast!'[1] shouted another. Men rushed from all parts of the cathedral. In the press of bodies, according to one account, the Reformer was able to wriggle free and take to his heels. Clearly, Dusgate was courting the flame. Only a belief that risking one's life for one's faith is a fructifying act—a means of honouring Christ's Gospel—can explain such recklessness.

Very early one morning, around five o'clock, a certain Catholic of the city of Exeter, called 'W.S' by Foxe, was hurrying through autumnal mists to early mass. At Stile Gate, one of the smaller gates to the cathedral yard, he nearly fell over a boy attaching bills to the railings. The heretic! The boy tried to bolt, but a jubilant W.S. grabbed him by the scruff of the neck and half-walked, half-dragged him to the office of the mayor. Once there, the boy was recognized as the servant of Benet, the schoolmaster. Within hours Dusgate was arrested. The next morning he was brought before the cathedral canons and officers of the civil authority. Among other things he was asked why he had posted 'bills of blasphemy' rather than proclaiming his heresy out loud. The forthrightness of his reply still astounds. From the years of anonymity, and the hard-won experience of religious exile, had come the courage to defy authority, and the patience to suffer whatever that authority chose to inflict:

> I put up the bills so that many would read and hear what abominable blasphemers you are, and that many might know your antichrist, the pope, to be that boar out of the wood, which destroys and throws down the hedges of God's church. For if I had been heard to speak one word, I should have been clapped fast in prison, and the matter of God hidden. But now I trust more of your blasphemous doings will thereby be opened and come to light. For God will so have it, and will no longer suffer you.[2]

Dusgate was transferred to the bishop's prison, where he was clapped in irons and weighted with chains 'with as much favour as a dog should find'.[3] Bishop Vesey, knowing the propaganda value of a recanted heretic exceeded that of a dead one, embarked on a concerted campaign to coax an abjuration

---

1   Ibid.
2   Ibid. 22.
3   Ibid.

from his prisoner. The first wave, so to speak, was led by Dr Brewer, Vesey's chancellor; the second by Gregory Basset. A story like Basset's, troublesome and tragic in equal measure, can haunt the Christian conscience. It forces us, not for the first time in these accounts, to deal with 'that' question: What Would I Have Done? For Basset was a convert from Catholicism. He too, like Dusgate, like Frith, like Latimer and the others, had imbibed the teaching of Luther. He had received into his heart the seed of the Gospel. He rejected the institutional apparatus of Romanism and accorded all authority in life and religion to the Word. These beliefs, and the stridency of his witness, especially to the young, saw him arrested and thrown into Bristol gaol. Through many a lonely and pain-racked night he stood firm in the Saviour's cause. 'He lay in prison long', reports Foxe, 'and was almost famished'.[1]

One morning Basset was shown a great pan full of burning coals. Any failure to admit his heresy—he was told—and both his hands would be thrust into the coals. Basset, broken mentally and physically, recanted: 'and became afterwards a mortal enemy to the truth all his life'.[2] Rather than taking his humiliation to the Cross of Christ, where he might find peace with God, he chose to rely for salvation on his own efforts. Christ's finished and perfect work was traded in for the wardenship of the house of Franciscans. Basset's is a salutary tale, and a terrifying one. It tells us that the worst sort of betrayal must involve love. It tells us that our bond with Christ, the one bond that should be beyond betrayal, isn't. In the wake of his recantation, Basset placed all his erudition at the disposal of the priests. His attempts to persuade Dusgate to match his apostasy became so unhinged that for eight days 'he would not depart the prison, but lay there night and day'.[3] Dusgate faced him, and the monks and friars who came after, with boldness and no little asperity. Taken to task by a Dominican ('God knoweth', writes Foxe, 'a blockhead')[4] for his views on monastic piety, Dusgate remonstrated that 'by the merits of your orders you make many brethren and sisters: you take yearly money off them, you bury them in your coats, and in shrift you beguile them'.[5] The pope, he repeated, was 'antichrist, the Thief, the Mercenary, and the Murderer of

---

1   Ibid. 20.
2   Ibid. 22.
3   Ibid.
4   Ibid. 24.
5   Ibid.

Christ's flock'.[1] The professionally religious were '[making] lying sermons to
the people, to maintain your false traditions and foul gains'.[2] The cut-and-
thrust of doctrinal debate seems to have had an analgesic effect on Dusgate.
What emerges is an all-embracing certainty that despite the opposition of
the world, Christ reigns wherever His Gospel is preached. The glory of the
children of God lies beyond this earthly realm:

> He is my only way, who says 'I am the way, the truth and the life'.
> In His way I will walk, His doings shall be my example: not yours, nor
> your false pope's. His truth will I embrace: not the lies of your pope's.
> His everlasting life will I seek, the true reward of all faithful people.
> Away from me, I pray you. Vex my soul no longer. You shall not prevail.
> There is no good example in you, no truth in you, no life to be hoped
> for at your hands. You are all more vain than vanity itself. If I should
> hear and follow you this day, everlasting death should hang over me: a
> just reward for all them that love the life of this world. Away from me.
> Your company suits me not.[3]

On 22 December 1531 Dusgate was tried in a spiritual court. The infamous
statute *de Haeretico Comburendo*, first enacted under Henry IV in 1401, had been
dusted off by lord chancellor Thomas More. Perhaps only John Fisher, bishop
of Rochester, could match More's furious anti-Lutheranism. As propagandists
for papal and conciliar government, More and Fisher stood for external
ritual against inner prayer; for inherited custom against the inviolability of
the Word. No duty came above protecting 'the common faith and belief of
the holy church'.[4] In the cause of expediting the immediate destruction of
one of 'our evangelycall Englysshe heretykes',[5] no stone was left unturned,
no bending of the legal framework considered too cavalier. Under cover
of More, bishop Vesey handed Dusgate over to the civil authority—to Sir
Thomas Dennis, sheriff of Devonshire—for burning.

Thomas Dusgate was brought to the stake on 15 January 1531. He was
reckoned about fifty years old. The sheriff, keen to purge Exeter of heresy
by means of a spectacle that would terrify all who observed it, had petitioned

---

1   Ibid. 23.
2   Ibid.
3   Ibid. 24.
4   Quoted in Peter Ackroyd, *The Life of Thomas More* (London, 1998), 274.
5   Ibid. 273.

the chamber of commerce to allow the execution to take place in the heart of the city. This was disallowed. Dusgate was transported by cart to Livery-dole, an ancient triangular site in Heavitree, about two miles away. He was led to a wooden platform. There he confirmed that God had called him for a purpose, and would enable him to fulfil it. He exhorted the crowd to flee evil desire, and the 'devices, fantasies and imaginations of man's inventions'.[1] He directed them to the message of salvation as set forth in Christ's own words. Such was his fundamental assurance, such was his compassion for those in darkness, that the sheriff's clerk did not doubt that the spiritual victory was Dusgate's. 'Truly', he intoned, 'this is a servant of God'. His was not a lone voice; the majority of the crowd, we are told, 'were astonished and in great admiration'.[2] As Dusgate was chained to the stake, two Catholics, Carew and Barnehouse, thinking that even now he might abjure, began to ply him with flattery. But seeing his spiritual peace, and eagerness for the next life, their artifice quickly unravelled. A splenetic Barnehouse stepped forward and snarled: 'Say, *Precor sanctum Mariam et omnes sanctos Dei*' ('Pray to holy Mary and all the saints of God'). To which the Reformer answered:

No, no; it is God only upon whose name we must call. And we have no other advocate unto Him but Jesus Christ, who died for us, and now sits at the right hand of His Father, to be an advocate for us. And by Him must we offer and make our prayers to God, if we will have them to take place and be heard.[3]

What happened next, its shocking nature, illustrates the basic tragedy of fallen human existence. Barnehouse grabbed a pike, skewered a nearby gorsebush, lit it, and pushed it into Dusgate's face. 'Ah, horrible heretic!' he screamed. 'Pray to our lady, and say Sancta Maria, or, by God's wounds, I will make you do it!' Dusgate did not flinch. His spiritual resistance was not broken, not impaired, but magnified; his assurance of eternal life, and tenacious hold on Scriptural texts, saw him rise above the torment inflicted on his body. He would cleave to Christ and suffer affliction with Him, for His sake. 'Alas!' he replied to Barnehouse, 'trouble me not'. And lifting his hands to heaven he prayed: 'Father, forgive them!'[4] How to understand

1 Foxe, v. 25.
2 Ibid.
3 Ibid.
4 Ibid.

such men. It wasn't a matter of preserving one's poise. Forget the Victorian stereotype. Forget self-righteous formality. The martyrs were not chary of emotion: far from it. But at the stake the overriding objective was to glorify the Gospel by giving a visible demonstration of how those who love the Lord withstand persecution. Every word, each act, was charged with self-awareness. Like Yeats' heroes, they '[Did] not break up their lines to weep'.[1] As for the Bible-haters, the little men like Barnehouse and Carew, their punishment would be spiritual, and would fall on the soul. As Calvin says: 'Tyrants may burn their flesh and their bones, but the blood remains to cry aloud for vengeance; and the intervening ages can never erase what has been written in the register of God's remembrance'.[2] The model was our Lord Jesus Christ Himself. The nearness of Him gave Dusgate everything necessary for perfect happiness. He knew, with absolute certainty, that he would share in the glory of those who suffered for His sake.

The call came to 'Fire the faggots!' Foxe's correspondent reports that many spectators, among them a shameful number of girls and women, began to tear up every shrub, and grab every branch they could lay their hands on, to throw into the flames. Soon the pile of burning and smoking wood reached Dusgate's midriff. His prayers continued to his death: 'he did never stir nor strive, but most patiently abode the cruelty of the fire'. On the edge of consciousness he was seen to lift his eyes to heaven. He whispered 'Lord, receive my spirit'.[3] Before long his body, charred and melting, toppled forward from its chain onto the fire.

In 1909 an obelisk of Dartmoor granite was erected to Dusgate's memory in Denmark Road, Exeter, near Livery Dole. A bronze panel depicts Dusgate banging on the door of Exeter cathedral. Also commemorated is Agnes Prest, the wife of a stonemason. Agnes left her husband over his refusal to accept her evangelical faith. When forced to return to the matrimonial home, she was reported by her neighbours and brought before James Turberville, bishop of Exeter. Under examination, she refused to affirm the doctrine of transubstantiation, and was burned to death on 15 August 1557.

The following inscriptions grace two bronze panels affixed on opposite sides of the base of the obelisk:

---

1   W. B. Yeats, 'Lapis Lazuli. Quoted in John R. Knott, *Discourses of Martyrdom in English Literature* (Cambridge, 1993), 16.

2   Miller, 241.

3   Foxe, v. 25.

'In grateful remembrance of Thomas Benet M.A. [Dusgate] who suffered at Livery Dole AD 1531 for denying the supremacy of the Pope and of Agnes Prest who suffered on Southernhay AD 1557 for refusing to accept the doctrine of transubstantiation.

Faithful unto death'.

'To the glory of God & in honour of His faithful witnesses who near this spot yielded their bodies to be burned for love to Christ and in vindication of the principles of the Protestant Reformation this monument was erected by public subscription AD 1909.

They being dead yet speak'.

In the wake of Dusgate's martyrdom, Exeter's civil and religious élite could not feign indifference to the strife convulsing the nation. Ordinary believers were acutely aware of the issues at stake; in the market square points of doctrine were circulated as readily as goods. In 1534 the cause of Reform in the city was boosted by the arrival of Hugh Latimer, England's greatest preacher. Latimer made something of a specialty in these years of converting West Country monks. A year earlier, in Bristol, the leader of the local friars, John Hilsey, had forsaken idolatry during one of Latimer's sermons. Hilsey later became a favourite of Thomas Cromwell, and upon the execution of John Fisher was appointed to the see of Rochester. John Erley, another friar, this time from Gloucester, was arrested for his Latimer-inspired evangelicalism in the same period. But what Richard Rex has called the 'greatest triumph'[1] of Latimer's preaching tour came in 1534, in Exeter, with the conversion of John Cardmaker, warden of the house of Observant Franciscans.

Aside from the fact that he was a native of Exeter, nothing is known of Cardmaker's early years. But as he was admitted underage to one of only six houses of Observant Franciscans in the country, we can assume he was a gifted scholar with a decent grounding in Latin. In this period, devotional laxity and sexual impropriety were rife in the monasteries. The Observant Franciscans sought to reform themselves—and return to the spirit of their founder—through austerity, scholarship and the cultivation of piety. We might also conjecture, therefore, that young Cardmaker displayed a degree of self-denial rare among his peers. When next we hear of him he is supplicating the

---

1   *The Beginnings of English Protestantism*, ed. Marshall & Ryrie (Cambridge, 2002), 47.

university of Cambridge for a bachelor of theology degree. It is December
1532; Cardmaker is in his mid-thirties. His religious order had underwritten
the cost of sixteen years of study, at Oxford and at Cambridge. In 1533 he
received his degree and returned to the heartlands of his affinity: to Exeter,
to the house of Observant Franciscans. By the following year he had been
appointed warden.

Given the impact of Luther in 1520s Cambridge, the story that Cardmaker
was converted to the religion of the Reformed after hearing one sermon
in Exeter in 1534 seems fanciful. His university years embraced Luther's
seminal act at Wittenberg, Tyndale's translation of the New Testament, the
dissemination of Reformist texts in the university towns, the White Horse
meetings, the persecution of Robert Barnes, the execution of Bilney and
much else besides. Unless we accept the idea of a blinkered traditionalist at
university suddenly sprouting radical wings as the warden of a religious house,
the safest conclusion is that Latimer's sermon spoke to sympathies already
present in Cardmaker. Certainly there was no holding back *after* 1534. He
had tasted the grace and power of God. He had acquiesced to His Word.
By January 1536 he was licensed to preach. Three months later, under the
direction of Hilsey, now bishop of Rochester, he spoke in support of the
royal supremacy to the Crutched Friars in London.

In 1537 Cardmaker left his order to marry Katherine Testwood, a widow.
This was an annus mirabilis for the English Reformation. At the beginning
of the year, Thomas Cromwell, now vicegerent for religious affairs, declared
war on the tinkling rituals of Rome. He ordered an assembly of forty-one
divines, led by Cranmer, to draft new formularies of faith. This produced
the *Institution of a Christian Man*, widely known as the Bishops' Book. Its
appearance actuated the wholesale burning of relics and images so that
'the people should use no more idolatry unto them'.[1] In 1538 a new set of
injunctions decreed that within two years every church should possess and
display a copy of the Bible in English. It was to be chained to a lectern in
an open space, and made available to all: tutored and untutored alike. For
the first time in living memory, Christians were freed from the interpreting,
censoring tyranny of the priests. The translation was by Miles Coverdale,
working from Tyndale's original. In one fell swoop, suggests Peter Ackroyd,

1   Charles Wriothesley, *A Chronicle of England during the Reigns of the Tudors,* ed. W. D. Hamilton,
2 vols., (London, 1875–7).

Cromwell 'introduced into England a biblical culture of the word, as opposed to the predominantly visual culture of the later medieval world'.[1] By the spring of 1539 Henry was already blaming the accessibility of the Bible for all manner of 'murmur, malice and malignity'.[2] He decided to put the brakes on religious reform.

In 1540 John Cardmaker told a congregation at St Brides, Fleet Street, that 'it was as profitable to hear mass and see the sacrament as to kiss Judas' mouth'.[3] His honesty of purpose was transparent. In bondage to inherited custom from boyhood, he had emerged from the mist of years to embrace Scripture with an energy that was unflagging. In his heart was the impulse to see a Christian reshaping of England; in his sights were the unchecked ambitions of the Catholic affinity. The key players in that affinity, Thomas Howard, duke of Norfolk, and the bishops Stephen Gardiner and Cuthbert Tunstall, had availed themselves of Henry's idiosyncratic theology to fashion the Act of Six Articles. The passage of the act—styled 'the whip with six strings' by the Reformed—marked the triumph of tradition, and brought to an end to the Scripture-dominated innovations of the 1530s. The Act of Six Articles was the king's own declaration of faith; it ushered in a reactionary cycle that would last until his death. The doctrines of transubstantiation, communion in both kinds, auricular confession, private masses and clerical celibacy—all mainstays of pre-Reformation popular devotion—were reinstalled as pillars of the Tudor church. Any denial of their efficacy was punishable by death. By 1543, when Cardmaker was made minister of St Brides, Cromwell had been condemned without trial and beheaded on Tower Hill. Robert Barnes, William Jerome and Thomas Garrard had been burned to death at Smithfield. And by the Act for the Advancement of True Religion, Henry had restricted the right to read the Bible to clerics and noblemen, and to the wealthier merchants. Women outside the gentry and nobility were forbidden to read it at all. Gentlewomen and those of noble birth might read it, but only in private. A far cry from William Tyndale's aspiration, voiced to a cavilling priest in 1523, that 'If God spare my life, ere many years pass, I will cause a boy that driveth the plough shall know more of the Scriptures than thou dost'.[4]

1   *The History of England* (London, 2012), ii.131.
2   Ibid. 140.
3   John Foxe, *Acts &Monuments* (London, 1570), ii. 1379.
4   Quoted in Marcus Loane, *Masters of the Reformation* (London, rep. 1956), 53.

In March and April 1546, Edward Crome, called by Nicholas Ridley a 'fatherly example of patience and constancy, and all manner of true godliness',[1] rose in a number of London pulpits to impugn the mass, deny the existence of purgatory and affirm the doctrine of justification by faith alone. As a result, he and a number of known associates, including Latimer, Nicholas Shaxton, formerly bishop of Salisbury, and John Cardmaker, were arraigned before the king's council at Greenwich. On 27 June Crome, for the second time, recanted his views. Shortly afterwards, 'in a particularly abject manner which permanently broke his evangelical spirit',[2] so did Shaxton. In September, Cardmaker, called 'Taylor' (his customary alias) by one council member, followed suit. By then, one of the grimmest episodes of the campaign against evangelicals in the late Henrician period had reached its conclusion.

Anne Askew was the second daughter of Sir William Askew, a Lincolnshire landowner. Her brother Edward was in service to Cranmer and a cupbearer to Henry VIII. Well-educated and devoted to Scripture-reading, Anne was compelled by her father, sometime before 1540, to wed Thomas Kyme, the former fiancé of her deceased sister. Cracks in the marriage immediately began to show, not least because Kyme, a dyed-in-the-wool Romanist, could not stop Anne collecting and distributing Reformist tracts. In 1544, egged on by local priests, Kyme drove Anne from their home. She first tried to obtain a divorce in the bishop's court in Lincoln; later she turned to the Court of Chancery in London. Her first appeal was to Paul's directive to the church in Corinth: *But if the unbelieving depart, let him depart: a brother or sister is not in subjection in such things.*[3] The petition was denied. But she moved to London and soon made friends at Court, particularly among the women close to Katherine Parr, Henry's religiously radical sixth wife. D'Aubigné tells us 'the queen frequently received Anne and other Christian women in private apartments'.[4] Katherine appears to have formed her Reformist views as a result of the Catholic rebellion known as the Pilgrimage of Grace.[5] A heaven-sent opportunity to advance those views arrived when Henry left

1   *Letters of the Martyrs,* ed. Coverdale (London, 1837), 44.
2   MacCulloch, 353.
3   1 Corinthians 7:15.
4   *The Reformation in England* (London, rep. 1963), ii. 463.
5   An uprising in the North in support of the Old Faith; it began with riots in Lincolnshire in October 1536 and soon spread to the Ridings of Yorkshire. Katherine herself was held hostage for a time at Snape Castle.

England to lay siege to Boulogne in 1544. As regent, Katherine met daily with Thomas Cranmer. With his unstated approval she began to host a kind of Reformed salon. Every afternoon, for at least two hours, scholars such as Latimer, Ascham and Ridley were invited to lead talks on Bible topics. The courtier-supporters present included a number of what might be called tacit Lutherans: Lady Denny, Lady Lane, Lady Hertford, Lady Tyrwhitt and Catherine Willoughby, duchess of Suffolk, chief among them. 'Every day is like a Sunday', wrote one attendee, '[which is] a thing hitherto unheard of, especially in a royal palace'.[1]

In 1546 Katherine wrote a famous letter to the fellows of Cambridge University, imploring them to make the town as famous for Gospel-inspired learning as Athens had been for natural and moral philosophy. In 1548, by now married to Thomas Seymour, Katherine Parr died of puerperal fever six days after giving birth to her only child. Her overtly Reformed funeral, composed of Bible-readings and psalm-singing, with a sermon preached by Miles Coverdale, has been called 'the first such for royalty in England'.[2] Along with her patronage of the Bible-men, her love of learning, bounteous spirit and diligent love of God and neighbour all mark her out as a notable figure. Her influence was perpetuated in the lives of her stepchildren Edward VI and Elizabeth I, and most especially in the person and beliefs of her brilliant ward, Lady Jane Grey.

Once settled in London, Anne Askew continued to embody the deep spiritual earnestness of the Reformation. By early 1545 word of her 'Gospelling' had reached the ears of Edmund Bonner, the bishop of London. A bluestocking handing out tracts, especially one 'young and remarkably beautiful', was not going to pass unnoticed. Among other things she had been overheard saying she 'would sooner read five lines in the Bible than hear five masses in the church'.[3] On Bonner's instructions, a spy called Wadlow was lodged in the house next door to Anne. Wadlow, however, was disarmed by the intense young evangelical. She was the 'devoutest and godliest woman I ever knew' he reported. '[At] midnight she beginneth to pray, and ceaseth not in many hours after, while I and others sleep or do worse'.[4]

---

1   Quoted in David Starkey, *Six Wives* (London, rep. 2004), 749.

2   Janel Mueller, *The Oxford Encyclopedia of the Reformation*, ed. Hillerbrand (New York, 1996), iii. 222.

3   Foxe (1837), v. 538.

4   From an account by John Louth, quoted in Ackroyd, *The History of England* (London,

According to her own extraordinarily vivid account of her ordeal, Anne
was first arrested in March 1545. She was questioned by Christopher Dare,
the judge at her heresy hearing, then handed over to the lord mayor, Martin
Bowes, and the bishop's chancellor. A fine intelligence shines through all her
replies. One detects no hint of vanity, only a heightened form of female self-
governance. Bowes forwarded an hypothesis: if a mouse eats a consecrated
wafer, does it receive the body of our Lord? Anne was not about to fall into
so obvious a trap. She 'made them no answer, but smiled'.[1] Told that the
apostle Paul forbade women to talk or speak of the Word, Anne suggested that
her examiners reacquaint themselves with his first letter to the Corinthians.
'How many women', she enquired, 'have you seen go into the pulpit to
preach?' 'Never any', comes the dragged-out reply. 'Then you ought to find
no fault in poor women', Anne declares, 'except they have offended the law'.[2]

Anne's intrepidity saw her cast into the Counter, a gaol under the
jurisdiction of the City of London. A priest was sent, wrote Anne, 'to give
me good counsel, which he did not'.[3] After twelve days' solitary confinement
her cousin, a lawyer called Christopher Brittayn, was able to visit her. Anne
had always been delicate and sickly; nothing in her background had equipped
her to cope with incarceration. Seeing her physical deterioration, Brittayn
implored the lord mayor to grant her bail. As a result, the following afternoon,
she was brought before Bonner and John Wymesley, the bishop's archdeacon.
She was clutching a treatise by John Frith. Wymesley snatched it from her
hand. 'Such books as this', he said, 'have brought you to the trouble you
are in. Beware, for he who wrote it burned in Smithfield'. Anne did not
waver. She would not be bullied; nor would she disown Frith. She opined
that criticising books before reading them was 'a token apparent of a very
slender wit'.[4] Bonner's approach was more sagacious. He positioned himself
as her protector. She was, he said, 'free to utter the bottom of [her] heart
in any way'.[5] Anne wasn't fooled. Asked 'why [she] had so few words', she
countered meekly that 'God has given me the gift of knowledge, but not of

2012), ii. 172. Wadlow is described as 'one great papiste of Wykam College ... a coursytore of
the Chawncery'.
    1   *The Examinations of Anne Askew,* ed. Elaine Beilin (Oxford, 1996), 167.
    2   Beilin, 30.
    3   Foxe, v. 538.
    4   Beilin, 42–43.
    5   Ibid. 44.

utterance. And Solomon says that a woman of few words is a gift of God'.[1] John Bale, Anne's first editor, reminded his readers that Christ, brought before the Sanhedrin, kept silent and said nothing until 'he was compelled by the living God, to speak'. And just as Caiaphas, the high priest, procured the death of Christ by his questions, so 'this bloody bishop Bonner, of the same wicked generation, did later, by this faithful woman'.[2] When her approval of private masses was sought Anne retorted 'O Lord, what idolatry is this?—[to] believe more in private masses than in the healthsome death of the dear Son of God'. Bonner's dovish mask slipped. 'What kind of answer is this?' he stormed. 'It is a mean one', admitted Anne, 'but good enough for the question'.[3]

Before her removal to London, Anne had made a six-day visit to Lincoln, the purpose of which was to discuss doctrine with the very clergy she had been told would 'assault me and put me in great trouble'.[4] She was seen daily in the cathedral, always reading the Bible. Under the terms of the Act for the Advancement of True Religion she could be prosecuted. The application of the Act was far less draconian than for the Six Articles, but it still affected the climate of Reform. In Lincoln minster that climate was distinctly chilly. Groups of priests, up to six at a time, encircled Anne like wolves. They gave every indication of wanting to talk to her. 'Yet', Anne told Bonner regretfully, 'they went their ways again without speaking'. What?—did none engage with her, asked the horrified bishop. She recalled one cleric who did. 'And what did he say?' enquired Bonner. 'His words were of so small effect', said Anne, 'that I do not now remember them'.[5]

After several fractious exchanges, Anne was asked to put her name to a confession of faith: one that upheld the mass. Instead of just signing the document, as Bonner had directed, she wrote: 'I, Anne Askew, do believe all manner of things contained in the catholic church'. The bishop was fully aware that for an evangelical the Reformed church is the universal church: the only, in fact, 'catholic' church. On reading her additions, Bonner left the room in a filthy mood. 'She is a woman', barked the bishop, 'and I am nothing deceived in her'. This alerted Christopher Brittayn to a chink in his armour.

---

1   Ibid. 51.
2   Ibid.
3   Ibid. 52.
4   Ibid. 56.
5   Ibid. 57.

'Take her as a woman', urged the lawyer, 'and do not set her weak woman's wit to your lordship's great wisdom'.[1] It worked. On the provision of sureties Anne was released. But she would not surrender the role for which she was sure God had destined her. Within a year she was rearrested and brought before Thomas Wriothesley, the lord chancellor, and Stephen Gardiner, the bishop of Winchester, at Greenwich. Gardiner was desperate for Anne to betray her friends. He had mentioned Katherine Parr's heretical leanings to Henry, and how 'perilous a matter it is to cherish a serpent within his own bosom'.[2] Wriothesley immediately pressed Anne for her view of the Lord's Supper. 'I believe', she said, 'that so oft as I, in a Christian congregation, do receive the bread in remembrance of Christ's death, and with thanksgiving, I receive therewith the fruits of His most glorious passion'. This was not nearly heretical enough for Gardiner, who demanded more detail. Her reply was untrammelled by wordplay; it spoke of a life endowed with purpose, of the liberty of grace. 'I will not sing a new song of the Lord', she said, 'in a strange land'.[3] Gardiner accused her of speaking in parables. Again, the recourse was to Scripture. 'It is best for you', she told him, 'for if I tell you the truth you will not believe me'.[4] Gardiner was disdainful. He derided her for repeating verses from the Bible like a parrot. Anne, knowing that 'the Word partakes of the nature of God Himself',[5] was perfectly composed. 'I am ready to suffer all things at your hands', she continued. 'Not only your rebukes, but all that shall follow besides, yea, and all that gladly'.[6]

Anne's interrogation took five hours. The next day Gardiner assured her that she would be burned to death for her beliefs. Anne answered that 'I have searched all the Scriptures, yet could I never find that either Christ or His apostles put any creature to death'.[7] On 20 June 1546 she was taken to Newgate gaol. By all accounts she was now extremely sick. She wrote that 'in all my life before, I was never in such pain. Thus the Lord [does] strengthen you in the truth. Pray, pray, pray'. While at Newgate she composed an affecting ballad. One verse runs:

---

1   Ibid. 62.
2   Quoted in Ackroyd, *The History of England* (London, 2012), ii. 172.
3   Beilin, 93; Psalm 137:4.
4   Quoted in Ackroyd, 173; See John 8:45.
5   Miller, 21.
6   Beilin, 94.
7   Ibid. 98.

> I saw a royal throne
> Where Justice should have sit
> But in her stead was one
> Of angry cruel wit.[1]

Following her condemnation for heresy at the Guildhall, Anne was taken 'to the sign of the crown': an inn identified by the sign over its door. There she was met by Sir Richard Rich, a member of the Privy Council. Rich was described by Thomas More as 'light of his tongue, a great dicer and gamester, and not of any commendable fame'.[2] His utter lack of character served him admirably in the labyrinth of Tudor politics. After betraying first the Catholic More, then the Reformed Cromwell, Rich became Baron Rich—and later lord chancellor—under the strongly anti-papal Edward VI. He was still around to help restore Catholicism under Bloody Mary. But in June 1546, Rich was Gardiner's man. His job was to prove a link between Anne and Katherine Parr's entourage, in advance of Gardiner's move against the queen herself. Anne had fallen into their laps. She was isolated. Unlike her male co-religionists, she had no constituency. She did not belong to one of the great universities. She had no official role within the church. A well-born girl, certainly, but not a noblewoman. A reliable witness to the evangelical intensity of the queen's household, she was outside the protection of that household.

Having failed to wring any kind of testimony from Anne, Rich brought on his dancing bear, the wretched Nicholas Shaxton. Disgrace, like misery, enjoys company. Shaxton begged Anne to repudiate her beliefs as he had done. But Anne was made of sterner stuff than the former bishop. If the choice was to burn or forsake the doctrine of God she would choose the former. She told him bluntly, not proudly, that it would 'have been better for him never to have been born'.[3] Rich was incandescent; Shaxton had been the gambler's trump card. He was unused to failing his paymasters. At his bidding Anne was sent to the Tower of London. On the morning of 29 June, she was taken from her cell to the White Tower.

The White Tower has four floors; the ground floor, the north end of which is actually below ground, has no windows. There is a circular well,

---

1 Ibid. 150.
2 Quoted in Peter Ackroyd, *The Life of Thomas More* (London, 1998), 384.
3 Beilin, 119.

lined with ashlar. The two larger rooms were used as dungeons; the third was
a torture chamber. The floors were of rough earth. It was to this fetid place
that Anne was led by Richard Rich and lord chancellor Thomas Wriothesley.
Also on hand were Sir Anthony Knevet, the lieutenant of the Tower, and
a guard. Anne was shown a gruesome rack known as 'the duke of Exeter's
daughter'. This was a wooden frame with a roller at each end to which
wrists and ankles were tied. When the rollers were rotated victims would
rise several inches until they were taut. Still the audacity of Anne's witness
held firm. Wriothesley repeatedly accused her of being 'maynteyned' by
associates at Court. Someone, he insisted, had brought money to the prison
to improve her living conditions. A simple enough matter, said Anne. Her
maid had gone into the streets to collect money from the working poor, 'but
who they were I never knew'.[1] In her own words she 'confessed no ladies
or gentlewomen to be of my opinion'.[2]

Eventually Anne was told to remove all her clothing except her shift (a
loose undergarment). Under Knevet's supervision she was placed on the rack,
and stretched until her bones were almost broken. At this point a distressed
Knevet, 'tendering the weakness of the woman',[3] refused point blank to
rack her any more. Much to the disgust of Wriothesley and Rich he started
to take her down. Wriothesley grabbed his arm and told him that unless he
recommenced the racking, his disobedience would be reported to the king.
Still Knevet refused. But now, fearing for his own skin, he left the Tower
and hastened to Greenwich. He wanted to put his version of events on
record; and, if necessary, beg the king's pardon. This left Anne Askew to the
lethal machinations of Wriothesley and Rich. Those two pillars of the state,
'throwing off their gowns, would needs play the tormentors themselves'.[4]
Stung by Anne's silence to increasing levels of fury, the two men, quite
illegally, grasped a handle each and set to work. According to Anne, 'because
I lay still, and did not cry, my lord chancellor and master Rich took pains
to rack me with their own hands, till I was nearly dead'.[5] By the time they
were finished Anne was, to all intents and purposes, crippled: her shoulders
and hips torn from their sockets, elbows dislocated, knees broken.

---

1   Ibid. 124.
2   Ibid. 127.
3   Foxe, v. 548.
4   Ibid.
5   Beilin, 127.

When a horrified Knevet returned from his mission to Greenwich he had Anne lifted off the rack. She immediately fainted. When she came to she found herself laid out on a damp stone floor. Wriothesley was leaning over her, dripping honeyed words into her ear, attempting by pretence of pity 'to overcome the resolution which his horrible barbarities had not been able to subdue'.[1] This discussion lasted, recalled Anne, 'for two long hours', during which she exercised her Bible knowledge and 'my Lord God (I thank His everlasting goodness) gave me grace to persevere and will do, I hope, to the very end'.[2] Afterwards she was carried to a house somewhere within the Tower enclosure. The lord chancellor sent word that if she would only conform to the authority of the church she would want for nothing. But the comforts Anne sought were no longer of this realm. Her reply to Wriothesley was that 'I would rather die than break my faith'. To a correspondent she wrote: 'Thus the Lord open the eyes of their blind hearts, that the truth may take place. Farewell dear friend, and pray, pray, pray'.[3]

On 16 July 1546 Anne Askew was burned to death in Smithfield. Too crippled to walk, and wearing only the shift she was tortured in, she was carried to the stake in a chair. Shaxton was instructed to preach. Anne was attentive, nodding whenever Scripture was appealed to, or exclaiming 'There he misseth, and speaketh without the book'[4] when error crept in. When the faggots were lit, according to the account of some Dutch merchants, 'the sky abhorring so wicked an act, suddenly altered colour, and the clouds from above gave a thunderclap'.[5] An onlooker who called out 'A vengeance on all you that thus doth burn Christ's member'[6] was beaten by a Catholic carter. Anne, however, was beyond strife or fear or uncertainty. She had braved the storms, and was bound for regions of unfading glory. Foxe records that 'being compassed in with flames of fire, as a blessed sacrifice unto God, she slept in the Lord AD 1546, leaving behind her a singular example of Christian constancy for all men to follow'.[7]

Seven months later Henry VIII was dead. Edward VI, a grave and devout

---

1 J. A. Wylie, *The History of Protestantism* (London, 1870), iii. 406.
2 Beilin, 130.
3 Ibid. 132.
4 Foxe, v. 550.
5 John Bale, quoted in Beilin, 154.
6 Quoted in Ackroyd, *The History of England* (London, 2012), ii. 173.
7 Foxe, v. 550.

boy of ten, succeeded to the throne. The reign of terror that had consumed
sweet Anne Askew was over. The country was embarked upon its great
experiment in Reformation. 'A new face of things began now to appear',
wrote Foxe, 'as it were in a stage new players coming in, the old being
thrust out'. Over the next six years a small army of European scholars would
make their way to England. Many home-grown divines—those who had
recanted like Crome and Cardmaker, or kept their radicalism under wraps,
like Cranmer and Ridley—began to preach, without inhibition, the Word
as the foundation of all true religion. The effects were immediate, and
oftentimes disturbing. The power and efficacy of Cardmaker's oratory in
one London pulpit prompted one gang of Catholics to 'cut and mangle his
gown with their knives'.[1]

In 1550 Cardmaker was made prebendary and chancellor of Wells. There
he formed a close alliance with the energetic bishop (since 1548) of Bath
and Wells, William Barlow. Variously described as a 'weathercock Reformer'
and 'a man of much motion and promotion',[2] Barlow had already served
as bishop of St Asaph (1535) and St David's (1536). In reviewing the Welsh
reaction to Barlow, Glanmor Williams gets nearest, perhaps, to an accurate
portrait of a great survivor and complex individual. 'Barlow himself', he
writes, 'fanatical, iconoclastic, rash, and often unscrupulous, but a courageous
and not insincere innovator withal, commands attention if not respect'.[3]
The light of innovation, already flickering in 1550, died with Edward VI's
passing in 1553. The English church was plunged into its dark age. A variant
on the test of Christian character met by Anne Askew, minus the element
of torture, now awaited Cardmaker in the reign of Mary.

On 18 April 1554 Cardmaker was deprived of his livings. The next month
he and Barlow were taken into custody, then bailed. In November, frantic
with fear, they fled to London in secular disguise. Bent on 'going over sea
like merchants'[4] they were arrested by agents of the Crown at the London
docks and imprisoned in the Fleet gaol. By this time it is estimated that
there were around eighty Reformers in custody, divided between the Fleet,
the King's Bench, the Marshalsea and other prisons. The keepers of these
prisons were told to 'make perfect books of the names of all the prisoners

---

1 Foxe, vii. 77.
2 Thomas Fuller, quoted in Hillerbrand, i. 121.
3 *Welsh Reformation Essays* (Cardiff, 1967), 111.
4 *Diary of Henry Machyn* (London, rep. 1848), 75.

under their charge, together with the causes of their committing'.[1] Once the records were passed to the Council at Westminster, each man was assigned a time and place to be tried before Gardiner—now lord chancellor—and a panel of privy councillors and bishops. Barlow and Cardmaker were brought to the church of St Mary Overy's at the end of January 1555. Andrew Brown reports that they 'tried to placate their interrogators by making ambiguous or submissive replies'.[2] Critically, at the end of the interview, Barlow did not deny that he had recanted. Gardiner was cock-a-hoop. He dropped Barlow's name into all subsequent hearings, holding the bishop up as an example for others to follow. None did: apart from Cardmaker. He was remanded to the Comptor gaol to await release upon his formal acceptance of 'transubstantiation and certain other articles'.[3] As for Barlow, he was allowed to sail to Emden, where he ministered to a large English congregation. From there he went to Wesel and thence to Weinheim (near Heidelberg) as part of the duchess of Suffolk's household. On 18 December 1559, having returned to England with letters from Albert of Brandenburg and Philipp Melanchthon, he was made bishop of Chichester.

Once in the Comptor, Cardmaker was joined by Laurence Saunders, the rector of All Hallows, Bread Street, fresh from his own hearing. When offered his freedom in return for his signature on a form upholding the sacrificial mass, Saunders said that 'I may not buy liberty at such a price'. The series of threats which followed were met with equanimity and proclamations of God's electing love. Gardiner finally dismissed him with a promise that he would burn 'within seven days'.[4] In the hours and days ahead, Cardmaker engaged with his fellow Reformer in what Foxe pleasingly calls 'Christian conference'.[5] By the time of their parting, Saunders' inward joy and peace of conscience, allied to his careful use of Scripture, had set Cardmaker free. Nothing could disturb his sense of God's favour. Perhaps, as prebendary and chancellor of Wells, he had sought his identity in the robes of office. Perhaps the power of human personality, as represented by William Barlow, had caused him to forget that *there is no power but of God: and the powers that*

---

1   *Acts of the Privy Council of England* (1890–1907), v. 91. See Andrew Brown, *Robert Ferrar: Yorkshire Monk, Reformation Bishop, and Martyr in Wales* (London, 1997), 232.

2   Brown, 232–233.

3   Foxe, vii. 78.

4   Foxe, vi. 626.

5   Foxe, vii. 78.

be, are ordained of God (Romans 13:1). No man can serve two masters.[1] But in his cell at the Comptor, a renewed sense of the connectedness of affliction and faith was visited upon Cardmaker.

Certain that Cardmaker 'was become theirs'[2] Bonner and the bishops first listed the articles against him: and then waited confidently for his written recantation. Of the eight articles, no less than four concerned the doctrine of transubstantiation. In every reply Cardmaker affirmed the excellence of the Christian faith and the superiority of its Reformed model. The following day, in a separate letter to Bonner, he enlarged upon his understanding of the Supper. At the original hearing he had followed Barlow's lead. No more. He was finished with sophistry. The carnal matter of Christ is not present: 'so I say', he concluded, 'that Christ is present spiritually too, and in all them which worthily receive the sacrament, so that my denial is still of the real, carnal and corporeal presence in the sacrament, and not of the sacramental, nor spiritual presence. This have I thought good to add to my former answer, because no man should misunderstand it'.[3] No man could, or did. Least of all Bonner. In a last desperate attempt to reverse this reversal, the bishop told Thomas Martin, a Catholic theologian, to engage Cardmaker in written disputation. Martin's defence of the mass only served to steel Cardmaker's resolve. On 25 May 1555 he was condemned by Bonner and committed into the hands of the sheriff of London.

Five days later, alongside John Warne, a London upholsterer, Cardmaker was led to the stake in Smithfield. The atmosphere was charged with subversive energy. Given his two previous abjurations, the Catholics in the crowd were confident that Cardmaker would falter. An equal number of Reformed were praying he would not. To intensify the strain on Cardmaker, Warne was brought to the stake first. Wood and reeds were piled about him with theatrical precision. Every word, every glance, every drawn-out action, was designed to induce panic. As Warne made his prayers, Cardmaker was taken to one side. He was seen conversing animatedly with his captors. The Bible-men were crestfallen. In the words of Foxe's informant, 'beholding this manner of doing, [they] were in a marvellous dump and sadness, thinking indeed that Cardmaker should now recant'.[4] When he knelt down in silent

---

1   Matthew 6:24.
2   Foxe, vii. 78.
3   Ibid. 80.
4   Ibid. 82.

prayer, many assumed he was acknowledging his alienation from God. Who knows?—perhaps he was. But when he rose, instead of turning back to the Catholic group, he began to undress. In his undershirt he kissed the stake, then took Warne by the hand and 'comforted him heartily'. His supporters were ecstatic. 'The Lord strengthen you, Cardmaker', they cried out. 'The Lord Jesus receive thy spirit!'[1]

The fires were lit. A Venetian ambassador heard shouts and cheers echoing around Smithfield long after Cardmaker and Warne had ascended to glory.

1   Ibid.

III

JOHN FRITH,
John Rogers

In John Frith, writes J.H. Merle d'Aubigné, Cambridge University gave England 'a teacher who might be placed beside, and perhaps even above, Latimer and Tyndale'.[1] Carl Trueman affirms Frith's status as 'the great loss of the English Reformation'.[2] A.G. Dickens agrees that 'had he survived, his must have become one of the great names of the age'.[3] A remarkably intelligent young man, eloquent and persuasive, Frith was more than usually aware of the emptiness of any learning that did not have as its goal the furtherance of God's kingdom. A feature of his reforming life was its moderation. His sweet nature recoiled from the factionalism of his day. 'The opinions for which men go to war', he once wrote, 'do not deserve those great tragedies of which they make us spectators. Let there be no longer any question among us of Zwinglians or Lutherans, for neither Zwingli nor Luther died for us, and we must be one in Jesus Christ'.[4] What mattered was the practical outworking of our salvation: bringing glory to God by caring for one another. No one is more in need than the unregenerate man or woman. Thus, 'if I perceive my neighbour likely to perish for lack of Christ's doctrine, then am I bound to instruct him with the knowledge that God has given me, or else his blood shall be required of my hand'.[5] In his short life Frith was asked searching questions about our duties towards the poor and oppressed, and about what

---

1   *The Reformation in England* (London, rep. 1963), ii. 53.
2   *Luther's Legacy: Salvation & the English Reformers 1525–1556* (Oxford, 1994), 2.
3   *The English Reformation* (London, 1967; revised edition), 115f.
4   Quoted in D'Aubigné, ii. 125.
5   *The Work of John Frith*, ed. N.T. Wright (Appleford, 1978), 269.

it means, in the fullest sense, to 'honour, praise and thank' the author of our salvation:

> I answer that His honour, praise and thanks is nothing else but the fulfilling of His commandments. If you ask me what His commandments are, as touching the bestowing of your goods? I answer, His commandments are that you bestow them in the works of mercy, and that shall He lay to your charge at the day of judgement. He shall ask you, whether you have fed the hungry, and given drink to the thirsty, and not whether you have builded abbeys and chantries. He shall ask you whether you have harboured the harbourless, and clothed the naked, and not whether you have gilded images, or given copes to churches. He shall ask you whether you have visited the sick, and gone to the prisoners, and not whether you have gone on a pilgrimage to Walsingham or Canterbury. [1]

The kind of indomitability and drive we associate with Luther or Calvin, Zwingli or Bucer, was less conspicuous in Frith. But, says d'Aubigné, he was imbued with 'less strong but perhaps more amiable features in his character; he taught with gentleness those who were opposed to the truth'. [2] There was something about Frith's equanimity, his silence, his godliness, which unwittingly showed up lesser men. In a rapidly changing world he was bent on understanding others. But this should not be interpreted as a craving for harmony at all costs. Even to define his approach as tolerant—in that word's modern sense, as a kind of glib accommodation—rather misses the point. Frith was quite sure what he stood for, and what he stood against. His serenity concealed a daily search for meaning. His views on purgatory and the Lord's Supper would lead to the stake. But his desire to see a living faith encompassing as many people as possible bred a willingness to engage with different strains of thought. His soul cried out for those in darkness. For Frith, setting out his own position was only half the battle. He also wanted to win over those who rejected that position. 'Frith always had in mind', writes Clebsch, 'not to vanquish his enemies but to praise his Creator and Redeemer'. [3] He recognized, as acutely as any Reformer, English or

---

1   Ibid. 277–278.
2   Ibid.
3   William Clebsch, *England's Earliest Protestants* (Westport, 1964), 7.

Continental, the incompleteness of all human attempts to understand the mind of God.

John Frith was born and baptized in 1503 in Westerham in Kent, the son of an innkeeper. He is known to have attended a grammar school in the nearby town of Sevenoaks. The intention of such schools, usually founded by wealthy merchants, or by municipal guilds, was to equip educable boys for careers in commerce. The fact that lessons were in English rather than Latin is thought by many to have accelerated the progress of Reform. From Sevenoaks Frith was sent to Eton, probably at the age of fourteen: his 'marvellous instinctions and love unto learning'[1] were apparent to all. In 1522/23 he went up to Cambridge, first as scholar to Queen's. He removed to King's in 1524/25 and was admitted Bachelor of Arts. At Cambridge, Frith became 'an exquisite learned man'.[2] He excelled in every subject, including mathematics: d'Aubigné even calls him 'the mathematician of King's'.[3] Though a scholastic curriculum was still in place—Peter Lombard's *Sentences*[4] was still being taught—a gradual shift to humanist and increasingly biblical learning had begun. New lecturers in Greek and Hebrew were appointed. Frith encountered the works of Luther and Melanchthon for the first time; also, in all likelihood, those of Oecolampadius: the greatest single influence on his theology. He may have seen himself as a proto-Reformer. But he saw no reason to challenge those aspects of the curriculum that helped him turn his ideas into understanding. He pored over the great works of classical literature; his explorations into moral philosophy, logic and rhetoric went on. As did his efforts to distinguish truth from feeling, to put moral obligation in order of precedent.

In 1525 Frith was placed first in the *Ordo Senioritatis*, the published list of BA students. But his days at the university in the Fens were numbered. In 1525–6 he was among the group of star scholars poached by Wolsey to form the intellectual nexus of the expensively constructed, sumptuously equipped Cardinal College (later Christ Church) in Oxford. Others in the group included John Clarke, John Fryer and Henry Sumner. Also transferred to Oxford—to St. Mary's, the new monastic college—were several of the more gifted Augustinians. Among them was Robert Ferrar (q.v.), the future

---

1 John Foxe, *Acts & Monuments* (1838), v. 4.
2 Ibid.
3 D'Aubigné, i. 195.
4 The standard textbook of Roman Catholic theology.

bishop and martyr of St David's. What the cardinal had somehow failed to notice was how many of these talented young men were committed to the reform of the church. 'Every man', wrote Frith, 'which hath the light of God's Word revelated unto him, is sent whensoever he seeth necessity, and hath cure of his neighbour's soul'.[1] This was the radical affinity to which Frith adhered. Together they circulated tracts, formed study-groups, and taught the new theology publicly, including the doctrine of justification *sola fide*. As 'a Christian man which saith nothing but that Scripture confirmeth'[2] Frith's comfort, and Frith's joy, was to see the eternal consequences of the Cross applied not only to the life of the church, but to individual lives:

> It is not therefore sufficient to believe that He is a Saviour and Redeemer, but that He is a Saviour and Redeemer unto *you*. And this you cannot confess, unless you acknowledge yourself to be a sinner, for he that thinks himself no sinner needs no Saviour and Redeemer ... He that believes not God has made Him a liar, because he believes not the record that God has given of His Son. And this it that record, that God has given us eternal life, and this life is in His Son, which was made our beast, bearing our sins upon His own back, made obedient unto the death, offering up our iniquities (as a sacrifice) unto His Father, being our mediator and atonement between His Father and us ... So that sin has no power over us, nor can condemn us; for our satisfaction is made in Christ, who died for us that were wicked ... For by grace are you made safe through faith (Eph. 2: 8–9) and that not of yourselves, for it is the gift of God, and cometh not of works, lest any man should boast himself.[3]

Aiding and abetting the undergraduates was Thomas Garrard, the lynchpin of a highly-organized book-smuggling operation, bringing in pamphlets and tracts from the Low Countries. In February 1528 his activities were uncovered. A number of Cardinal College men 'were therefore accused of heresy unto the cardinal, and cast into a prison, within a deep cave under the ground of the same college, where their salt fish was laid'.[4] Over the six months of their incarceration, three of the students, including John Clarke, their leader, fell victim to 'sweating sickness' and died within a week of

---

1   Wright, 269.
2   Ibid. 253.
3   Ibid. 460–462.
4   Foxe, v. 5.

one another. Wolsey, fearful of creating martyrs, had Frith and the others released on the condition that they didn't travel more than ten miles from Oxford. The precise details of Frith's movements in the aftermath of the salt cellar are unclear. But by December 1528 he is living in Antwerp, helping William Tyndale revise his New Testament and Pentateuch. Frith's first meeting with Tyndale appears to have been much earlier, before Cardinal College, towards the end of his time at Cambridge. Though never himself a student at Cambridge, the begetter of the Bible in English was instrumental in Frith's conversion.[1] 'Through Tyndale's instructions', reports Foxe, 'he first received with his heart the seed of the Gospel and sincere godliness'.[2] That Gospel, for Frith, became the foundation of all true religion. Tyndale convinced him it was a gift of God Himself, not a work of art; its authority could not be abrogated by pope, church or tradition. By the time Tyndale left England in April 1524, Frith was independently affirming that 'I will consecrate my life wholly to the church of Jesus Christ. To be a good man, you must give a great part of yourself to your parents, a greater part to your country; but the greatest part of all to the church of the Lord'.[3]

By the time of Frith's arrival in Antwerp, Tyndale's New Testament, completed using Erasmus' Greek New Testament as a primary source, along with the Vulgate and Luther's German Bible, had 'opened the eyes of the whole English nation, which before were many years shut up in darkness'.[4] Often hidden in bales of cloth, the books arrived under cloak of night in the London docks. To store them was both impractical and fraught with danger, so Garrard and his friends would depart at dawn for the university towns and main religious houses. Tyndale, meanwhile, was living a hand-to-mouth existence, moving from Hamburg to Cologne to Worms, keeping one step ahead of spies and agents while seeking different printers for his work. But by 1528 he was settled among Antwerp's English cloth-merchant community. This afforded him a semblance of security while he set about

---

1   Foxe credited Tyndale with time at Cambridge in the first edition of *A&M*, but omitted that claim in later editions. There is no sign of Tyndale in the records of those who studied at Cambridge in the sixteenth century. Nor is there any mention of Tyndale in the writings of Bale and Cranmer, both of whom would have coincided with Tyndale had he been to the university.

2   Foxe, v. 4.

3   Quoted in D'Aubigné, i. 195.

4   Foxe, v. 121.

his translation of the Old Testament and the writing of other theological and polemical works.

In addition to checking Tyndale's manuscripts, Frith took on the role of supervising production and liaising between Tyndale and his printers, thus allowing the older man to concentrate fully upon his magnum opus. That so precocious a scholar and so personable an individual as Frith was sharing the weight of his labours transformed Tyndale's lonely exile. Tyndale later wrote to Frith that 'God has made me ill-favoured in this world, and without grace in the sight of men, speechless and rude, dull and slow-witted. Your post shall be to supply what is lacking in me'.[1] By the spring of 1529, Frith had a translation of Luther's anti-papal octavo *Revelation of the Antichrist* under his belt. He was also translating and reworking Melanchthon's *Antithesis between Christ and the Pope*. In the same year, using the pseudonym 'Richard Brightwell', he presented his own *Epistle to the Christian Reader*. The three sections were printed in a single volume by Martin de Keyser in Antwerp (otherwise 'Hans Luft of Marburg'). To these was added a treatise entitled *Antithesis, where are compared together Christ's Acts and our Holy Father the Pope's*. Seventy-eight deeds or utterances of Christ are contrasted and compared with those of the pope. In a heart-rending coda, Frith urged that the carnal kingdom of antichrist be vanquished by love rather than by hostility: an irenicism at odds with the more abrasive approach of his contemporary (at Cambridge) and fellow exile (in Wittenberg) Robert Barnes. It is this aspect of Frith's personality that seems most current and modern. For Tyndale's young helper, entering into discussions with those who held different views was not a choice but a necessity.

In October 1529 he attended the Marburg Colloquy, convened between Luther and Zwingli to discuss their differing views of the Lord's Supper. Here Frith was given a Lutheran thesis on faith and good works by Patrick Hamilton, a young Scot loved as much for his unimpeachable morality as for his scholarship. Hamilton fled Scotland after being accused of heresy by archbishop James Beaton, and spent a year at Marburg University. Seeing in Hamilton's words a singular devotion to the person and teaching of Christ, Frith immediately set about a translation of his thesis. What would come to be known as 'Patrick's Places', sensitively rendered from the original Latin, would become, after Hamilton's burning in February 1529, widely-loved as

---

1   Quoted in Brian H. Edwards, *God's Outlaw* (Darlington, 2002), 134.

a meditation on justification by faith. As well, it exploded any idea of the
Reformed despising good works. For Frith and Hamilton works were the
unconscious overflow of a living faith. They cannot justify the ungodly, nor
are they a price paid for sin, but are done from love of God, to God's glory:

> But we teach you how [works] ought to be done, and that they are
> the fruits of faith, and mortify our members, and are profitable to our
> neighbour, and a testimony unto us that we are the children of our
> heavenly Father. As an example, I say, that neither the sun or moon do
> justify us, or purchase remission of our sins, and yet [I would not] deny
> or destroy the sun and the moon, for without them we can have no
> light, and we cannot be without them.[1]

During Lent 1531 Frith returned to England. The trip could hardly
have lifted his spirits. Thomas More had by now succeeded Wolsey as lord
chancellor. Unlike Wolsey, More was a torturer and man-burner; the judicial
functions of his office were weapons to war against heresy. A rising tide of
arrests culminated with Bilney perishing in the flames in Norwich in August,
and the Benedictine monk Richard Bayfield in Smithfield in December. At
his trial Bayfield had admitted reading Frith's *A Disputation of Purgatory* 'to
himself alone'.[2] Such an act was guaranteed to attract the hostility of More,
who wrote in the aftermath of Bayfield's martyrdom that 'There should have
been more burned by a great many than there have been within this seven
year last passed, the lack whereof I fear me will make more burned within
this seven year next coming than else should have needed to have been
burned in seven score'.[3] Frith's response, on returning to Antwerp, was to
develop and put down on paper his ideas about the function of works within
the Christian life.[4] In the same period he took a wife; Stephen Vaughan,
latterly Henry VIII's agent on the Continent, told Thomas Cromwell that
Frith 'is very lately married in Holland, and there dwelleth, but in what place
I cannot tell'.[5] It was not, it seems, a love match. According to Vaughan,
Frith was 'driven [to marriage] through poverty, which is to be pitied, his

1   Wright, 239.
2   Foxe, iv. 683.
3   Tyndale, *Works* (London, 1850), iii. 97n.
4   Some of these ideas are contained within Frith's commentary on *Tracy's Testament*, discovered
among the papers of William Tyndale.
5   Quoted in Moynahan, *If God Spare my Life* (London, 2002), 278.

qualities considered'.[1] *A Disputation of Purgatory* had, by this time, taken a wrecking-ball to Vaughan's plans to persuade Frith to forsake Tyndale and serve the king.

A treatise in three books, the *Disputation* attacked purgatory on the basis that no proof could be found in Scripture for its existence. The Council of Trent, in various phases from 1545 to 1563, confirmed that 'there is a purgatory and the souls that are detained there are helped by the prayers of the faithful but most especially by the sacrifice of the altar'. Other 'helps' included the sale of indulgences. All of which caused redemption to rest upon human repentance and effort. Why, said Frith, with so many priests saying so many masses, purgatory should be quite empty! His treatise was interpreted as a personal attack on More and John Fisher, the Luther-baiting bishop of Rochester. While in the Low Countries, Frith had studied books in defence of purgatory by both men, and another by John Rastell, a lawyer, printer, and More's brother-in-law. 'A purgatory!' exclaimed Frith. 'There is not only one, there are two. The first is the Word of God, the second is the Cross of Christ: I do not mean the cross of wood, but the cross of tribulation. But the lives of the papists are so wicked that they have invented a third'.[2] More, in his *Supplication of Souls,* made some use of the Vulgate.[3] For the most part, however, both he and Fisher relied on tradition as embodied in conciliar decrees and patristics.[4] Frith was not impressed. There must be 'a judge to discern between truth and falsehood':

And who should that be?—the pope? Certainly not, for he being a man, as the doctors were, may err as they did. Our judge, therefore, must not be partial, flexible, nor ignorant. And so are all natural men excluded. But he must be unalterable, even searching the bottom and ground of all things. Who must that be? Verily, the Scripture and Word of God, which was given by His Son, confirmed and sealed by the Holy Spirit, and testified by miracles and blood of all martyrs. This Word is the judge that must examine the matter, the perfect touchstone that

1   Quoted in Brian Raynor, *John Frith: Scholar and Martyr* (Sevenoaks, 2000), 97.
2   Quoted in D'Aubigné, ii. 126.
3   A Latin version of the Bible, mainly the work of St Jerome, which achieved widespread influence in the Middle Ages.
4   The branch of theology concerned with the writings of the church fathers, typically those who were active after the writing of the New Testament, and before the end of the 8th century.

tries all things, and day that discloses all juggling mists. If the doctors say anything not dissonant from this Word, then it is admitted and held for truth. But if any of their doctrine discord from it, it is to be abhorred, and held accursed.[1]

Frith saw that the familiar practice of the religious élite settling religious issues between themselves had led to glaring inconsistencies. Thus, despite being its 'chiefest friends, proctors and patrons',[2] More and Fisher had wildly differing conceptions of purgatory: both as a place and a condition of existence. So while More says there is water in purgatory, Fisher denies it. To More, 'the ministers of punishment are devils'; no, writes Fisher, 'the ministers of punishment are angels'. And More's view 'that both the grace and charity of them that lie in the pains of purgatory are increased', is contrasted with Fisher's that 'the souls in purgatory obtain there neither more faith, nor grace, nor charity, than they brought in with them'.[3] Frith's criticism is devoid of self-advertisement; or, indeed, rancour. 'These things considered', he writes, 'it made my heart yearn, and fully to consent, that this their painful purgatory was but a vain imagination, and that is has for a long time deceived the people, and milked them of their money'.[4] He commends instead the words of Christ: 'Come unto me, all ye that are weary and laden, and I will ease you' (Matthew 11:28). And asks, with more than a hint of wistful solicitude: 'Wilt thou send us, Lord, into purgatory? Forsooth there is little ease, if the fire be so hot as our prelates have feigned it'.[5]

If More's failure to utilize the Latin or Greek texts of Erasmus was evidence of bad scholarship, his doctrine was far, far worse. It effaced the Cross from the mind of Christ, from His Word, from history: 'The Scripture', writes Frith, 'knows no other satisfaction to be made for sin towards God, but only the blood of His Son Jesus Christ; for if there were another satisfaction, then Christ died in vain: yes, and he that seeks any other satisfaction for his sin (towards God) than Christ's blood (which must be received with a repenting heart through faith) despises Christ's blood and treads it under his feet. And

---

1 Wright, 189–90.

2 Ibid. 89.

3 Ibid. Richard Rex, Fisher's biographer, writes that 'in principle the position ascribed by Frith to Fisher is more mainstream than that ascribed him to More' *(from a letter to the author)*.

4 Ibid. 89–90.

5 Ibid. 115.

so is the first part of Master More's solution false, that they should be shut in purgatory to make satisfaction'.[1] As we've seen, Frith's theology of death and life admitted two purgatories: two, as it were, *legitimate* purgatories. The first related to the Word of God, the second to the Cross of Christ. The former was a purgatory of the heart, wherein the Holy Spirit, working through the Word, brings us to faith 'and gives us a will and gladness to do whatever our most merciful Father commands us'. Such a purgatory 'obtains to no man, but through faith, for the unfaithful are not purged by the Word of God, as the Scribes and Pharisees were nothing better for hearing His Word, but rather the worse, for it was a testimony against them unto their condemnation'.[2] And in place of a mechanism that downplays moral agency and accountability, Frith erects '[our] spiritual Cross, which is adversity, tribulation, worldly depression etc'.[3] By such trials are we tested in order that the things that do not belong to the essence of faith fall away. Thus to the purification of our souls is added the sanctifying effects of a process of mental suffering and bodily disintegration: 'the Cross of tribulation to which God has nailed us'.[4] Upon death the last vestige of sin is removed.

No English Reformer had provided such a masterful defence of his views; Frith had, by common consent, 'beaten Thomas More in controversy'.[5] An infuriated More told friends of his determination to 'pluck as I trust the most glorious feathers from his gay peacock's tail'. In the months ahead his hatred of Frith and the 'corrupt canker' of Frithian heresy became so intense it bordered on the pathological. Should he return home, every expression of More's murderous intent—his network of informers, bribery of officials, use of torture and double agents—would be brought to bear against him. Frith knew all of this. But, writes d'Aubigné, 'Humble before the Lord, mild before men, and even in appearance somewhat timid, Frith in the face of danger displayed an intrepid courage'.[6] In July 1532 he crossed the sea to England for the last time.

Frith landed somewhere on the Essex coast. By foot and by cart he proceeded to Reading, where, unwashed and in rags, he was set in the

---

1   Ibid. 177.
2   Wright, 90.
3   Ibid. 91.
4   Quoted in Raynor, 65.
5   Carl Trueman, *Luther's Legacy* (Oxford, 1994), 3.
6   Quoted in Raynor, 224.

stocks as a rogue and a vagabond. Fearing More's men, he declined to give his name, but begged for the local schoolmaster to be brought to him. By the time Leonard Cox, by chance a fellow Etonian, arrived, Frith was 'almost pined with hunger', and began 'in the Latin tongue [to] bewail his captivity'.[1] Hearing a vagrant faultlessly reciting parts of Homer's *Iliad* in the original Greek was a novel experience for Cox. He scurried off to petition the town's governors, and Frith was soon unshackled. His freedom was short-lived. Stokesley, bishop of London, had gotten wind of his return and sent agents to comb the countryside of Berkshire and Oxfordshire. A reward was put on Frith's head. Coast roads were watched, new informers recruited. In October 1532 the Reformer was seized at Milton Shore, near Southend, while attempting to buy a passage back to Antwerp. He had been taken by Stokesley's men, but to the bishop's immense frustration neither he—nor, in fact, More—was allowed to keep him. Instead Thomas Cromwell, who could always be relied upon to shelter Reformers, claimed Frith for himself and arranged for him to be kept in the Tower of London, unchained and held in loose confinement. There he would spend the last year of his life.

Soon after his arrest, events moved in a direction favourable to Frith. Following the pope's refusal to grant an annulment of Henry VIII's marriage to Catherine, the king's cause needed some serious underpinning. Frith's natural charm, and capacity for moderation and originality, were recommended to the monarch. As early as May 1531 Cromwell had written to his agent Stephen Vaughan that 'as touching Frith ... [the king] hopes that he might be recalled to the right way, and he instructs you to speak with Frith if you are able, and to urge him to leave his wilful opinions, and like a good Christian to return to his native country, where he assuredly shall find the king's highness most merciful, and benignly upon his conversation disposed to accept him to his grace and mercy'.[2] Frith's opinions mattered. Despite his incarceration they were actively sought. The duke of Norfolk, the most Catholic of Henry's privy councillors, even suggested there was 'no fitter or better qualified man to send abroad on an embassy to a great prince'.[3] It is difficult to imagine Norfolk saying similar things about, say, Robert

1 Foxe, v. 5.
2 Quoted in Raynor, 97.
3 Quoted in Moynahan, 279.

Barnes: this despite the fact that Barnes was willing, where Frith was not, to entertain royal headship as a theological idea.

Frith was treated with unprecedented leniency in the Tower. He was even allowed, according to John Strype, 'to go at liberty in the night to consult with godly men'.[1] While thus confined, Frith was able to write two or three short treatises on the new faith. One of these would lead directly to his downfall. Frith was enjoined by 'a friend' to commit his views on the Lord's Supper to paper. 'I was loath to take the matter in hand', wrote Frith later, 'yet to fulfil his instant intercession, I took upon me to touch this terrible tragedy, and wrote a treatise, which, besides my painful imprisonment, is like to purchase me most cruel death'.[2] The so-called friend passed it on to William Holt, a London tailor. Holt hailed the next boat to Chelsea, and placed the treatise in the hands of Thomas More. It was, in fact, a set-up. The now ex-lord chancellor, acting through his double-agents, had induced Frith to air his opinions in order to derail Cromwell's positioning of him as a conciliatory figure—'one whom Henry VIII had desired to place near him'[3]—capable of mounting a scriptural defence of the split with Rome. More, still smarting from the intellectual drubbing he had received at Frith's hands, needed no convincing of the younger man's talents. But he now held all the evidence he needed to send him to the stake.

In 1523–25 the Swiss theologian Huldrych Zwingli, in setting out his understanding of the meaning of Christ's life and death, had denied outright His bodily presence in the Lord's Supper. At the Colloquy of Marburg (1529) Frith had observed the bitter rifts between Zwinglians and Lutherans. 'You must prove that the body of Christ is not here, when the Word says "This is my body"!' cried Luther at the Basel Reformer Oecolampadius. 'I do not want to hear reason ... God is above all mathematics. The words of God are to be adored and observed with awe'.[4] By the time of Marburg Frith had already begun his conversion to a view broadly in line with that of Oecolampadius.[5] In other words, it was not Christ's presence in the bread that saved, but His presence in the heart. The dogma of transubstantiation

---

1   Ibid. 280.

2   Ibid. 280–81.

3   D'Aubigné, ii. 126.

4   Quoted in Moynahan, 282.

5   Johannes Oecolampadius (1482–1531), Swiss Reformer, based in Basel. The first Reformer to have sanctioned lay participation in church government.

was abhorrent to His vision and voice; the Supper, argued Frith, must not be reduced to grossly physical terms. At the same time he opposed the construction of a 'bread only' theology. For the majority of those who self-identified as Zwinglians, the congregation was the body of Christ, the bread a bare sign. What happened at the Lord's Table was principally a congregational act of witness. Frith, taking the Oecolampadius line, emphasized instead a positive doctrine of real feeding on Christ. 'They speak well and faithfully', wrote Frith, 'which say that they go to the body and receive the body of Christ, and that they speak villainously and wickedly, which say that they only receive bread, or the sign of His body; for in saying so they reveal their infidelity'.[1] Elsewhere in his *Answer to More* Frith pauses in his exposition of 1 Corinthians to warn of the consequences of approaching the Lord's Table without a clear understanding of what is about to happen:

Wherefore whosoever doth eat of this bread and drink of this cup unworthily, is guilty of the body and blood of the Lord. He eateth this bread unworthily, which regardeth not the purpose for which Christ did institute it, which cometh not to it with spiritual hunger, to eat through faith His very body, which the bread representeth by the breaking and distributing of it: which cometh not with a merry heart, giving God hearty thanks for their deliverance from sin: which do not much more eat in their heart the death of His body, than they do the bread with their mouth.[2]

Typically, however, Frith was prepared to accommodate himself to the views of others. 'His rule regarding ceremonies', says Clebsch, 'was to avoid offending his weaker brother'.[3] Carl Trueman comments that Frith was not 'much concerned to deny that Christ is physically present in the eucharist', for 'such presence is not important to salvation'.[4] Aware that More and Stephen Gardiner, the bishop of Winchester, would stop at nothing to set the Reformed at each other's throats, Tyndale cautioned Frith to leave the subject alone. 'Mine heart's desire in the Saviour Jesus', wrote Tyndale to his young friend, 'is that you arm yourself with patience, and be cold, sober, wise, and circumspect; and that you keep a-low by the ground, avoiding high

1 Wright, 447.
2 Ibid. 437.
3 Clebsch, 121.
4 Trueman, 151.

questions that pass the common capacity ... Of the presence of Christ's body in the sacrament meddle as little as you can, that there appear no division among us. Barnes will be hot against you'.[1] Robert Barnes held to a strongly Lutheran view of the Supper. Addressing Frith as 'brother Jacob, beloved of my heart', Tyndale pleaded with him to 'act in fear, and not in boldness'.[2] But it was too late. Not only did More hold three copies of Frith's treatise, he soon acquired a copy of Tyndale's letter as well. He was triumphant: 'I wish me sore that Christ will kindle a fire of faggots for [Frith]', enthused 'Saint' Thomas, 'and make him therein sweat the blood out of his body here, and straight from hence send his soul forever into the fire of hell'.[3]

Having lost much of his influence with the king since resigning the lord chancellorship in May 1532, Thomas More was no longer in a position to molest Frith personally. But his command of court-craft, and understanding of Henry's complex character, remained intact. As a means of attacking Frith, and discrediting Cromwell, *A Letter of Sir Thomas More, Knight, impugning the erroneous writing of John Frith against the blessed Sacrament of the Altar* was wickedly effective. A master of English prose, More contrived to fawn on Henry for being 'a most faithful Catholic prince for the avoiding of pestilent books',[4] while chivvying him to do more to root out heresy. Full of, in Frith's own phrase, 'painted poetry, and crafty conveyance',[5] the *Letter* depicted Frith's work as 'a false foolish treatise against the blessed sacrament of the altar'.[6] Frith himself, said More, was an even greater threat to the realm than Luther: a sponge for all the poison spewed out by Oecolampadius and Tyndale. Using the metaphor of a bonfire that 'beginneth to reek out at some corner ... burneth up whole towns, and wasteth whole countries ... lieth lurking sly; in some old rotten timber under cellars and ceilings',[7] More amplified his hatred of the Reformed in general, and of Frith in particular, to ear-splitting levels.

His timing was exquisite. Having named himself Supreme Head of the English church, Henry was morbidly sensitive to accusations of colluding with

---

1   Foxe, v. 133.
2   Ibid.
3   *Complete Works of Thomas More* (New Haven & London, 1979), ix. 122.
4   Quoted in Moynahan, 284.
5   Wright, 267.
6   *Complete Works*, ix. 123. See Peter Ackroyd, *The Life of Thomas More* (London, rep. 1999), 324.
7   *Complete Works*, vii. 234.

heretics. He yearned to be seen as true defender of the faith. And that is why, as Peter Ackroyd puts it, 'he still needed the tacit support of Thomas More, even in retirement, and why he could not allow himself to be compromised by Cromwell's association with the "bretherne".'[1] For More, the burning of Frith—albeit an excellent thing in itself—was first and foremost a shot across Cromwell's bows. MacCulloch writes that 'as the breach with Rome widened, it was important to be firm against such "sacramentaries" as Frith in order that Henry's regime did not lose the loyalty of conservative leaders such as bishop Stokesley'.[2] There is a bogus quality to some of the odium heaped upon Frith. His writings reveal an imagination where the claims of truth coexist with a genuine desire to promote communion and community. N.T. Wright speculates to some effect that 'having learnt justification from Luther and the doctrine of Christ's presence from Oecolampadius, Frith discovered in [Martin] Bucer's work that tolerance of the views of others for the sake of which he was prepared to die'.[3] Even in his most polemical work, there is a reminder of the acts and duties of love:

Here ends the *Revelation of Antichrist*, which, although it be some deal fierce against the pope and his adherents, yet, good Christian brother, read it charitably. Move not thy patience. Overcome them rather with thy good and virtuous living than with force and exterior power. So shall you be the true son of thy Father which is in heaven, to whom only be the glory. Amen.[4]

Frith repeatedly maintained, while expounding his own views with the utmost vigour, that neither purgatory nor the Lord's Supper were articles of faith to be believed under pain of damnation. He drew a line between those aspects of the Christian faith that were integral to one's salvation, and others about which differences of opinion were allowable. As Foxe admits, Frith 'would never seem to strive against the papists, except he had been driven to it out of necessity'.[5] But a note of caution ought to be injected here. There is a delusive and anachronistic tendency within modern criticism to view Frith wholly in relation to the theology of tolerance. A lot of this,

---

1   *The Life of Thomas More* (London, rep. 1999), 324.
2   *Thomas Cranmer* (New Haven, 1996), 102.
3   Wright, 61–62.
4   Ibid. 37.
5   Foxe, v. 9–10.

one suspects, has to do with wish fulfilment: a determination among some
to detect in Frith an echo of their own religious uncertainty. But there is
an improbability, as Wright makes clear, 'about Frith, who could be very
dogmatic if he chose, dying as a martyr to the peculiarly twentieth-century
virtue of tolerance, which all too easily comes to mean a careless, *laissez-
faire* attitude of non interference, conditioned by philosophies in which all
values are relative'.[1] In Frith, as much as in any Reformer, we see a solid
determination to oppose anything that stifles the purpose of Christ's ministry,
no matter what the personal cost. Yes, his instincts were irenic and inclusivist.
But Frith insisted that we commit to belief before we commit to community.
We must seek the face of God, not the warmed-up wisdom of men. He
was never afraid to hold an opinion or to express it, believing with all his
heart that one day 'the Word of God shall blow away from the face of the
earth the dark clouds and mists of men's inventions, and shall scour away
the rust of fleshly understanding of the Scriptures'.[2] If the doctrine of love
is at the centre of his theology—as we might, I believe, say that it is—it is
emphatically biblical, not platitudinous, love.

Upon revisiting Frith, it is hard to understand why he is such a neglected
figure. His reputation among his contemporaries, and near-contemporaries,
was sky-high. His writing is scholarly, exact and closely argued, as it had to
be. Yet whole passages have a buoyancy to them, a dancingness: a kind of
condensed energy. He is self-effacing. A penchant for alliteration never grates.
And he is often amusing: the going rate for leaving purgatory is 'more painful
to the poor, yet it is more profitable to the prelates':[3] their doctrines 'have
golden tails, for money is ever the end'.[4] In his *Bulwark against Rastell*, Frith
likens his dialogue with Thomas More's brother-in-law to a tennis match:

> God give me leave to keep the court with him. He shall win but little,
> unless he convey his balls more craftily. And yet, truth to tell, we play
> not on even hand. For I am in a manner as a man bound to a post, and
> cannot well bestow me in my play, as if I were at liberty. For I may not
> have such books as are necessary for me, neither yet pen, ink, nor paper,
> but only secretly... I hear the keys ring at the doors, straight all must be

---

1   Wright, 75.
2   Ibid. 208.
3   Ibid. 114. See also Introduction.
4   Ibid. 306.

conveyed out of the way (and then if any notable thing had been in my mind, it be clean lost)'.[1]

The style seems modern: more modern, curiously, than a lot of Puritan writing. At no point does he seem removed from those he is addressing. He writes lovingly of doctrine, but is never doctrinaire. He doesn't begin with a theory and then fit Scripture around it. All of which contributes, in the opinion of Clebsch, to 'a more consistent, and more consistently theological, literary corpus than any of his fellow-workers achieved'.[2]

Shortly before his death, still voicing his opposition to the adoration of the sacrament, Frith wrote that 'all the Germans and Almains, both of Luther's side, and Oecolampadius, do wholly approve my matter. And surely I think that no man that hath a pure conscience, but he will think that I die righteously; for that this transubstantiation should be a necessary article of the faith, I think that no man can say it with a good conscience'.[3] But good consciences might be washed away in the tide of Tudor politics. Richard Curwen, one of the royal chaplains, was instructed by Stephen Gardiner, Frith's former tutor, to denounce Frith and his views in a sermon before the king. Frith was ordered by Henry himself to recant and held for examination before the bishops of London and Lincoln—and Gardiner himself—at St Paul's on 20 June 1533. He was even taken to Cranmer's house is Surrey, where he expounded the eucharistic doctrine of Oecolampadius. 'I myself sent for him three or four times', wailed the archbishop, 'to persuade him to leave that his imagination: but for all that we could do therein, he would not apply to any counsel'.[4] Every attempt to terrify him into compliance having failed, Frith's boldness gathered momentum. 'Let justice have its course', he declared, 'and the sentence be pronounced'.[5]

That sentence, delivered by bishop Stokesley, declared Frith 'obstinate and stiff-necked, willingly continuing in thy damnable opinions and heresies, and refusing to return again unto the true faith and unity of the Holy Mother Church'.[6] Having denied in writing that the doctrines of purgatory

---

1   Ibid. 242.
2   Clebsch, 7.
3   Wright, 455.
4   Quoted in MacCulloch, 101.
5   Quoted in D'Aubigné, ii. 144.
6   Foxe, v. 15.

and transubstantiation were necessary articles of faith, Frith was declared excommunicate and released into the hands of the secular powers, 'most earnestly requiring them in the truth of our Lord Jesus Christ that thy execution and punishment be not too extreme, nor yet the gentleness too much mitigated'.[1] Cast into Newgate, an iron band round his neck, weighed down with chains, Frith's first concern was to refute any suggestion that the Reformers lacked consistency among themselves. By the light of a guttering candle he wrote: 'I condemn neither those who follow Luther nor those who follow Oecolampadius, since both reject transubstantiation'.[2] Right to the end, he sought a common ground that did not sully the principles of the Reformation. 'I understand the church of God in a wide sense', he said. 'It contains all those whom we regard as members of Christ. It is a net thrown into the sea'.[3]

With Frith was Andrew Hewet, a young tailor's apprentice from Faversham in Kent. When his opinion on the Lord's Supper had been sought by the bishops, Hewet had replied: 'I think as Frith does'.[4] Stokesley was mightily amused. 'Why, Frith is a heretic', he jeered, 'and already judged to be burned. And unless you revoke your opinion, you shall be burned with him'. 'Truly', said Hewet, 'I am content'.[5] With Frith's execution fast-approaching, a letter arrived from Tyndale, enjoining him to contemplate God's merciful nature as revealed in Christ. 'If the pain be above your strength', wrote his mentor, 'pray to your Father in that name, and he shall ease your pain, or shorten it'.[6] He added a postscript: 'Sir, your wife is well content with the will of God, and would not, for her sake, have the glory of God hindered'.[7]

On 4 July 1533, Frith and Hewet were taken to Smithfield and tied to a stake, back to back. Frith took the lead in offering consoling perspectives on their plight. A conservative rector, Dr Cook, directed the crowd not to pray for the Reformers any more than they would for a dog. Frith smiled, and called upon his Lord and Redeemer to forgive the poor man. Cook's bombast, reports Foxe, 'did not a little move the people unto anger, and not

---

1   Ibid.
2   Quoted in D'Aubigné, ii. 144.
3   Ibid. 126.
4   Foxe, v. 15.
5   Ibid.
6   Foxe, v. 132.
7   Ibid.

without good cause. Thus the two blessed martyrs committed their souls into the hands of God'.[1] A cutting wind off the Thames drew the flame away from Frith, in the direction of Hewet. His companion's prompt deliverance meant more agonies for Frith, but strengthened and enabled by the Author of Life he 'seemed rather to rejoice for his fellow, than to be careful for himself'.[2] Eventually his blackened form slumped forward. Across the sea in Antwerp, upon hearing the latest news from England, William Tyndale set aside his pen and sobbed copious tears.

Until the day of his own martyrdom, in the Belgian town of Vilvoorde in the autumn of 1536, Tyndale never ceased to mourn the loss of one he called his 'dear son in the faith'.[3] He was, however, to enjoy for a brief period the fellowship of another Cambridge martyr: John Rogers of Pembroke Hall. Rogers was born in Deritend, in the parish of Aston in the West Midlands, the son of a lorimer: a presser and grinder of horse bits, spurs and other intricate iron objects. After graduating BA in 1526, he was awarded the benefice of Holy Trinity the Less in the City of London. When appointed chaplain to the English merchants in Antwerp in 1534, he adjusted quite naturally to the undemanding life of a Catholic priest. Everything changed when he met Tyndale. Under his guidance Rogers was introduced to better ways of pleasing God than kissing relics or embarking upon pilgrimages. The church of Rome, he now believed, taught doctrines plainly and directly against God's will: including that of clerical celibacy. Three years after his arrival in Antwerp he married Adriana de Weyden, a native of the port city. Unlike Frith's, the marriage was a love match. 'She was', writes Foxe, 'more richly endowed with virtue and soberness of life than with worldly treasures'.

Tyndale's special gift to Rogers was to convince him that until the Word of God was intelligible to the common man, England would never rise above its vague, intermittent and inert hankerings after faith. In the late autumn of 1536, his conscience pricked by reports of Tyndale's strangulation and burning near Brussels, Rogers stepped up his efforts to incorporate Tyndale's as yet unpublished translation of the Old Testament—from Joshua to 2 Chronicles—into a complete English Bible. He used Miles Coverdale's translation for the remaining books and the Apocrypha. Aside from the

1 Ibid. 18.
2 Ibid. 15.
3 Quoted in Moynahan, 277.

Prayer of Manasses, which he found in a French Bible of 1535, Rogers did
little, if any, of the work of translation. But he edited the text and supplied
a preface and marginal notes. The Matthew Bible, sometimes known as
Matthew's Version,[1] was published in Antwerp in 1537 by Jacobus van
Meteren, Adriana's uncle.

After three years on the banks of the Scheldt, Rogers decamped to
Wittenberg. Like Barnes before him he matriculated at the university and
formed close ties with Luther and, especially, with Melanchthon. With
Melanchthon's support, he spent four and a half years as the superintendent
of a church in the north of Germany. He returned to England in 1548.
After publishing a well-received translation of Melanchthon, Rogers was
presented to the livings of St Margaret Moses and St Sepulchre: this placed
him in important London pulpits. By 1551, already a prebend of St Paul's,
he had been appointed divinity lecturer by the dean and chapter. As a rising
man in the church, Rogers might have been expected to avoid ruffling the
feathers of senior bishops. Instead he preached hotly against the acquisition of
monastic lands by peers and gentry who, while cosying up to the Reformers,
were actually feathering their own nests. His remarks cut so deeply he was
summoned before the Privy Council. He also demonstrated his independency
by endorsing the views of John Hooper and Robert Ferrar on the subject
of clerical vestments. Both men felt that as modesty and fear were the
proper attitudes before God, traditional liturgical dress—with all its gaudy
accoutrements—ought to be done away with. Rogers himself always favoured
a simple round hat rather than the customary angled cap.

After a 'godly and vehement' sermon at Paul's Cross, shortly after the
accession of Mary Tudor—in which hearers were exhorted to 'beware of
all pestilent popery, idolatry and superstition'[2]—Rogers was called before a
Privy Council packed with haters of the Bible-men. Released then rearrested,
he was placed under house arrest before being taken to Newgate. A year
later he was twice examined by a panel presided over by Stephen Gardiner.
On 22 January, asked whether he would accept the religious, judicial and
administrative authority of the pope, Rogers declared that Christ alone was
head of the church. When he attempted to draw Gardiner into debate, the
lord chancellor insisted that the Bible forbad him 'to use any conferring and

---

1   Rogers' pseudonym was 'Thomas Matthew'.
2   Foxe, vi. 592.

trial with thee. For St Paul teacheth me that I should shun and eschew a heretic after one or two monitions, knowing that such a one is overthrown, and is faulty, insomuch as he is condemned by his own judgement'. To which Rogers replied: 'I deny I am a heretic. Prove that first, and then allege your text'.[1]

On 29 January 1555 John Rogers was convicted of heresy. He might have fled to the Continent, but chose to remain and risk all in Christ's cause. After sentence of death was pronounced, he spoke thus:

Well, my lord, here I stand before God and you, and all this honourable audience, and take Him to witness, that I never wittingly nor willingly taught any false doctrine; and therefore have I a good conscience before God and before all good men. I am not afraid, but I shall come before a judge that is righteous, before whom I shall be as good a man as you; and I do not doubt but that I shall be found there a true member of the true catholic church of Christ and everlastingly saved. And as for your false church, you need not excommunicate me from it. I have not been in it these twenty years, the Lord be praised.[2]

Rogers was brought to the stake on 4 February 1555, the first of the Reformers to burn under Mary I. On the 8th, John Bradford wrote—in a letter to Cranmer, Latimer and Ridley—that his good friend Rogers 'hath broken the ice valiantly'.[3] According to a report sent to Foxe, Rogers slept so soundly on his last night that 'scarce with much shaking could [he] be awakened'.[4] All through his incarceration he had displayed the characteristics of kindness and loyalty that were so much a feature of his walk with God. John Hooper wrote that 'there was never little fellow better would stick to a man than [Rogers] would stick to him'. En route for Smithfield, he recited Psalm 51: David, after confessing his sin, implores God to 'take not thine Holy Spirit from me' and to accept the burnt offering of the righteous. As the faggots were lit, a royal pardon was presented and Rogers' abjuration sought. He refused, exhorting onlookers to depend entirely on the doctrine of Christ. Foxe relates that 'after lifting up his hands unto heaven, not removing the same until such time as the devouring fire had consumed them—most

1 Ibid. 594–595.
2 Ibid. 602.
3 *The Writings of John Bradford* (Edinburgh, fac. 1979), ii. 190.
4 Foxe, vi. 609.

mildly this happy martyr yielded up his spirit into the hands of his heavenly Father'.[1] Antoine de Noailles, the French ambassador to London, left this account:

> This day was performed the confirmation of the alliance between the pope and this kingdom, by a public and solemn sacrifice of a preaching doctor named Rogers, who has been burned alive for being a Lutheran; but he died persisting in his opinion. At this conduct, the greatest part of the people took such pleasure that they were not afraid to make him many exclamations to strengthen his courage. Even his children assisted at it, comforting him in such a manner that it seemed as if he had been led to a wedding.[2]

---

1   Ibid. 611.
2   *DNB*, 17.128–9.

IV

THOMAS BILNEY

Among the first-generation English Reformers, Thomas Bilney was the best-loved and most influential; 'the moving spirit', writes William Clebsch, 'of the Cambridge circle of Lutherans'.[1] Hugh Latimer, John Lambert and Robert Barnes were all guided to the fold of Christ by 'Little Bilney'. His zeal for the Gospel, gentle disposition and compassion for those struggling in darkness shine through every account of his life. Once directed in the ways of the Lord, writes Foxe, Bilney was filled 'with an incredible desire to allure many unto the same, desiring nothing more than that he might stir up and encourage any to the love of Christ'.[2] So far, so admirable. But he was also described as 'a man of timorous conscience' whose views on the mass and transubstantiation 'never differed from the most gross Catholics'.[3] For Greg Walker, in his seminal essay on the Bilney trial, he is a 'shadowy figure', who at his first trial for heresy proved 'more schemer than saint'.[4] Another is certain 'that he was neither a Protestant nor particularly heretical'.[5]

Given the part played by Bilney in the construction of an English Reformed identity, such conjecture is, to say the least, unsettling. Are his repeated protestations of loyalty to the established church really compatible with being 'persuaded by God's holy Word'?[6] How far outside the sphere of medieval orthodoxy did he actually stray? He was a popular preacher and devoted to pastoral work. In his private habits he was the very model of pious living. But

---

1   William Clebsch, *England's Earliest Protestants 1520–1535* (New Haven, 1964), 278.

2   John Foxe, *Acts & Monuments* (1837), iv. 620.

3   Ibid. 649.

4   Greg Walker, 'The 1527 Heresy Trial of Thomas Bilney Reconsidered', *Journal of Ecclesiastical History*, vol. 40, no. 2 (April 1989), 238.

5   Muriel C. McClendon, *The Quiet Reformation: Magistrates and the Emergence of Protestantism in Tudor Norwich* (Stanford, 1999), 64.

6   Foxe, iv. 653.

how credible is it to describe him as 'stand[ing] in the place of honour at the head of the English Reformation'?[1] Was he dissenter—or dissembler? Or a combination of both? Perhaps, in the conflicted theology that accompanied Thomas Bilney to the stake in Norwich in 1531, we might discern the fault lines of Henrician evangelicalism itself.

He was born in Norfolk, probably in Norwich, though the village of East Bilney is another possibility. The year of his birth is uncertain, but 1495 is usually cited. Both parents outlived their son. By 1510, or thereabouts, Bilney is at Cambridge, reading law at Trinity Hall. But the Norfolk tie-in is important in at least one respect. In the first quarter of the sixteenth century Lollardy was deeply entrenched in the county. Lollards regarded themselves as an élite fellowship of 'known men': the elect, known to God and to one another. The practical bent of their teaching owed much to their obsessive reading of the letter of James, called by E.G. Rupp 'the handbook of the known men'.[2] Being a clandestine, decentralized movement, a church without walls, Lollardy had many regional variations. It drew upon a variety of ideas. At its core, however, dwelt a visceral hostility to pilgrimages, to the mediation of saints, to the veneration of images. These were the practices attacked by Bilney from pulpits in London and East Anglia in 1527. 'Jews and Saracens', he declared, 'would have become Christian men long ago, had it not been for the idolatry of Christian men, in offering of candles, wax, and money, to stocks and stones'.[3] Such invectives against the appendages of idolatry constituted, says Foxe, the 'whole sum of [Bilney's] preaching and doctrine'.[4] Does this make Bilney a Lollard? Almost certainly not. Such ideas, after all, were hardly the preserve of Lollardy. Humanists as well as Lutherans expressed them with equal force. But the tenor of his sermons suggests at least some Lollard influence, and certainly won him an ardent Lollard following.

All of this, however, was in the future. In 1516, six years into his university career, a guilt-wracked young scholar sat in his rooms at Trinity Hall with 'small force of strength left in me (who by nature was but weak), small store of money, and very little wit or understanding'.[5] A spirit of confusion had

1   Marcus Loane, *Masters of the Reformation* (London, 1956), 26.
2   *Studies in the Making of the English Reformed Tradition* (Cambridge, 1947), 5.
3   Foxe, iv. 627.
4   Ibid. 649.
5   Ibid. 635.

overtaken him. He could not work; he could hardly rest. He brooded endlessly on his sinful nature and worked himself into a spiritual darkening from which, it seemed, he would never re-emerge. He took his angst to the priests ('unlearned hearers of confession')[1] who prescribed regular fasting, vigils, masses and expensive indulgences. This relieved him of his money: little else. His morbidity increased. Looking back on his breakdown, Bilney compared himself to the woman 'that was twelve years vexed with the bloody flux [that] had consumed all she had, and felt no help, but was still worse and worse, until such time as she came at last to Christ'.[2] Several descriptions of Bilney, from Foxe and others, hint at a neurotic element in his makeup. Despite this burden, or because of it, he was as threatened by isolation as others were by intimacy. His whole being threw out tendrils, as it were, towards the outer world. Such vacillations between faith and fear, strength and weakness, set him apart from more obviously resilient figures in Reformation history. He was, observes Loane, 'as gentle as Luther was rugged'.[3] This might explain the very different moral reasoning that underpinned his defence at his trial. Bilney would ever seek his identity in attachment, and reach for other hands to grip his own. In an atmosphere where the pursuit of knowledge turned too easily into a pursuit of self-exultation, he dedicated himself to the ideal of a holy life. He never slept for more than four hours. He ate one meal a day. His search for emotional stability, and desire to purge himself of unsuitable thoughts, instilled a strong aversion to the arts and music, whether it was the 'dainty singing' of Cambridge choirs, or chordal pieces played by his neighbour, and future bishop of Ely, Thomas Thirlby.[4]

One day at Trinity Hall, Bilney happened upon a group of students debating Erasmus' *Novum Instrumentum*, his Latin translation of the New Testament. 'If you approach the Scriptures in all humility', wrote the most renowned scholar of his age, 'you will perceive you have been breathed upon by the holy will'.[5] Bilney's gaunt, wasted features were stirred to their roots. 'At last', he enthused, 'I heard speak of Jesus'.[6] Erasmus, it is important to remember, was no Protestant. He would mock Luther for 'making everything public

---

1   Ibid.
2   Ibid. See Luke 8: 43–48.
3   Ibid. 27.
4   See Foxe, iv. 621.
5   Quoted in Peter Ackroyd, *The History of England*, (London, 2012), ii. 26.
6   Foxe, iv. 635.

and giving even cobblers a share in what is normally handled by scholars'.[1]
But his pioneering work, with its purer method of enquiry, shot an arrow
into the black heart of the Magisterium, the teaching authority of the
Catholic Church. The reaction of the college authorities was immediate
and uncompromising. Any attempt to bring the book (or its second edition,
the *Novum Testamentum*) into the university 'by horse or by boat, on wheels
or on foot',[2] was forbidden. But copies might still be bought, if you knew
where to look, and who to talk to. Alone in his room, door locked, the
outlawed text in front of him, Bilney was beguiled by the beauty of Erasmus'
Latinity. But then his eyes settled on some words of Paul ('Oh most sweet and
comfortable sentence to my soul!') contained in the first letter to Timothy:
*It is a true saying, and worthy of all men to be embraced, that Christ Jesus came
into the world to save sinners; of whom I am the chief and principal.*[3] It is easy to
sense a brightness of fever in his eyes; a hectic flush upon his cheeks. 'This
one sentence', said Bilney, 'through God's instruction and inward working,
which I did not then perceive, did so exhilarate my heart, being wounded
with the guilt of my sins, and being almost in despair, that immediately I
felt a marvellous comfort and quietness, insomuch that my bruised bones
leaped for joy'.[4]

This inrush of emotion immediately penetrated his intellectual world. In
the years ahead Bilney was to articulate an understanding of God, and of
his own relation to Him, that made him a conspicuous agent of the Gospel.
He joined an eclectic group of scholars who met at the White Horse Inn:
styled 'Little Germany' by the townsfolk. All Bilney's intensity of feeling, his
eloquence and charm, was poured into debates sparked by the arrival, via
the port of Kings Lynn and other waterways, of Luther's tracts. He shone in
this kind of gathering. God sent him souls to educate for heaven, and a new
serenity. He also began his famous ministry to the sick and suffering of the
town. He went to the leper houses, taking fresh linen and preaching Christ's
unfailing love. He visited the gaol. But when the time came for the Bible-
men to declare themselves, they chose Robert Barnes as their mouthpiece.
Richard Rex has said that in the 1520s 'all we see of the Reformation in

---

1   Quoted in James McConica, *The Oxford Encyclopedia of the Reformation*, ed. Hillerbrand
(New York, 1996), ii. 58.

2   Quoted in Loane, 7.

3   I Timothy 1:15.

4   Foxe, vi. 635.

Cambridge is Luther'.[1] Luther was an Augustinian. So was Barnes. After his conversion, and at least until the 1534 edition of *A Supplication*, Barnes' theology summoned no originality: he was straightforwardly Lutheran. For the early makers of the English Reformation that was an advantage. The only definitive thing that can be said about Bilney in this period was that he was devoted to Bible-reading.

In 1525, Bilney convinced a 'not altogether willing Barnes'[2] to preach the set-piece Christmas Eve sermon at St Edward's church in Cambridge. St Edward's was the parish church of Trinity Hall and Clare Hall. Bilney (of Trinity Hall), along with Latimer (of Clare), was a regular, and very popular, preacher. That Bilney was unwilling to preach might indicate a reluctance, shown later at his trial, to publicly state opinions he was airing in private. Barnes' sermon itself, a punchy critique of clerical abuses, was based on the epistle for the fourth Sunday in Advent. According to Foxe he 'postilled the whole epistle following the Scriptures and Luther's postil'.[3] Overnight Barnes became England's leading Lutheran. He was arrested on 5 February 1526. Exile awaited, and, before his martyrdom in 1540, a unique career as a polemicist and diplomat. After Christmas Eve 1525, for Barnes and for the English Reformation, there was no going back. In the case of Bilney, however, there is no evidence of him going forward either. His theological position remained ambiguous. While Barnes expounded doctrine in the full light of day, Bilney was content to operate in the shadows.

In the wake of Barnes' trial both Latimer and Bilney were summonsed by Thomas Wolsey, papal *legate a latere*, cardinal archbishop of York, and lord chancellor of England. Wolsey, unlike his self-scourging successor (as chancellor) Thomas More, was a pragmatist with no instinct for cruelty. In all his dealings with the Bible-men he 'left unexplored no avenue towards abjuration'.[4] After Bilney's wide-eyed denial of Lutheran sympathies, he displayed a remarkable degree of largesse. As reported by More, Wolsey, accepting '[Bilney's] denial with a corporal oath that he should from that time forth be no setter forth of heresies, but in his preachings and readings impugn them, dismissed him very benignly; and of his liberal bounty gave

1 'The Early Impact of Reformation Theology at Cambridge University, 1521–1547', *Reformation & Renaissance Review* 2 (Cambridge, 1999), 42.
2 Korey Maas, *The Reformation and Robert Barnes* (Woodbridge, 2010), 14.
3 Foxe, v. 415.
4 Clebsch, 279.

him also money for his costs'.[1] He was not asked to recant. Quite an outcome; and further evidence of Bilney's ability to overcome opposition by the force of his personal magnetism.

In May 1527, along with Thomas Arthur, Bilney, nerved by his reading of Scripture to unusual candour, embarked on a preaching tour of the eastern counties. At St George's chapel in Ipswich he satirized the commonly held belief 'that to be buried in St Francis' cowl [monk's hood] should remit four parts of penance'.[2] And popular shrines like Walsingham, he said, only existed 'to blind the poor people'.[3] His claims for inward faith over external form saw him manhandled from the pulpit. Such melodrama only increased his celebrity. Crowds were soon flocking to hear him in towns and villages throughout the see of Norwich. An appalled Thomas More spoke of two men 'who would not hesitate to travel twenty miles to hear Bilney deliver a sermon';[4] John Pykas, a Colchester baker, described one sermon as 'most ghostly made and best for his purpose and opinions as any that he ever heard in his life'.[5] Many were inspired to private acts of iconoclasm. In due course, like a repertory company doing good business in the provinces, Bilney headed for London. In Bishopsgate, Newington, Kensington and Chelsea, his assault on the invocation of saints and image worship sparked near-riots. He was finally arrested after a Whitsuntide sermon at the City church of St Magnus the Martyr, where he urged the king to 'destroy and burn the images of saints set up in churches'.[6]

Until the advent of Thomas More, who used the powers of the lord chancellorship to wage a private war against the 'newfangly minded',[7] there was no consensus about where to draw the line on Lutheran opinion. But wherever the line was in 1527, Bilney had crossed it. He and Arthur were cast into the bishop of London's coal-house before being taken to the Tower to await trial.

---

1   Quoted in Loane, 16.

2   Foxe, iv. 627.

3   Ibid.

4   Quoted in Korey Maas, 'Thomas Bilney: Simple Good Soul?', *Tyndale Society Journal* 27 (Oxford, July 2004), 8–20.

5   Quoted in Patrick Collinson, 'Night schools, conventicles and churches' in *The Beginnings of English Protestantism,* ed. Marshall & Ryrie (Cambridge, 2002), 227.

6   Foxe, iv. 627.

7   Quoted in Peter Ackroyd, *The Life of Thomas More* (London, rep. 1999), 271.

The tour of East Anglia and the diocese of London was the apotheosis of Bilney's preaching ministry. Many were converted. But converted to what, exactly? In his lengthy dialogue with John Brusierd, a Franciscan monk, preserved by Foxe, Bilney pitches his theological tent well within the boundary of Lollard-inflected Catholicism. To get at his core beliefs, to understand what it was he was prepared to hazard life and limb for, is a tricky business. What we're left with is a rejection of image worship, and of trusting in man's merits. We read something adjacent to, but by no means identical with, Luther's doctrine of justification by faith alone. There is little else to contradict A.G. Dickens' view that when we hear of someone being converted by Bilney, 'this may mean little more than the fact that he first brought home to them the full meaning of a personal religion'.[1] The confusion over Bilney has been put down, at least in part, to the fact that he wrote so little. But we have the Brusierd dialogue. We have the 1527 trial transcripts and five long letters to the bishop of London. By way of comparison, Lady Jane Grey's written legacy consists of three letters (two very short), one prayer and her own briskly decisive dialogue with a Catholic priest. Yet we have a complete, even exhaustive, picture of the Christian life of England's outstanding female scholar: its basis, its pattern, its content. The contrast here, for some, is between Jane's fierce personal integrity, alive and intact in the public world of social power, and the irresolution that marked Bilney's own behaviour outside 'the private school of friendship'.[2] His timid soul quaked at the polarization of the English Reformation. The suspicion remains that his happiness was rooted in personal experience: in his own religious self-consciousness.

On 27 November 1527, Bilney was summonsed before Wolsey and assorted divines at the Chapter House at Westminster. The cardinal first raised the issue of Bilney's oath, sworn a year before, not to teach Lutheran doctrine. Bilney did not deny taking the oath. But, he said, as it had been sworn in a private interview with Wolsey, and not officially in a court of law, he had not considered it binding on his conscience. Wolsey, not unnaturally, took this as a slap in the face. Bilney had betrayed his trust; he had used his scholarly status to mislead. The cardinal insisted that Bilney take a second oath. He had to swear to answer the articles presented to him 'without any

---

1   *The English Reformation* (London, 1967), 118.
2   Loane, 26.

craft, qualifying, or leaving out any part of the truth'.[1] Given the setting, and the legal basis upon which the hearing had been convened, the oath was unnecessary. But Wolsey wanted to wound Bilney, to give notice that he was calling his integrity into question. The second oath, writes Loane, 'was meant to humiliate as well as to correct'.[2] At this point, whether through disgust with Bilney, or self-recrimination, or perhaps because he really was 'occupied [with] the affairs of the realm',[3] Wolsey departed.

Bilney was left in the hands of Cuthbert Tunstall, a one-time diplomat and chancellor to William Warham, archbishop of Canterbury. Tunstall is one of the more unusual figures in the hierarchy of the Tudor church. A humanist trained as a lawyer in Italy, and the author of a well-used mathematical treatise, he was moderate in everything aside from his desire to please his king and return the church to a spiritually comatose state. By 1522, when he became bishop of London, most of the cultural values he had espoused as a humanist had fallen by the wayside. In 1523 he led the campaign to destroy every copy of Tyndale's works. But he would always favour toleration and mediation over bullying and coercion. According to Thomas Mayer, 'he put a high premium on both learning and intellectual and religious modesty'.[4] Tunstall knew how to compromise in order to achieve his goals. In respect of Bilney, that goal was a willing confession.

Bilney had assured Wolsey that he had not 'preached or taught any of Luther's opinions, or any others contrary to the Catholic church'.[5] Before Tunstall, following a five-day adjournment, he agreed that Luther was 'a wicked and detestable heretic'.[6] He upheld the primacy of the Roman See; he endorsed the doctrine of the keys. He couldn't wait, it seemed, to get out of his own way. He also made the jaw-dropping concession that the worship of images might be justified because 'when they are the books of laymen it is proper to revere them'.[7] The bishops then took depositions from those who had heard Bilney's denunciation of image worship, pilgrimages and prayers to saints at St Magnus. Bilney denied saying any of it. He told lies, in fact.

---

1 Foxe, iv. 622.
2 Loane, 19.
3 Foxe, iv. 622.
4 Hillerbrand, iv. 183.
5 Foxe, iv. 622.
6 Ibid. 624–625.
7 Ibid. 626.

More witness statements were brought forward, from Newington and Ipswich as well as St Magnus. The sheer weight of the evidence stacking up against him forced Bilney to change tack. He opted for memory loss; he couldn't remember, he said, what he had preached. This fooled no one, but left the trial with nowhere to go. In effect, Bilney was throwing down a challenge to Tunstall: give me a slap on the wrist, and let me go, or pass me over to the secular power. But that was only one part of Bilney's strategy: the public part. In typical Bilney fashion he also wrote directly to the bishop. His five letters are intensely personal, autobiographical affairs, fawning towards Tunstall and designed to draw the bishop into a social relationship:

> I began to doubt, for what intent [you] should require [explanation] of [me]: an old soldier of a young beginner; the chief pastor of London of a poor silly sheep ... I would to God you would give me leave privately to talk with you, that I might speak freely that which I have learned in the holy scriptures for the consolation of my conscience; which if you will do, I trust you shall not repent you. All things shall be submitted unto your judgement; who... if I shall be found in any error (as indeed I am a man), you, as spiritual, shall restore me through the spirit of gentleness.[1]

Tunstall was not charmed. He refused Bilney's invitation. Instead, he asked him to set down on paper a summary of the doctrine which he, Thomas Bilney, understood to be contained in God's Word, and that ought to be preached by all. In short, Tunstall 'requested precisely the declaration of belief which Bilney refused to provide in open court'.[2] Bilney immediately declared this 'a burden too heavy for my strength'.[3] He begged Tunstall's indulgence. The rest of his reply was fleshed out with strictures against false teaching, panegyrics to Christ, and fervent appeals for pastors and bishops to 'preach the Gospel unto every creature'.[4] As truths, these were unimpeachable. There was nothing, not a sentence, not a syllable, in Bilney's correspondence that a Lutheran or a Lollard or, more to the point, a Catholic of Tunstall's stripe could take issue with. Bilney suggests a great deal, reveals close to nothing. By the close of the third letter his inspiration was starting to flag.

---

1   Ibid. 638. See Walker, 237.
2   Walker, 237.
3   Foxe, iv. 639.
4   Ibid. 640. See Matthew 28:19.

He offers his most novel reason yet for his obfuscation, before switching to
a well-worn theme:

> The want of paper will not suffer me to write any more, and I had
> rather to speak it in private talk unto yourself; whereunto if you would
> admit me, I trust you shall not repent you thereof: and unto me (Christ
> I take to my witness) it would be a great comfort, in whom I wish you,
> with all your flock, heartily well to fare.[1]

On 3 December 1527 Tunstall presented a summary of the evidences
against Bilney. He also, 'in discharge of my conscience',[2] set Bilney's letters
before the court. Called upon to confess his heresy, Bilney refused. The next
day, showing considerable scruple, Tunstall asked his fellow judges to study
each witness statement, as well as Bilney's reply to every article laid against
him. Again, Bilney was invited to abjure his errors. Again he declined, and
robustly; he would 'stand to his conscience'.[3] The court readied itself for
the passing of the sentence. But to the bafflement of many, including his
fellow judges, Tunstall called a recess. Bilney was instructed to 'depart into
a void place, and there to deliberate with himself'.[4] One can only speculate
about what was going on here. It seems unlikely that someone as astute as
Tunstall, as politically adept, as socially savvy, had not observed the wheels
of fear and pathos that turned within the heart of the prisoner. We should
remind ourselves that Tunstall was no man-burner. What he wanted was a
voluntary confession. So far, Bilney had been carried along by the energy of
the trial proceedings. It was time to make a tactical change; to slow things
down. Every instinct told him to give Bilney time to think, room to weaken;
to throw him, in silence and in solitude, entirely upon his own resources.

But when he reappeared, Bilney was resolute. To Tunstall's request that
he return to the unity of the church, he replied, in clear and perfectly
modulated Latin, 'Let judgement be done in the name of the Lord'. He was
the epitome of harried virtue. Tunstall could only urge him once again to
submit. 'This is the day that the Lord has made', answered Bilney. 'We will
rejoice and be glad in it'.[5] His fellow judges now looked to Tunstall to call

---

1   Ibid. 641.
2   Ibid. 623.
3   Ibid. 631.
4   Ibid.
5   Ibid.

time on the heretic-scholar. But what they deemed intractable he considered tactical, and their untenable was his unconcluded. He would not abandon his strategy; nor, however, would Bilney be pandered to. Tunstall removed his cap and intoned 'In the name of the Father and the Son and the Holy Spirit ... let God arise and let His enemies be scattered'. He made the sign of the cross on his forehead and breast, and told the defendant that 'by the consent and counsel of my brethren here present, [I] do pronounce thee, Thomas Bilney, who hast been accused of divers articles, to be convicted of heresy'. A momentary pause, then: 'And for the rest of the sentence, we take deliberation until tomorrow'.

The following morning, still insistent that he was 'not separate from the Church',[1] Bilney invoked the medieval process of compurgation. Also called 'the wager of law', and seen frequently in Welsh courts, compurgation allowed a defendant to prove his innocence, or non-liability to prosecution, by bringing forward a number of witnesses, usually twelve, to attest to his truthfulness. Bilney spoke of an army of friends, thirty men for each hostile witness, who would vouch for his orthodoxy. Tunstall was immovable. It was too late, he said, for fresh witnesses. Bilney—now likening himself to the much-wronged Susanna in the apocryphal thirteenth chapter of Daniel— begged him to reconsider. It was odd behaviour. After a quick consultation with his fellow judges Tunstall announced 'it was not lawful to hear a petition which was against the law'.[2] With his strategy falling apart, Bilney requested, in a telling phrase, the company of those 'in whom his trust was'.[3] Tunstall was quite happy to see Bilney's friends adding their anxiety to his. The prisoner was granted two days to arrive at 'a plain determinate answer what he would do in the premises'.[4] On 7 December 1527 Bilney was escorted to the Chapter House for the last time. Sleepless nights had framed his eyes with a semicircle of ill-health; the most awful emanation came off him. At nine o'clock he was asked again whether he would 'revoke the errors and heresies whereof he stood accused, detected and convicted'.[5] The heart-tugging of his friends, and his own proneness to self-pity, had combined to sap the last of his strength. 'Under the pretext of being useful to Jesus Christ

---

1 Ibid.
2 Ibid. 632.
3 Ibid.
4 Ibid.
5 Ibid.

for many years', reflects d'Aubigné, 'Bilney disobeyed Him at the present moment'.[1] Having appealed to Tunstall to 'deal gently'[2] with him, Bilney recanted in stages: first in private, to the bishop and his panel, then publicly before the court. The next morning he was led to Paul's Cross. A faggot (bundle of twigs) was placed upon his shoulder; his black cap, the mark of his vocation, was pulled from his head. Finally, inert and spiritless, he was forced to listen as a priest extolled the infallible teaching authority of popes and councils. At the sermon's conclusion he was returned to prison. And there he lay, according to Latimer, 'in a burning hell of despair'.

In the aftermath of the trial, doubt was cast on the legitimacy of Bilney's abjuration. The former law student, it was suggested, had colluded with the judges, through the agency of his friends, to concoct a form of words that, while satisfying Tunstall's wish for a public renunciation of heresy, avoided a clear admission of guilt on Bilney's part. Thomas More, whose hatred of 'seditiosa dogmata', and desire to see the Reformed go 'straight from the short fire to the fire everlasting',[3] was outraged. For weeks he moped about an abjuration 'whereof I never saw the like nor in so plain a case never would, were I the judge, suffer the like hereafter';[4] the trial and its outcome, he said, was 'so strange that the like hath been very seldom seen'.[5]

Dozens of formal recantations were made under Henry, even more in the reign of Mary. Bilney's is preserved in the Guildhall library. Only a thwarted man-burner could read it and smell conspiracy. Bilney disavows 'all manner of heresies and articles following whereupon I am now defamed noted vehemently suspected and convicted'. He lauds 'the true Catholic and apostolic faith' and vows 'by the grace of God hereafter ever to persevere and abide in the true doctrine of the holy church'.[6] Historical continuity and traditional ritual is upheld; the Lollard cum Lutheran basis of his recent preaching renounced. The divine origin of 'our Mother the Holy Church of Rome' is proved by 'myracles dayly shewed', and reinforced by pilgrimages and image worship. As for the pope, he is the successor of St Peter and the

---

1   *The Reformation in England*, (London, rep. 1962), i. 295.

2   Foxe, iv. 632.

3   Quoted in Peter Ackroyd, *Thomas More* (London, 1998), 292.

4   Thomas More, *A Dialogue Concerning Heresies,* ed. W. S. Campbell (London, 1929), 196. Quoted in Walker, 223.

5   Ibid. 202. See Walker, 223.

6   Guildhall Library, MS 9531/10 fol. 120r.

paradigm for all earthly law and authority. One looks in vain for anything that might support the conclusion that Tunstall was somehow outwitted. But the bishop was no fool: and no sadist. His only aim was to undermine religious and political dissent. In this, at least in the short term, he was successful. Bilney, on the other hand, was crushed under the weight of bitter defeat: 'He thought', wrote Latimer, 'that all the whole Scriptures were against him, and sounded to his condemnation'.[1] Hardly the bearing of a winning strategist. Some said that in his oath of abjuration Bilney simply foreswore as heretical the views he claimed never to have entertained in the first place. But Bilney knew that that was nonsense: as did the bishops, as did every member of every congregation on his ill-starred tour. Having lied about his heterodoxy he had feigned amnesia. At the end of the trial, even he seems to have accepted the justice of his conviction. Therein lies the enigma of Thomas Bilney. What on earth was he thinking of?

To unlock the most troubling aspect of the Bilney trial, we could do worse than look at his Bible. This was a Latin translation, commonly called the Vulgate ('Book in the Common Tongue'), mainly the work of Jerome (c. 345–420). Ratified by the medieval church not long after its first appearance, the Council of Trent would later pronounce the Vulgate the only authentic Latin text of the Scriptures. Bilney's copy, which the present author has handled, is lodged in the library of Corpus Christi College in Cambridge. It was printed in Lyons in 1520. There are various inscriptions on the title page, including one that reads: 'Master Willon, former Fellow of this College, gave this book to the College of Corpus Christi to be kept in the inner library, 1588. It was once the book of Bilney the martyr, and by him the Notes were written which run in it'.[2] Bilney's annotations, in black ink, pepper the margins. These are impromptu thoughts, devoid of pretence, written for himself alone. No thought is given to posterity. Taken together they give a fascinating insight into his spiritual and intellectual concerns. In the eighth chapter of Isaiah he warns against vain revelations, saying: 'One ought to trust the law rather than wonders'.[3] Certain of the Notes give weight to papal authority: but, says Bilney, 'one can deduce how vain is that saying which is advanced: that the Catholic Church cannot err'.[4] In the Book of

---

1 Foxe, iv. 641.
2 See J. Y. Batley, On a Reformer's Latin Bible (Cambridge, 1940), 17.
3 Ibid. 28.
4 Ibid. 36.

Job he reads into the corrupted witness of Eliphaz[1] a warning against the invocation of saints. The law of leprous garments, outlined in the thirteenth chapter of Leviticus, apparently justifies the confessional. 'Renewed sin that must grow old', writes Bilney, 'hence perhaps one should gather that men ought to show their sins to priests'.[2] Elsewhere he questions, but refrains from criticizing, expressions of traditional belief.

But the most intriguing entries occur in 1 Samuel and in the Book of Jeremiah. In the former, adjacent to the verses where Michal lies to Saul's messengers,[3] we read that David's wife 'practices deceit blamelessly'.[4] And in the margin of the twenty-eighth chapter of Jeremiah, Bilney commends what he calls the prophet's 'pious lie'.[5] Whether or not we're under an obligation to tell the truth at all times is an interesting pool to dip into, Christianly-speaking. Calvin, a fervent defender of absolute truthfulness, argued that the midwives who lied to save Israelite babies ought to have told the truth in order to make a witness to Pharaoh. R.J. Rushdoony, for one, dismisses such views as 'pharisaic nonsense'.[6] But our immediate concern is not with theology, but with motivation. *Why* was Bilney so attentive to this issue? Was he seeking a doctrine of dissimulation? If he was, he was placing himself outside of the kind of ethical relationship with our neighbour that Calvin, and English Reformers like John Frith, would have regarded as foundational. Ultimately it is the calculated way in which he violates the Ninth Commandment, or—looked at from a different angle—differentiates between godliness and morality, that makes Bilney unique in these accounts. All the others, albeit at different stages, and in different ways, had used personal affliction as a platform for biblical witness. Not Bilney. Not yet.

The Reformer who returned to Cambridge in the spring of 1529 cut a forlorn figure. He was burdened by remorse, locked, it seemed, in a private aura of unregeneration; immured in his own effluvium of hell. His friends, alarmed at signs of mental fragility, took turns to lodge with him night and day. The Bible, once his strength and stay, now reduced him to incoherence and misery. When he heard familiar verses read out, reports Latimer, 'it was

1 See Job 42.
2 Batley, 42.
3 See 1 Samuel 19.
4 Batley, 47.
5 Batley, 48.
6 *The Institutes of Biblical Law* (Philadelphia, 1973), 546.

as though a man should run him through the heart like a sword'.[1] But slowly, over the course of about two years, Bilney began to recover. He shook off his lethargy in worship and prayer. He resumed his ministry to the outcasts of Cambridge; reaching across to them this time, not down, seeing in their material needs the very nature of his own dependency upon God. And with Latimer his companion, he walked upon Heretics' Hill, and embarked afresh on a humble, reverent exploration of what God has revealed of Himself in Scripture. 'He came again',[2] said Latimer, like one rising from the dead.

One night, early in 1531, Bilney told his friends he was 'going up to Jerusalem'.[3] At ten o'clock, beneath the soft effulgence of the moon, the gate of Trinity Hall clanked behind him for the last time. This leaving seems somehow emblematic of Bilney's whole career: 'a dangerous progress in darkness and loneliness'.[4] When next we hear of him he is in Norfolk, preaching outdoors his vision of a church purified of outward corruption. To Katherine Manne, an anchoress at the Dominican friary in Norwich, he gave copies of Tyndale's New Testament and *The Obedience of the Christian Man*. In sorrow and self-exculpation he visited those who had felt most let down by his recantation. He had, he declared, 'known the terrors of the Lord'. He confessed his weakness. But with a querulous, self-commiserating air, he still contrived to park the lion's share of the blame at the door of his 'fleshly friends'.[5] Many of these had loved and cared for him since his release. With Bilney, it seems, any praise needs to be qualified. For all his fevered reading of the Scriptures, a disinclination to hold himself accountable for his actions insinuates itself time and again.

In Norfolk, and later at Greenwich, Bilney violated the embargo on preaching handed down at his 1527 trial. On his return from London he was arrested by bishop's officers and convicted as a relapsed heretic. This provoked a maliciously gleeful intervention by Thomas More. The greatest hater of the English Reformation was now lord chancellor. Unlike Wolsey, 'Saint' Thomas saw any questioning of the established order as a crime against God. Still seething over Bilney's escape in 1527, he told the sheriffs to 'Go your ways and burn him first; and then afterwards come to me for a bill of my

1 Foxe, iv. 641.
2 Ibid.
3 Ibid. 642.
4 Batley, 10.
5 Foxe, iv. 642.

hand'.[1] Bilney's next appeal was to the king. What Bilney expected from his petition is unclear. For some it was an audacious attempt to identify himself with Henry's own theological vagaries. For others, he was addressing his own conscience ('and a very eccentric conscience it was').[2] Perhaps he just wanted to bear better fruit unto God than he had managed at his trial. But *a wise man's heart discerns both time and judgement* (Ecclesiastes 8:5). Whatever else he was, in strength and in weakness, Bilney was seldom wise.

The petition failed, and he was gaoled, awaiting execution, in the dank undercroft of Norwich Guildhall.

His friend Thomas Necton, one of two sheriffs of Norwich, ensured his living conditions were at least tolerable. Also that he had sufficient ink and paper to write home to his parents. He composed several homilies. He made confession, received absolution, heard mass and took communion. Through Necton's offices, a group of friends was able to share his last evening. Among them was Matthew Parker, Martin Bucer's protégé and a future archbishop of Canterbury. As they sat around Bilney's cell, convivially supping mugs of ale, someone ventured a hope that the Holy Spirit might cool the next day's fire. Bilney's eyes settled on the candle in front of him. After a moment's consideration, he rolled his palm over the glow. Then, to a collective gasp, he dropped his index finger into the flame. He held it there, motionless, until it melted down to the joint. 'I feel by experience', he said:

> [And] have known it long by philosophy, that fire, by God's ordinance, is naturally hot. But yet I am persuaded by God's holy Word, and in the experience of some spoken of in the same, that in the flame they felt no heat, and in the fire they felt no consumption. And I constantly believe that howsoever the stubble of this my body shall be wasted by it, yet my soul and my spirit shall be purged thereby: a pain for the time, whereon notwithstanding joy unspeakable.[3]

By condescending grace, it does appear that Bilney was enabled, in the last weeks of his life, to abandon his often debilitating preoccupation with self. The nearness of God gave him everything he needed. Because God is steadfast he could be steadfast too. On 19 August 1531 he was taken, probably

---

1   Ibid. 650.
2   Batley, 11.
3   Foxe, iv. 653.

by boat, to Lollards' Pit, a spot of sterile savagery close to Bishopsgate. A great wind was blowing. For his 'ghostly comfort' Bilney was allowed to choose—again, the hand of Necton is evident—a friend to accompany him. He asked for Dr Warner, vicar of Winterton. A medieval bridge, along which Bilney is likely to have processed, survives to this day; Lollards' Pit itself, a scooped-out piece of ground at the foot of St Leonards Hill, is now the site of a DIY centre. But with a pinch of imagination, we can still conjure the scene that greeted Bilney's eyes: the slow-moving river is unchanged, so too the distant spire of the cathedral. A grazing shaft of sun still hits the underside of Bishopsgate Bridge. The surrounding slopes, in the hot summer of 1531, were thick with spectators, turning the site into a ragged amphitheatre. Along with the curious, the partisan and the naturally ghoulish, the crowd was swelled by those whose presence had been bought by the bishop with the offer of forty days' indulgence.

Bilney, a pale, waiflike figure, clad in a coarse gown with open sleeves, descended into a circular hollow. As the sheriff's men made their final preparations, his only concern was to erect his mind and senses to heaven. He restated his belief 'Credo Ecclesiam Catholicam'. He is supposed to have read out another recantation. Letting his gown slip from his shoulders, 'his hair being piteously mangled',[1] he knelt before the stake and was heard to repeat, three times over, 'And enter not into judgement with thy servant; for in thy sight shall no man living be justified'.[2] All was ready. He undressed to his underclothes. Amidst the swirl and din he was half-pulled, half-lifted onto a ledge just above the woodpile. According to one account, Bilney aided his captors by holding one end of the chain that was drawn around his midriff. He straightened his back against the stake. Once secured, a staple was driven through the chain to make it firm. As more reeds were banked up against Bilney's body, Doctor Warner, the tears streaming down his face, spoke his final farewell. The martyr 'did most gently smile': 'Oh, Doctor', he begged his friend, 'feed your flock, feed your flock: that when the Lord cometh, he may find you so doing'. He bowed his head: 'Farewell, good Master Doctor, and pray for me'. Warner was emotionally spent; there were no words left. Not minded to watch Bilney burn, he departed Lollards' Pit

---

1 Ibid. 654.
2 Ibid. 655.

'sobbing and weeping'.[1] Next to gather at the stake was a group of friars. Their greed had figured prominently in Bilney's preaching. Hearing stirrings of support for Bilney rising up from the crowd, panic was struck into their hearts. With taunts raining down, they begged Bilney to exonerate them of wrongdoing, lest their income, made up of charitable alms, suffer. Bilney, his release from the entropy of dwindling existence assured, did not hesitate to give them what they wanted: 'I pray you good people', he called out, 'be never the worse to these men for my sake, as though they should be the authors of my death; it was not they!'[2]

A torch was set to the reeds. Out of a billow of smoke, a flame shot upwards, enveloping Bilney as he struck his breast and cried first 'Jesus!' then 'Credo!' A wind that had been spoiling ripening cornfields for days swirled around the Pit; three times it parted the blaze, three times the disfigured, blackened form of Bilney was displayed before the multitude, eliciting gasps and screams and wild halloos. Eventually the fire took hold; Bilney's breath went in and out in long parched shudders, and then he fell forward, his flesh sucking upon the chain. The vile melodrama of suffering at a end, a sheriff's man struck out with an iron bar the staple behind the post. The remains of Thomas Bilney, scholar of Trinity Hall, collapsed into ashes and dirt.

In trying to arrive at the truth about Thomas Bilney one is pulling at broken strings. Once fact has been winnowed from opinion, there are worse options, it seems to me, than to accept that all reconstructions of the past remain irretrievable; and therefore imaginative. But what *can* we know, or at least surmise? Clearly, and contrary to the popular view, this was no Candide, searching for truth as the eternal innocent. No one in these accounts performed as egregiously as he. After his final arrest, in fact, he seemed to welcome the abbreviation of his life as an atoning act: a chance to break free of his often tortuous negotiations with himself. With the approach of death, Bilney found a strength and clarity that had eluded him in life. As far the ruling principles of his thought are concerned, there seems little doubt that while he embraced the iconophobia and iconoclasm of Lollardy and (later) Lutheranism—'Saints in heaven need no light', he said, 'and the images have no eyes to see'[3]—his pathology of self-examination, and constitutional

---

1   Ibid.

2   Ibid.

3   Quoted in Ackroyd, *The History of England*, iii. 49.

timidity, left him unwilling to abandon either the social formation or the mystical tradition of Catholicism.

Bilney is known to have preached human righteousness as a fiction; Christ alone 'is the door whereby we must come to the Father'.[1] But on that other key issue of the Reformation, he went to the stake a perfectly orthodox believer in the doctrine of transubstantiation. In other words he identified the signs—the bread and wine of the eucharist—with the things they signify. At the moment of consecration, said Bilney, the substance of bread and wine is converted into the actual body and blood of Christ: into carnal matter. His appropriation of the truths of Scripture sits uneasily alongside this belief. As does his refusal to be openly, or even clandestinely, at odds with Rome. He knew the same truth as other Reformers; his life consisted of how he chose to distort it. In the realm of ethics he never became evangelical. Beyond this, nothing can be pressed too far.

In the aftermath of his martyrdom, all sorts of rumours started to circulate regarding Bilney's recantation at Lollards' Pit. Some said he hadn't recanted at all. One witness, alderman John Curat, insisted he had, but that he had not actually heard it himself: he had stooped down to lace his shoe at the vital moment. The mayor of Norwich, Edward Rede, while dismissing Curat's account, muddied the waters still further with his assertion that Bilney held no heretical opinions, and had nothing to recant. All of which gave rise to a Star Chamber investigation, convened under lord chancellor Thomas More in November 1531. By December 5, Rede was qualifying madly. Finally he admitted to seeing Bilney's written revocation. Even this, however, cannot be regarded as definitive. Given More's determination to present Bilney's recantation as a triumph of the true faith, Rede may well have been fighting for his life. But what no one seems to have doubted at the time was the sincerity of Bilney's own belief that he was 'not separate from the Church'. In the end, perhaps we ought to be as distrustful of the shabby gift of disillusion as of the sought memory that tells us what we wish to know. Let us summon instead a proper expression of generosity. In the summer of 1531, at Lollards' Pit in Norwich, Thomas Bilney, pushed and pulled about by the forces of tyranny, was *raised up incorruptible* (1 Corinthians 15:52) to the house and home of his Father. Nothing counts too much besides that fact.

---

1   Foxe, iv. 635.

V

JOHN LAMBERT

The events that culminated in the death of John Lambert symbolize a collective failure, in the Henrician period, to mend theological fences. His persecution and execution shattered the appearance of unanimity in the Reformed camp. No one comes out of the Lambert episode well: certainly not Thomas Cranmer, whose innate caution and tendency to defer in all things to the majesty of the crown were never more in evidence. The part played by Robert Barnes in Lambert's downfall is more easily understood, and perhaps more easily forgiven: Barnes was always Barnes, impassioned and uncompromising, and as a Lutheran could not be expected to find his old friend's sacramentarian views anything other than offensive. But one is still made uneasy by John Foxe's decision to excise any mention of Lambert's death from his otherwise comprehensive account of Barnes' career. Not for the first time, as well, one is forced to ponder the lack of a radical edge which might have led Englishmen to embrace the kind of Reformation being enacted on the European mainland. In the absence of a single presiding genius to unite around—a Calvin, for example, whose grandeur of soul enabled him to enlighten minds with lucidity and beauty, but also 'to smite the evil-doers with the lightnings of his wrath'[1]—the godly company looked to Cranmer for leadership. Then as now, the crippling uncertainty of an archbishop became a mirror held up to the English church.

John Lambert was born in Norfolk, probably in Norwich, in the last decade of the fifteenth century. Though his family name was Nicholson, he was already calling himself Lambert by the time he took a bachelor's degree at Cambridge in 1519/1520. On the nomination of Catherine of Aragon, and despite certain objections by the college authorities, he is recorded as a fellow of Queens' College at the beginning of the Michaelmas term of 1521.

---

1 J.A. Wylie, *The History of Protestantism* (London, 1878), iii. 418.

In the early 1520s he is thought to have attended the famous gatherings at the White Horse Inn, where the intellectually curious met to discuss and debate the new ideas emanating from Germany. Though Thomas Bilney is usually credited with Lambert's conversion, it is impossible to point to a single pivotal experience, or conversation, that led Lambert to fix his faith on Christ alone. So much in the religious life is cumulative. But when Lambert left Cambridge, sometime after Easter 1522, he was certain that the church's doctrine, no less than her morals, cried out for Reformation. He was ordained—according to certain replies made to William Warham, archbishop of Canterbury—in Norwich. There is no record of his whereabouts for the next four years. But his scholarship gathered depth and substance, and the more he learned the more he leaned upon the self-authenticating Word. He saw, and with blistering clarity, his inability to contribute anything towards his salvation. His only hope was in the perfect sacrifice of the perfect Saviour.

When next we hear of John Lambert it is Sunday 28 October 1526. He is in the crowd at Paul's Cross, observing the ritual burning of William Tyndale's New Testament. The bishop of London, Cuthbert Tunstall, hurled invective at the translation, branding it *doctrinam peregrinam*, 'strange doctrine', and calling attention to its 'errors three thousand and more'.[1] Lambert wrote that 'truly my heart lamented greatly to hear a great man preaching against it, who showed forth certain things he noted for hideous errors to be in it, that I, yes and not only I, but likewise did many others, think verily to be none. But (alack for pity!) malice cannot say well. God help us all, and amend it'.[2] Afterward, 'being forced by violence of the time',[3] Lambert fled to Antwerp, eventually becoming chaplain to the English merchants. He met and formed friendships with Tyndale and John Frith, though it cannot be said with any degree of certainty that he collaborated in biblical translation. But from the pulpit of the English House Lambert blasted the pretensions of the papacy. He emphasized the continuity of the Gospel with the Old Testament. He urged his congregation to believe everything written in the law and the prophets.

Lambert's time in Antwerp was ended at the behest of Thomas More. The lord chancellor's amicable relationship with the city government (he

---

1   Quoted in Brian Moynahan, *If God Spare my Life* (London, 2002), 101.
2   Ibid. 102.
3   John Foxe, *Acts & Monuments* (1838), v. 181.

had earlier secured the right of English merchants to trade in the Antwerp market) gave him all the leverage he needed to have Lambert arrested for heresy and brought back to England. On 27 March 1531 he was examined before a representative assembly of clergy. No record of those deliberations has been preserved, but Lambert remained in prison throughout the period 1531/2. He was subsequently examined at Lambeth and brought to William Warham's palace at Orford, near Sevenoaks. And there, before the archbishop himself, Lambert was called upon to respond to forty-five separate articles. Warham was the last archbishop of Canterbury before the definitive breach with Rome. A cultured, kindly man, and an active patron of Erasmus, Warham never made the transition from humanist to Reformer. In February 1532 he called for an end to antipapal legislation. He let it be known that he opposed the annulment of Henry's marriage to Catherine of Aragon. In the opulent setting of the palace chapel, fussed over by his minions, Warham asked Lambert whether he had ever before been suspected of heresy. Lambert replied that as some had thought ill of Christ, why should he fear if others 'suspect me amiss, and evil report of me?'[1] He already had a sense of rôle. He was then asked if he had read or kept any of Martin Luther's works. 'Yes', said Lambert, 'and I thank God that I ever did so, for by them God hath shown me, and a vast multitude of others also, such light as the darkness cannot abide'.[2] Luther, he argued, desired above all else that his writings, along with those of his opponents, be translated into all languages, 'whereby men should better judge what the truth is'.[3] But this aspiration was repeatedly shot down by an 'over-rich prelacy, who are so drowned in voluptuous living that they cannot attend to study God's Scripture, nor preach the same, which should be the principal part of their office'.[4] The other articles related to his rejection of papal-Catholic dogma. He points up the absence of any Scriptural mandate for clerical celibacy, denies the doctrine of purgatory, and takes issue with Warham's assertion that images and relics are 'sufficient to keep Christ and his saints in remembrance'.[5] And although he side-stepped questions on the Lord's Supper, Lambert was quick to praise *Unio Dissidentium (1527)*, an anthology of patristic quotations weighted in favour of a memorial view of

---

1   Ibid. 184.
2   Ibid.
3   Ibid.
4   Ibid.
5   Quoted in J. H. Merle d'Aubigné, *The Reformation in England* (London, rep. 1963), ii. 86.

Christ's presence. Elsewhere he is certain that 'faith only does justify, and work salvation, before a man do any other good works'.[1]

The outcome of these disputations is unclear, but Lambert was taken back to prison and only discharged upon Warham's death on 22 August 1532. With the Reformist Anne Boleyn presented as the king's consort, Lambert was able to return to London unmolested. He found work tutoring children in Latin and Greek. He contemplated getting married. Before archbishop Warham, Lambert had directed no man to 'pass his life without marriage, except those who have it given them, by the singular grace of God, to live chaste'.[2] Let no one, he insisted, be coerced into either singleness or wedlock. His priority was to see all people walking holily in the world, in the service and fear of God. Even eunuchs merited respect, he said: 'that have so made themselves, for love of the kingdom of heaven'.[3] In the end Lambert remained a bachelor, events, according to Foxe, 'both intercept[ing] his marriage, and also his freedom'. He may have joined the Worshipful Company of Grocers: one of the 'Great Twelve' City Livery Companies. This has led to speculation that he left the priesthood. The data, however, is scant and cannot be pushed too far. What is plain is that the habit of serenity had not diluted his Reforming zeal. Some time before 13 March 1536 he was accused of heresy by Thomas Howard, duke of Norfolk, and required to explain his views on the worship of the saints.

That Lambert's examination on this issue was again entrusted to the senior prelate of the English church is a fair indicator of his standing among the 'evangelycall fraternyte'. Cranmer, elevated to the see of Canterbury on Warham's death, was joined on a specially convened panel by bishops Shaxton and Latimer. Cranmer was in the midst of one of those fluctuating lapses that wasted the hope and strength of Reformation in England. He recognized the threat Swiss-style theology posed to his piecemeal programme of Reform: a programme already undermined by factional politics and changes in the king's mood. But Lambert's facts were marshalled, his resolutions formed. He would not backtrack on replies given to Warham. Men departed should not be venerated as guardians and benefactors. How can saints, joyously free of human worries, be affected in any way by human need? Their presence in

---

1   Foxe, v. 216.
2   Ibid. 187.
3   Ibid.

heaven was itself dependent on God's mercy. To appeal to saints, or worship their actions, endeavours or suffering, was to reject the very uniqueness of God in Christ. Why, the saints and angels themselves, declared Lambert, 'would not that we should build any churches in reverence of them; but would that with them we should honour the original Maker and Performer of all'.[1] The bishops fulminated and fretted, but failed to find any Scripture to condemn him by. He was released, and spent the next two years preaching, in every evangelical setting imaginable, the mutual relation between faith and the Word of God.

And then, in the autumn of 1538, Lambert attended a service at St Peter's church in London. The preacher, the well-known evangelical John Taylor[2], affirmed the actual presence of Christ in the bread and wine of the Lord's Supper. Lambert had by this date aligned himself with a broadly Zwinglian outlook: the words 'this is my body' (Matthew 26:26) were to be understood in a purely symbolic sense. At the end of the service Lambert approached Taylor, who declared a willingness to discuss, at a later date, the finer points of his sermon. In preparation, Lambert drafted ten arguments against sacramental materialism. These, says Foxe, 'he comprehended in writing, proving the truth of his cause, partly by Scriptures, and partly by good reason and the doctors'.[3] But Taylor had no intention of keeping his appointment with Lambert. Instead he scuttled across town to brief Robert Barnes. The fiery Lutheran then dragged Cranmer into the fray. Throughout the 1530s the archbishop—who was to change his mind on the Lord's Supper three times—retained a belief in the Real Presence. Nor had he excused Lambert's stinging attack on the worship of saints. Lambert was summoned to Lambeth Palace. And there, along with Barnes, Taylor and Latimer, Cranmer attempted to unburden the ex-chaplain of Antwerp of his offensive views. Lambert was unwavering. His every entreaty having failed, Cranmer had the vexatious 'sacramentary' confined to Lambeth. And then Lambert made his fatal mistake. He appealed to the king.

Lambert could hardly have chosen a less propitious time for his grand gesture. In the autumn of 1538 Henry VIII was still trusting in his God-given *imperium*. But his theological convictions had calcified into something like

1 Ibid. 197.
2 Later bishop of Lincoln under Edward VI.
3 Foxe, v. 227.

Catholicism minus the pope. The sacrament of the altar, private masses and clerical celibacy were all being bedded into government policy; in the summer of 1539 they would be enshrined as indelible attributes of the Christian church.[1] Lambert's precipitous action played directly into the hands of Stephen Gardiner, bishop of Winchester. Gardiner, writes David Starkey, 'was that rarest of things, a reactionary with a clear sense of strategy, and the will and boldness to carry it out'.[2] He saw, with perfect clarity, that although the intellectual roots of the Reformation lay in Europe, the English experience, with Henry as the sole arbiter of religious policy, might be reconstructed as a partial, state-directed process. The royal supremacy itself would protect Catholic orthodoxy. In a private audience, Gardiner spoke equally to the king's fears and to his vanity. Upon the break with Rome, Francis I of France, and Charles V, the Holy Roman Emperor, had heaped opprobrium upon England and Henry. An invasion fleet, it was rumoured, had gathered in the ports of the Low Countries. Gardiner counselled his king that the Catholic princes' hostility, and the anxiety that stoked it, might evaporate 'if only in this matter of Lambert he would manifest unto the people how stoutly he would resist heretics'.[3] His rhetoric fired a spectacular display of hubris, with Henry identifying himself with the prayers of a burdened king in the Psalms. A decree was issued. Lambert would be tried at Westminster with Henry presiding in person. The Reformation in England had reached an early fork in the road.

Foxe reports that on the day of Lambert's trial, 16 November 1538, 'a great assembly of nobles was gathered from all parts of the realm, not without much wonder and expectation in this so strange a case'.[4] Amidst huge crowds and chivalric ballyhoo, Henry processed into the King's Hall at York Place dressed—to convey his purity—in white silk. In attendance were all the leading bishops, justices and MPs: John Husee, in a letter to Lord Lisle, speaks of the hall being full to bursting, bedecked with 'scaffolds, bars and seats' on all sides. The trial of Lambert, writes MacCulloch, 'may be reckoned an addition to the sequence of great Tudor Councils'.[5] The outcome was, of course, preordained; Henry had already backtracked on the radicalism of the

---

1   The Act of Six Articles.

2   *Six Wives* (London, 2004), 721.

3   Foxe, v. 228.

4   Ibid. 229.

5   MacCulloch, 233.

1530s. He was making copious emendations to drafts of what would become the Act of Six Articles. The trial of Lambert was a political set-up, an exercise in statecraft, devoid of justice. For Henry it was also a platform to present himself as the master of his own church: the authorizing force for all things spiritual and temporal. In his way stood John Lambert, assailed by 'many and great perplexities, vexed on the one side with checks and taunts, and pressed on the other side with the authority and threats of the personages'.[1] No one dared risk the king's displeasure. Certainly not Sir Thomas Elyot, who addressed Henry in a fawning preface to his Latin-English dictionary:

A divine influence or spark of divinity which late appeared to all them that beheld your Grace sitting in the throne of your royal estate as Supreme Head of the Church of England next under Christ, about the division and condemnation of the pernicious errors of the most detestable heretic, John Nicholson, called also Lambert.

Foxe offers a typically clear-headed account. After the bishop of Chichester had outlined the prosecution case, Henry stood up and glowered at Lambert 'as if [he] were threatening some grievous thing to him'.[2] Upon being asked his name the Reformer admitted to two: Nicholson as well as Lambert. 'What', blustered the king, 'have you two names? I would not trust you, having two names, although you were my brother'.[3] Lambert's reply was respectful yet pointed: 'Oh most noble prince', he said, 'your bishops forced me of necessity to change my name'.[4] After several profitless exchanges, Henry turned to the issue of the Lord's Supper. Therein, he knew, was planted the seed of Lambert's destruction. Lambert, however, was grateful that the king 'would not disdain to hear and understand the controversies of religion'.[5] His naivety was instantly stamped upon; Henry had come to condemn, not to listen. He shifted upon the throne. 'Answer as touching the sacrament of the altar!' he cried, and tore off his pearl-and-feather cap. 'Do you say that it is the body of Christ, or will you deny it?'[6] Lambert, visibly rattled, was silent for several moments. His next utterance, he knew, would follow him

---

1 Foxe, v. 233.
2 Ibid. 230.
3 Ibid.
4 Ibid.
5 Ibid.
6 Ibid.

into eternity. But when at last he spoke his voice was clear and composed: 'I answer with Augustine, that it is the body of Christ after a certain manner'.[1] The king leaned forward, fervent and hostile. 'Answer me neither out of Augustine nor by the authority of any other' was his instruction. 'Tell me plainly whether *you* say it is the body of Christ or not'.[2] Lambert plunged: 'Then I deny it to be the body of Christ'.[3] 'Mark well', cried the king, 'for now you shall be condemned by Christ's own words: *Hoc est corpus meum* ("this is my body")!'[4]

With his actor's instinct for high drama, Henry sat back. All about him hands shot up in nervous acclamation. Cranmer stepped forward. Taking the conversion of Paul as his text, the archbishop questioned Lambert's assertion that Christ's body cannot be in two places at once: in heaven *and* in the bread of the sacrament. Why, said Cranmer, Paul saw Christ near Damascus at the same time as Christ was certainly in heaven—'and if [the body of Christ] may be in two places, why by the like reason may it not be in many places?'[5] Lambert answered that Scripture records that *there shined round him a light from heaven, and he said 'Who art thou, Lord? And the Lord said, I am Jesus whom thou persecutest* (Acts 9:3–4). Christ remained always in heaven said Lambert, although He 'might speak unto Paul, and be heard upon earth'.[6] Yes, Paul and his companions heard His voice. But they saw no body. They saw a light. Though dismissive of his theology, Cranmer did not stoop to browbeating Lambert. 'Brother Lambert', he said, 'let this matter be handled between us indifferently, that if I do convince this your argument to be false by the Scriptures, you will willingly refuse the same; but if you will prove it true by the manifest testimonies of the Scriptures, I do promise, I will willingly embrace the same'.[7] Once more the enigma of Cranmer is writ large. Many have praised his moderation during his examination of Lambert. The same moderation was present in 1533, when Cranmer presided over the burning of John Frith. No matter how fair-minded he appears, it is impossible to overlook Cranmer's complicity in these events. Having submitted his

---

1   Ibid.
2   Ibid.
3   Ibid.
4   Ibid.
5   Ibid. 231.
6   Ibid.
7   Ibid.

conscience to the king's pleasure, and diligently, in his own phrase of 1555, 'maintained the papist's doctrine',[1] the most frustrating churchman of the Tudor age resumed his seat.

A gaggle of bishops, including Gardiner, Tunstall and Stokesley, the boorish bishop of London, then took up cudgels against Lambert. Stokesley, who later boasted of sending fifty heretics to their deaths under Mary, returned to the issue of the substance, or inner reality, of the eucharistic elements. In his replies Lambert invoked what he called 'the perpetual rule' of the philosophers: 'the qualities and accidents in natural things', he said, 'should remain in their own proper nature'.[2] His words created fresh uproar. To tolerate an attack on transubstantiation was to risk the degradation of divinity, and with it the extinction of everything that mattered, whether in life, or death, or eternity. For Catholics, to attack the doctrine of transubstantiation was to attack Christendom itself: if modern readers are to understand the Reformation at all, they must first understand this. As the bishops took turns to belabour Lambert, the better to impress their king, the Reformer, who had been on his feet for at least five hours, lapsed into an exhausted silence. As the light faded and torches were lit, he told Henry that 'I commend my soul into the hands of God, but my body I yield and submit unto your clemency'.[3] Henry was implacable. 'If you commit yourself unto my judgement', he said, 'you must die, for I will not be a patron to heretics'.[4] It was a doom-laden moment. The king beckoned Thomas Cromwell, vicar-general and vicegerent. Cromwell then read out the sentence of condemnation. Thus, in a grim irony remarked upon by Foxe in later editions of his book, the destruction of the Gospel-loving Lambert was wrought 'by no other ministers than gospellers themselves, Taylor, Barnes, Cranmer and Cromwell, who afterwards, in a manner, all suffered the like for the gospel's sake'.[5]

Shortly after dawn on 20 November 1538, John Lambert was taken to the house of Thomas Cromwell. The king's chief minister abased himself and begged Lambert's forgiveness. Lambert breakfasted, amiably enough we are told, with Cromwell's staff before departing for Smithfield. The insupportable blunderings and wanton savagery he endured at Smithfield remind us that

---

1   MacCulloch, 234.
2   Foxe, v. 233.
3   Ibid. 234.
4   Ibid.
5   Ibid.

the unimaginable can occur. No other Reformer, in the opinion of Foxe, was 'so cruelly and piteously handled'.[1] He was set upon a woodpile so shabbily constructed that his thighs and legs were burned off. As his stumps smouldered, his tormentors used pikes to hoist his body out of reach of the flames; he was then lowered onto the rekindled fire. Amidst this witless barbarity, Lambert's supreme concern was to see God's rule manifested in the lives of his countrymen. 'None but Christ', he cried out, his hands fully alight, 'none but Christ!'[2] When they were convinced he had breathed his last, the sheriff's men shook him loose from their pikes. His body fell into the ashes. The crowd, horrified and disbelieving, eventually drifted away, the manner of Lambert's passing inspiring valedictory thoughts that endured far beyond the stilling of his voice.

---

1   Ibid. 236.
2   Ibid.

VI

GEORGE MARSH

Smithills Hall stands in 120 acres of prime parkland on the edge of the West Pennine moors. One of the oldest manor houses in the north, constructed of rough-hewn stone, Smithills was the family seat of Sir Ralph Radcliffe (d. 1406), High Sheriff of Lancashire and twice its Member of Parliament. Sir Ralph's heirs held the property until 1485, when it passed to the newly-wealthy Bartons, a family of sheep farmers. In 1963 Smithills opened as a museum; it was also, for a period, a residential home and day centre. On a fresh golden afternoon, few visitors around, the house feels smaller than its size, and brimful of history. The paths trodden by the footsteps of ages are gone, broken up. But in the high gable, the oak-timbered hall, the ascending diagonal of a mullion, meaning is drawn from silence, a quality of light, a nostalgia. A light drizzle begins to fall. As the smell of old wood and damp stone merges with the dusk, the mind is subject to a number of thoughts and imaginings, phantom flickerings from obscurity to obscurity. At the entrance to the withdrawing room, protected by a metal shutter, is the outline of a stamped foot on a flagstone. This is the famous 'footprint of faith', left, according to tradition, by George Marsh in 1554 and said to bleed each year on the anniversary of his death. All nonsense of course: and the worst insult to Marsh imaginable, given the repugnance he felt toward the veneration of relics. But still, this evening, this wet October evening, amidst the whispering gusts of past lives, in such an unaccountable atmosphere, the questions the footprint poses do not seem inconsequential.

He was born at Broadgate Farm, in the district of Deane, near Bolton in Lancashire, in about 1515. An intelligent child, attentive and curious, he was judged capable, at around the age of seven, of meeting the demands of a grammar school education. The primary purpose of these schools was to provide boys with a working knowledge of Latin grammar—hence 'grammar' school—both in language and literature. For young Marsh this meant less contact with the 'honest trade'[1] of Richard his father. His school day would have lasted from six in the morning till six in the evening. As books were rare, and paper expensive, a good memory was vital: a schoolboy of the period learnt by repeating and retaining his teacher's words. The fact of his education points to a stable background and relatively well-to-do parents. Until his late twenties, George Marsh was a farmer. He raised livestock. He fretted over weather and disease. He toiled in meadow and woodland, hedgerow and ditch. Though arduous, and hard to romanticize, the life had a completeness to it: something rooted and rhythmic, and honourable in nature's way. When he was twenty-five he married. His wife's early death ('a painful cross to my flesh') seems to have had a transfigurative effect. Henceforth he would give expression to his other self: the inner man, the seeker after truth. He would outsoar the shadow of loss and begin a new life. It was a decision both poignant and intensely forward-looking. In 1551, having made ample provision for his children, Marsh left Lancashire for Cambridge. In the same year his name was written in the matriculation roll of Christ's College.

Little is known of Marsh's academic career. One source has him proceeding to the degree of MA, but the date is wrong and no award can be verified. What is certain is that he came vitally under the influence of the main reforming doctrines. Marsh was not an original thinker. His theological master was Wittenberg's Philipp Melanchthon, who, by the early 1550s, was reaching the height of his influence. Marsh seems to have been particularly struck by Melanchthon's contribution to debates over the Lord's Supper, and by his understanding of the use of law as it related to the common life of believers. Indeed, even after his arrest in 1554, Marsh was directing well-wishers to the writing of Melanchthon: 'whose judgement in these matters of religion I do chiefly follow and lean unto',[2] rather than advertising his own views. Barely a year after his arrival at Cambridge, Marsh was ordained by Nicholas Ridley, bishop of London. These were exciting, formative days, days when a young(ish) scholar, especially one with a love of biblical text, might identify himself with what he believed was right. From mid-January to mid-April 1552, Parliament passed laws authorizing the use of a revised Book of Common Prayer. This contained everything necessary for public

---

1   John Foxe, *Acts & Monuments* (1838), vii. 39.
2   Ibid. 54.

worship, throughout the year and from birth to death. Following critiques by Martin Bucer and Peter Martyr Vermigli, regius professors at Cambridge and Oxford respectively, the Prayer Book replaced 'vain and superstitious fables' with readings from Scripture. Holy Communion, a means of spiritual union with Christ, changing people not things, was reinforced by the Decalogue. The mass-practice of Rome was openly scorned, along with the pope's assumption of absolute and oracular authority. Edward VI, the 'young Josiah', now in the sixth year of his reign, had described the pontiff as 'the true son of the devil, a bad man, an antichrist and abominable tyrant'.[1]

Up and down the land, individual believers were refuting the efficacy of virtuous deeds, vocal prayer and external devotion. Instead they praised the all-sufficiency of Christ's death. In the university towns, amidst the swirl of event and change and potentiality, men of wide and awakened interests were recasting every idea, every conviction in the light of Scripture. It had all the quality of revelation. The aim was to return to the purity, simplicity and rationality of apostolic times. A co-ordinated programme of preaching, pastoral care and education would see a national community transformed into a Christian commonwealth, a *res publica Christiana*, ordered according to Christ's law manifested in the Bible: a Bible which ordinary men and women might read, and understand, and act upon.

From the spring of 1553, the bent of Marsh's mind ceases to be a matter for conjecture. He became, in close succession, the curate for two evangelical hot-spots: Church Langton in Leicestershire, and All Hallows, Bread Street, in the City of London. This rapid rise, for one with little pastoral experience, and no great academic achievement, is explained by the bond of interest and friendship Marsh shared with Laurence Saunders (q.v.). A Reformer of massive divinity, and a personality of exceptional warmth, Saunders was rector for both Langton and Bread Street. To Marsh, he was ever 'my most loving and most gentle master';[2] Saunders, in turn, recognized a kindred spirit: one whose joy at possessing the gift of faith increased every time the gift was shared. But Marsh, no less than Saunders, knew the times were evil and the days short. Even above peace, he loved righteousness and hated iniquity. Like a 'full faithful shepherd', we are told, '[he] kept his sheep from

---

1 From a treatise *Against the Primacy of the Pope* quoted in Peter Ackroyd, *The History of England*, (London, 2012), ii. 223.

2 Foxe, vii. 54.

the poisonous infection of the popish wolves'.[1] But what united Saunders and Marsh above all else was what Marsh called, in one of his letters, 'the true touch-stone, which is the Word of God'.[2] Their common purpose was to liberate that Word from the shackles of obscurantism and tradition: to restore its relation to grace and its application to the full-orbed reality of human affairs: of truth and feeling, pith and stomach, bone and muscle.

Though Cambridge remained his base, Marsh was bidden by conscience to ride, at regular intervals, back to his old stamping grounds in Lancashire. As Saunders also preached there in the period 1552/3, it is safe to assume that the two co-ordinated their visits. In pulpits in the Deane valley, in Rumworth, in Bolton, Bury and Eccles, the doctrine of justification by faith alone in a crucified—yet living—Christ was triumphantly proclaimed. In eradicating abuses, in promoting holiness and purifying doctrine, the Reformers cut like a knife through the entanglements of medievalism. A debased system of mediatorship, extending from the virgin to a well-placed saint, from pope to local priest, was replaced by a direct relationship between individuals and their Saviour. The abscondite, gracious God could be known, and known personally. It was a brilliant phase in the history of England. And then came the fateful summer of 1553. The death of Edward VI, and the accession of Mary Tudor, saw a volte-face and a creeping restoration of Catholic rite and ritual. Altars, roods and images were back in place. But Marsh continued to preach, in private houses and in churches, impervious to the concentration of traditionalist forces building up. His heart was formed for God's service. A notable convert was Geoffrey Hurst, a nail maker of Shakerley, who, strengthened by his reading of Tyndale's New Testament, began handing out Reformist tracts and preaching in the open air. He was later tried for heresy and imprisoned at Lancaster Castle. Only Mary's death, in 1558, prevented him from following Marsh to the stake. Hurst is believed to have married Alice, Marsh's sister. Whether this was before, or after, his conversion is unclear.

Before long, reports of Marsh's activity reached the ear of Edward Stanley, earl of Derby and a leading light of the conservative faction. Over and above matters of religion, Derby believed in the principle, and power, of inherited tradition. A great rebuker and despiser of the common people, Derby was horrified by the idea that Christian thinking could be done by anyone on the

---

1   Ibid. 55.
2   Ibid.

basis of one freely obtainable text: the Bible. In addition, his family's brand of witless feudality had been well-served by the elitist structures of Rome, while the Reformers' attempts to preserve church property for church use, for the salaries of preachers, and for poor relief—rather than handing it over to the nobility in the example set by Henry VIII—struck at his self-interest. In the midst of the succession crisis involving Lady Jane Grey, Derby had marched to Mary's aid with two thousand men; in its aftermath he became a Privy Councillor and Lord High Steward. He also served as a commissioner at Lady Jane's trial. As such he was complicit in sending to the block a seventeen-year-old girl, one of the wonders of her age, endowed with every quality of meritorious femininity. Not only was Jane locked in the Tower, she was demeaned: the government insisting that she walk through the streets to her trial at the Guild Hall. Her youth and frailty accentuated by hundreds of men with spears lining the route, Jane was spattered by mud, derided and gawped at. But she was strong in faith: 'I shall be delivered', she wrote to her sister, 'of this corruption and put on incorruption'.[1] Throughout her *via dolorosa*, dressed entirely in black, she read from an open Bible. Derby's part in her destruction seems to have primed a more general appetite for hunting evangelicals. After Jane, his name appears in the records of at least six more martyrdoms.

In early March 1554 Derby sent word to Robert Barton of Smithills Hall, the local Justice of the Peace, that Marsh was to be captured and held, to await examination on a charge of heresy. But first he had to be found. As Marsh was in Deane, visiting his mother, this shouldn't have proved too difficult. Barton's men, however, led by his servant Roger Wrinstone, chased a succession of false leads as far as Bolton. By such means does God accomplish his purposes. Because Marsh had not returned to Lancashire to visit or to preach. He had come to say goodbye. The complex of motives from which he acted must be viewed against a backdrop of the re-Catholicization of England. At the beginning of 1554, Mary's advisors had negotiated a treaty with Spain, the terms of which allowed her to wed Prince Philip, the son of the Holy Roman Emperor. A rebellion against the marriage, led by Sir Thomas Wyatt of Kent, had been roundly defeated.[2] In its aftermath, the

---

1   From a letter to her sister Katherine, quoted in Eric Ives, *Lady Jane Grey* (Malden, 2009), 272.
2   With Wyatt at the head of a force of 3000 men marching on London, Mary made a stirring speech at Guildhall. The city gates were closed, and Wyatt's men deserted him.

ill-starred Jane Grey was beheaded. Princess Elizabeth was conveyed to the Tower. Married priests were deprived of their livings. John Bradford was taken from the Tower and thrown into the King's Bench prison alongside Robert Ferrar. In April they would be joined by Rowland Taylor. As Barton's men scoured Bolton for Marsh, Ridley, Latimer and Cranmer were en route for Oxford and the Bocardo prison: their show trial would begin on 14 April. Laurence Saunders, Marsh's dearest friend, languished in the Marshalsea.

On 12 March, at his mother's house in Deane, Marsh's deliberations on his future reached a pitch of nervous intensity. How might he save himself? The accession of Mary was the death knell for reforming ideas. The land was under papal interdict. He was denied the pulpit. He feared bodily harm: why would he not? He wanted to spare his family, especially his mother, further anguish. The only way out—for himself, for them—was to seek refuge on the Continent. With the financial backing of certain London merchants, many of the Bible-men had left already. As the time of burnings began, hundreds more would follow, joining exile communities in Emden, Strasbourg, Wesel, Worms, Frankfurt, Basel, Geneva and Zürich. Marsh's preferred option, to go to Denmark, made perfect sense. Christian III, king of the Danes, was a Lutheran to his fingertips; Philipp Melanchthon, Marsh's theological hero, was his adviser. In 1521 Christian had attended the Diet of Worms, where Luther's electrifying defence of his doctrine ('my conscience is captive to the Word of God') converted many. The king's links to Reformist England came through his chaplain Joannes Macchabaeus (John McAlpine), the brother-in-law of Miles Coverdale. Christian would intervene in April 1554 to save the imprisoned Coverdale's life.

A man of moral as well as intellectual stature, Christian had absorbed all of Melanchthon's ideas about the responsibilities of rulers, both religious and dynastic. His was an intensely practical vision. What might be termed the theology of welfare was transformed; an altar-bound Christ, gilded and grieving, gave way to a social Christ, an evangelical Christ, reaching out to the sick and downtrodden. A 'poor chest' became a feature of every parish. Sumptuary laws[1] were enacted, begging discouraged. Hospitals were built. In the universities, languages and history took precedence over Aristotle and the scholastics. The truth of any teaching was judged by its fidelity to the *analogia fidei*, the rule of faith. Christian III was, in all the ways that matter, an

---

1   Laws that circumscribe expenditure on food and personal items.

heroic figure. Nor was his a voice in the wilderness. His sense of rulers being accountable for the spiritual well-being of their subjects was shared, among others, by Landgrave Philipp of Hesse and Albert of Prussia. So in leaving England Marsh was not only, after Christ's injunction, fleeing persecution.[1] He was departing from what he knew to be wrong, and identifying himself with what he knew to be right: a brave new world being fashioned in northern Europe by biblicist princes.

At the prompting of his mother, Marsh resolved to leave England 'after a week then next ensuing'.[2] Only then, with one foot on the threshold of defection, did Marsh learn of the warrant issued for his arrest. It changed everything. No warrant—and no charge—and his enemies would have been left with the fact of his flight, and their own hypothesis to account for it. But now, if he went, it would be reported that he had refused an opportunity to defend his doctrine. The priests would portray him as a purveyor of novelty: high-idealled maybe, but wrong-headed and weak-willed. In the affections of those he'd preached to, and conversed with, he would have a much less secure place. Some might suspect him, at least in private, of running away, not only from 'the country, and my nearest and dearest friends, but much rather from Christ's Holy Word'.[3] What's more, thought Marsh, they might be right.

At dusk he left his mother's house to meet a friend on Deane Moor. As sunset hues merged into the remnant of the day, Marsh fell to his knees. It was not the act of one at his wit's end. Marsh still had options. He was not falling apart. No, upon Deane Moor he simply rendered obedience to Christ Jesus. 'Obedience', wrote John Calvin, 'is the end of our calling'.[4] Rather than stir himself up to new heights of emotion, as you or I might have done, Marsh simply *believed*: believed he was in the arms of One greater than his fears. For the Reformers, faith *meant* to believe; it 'purifieth the heart', wrote John Frith, 'and giveth us a will and gladness to do whatsoever our most merciful Father commandeth us'.[5] Marsh exercised his belief at the point of need, seeking God's will by prayer and supplication, and with thanksgiving: embracing it, aligning himself to it, in the certain knowledge that *God hath*

---

1 Matthew 10:23
2 Foxe, vii. 40.
3 Ibid.
4 *Calvin's Wisdom,* ed. Graham Miller (Edinburgh, 1992), 228.
5 *The Work of John Frith,* ed. N. T. Wright (Appleford, 1978), 90.

not given to us the spirit of fear, but of power, and of love, and of a sound mind
(2 Timothy 1:7). Among the heath-clad hills he poured out 'the cogitations
and counsels of mine own mind', and returned home 'doubt[ing] not but
God (according as our prayer and trust was) would give me such wisdom
and counsel as should be most to His honour and glory'.[1]

Back at the house, Barton's band, led by Roger Wrinstone, turned up at
last. Along with the confusingly-named William Marsh, George's brother
bore the brunt of their retributive rage. In the end, in a deep inward turning
of the spirit, he agreed to bring the Reformer to Smithills 'the next day'.[2] As
soon as Wrinstone had left he went to find his brother in Adderton. When
George returned he beheld a house in uproar: an absent brother, a weeping
mother, his worst fears realized. His response was to detach himself, and
the danger he represented, without delay from the ones he loved. He rode
off to the house of a friend, not far from the church at Deane. Once again
he was confused, conflicted; his mind roared with speculation. And there
he called upon God, and took some 'ill rest'.[3] When he awoke, everything
around him, the whole crooked sequence of life, and his own little part of
it, was irrevocably altered. A quality of certitude entered his soul. As patches
of the new day blended with the old, the immensities and infinities of God
in Christ sounded in his heart like a great music: not loud, but all-pervasive,
filling the earth, the air, the trees, the sky. The perplexities of suffering were
ended. And when letters arrived from a faithful friend begging him not to
flee abroad, but to 'abide and boldly confess the faith of Jesus Christ', the
path before him was instantly confirmed to his soul: 'I would not fly' he
wrote, 'but go to master Barton, who did seek me, and there present myself,
and patiently bear such Cross as it should please God to lay on my shoulders.
Whereupon my mind and conscience, afore being much unquieted and
troubled, was now merry and in quiet estate'.[4] Before leaving for Smithills
with his brother and William Marsh, he knelt by his bed. He gave thanks
for the assurance of faith, prayed for all without exception, and recited the
English Litany (1544). The first authorized vernacular service in English,
assembled by Cranmer, Luther-inflected throughout, and devoid of saint-
worship, the Litany—and especially its 'Exhortation to Prayer'—studiedly

---

1   Foxe, vii. 40.
2   Ibid.
3   Ibid.
4   Ibid.

evoked the Sermon on the Mount. We must acknowledge, it ran, 'that we thinke not the vertue of prayer to consist in multiplyeng of many wordes without faythe and godly devotion'. And later that God 'doth not regarde neither the swete sound of our voice, not the great number of our woords, but the ernest ferventnes of our hartes'.

En route to Smithills Marsh called on three friends, and his mother-in-law. Each was asked to 'comfort my mother and be good to my little children'.[1] He thought it unlikely he would see any of them again. When the last tears had been shed he mounted his horse, arriving at Smithills around nine o'clock in the morning.

The idea that Marsh underwent a no-holds-barred examination at Smithills, including being challenged to accept that the bread of the Supper was the actual flesh, blood and bone of Christ, can be bracketed with the apocryphal 'footprint of faith' story. Justice Barton had not the will, the inclination, the knowledge or the authority to stray onto such territory. He simply appraised Marsh of the charges against him, and instructed his (Marsh's) brother and William Marsh to deliver him to the earl ('or his council') at Lathom House by ten o'clock the next day. As his brother and William had crops to sow, Marsh asked Barton if someone else might be given the job. His request was denied. He was then released: effectively on his own recognizance. He went back to his mother's, changed his clothes, and, all the time praying, set off towards Ormskirk, riding roughly north-west. His brother and William joined him on the way. A mile and a half from Lathom they took lodgings. The following morning, a Wednesday, they reached Lathom House: a moated stone-built castle with eighteen towers, protected by walls six feet thick: the family seat of the earls of Derby.

Once admitted into the house, Marsh kicked his heels for most of the day. Around four o'clock, Roger Mekinson, a member of the household staff, brought him before a panel of nobles and clergy, presided over by the earl of Derby himself. In a great Tudor house such as Lathom, the Tudor personage left his Privy chamber, where he might entertain friends, or even the king, to hold audiences in the Presence chamber: a larger, well-timbered, often more elaborately adorned space. This is where Marsh faced his interrogators. After a period of silence he was asked for his name. Derby then put it to him that he 'was one of those that sowed evil seed and dissention among the people'.

---

1   Ibid.

Marsh denied it. He was asked whether he was a priest. No, he said. How, then, had he earned his living? He answered that he 'was a minister, served a cure, and taught a school'. Ah, said Derby, with clunking irony, 'this is a wonderful thing! Afore he said he was no priest, and now he confesseth himself to be one'.[1] But the doctrine of the priesthood of all believers, promulgated by Luther in 1520,[2] had jettisoned the sacramental character of ordination. To Marsh and his co-religionists, the mass was no sacrifice; it was a testament. 'What need is there of a priest', Luther had asked, 'when there is no need of a mediator or teacher?'[3] Marsh's role was to proclaim the Gospel of Christ through words and visible signs. 'By the laws now used in this realm', he confirmed, 'as far as I do know, I am [not a priest]'.[4] His instinct for an apt phrase would serve Marsh well. His words counted: he knew that. His trial was a providentially prescribed form of public witness. Quite apart from the men in front of him, he was speaking—preaching, in effect—to ordinary believers: consoling, encouraging, most of all reciting the ordinances of Christ, by which all might be instructed. None of which cut any ice with Derby. To him, Marsh's ordination was noteworthy because Nicholas Ridley had conducted the service, and Taylor, bishop of Lincoln, had assisted.[5] Such affiliations—at this time, in this company—were ample evidence of heresy. Derby had his point of leverage; a basis for lethal debate. Master Sherburn, the parson of Grappenhall, was on hand to deliver the preamble to many a Reformer's condemnation: 'But what is thy belief in the sacrament of the altar?'[6]

For Mary I, the burner of 287 Reformers, the sacrifice of the mass was the supreme element of faith to which all else was subject. That dread fact compels a pause. In 1215 the term *transubstantiatio* was granted dogmatic status by the Fourth Lateran Council. At the dawn of the Reformation, despite shifts of allegiance, refinements of language and outright challenges— notably from John Wycliffe in the late Middle Ages—transubstantiation was accounted the most perfect form of justification available in this life. In 1551, the Council of Trent, goaded into action by Luther, decreed once and for all

---

1 Ibid. 41.
2 Introduced in *To the Christian Nobility of the German Nation.*
3 Quoted in Richard Rex, *The Theology of John Fisher* (Cambridge, rep. 2003), 135.
4 Foxe, vii. 41.
5 Taylor had walked out of the mass celebrated at the beginning of the 1553 Parliament.
6 Foxe, vii. 41.

that the substance of bread and wine *was* transformed, at the priestly words of consecration, into Christ's actual body and blood. By manducation, therefore, or oral eating, the faithful were able to physically participate in Christ's nature. The nearly two hundred bishops who attended the Council of Trent were content to rest the whole edifice of the Church upon this dogma. Among the Reformed, in the same period, opinions were fiercely discrepant. Lines of division between the followers of Luther and Zwingli were drawn in heavy pencil; the debates marked by truculence and mutual distrust. Part of the reason for this, one suspects, is that the major Reformers, almost to a man, were former priests. Peter Martyr Vermigli, Regius Professor of Divinity at Oxford, was their most lucid expositor of the Supper. He observed the growing hostility and urged restraint. But not, at any stage, appeasement. A desire for unity, he said, must not be upraised into an article of faith. 'But perhaps ye think', wrote the Florentine, 'that the controversy about the eucharist is a certain small dissent: which is not so, seeing in it there is strife about the principal points of religion'.[1] There were questions of principle that appeals to brotherly love could not be allowed to override.

On one front, however, all branches of what would later be called Protestantism were in complete agreement. Transubstantiation was a papal imposture. Neither the Bible nor the church fathers ever mentioned the doctrine.

In his examinations before the earl of Derby, and in his prison letters, Marsh's aversion to spelling out his position on the Lord's Supper is plain. On one level this is perfectly understandable. Death was decreed for all who denied transubstantiation. Why connive at your own destruction? But his theological affinity with Melanchthon offers other, more complex reasons for this caution. Melancththon's warnings against transubstantiation date back to 1519.[2] But even after he became convinced that it was a perversion of Christ's testament, he was still affirming, at Marburg in 1529, an 'invisible corporal presence'. This was the age of diets and colloquies, all aimed at confessional consensus. In 1534, at Kassel in northern Hesse, Melanchthon agreed with Martin Bucer that Christ is present in the Supper, but 'in a sacramental way' (*auf sakramentliche Weise*).[3] It was a vital concession. In his

---

1 Quoted in Patrick Collinson, *Archbishop Grindal 1519–1583: The Struggle for a Reformed Church* (London, 1979), 42.

2 To his theses, in Wittenberg, for the baccalaureate in theology.

3 Quoted in Martin Greschat, *Martin Bucer: A Reformer and His Times* (Louisville, 2004), 134.

reworking of the Augsburg Confession (1530) and its Apology, issued in 1540, Melanchthon adopted Bucer's description of Christ's body and blood being 'truly exhibited' in the Supper—not, as before, 'truly present'. That body, that blood, were *with*—not in—the bread and wine.[1] Fourteen years later, in Lathom House, Marsh made the same point. Anyone who receives the consecrated elements, he said, 'did eat and drink Christ's body and blood, with all the benefits of His death and resurrection, to their eternal salvation; for Christ is ever present *with* (my italics) His sacrament'.[2] In a world where to be right about the Lord's Supper was to be right with God, Marsh, for good or ill, placed his confidence in sacramental union.

Melanchthon died in 1560. Twenty years later, he was still being derided, by dyed-in-the-wool types, as a crypto-Calvinist: 'the betrayer of Lutheranism'.[3] Those less fixated on the actual offering of Christ's body were dubbed 'Philippists'. Melanchthon's memory was attacked on the basis of his flexibility in matters he considered *adiaphora* ("things indifferent"). Even into the twentieth century, calling John Frith 'the Melanchthon of the English Reformation' was meant to underline Frith's allegiance to 'the theory of toleration'.[4] On the substantive issue, however, it must be pointed out that Melanchthon was never convinced that Christ's presence in the Supper depended on the state of the communicant's soul. In the sacramental debates of the 1530s, the theologians of north Germany, led by Luther and Melanchthon, and those of south Germany, led by Bucer, eventually lighted upon a formulation of the Lord's Supper broad enough to embrace every doctrine except transubstantiation. The southern Germans dropped any talk of participating in a memorial of Christ's crucifixion. They averted their eyes from the notorious *manducatio indignorum*, the 'eating of the unworthy': the idea that in the eucharist even unbelievers eat and drink Christ's body and blood. In May 1536, unabridged and unexpurgated, the *manducatio indignorum* was incorporated into the Wittenberg Concord by Melanchthon himself. All of which sets him at odds with Calvin and Bucer—and Peter Martyr Vermigli—and their conception of spiritual eating. Against this background, Marsh's refusal, before Derby, to answer what he calls 'hard and unprofitable

---

  1 'The Altered Augsburg Confession' (Lat. *Confessio Augustana Variata*).

  2 Foxe, vii. 41.

  3 Luther D. Peterson, *Oxford Encyclopedia of the Reformation*, ed. Hans Hillerbrand (New York, 1996), iii. 259.

  4 E. G. Rupp, *Studies in the Making of the English Protestant Tradition* (Cambridge, 1947), 10.

questions' takes on a real significance. As does his appeal to 'the saying of Paul, *Foolish and unlearned questions avoid, knowing they do but engender strife*'.[1] To parade doctrinal disunity in a public setting before a common enemy would have been self-indulgent and self-defeating. The overwhelming priority was to proclaim faith in Christ, in His reconciling act, in the renewed life of the justified sinner.

Behind Derby's striving to dictate to Marsh, to dominate him, sat a dogged determination to interpret his words and actions according to the necessities of the established order. Of the lacunae within his own understanding he made a combative virtue. For Marsh, on the other hand, any power, public or private, that did not acknowledge the vanity of human plans, and the indefeasible authority of the Bible, had alienated itself from the pursuit of heaven. Under cover of jurisprudence, he wrote, the council desired only 'to bring my body into danger of death, and to suck my blood'.[2] He was united to Christ, enslaved to God, and would not be tricked by 'philosophy and deceitful vanity after the traditions of men and ordinances of the world'.[3] This is what made the quarrel—every quarrel, in fact, in these accounts of the martyrs—so real: so vital, so mortal. In calling us to salvation, one form of high seriousness must prevail. The other must perish.

As the morning wore on, Derby's bombast congealed into something like hatred. To see rebellion manifested in the graceful figure of Jane Grey, cousin to Edward VI, was invidious. To see it written in the coarse features of a Lancashire farmer, albeit a highly educated one, was intolerable. What unsettled the Catholic lordlings was the manner in which the Reformation, with its relish for pure, apostolic Christianity, was freeing ordinary men and women from the dead hand of custom. In his most influential work, the *Loci theologici*, Melanchthon had set out his message concerning the believing sinner's acceptance by grace alone for the sake of Christ. The gift of grace, he said, bestows certainty. It is certain that the mercy of God is infinite: as is His truth. Everything believers are promised will be given to them, because this mercy, and this truth, are met together. From this proceeds a kind of annihilation: of self, of status, of any claim to personal merit. It is enough to be a member of Christ. And as a member of Christ one shouldn't settle

---

1   Foxe, vii. 42.
2   Ibid. 41.
3   Ibid. 42.

for less than the whole of the truth within the truth. The threat this message represented, not only to the pomp-devoted bishops, but to an influential segment of the landowning class, was just too real to be ignored.

By disposition Marsh was equipped to deal with anything Derby could throw at him. Towards the end of the first morning of the trial, thrown off balance—and 'much offended'[1]—by Marsh's inscrutability, the earl tried to force the pace. He sent for paper and ink. Marsh was ordered to set down his views on the Lord's Supper. At the first attempt he transcribed his earlier replies; at the second he wrote simply that 'further I [know] not'.[2] Derby's authority was paralysed. No amount of bellicose rhetoric could restore it. So he tried a different tack. He professed a willingness to offer mercy. In tones of effortful ingratiation he spoke of his desire to work for Marsh's good: to preserve him from harm. If only he would soften his stance. If only he'd return to the faith and unity of mother church: 'how glad he would be'.[3] In the Book of Acts, the uprightness of the apostle is thrown into sharp relief by the elasticity of his persecutors. Before Derby, Marsh would embody the same sense of high purpose. His faith—like Paul's, like Stephen's, like Barnabas's[4]—would be proved in affliction. But the first act of what would be a prolonged drama was over. Derby ordered his prisoner to be taken to one of the lodges on his estate: 'a cold, windy stone house, where there was little room'.[5] There he languished for two days. A guard brought food twice a day; otherwise he was alone. No bed was provided. At night, shivering with cold, he wrapped himself in scraps of tent canvas. He prayed, he studied, he meditated. He did all he could to amplify his mind into the realm of eternity.

On Palm Sunday 1554, around midday, Marsh was brought again before the panel. He talked about the Lord's Supper—for 'a good space', we are told—with the vicar of Prescot. No details of the discussion have been passed down. But this time, it seems, Marsh's language—at least as decoded by Prescot—was not considered ruinous. His understanding, said the priest, was 'sufficient for a beginner, and as one which did not profess a perfect knowledge in

---

1   Foxe, vii. 42.

2   Ibid.

3   Ibid.

4   Marsh, paraphrasing Acts 11:23–24, exhorted his flock in Church Langton to witness to each other as 'that good man, and full of the Holy Ghost, Barnabas, did the Antiochians, that with purpose of heart ye continually cleave unto the Lord'. Pauline language is found *passim* in Marsh's letters.

5   Foxe, vii. 42.

[the] matter, until such time as [he] had learned further'.[1] Derby was elated; Derby was relieved. So much so that Marsh was given the liberty of Lathom House. He could wander unmolested, talk to whomsoever he wished: even the servants. The earl doubted not that 'by the means and help of the vicar of Prescot', Marsh would be 'conformable in other things'.[2] A bed was sent to Marsh's lodge, with fine linen; a fire was lit in the grate. Once by himself, Marsh's mind threshed disconsolately. He'd been too clever by half: masking his words by indirection, doing all he could, short of denying Christ and His Word, to 'rid myself out of their hands'. In his efforts to evade specificity on doctrine he had compromised his Christian identity:

This considered, I cried more earnestly to God by prayer, desiring Him to strengthen me with His Holy Spirit, with boldness to confess him, and to deliver me from their enticing words, and that I were not spoiled through their philosophy and deceitful vanity after the traditions of men and ordinances of the world, and not after Christ.[3]

In a spirit of repentance, Marsh took his frailty to the throne of grace. Two days later, in a meeting with the panel's theological wing—the vicars of Prescot and Grappenhall—Marsh was asked what it was he found offensive about the mass. He replied 'the whole mass'. He saw in the use of Latin—recited or sung—a means for priests to present themselves as mediators between God and the main body of the faithful. Hadn't the apostle said that unless you speak plainly 'ye shall speak in the air'?[4] Rome, under a cloak of 'strange language',[5] had constructed an impious profanation of the death of Christ. In place of comprehensibility, in place of the sublimity of the human soul, was substituted an absurdist fantasy with 'manifold and intolerable abuses contained therein, contrary to Christ's priesthood and sacrifice'.[6] No storm of protest greeted these words. The regime's original policy, conceived by Stephen Gardiner, of exploring every avenue towards abjuration was still in place. Even after the first burning, of John Rogers in February 1555, the lord chancellor believed that the majority of evangelicals could be bullied

---

1   Ibid.
2   Ibid.
3   Ibid.
4   1 Corinthians 14: 9.
5   Foxe, vii. 42.
6   Ibid.

into silence. His queen was not persuaded. From the beginning of her reign, to the very end, Mary never doubted the merit of racking, famishing and burning heretics. Along with her closest adviser, papal legate cardinal Pole, she regarded them as putrid branches; they had to be cut off before their putrescence killed the whole tree. As the campaign of burnings intensified, Gardiner seems to have suggested some kind of moratorium. One death at the stake, it was said, was attracting more to the cause of Reform than a hundred sermons. Mary, however, was adamant: the executions must go on. Even in the weeks before her death, dangerously ill, she found time to write to a Hampshire sheriff, deploring his decision to pull a man from the flames after his first words of recantation.

At Lathom House, in the spring of 1554, the two priests sought 'gentle and far-sought'[1] means to blur the lines between their views and Marsh's. They derided literalism; Marsh mustn't, they said, substitute the definition of a thing for the thing itself. Credos of fluent obscurity fell from their lips. 'Sacrificium' and 'oblatio' were equated with thanksgiving and praise; the mass itself was 'a memorial of a sacrifice or oblation'.[2] On each point Marsh referred them to the agency of God's speaking: to the Bible. What it said disproved what their books 'do comment and gloss upon':[3] and what had been affirmed, as recently as 1551, by the Council of Trent: that Christ in the mass is offered and sacrificed 'for the sins and offences both of [the priest] and of the people; for them that were dead, and for the salvation of the living'.[4] To Reformers of every stripe this constituted a sinful robbing of God, to be resisted unto death if necessary. On the contiguous issue of the sacrament as a form of extended revelation, and of God's incarnation, Marsh kept a textual silence. His sense of connectedness—to Saunders, to the rest of the godly company, ultimately to God—had been forged by the Bible. Different minds had searched its contents, different conclusions had been drawn, especially with regard to Matthew 26:26: *hoc est corpus meum*, 'this is my body'. But that was no reason to doubt for a second the principle of the intelligibility of Scripture. The crucial point—certainly for Melanchthon, and one assumes for Marsh—was that Christ is not absent from His table. This was sufficient for evangelical solidarity: sufficient, too, to embrace the

---

1   Ibid.
2   Ibid.
3   Ibid.
4   Ibid. 43.

role of one guided by the Spirit of Truth. The lassitude of Palm Sunday was forgotten. With the priests immersed in their Jesuitical reasoning, Marsh was free to punch as many holes in transubstantiation, and in the concomitant doctrine of a sacrificing priesthood, as he wished. 'They sin willingly', he said:

[Which] of a set malice and purpose do withhold the truth in unrighteousness and lying, kicking against the manifest and open known truth, which although they do perfectly know that in all the world there is none other sacrifice for sin, but only that omni-sufficient sacrifice of Christ's death; yet, notwithstanding, they will not commit themselves wholly unto it, but rather despise it, allowing other sacrifices for sin, invented by the imagination of man, as we see by daily experience, unto whom, if they abide still in wickedness and sin, remaineth a most horrible and dreadful judgement.[1]

Before Derby, Marsh fought shy of admitting a convergence of earthly and celestial realities in the Supper. Before God his heart was opened up; before God he exercised his true confidence. Every morning Marsh prayed that 'If we hunger and thirst for righteousness, let us resort unto His table, for He is a most liberal feast-maker. He will set before us His own body, which is given to us to be our meat, and His precious blood, which was shed for us and for many, for the remission of sins, to be our drink'.[2]

On Maundy Thursday 1554, Marsh was presented with four articles, culled from summaries of doctrine used to force the compliance of Dr Edward Crome: the 'fashionable London cleric'[3] and fellow of Gonville Hall. In the matter of recantations, Crome was something of a dab hand. Twice in the reign of Henry VIII he agreed to retract, or at least modify, his criticisms of purgatory, fasting, confession, the merit derived from good works and the invocation of saints. Further down the line, in the spring of 1555, before the ashes of Rogers, Ferrar and Hooper were cold, he would again abjure to save his life. Crome was a brilliant scholar and a famous man. Marsh was neither of these things. But he was, perhaps, more conscious of the fadingness of human life. Left alone in his chamber to read the articles and weigh his fate, he emerged after half-an-hour to deny the mass, transubstantiation, communion

---

1 Ibid. 58.
2 Ibid. 68.
3 Eric Ives, *The Life and Death of Anne Boleyn* (Malden, 2004), 261.

in one kind and confession. His faith in Christ, he said, 'conceived by His holy Word, I neither could or would deny, alter, or change, for any living creature, whatsoever he were'.[1] Marsh would remain at Lathom until Low Sunday: that is, until the first Sunday after Easter. For the rest of his stay, the priests chose the rite of communion in one kind—in other words, giving ordinary people bread alone, not bread and wine—as the chief ground of their attack. The amount of attention paid to this issue by the Reformers is often overlooked; Luther, in his bracing *De captivitate Babylonica ecclesiae praeludium* ('Prelude on the Babylonian Captivity of the Church': 1520), placed it alongside transubstantiation and the mass as one of the 'three captivities' of the Lord's Supper.

Until the second decade of the 12th century, it was standard practice for the wafer and the chalice to be placed in the hands of clergy and laity alike: provided the latter had given adequate proofs of piety. But as every crumb of bread was reckoned co-terminous with His whole body, and every drop of wine with His blood, concerns arose about communicants spilling Christ on to the floors of churches. A crumb of bread might be picked up: not so a drop of wine. The church hierarchy was plunged into a series of agonized debates. In 1415, at the 13th Session of the Council of Constance, the grounds for offering the chalice to the laity were rejected. For Luther, a century later, this made a travesty of Christ's testament. 'The decisive thing for me', he wrote, 'is that Christ says "this is my blood, which is poured out for you and for many for the forgiveness of sins". Here you see very clearly that the blood is given to all those for whose sins it was shed. But who would dare to say that Christ's blood was not shed for the laity?'[2] Robert Barnes, England's best-known Lutheran, said that 'if you shall take away the parts of the sacraments at your pleasure, the consequence shall be that all at once the sacraments shall be destroyed, and Christ's Word set at nought'.[3] And in their stirring confession of faith, issued from the King's Bench prison in May 1554, Bradford, Taylor, Ferrar and Hooper described communion in one kind as 'a mutilation'; taking the cup away from the main body of the faithful was 'antichristian'.[4]

---

1   Foxe, vii. 43.

2   Quoted in Alister E. McGrath, *Reformation Thought: An Introduction* (Malden, 1999), 176–177.

3   *A Critical Edition of Robert Barnes's* 'A Supplication unto the Most Gracyous Prince Henry The. VIII. 1534:1531, ed. Douglas H. Parker (Toronto, 2008), 647.

4   See Andrew J. Brown, *Robert Ferrar: Yorkshire Monk, Reformation Bishop and Martyr in Wales*

At Lathom, the vicars of Grappenhall and Prescot did not appeal, in the first place, to conciliar decree. They opened their Bibles. They put it to Marsh that in Luke 24 and Acts 20 only the bread is referred to: there is no mention of wine. Marsh replied that the breaking of bread in Acts 20 'signified and meant the receiving of the sacrament, both of the body and blood of Christ, according to His institution'.[1] As for Luke 24:30 ('he sat at table with them, he took the bread, and blessed, and brake it, and gave it to them') that, he insisted, was an ordinary meal. It was an adequate defence: no more. So what was going on at Lathom? The low level of argumentation is puzzling. Marsh is called foolish, not wicked. Had his strange performance on Palm Sunday—his reluctance to delve too deeply into doctrine—been interpreted as a lack of intellectual heft? Marsh, we recall, might not have graduated from the university. Whatever the truth of this supposition, the priests' next ploy bordered on the risible. Marsh was given an encyclopedia of heresy, the work of Alfonso de Castro, a Franciscan monk known in some circles as the 'flagellum of heresy' (*azote de herejes*). His book, closer in tone to *The Perils of Pauline* than to a serious work of theology, detailed four hundred types of heresy, in alphabetical order, with helpful hints as to how the guilty might be whipped, battered or burnt. To have given the likes of, say, Ridley, or Bradford or Taylor, such a volume would have struck anyone as absurd. Marsh, however, was ordered to 'read and take counsel'[2] of it. But when the vicar of Prescot, cordial and greedy-eyed, went back to gauge its effect, he found a Reformer 'ground[ed] on the sure rock Christ'.[3] If Marsh's mind had been disquieted his soul had not. He declared the gulf between 'the blasphemous abuses and enormities of the Romish church',[4] and the Spirit of God, from whom the doctrine of the Gospel flowed, to be unbridgeable.

The vicar of Prescot's reaction was to call Marsh 'unlearned':[5] a calculated slur. Like most Catholics he deferred to a model of philosophical enquiry, of theological speculation, usually—if imprecisely—defined as *scholasticism*. A movement with its roots in the Middle Ages, scholasticism made extensive use of rationality and logic, especially in the works of Aristotle, to justify and

---

(London, 1997), 229.

1 Foxe, vii. 44.
2 Ibid.
3 Ibid. 56.
4 Ibid. 44.
5 Ibid.

systematize religious belief. As Alister McGrath puts it: 'The starting point of theology thus came to be general principles, not a specific historical event'.[1] The Reformed, meanwhile, had moved beyond the Erasmian humanism of the 1510s and 1520s,[2] with its mix of classical and Christian antiquity, to embrace a genuinely evangelical faith. Wolfgang Capito stated the case thus: 'Any good men ... limit the freedom of the Christian to the breadth of the Scriptures'.[3] Nothing of true value could be ascribed to the human intellect. Reason must not be imposed on revelation. The Creator God is not to 'be taken in this for a philosophical God ... but he is to be accepted as His own God who gave Himself up in pacts for the sake of the covenanted people'.[4] For Luther, Christ was the canon of the Scriptures: both Testaments were contained in Him. Catholicism, detained entirely on the surface of things, was incapable of excavating into such a reality. Melanchthon too placed the heart of truth in God: the unfettered pursuit of the former would lead to the latter. Providing for that pursuit was the whole purpose of learning. Calvin concurred: 'The true love of Christ is regulated by the observation of His doctrine as the only rule'.[5] In the same way, we see Marsh taking his stand on the divine origin of the Bible:

> I answered for my learning; I acknowledge myself to know nothing but Jesus Christ, even Him that was crucified, and that my faith was grounded upon God's Holy Word only, and such as, I doubted not, pleased God, and as I would stand in until the last day, God assisting me; and that I did not say or do anything either of stubbornness, self-wilfulness, vainglory, or any other worldly purpose, but with good conscience, and in the fear of God ... Then I said, I commit my cause unto God, who hath numbered the hairs of my head, and appointed the days of my life; saying, I am sure God, which is a righteous judge, would make inquisition for my blood, according as He hath promised.[6]

1   Alister E. McGrath, *Christian Theology: An Introduction* (Malden, 2001), 77.

2   Desiderius Erasmus (1446/9–1536). The most renowned scholar of the age, Erasmus argued that the church could be renewed and reformed by a return to the writings of the fathers and the Bible. His loyalty, however, was to the Catholic Church.

3   Quoted in James M. Kittelson, *Wolfgang Capito: From Humanist to Reformer* (Leiden, 1975), 93.

4   Ibid. 219.

5   *Calvin's Wisdom,* ed. Graham Miller (Edinburgh, 1992), 84.

6   Foxe, vii. 44.

Here is Marsh assuming the stance of an apostle. Marsh confident in the guidance of the Spirit. Marsh responding to the self-revelation of the God of heaven. Marsh honouring Christ by enthroning Him as King and Lord: *his* King and Lord, whose counsel controls whatever comes to pass. It was the most effective answer—the most open and heartfelt, the least conflicted—of his time at Lathom. Shortly before dawn on Low Sunday, Marsh was shaken out of sleep by his guard, Richard Scott. Two men were waiting with horses; ahead of them was a two-day ride to Lancaster Castle. At Broughton, north of Preston, they stopped for food and rest. In the morning Marsh was given over to local soldiery. On the approach to Lancaster, Marsh was supposed to have had his hands bound, his feet tied. But having observed their prisoner at supper, the soldiers decided, in Marsh's words, to 'take charge of me being loose, for they said I seemed to be an honest man'. Throughout these accounts—so full of dread, clamour and brutality—such decencies appear like blue sky glimpsed through a rainstorm. Nor, it seems, were the soldiers anxious to be rid of Marsh. After arriving in Lancaster, they kept him with them all night 'out of their gentleness'.[1] Marsh was only handed over to the gaoler the following morning.

On a chill, rainy morning, the walls of Lancaster Castle loom out of the mist in glistening medieval apparition. In its stone keep, battlements and massive inner walls, and in the monumental rock thrust of its gatehouse, all the might of Norman and Plantagenet kingship is embodied. Marsh was kept here for almost a year. Not, however, hidden away. From as far away as Cambridge, friends were able to visit. They brought news, food, even money. The local Reformed, seeing in Marsh's courage the fatherly favour of God, sought advice, and help with Bible-reading. Simpler souls were content with a few words of kindness. One man wrote of his indebtedness to Marsh for 'the great comfort' of 'see[ing] you take the Cross so thankfully'. Marsh in turn was thankful that his 'sweet Saviour Christ doth stir up the minds, not only of my familiar friends in times past, but also of sundry and divers heretofore unto me unknown and unacquainted'. Wait upon the Lord was his invariable instruction: 'faint not, and He will never fail you'.[2]

As Marsh's celebrity grew, so townspeople began to linger outside the window of his cell. Along with Thomas Warbarton, who would later shepherd

---

1   Ibid. 45.
2   Ibid. 67.

English exiles in Aargau, Marsh prayed from the English Litany before noon
and after; with other prayers added throughout the day. It was customary
for the two men to begin their readings around dusk 'with so high and
loud a voice, that people without in the streets might hear us'.[1] On several
occasions Marsh was shackled in irons and brought before the magistrates;
he was bullied and berated, and urged to betray 'a whole mess of good
gentlemen in Lancashire of [his] opinion'.[2] But Marsh had removed himself
from any concerns that removed him from Christ. When Parliament restored
the medieval statute *de heretico comburendo*, he would, he knew, be burned
to death. There was no time left for distractions. No time for the madness
of the world. What was left was completeness: a personality joined to the
acts and duties of love. A Christian's peace, he reflected, was 'taken for the
quietness and tranquillity of the conscience, being thoroughly persuaded
that through the only merits of Christ's death and blood-shedding, there
is an atonement and peace between God and us, so that God will no more
impute our sins unto us, nor yet condemn us'.[3]

One gauge of Marsh's stature was the steady stream of priests—up to six
at a time—trying to convert him. Watchful chancers, quick improvisers and
duplicitous supplicants: all beat a path to his cell. But no-one took as close,
or as morbid, an interest in Marsh as George Cotes, the bishop of Chester.
Cotes swept into Lancaster like a one-man mob. Any curate shown to be
sympathetic to Reform was ejected. In the midst of men and women newly
established in the philosophy of Christ, Cotes preached that nothing stood
above the identity and unity of the Catholic Church, and the powerful
tradition of its teaching. Thomas More believed that faith was inculcated
by consensus and tradition 'and so comen downe to our days by contynuall
successyon'.[4] That was the prism through which Cotes viewed both current
affairs and universal history. The Bible-men were 'frenzy-fools', convulsing
their environment and subverting the Councils of the Church by means
of radical theology and popular violence. Anything that might critique or
supplement his own habits of mind was heretical to Cotes. With characteristic
brio he set about extirpating every trace of reform from his diocese. Empty
formalism was accompanied by an empty heart; Marsh's cell-bound witness

1   Ibid. 47.
2   Ibid. 46.
3   Ibid. 64–65.
4   Quoted in Peter Ackroyd, *The Life of Thomas More* (London, 1998), 275.

was ended, his gaoler rebuked for his kindness. Cotes gave instructions that Marsh be 'more strictly kept and dieted'.[1] In March 1555, with the Revival of Heresy Acts passed, Marsh was transferred to Chester. The carousel had taken its final turn.

Marsh appeared before Cotes on three occasions. First he was brought to the bishop's palace, to a private chamber, 'nobody being present but they twain'.[2] The next two were set-piece events, conducted three weeks apart in the Lady Chapel of Chester cathedral. Before a stone shrine of Werburgh, the first-century saint, Marsh faced a panel comprising Cotes, Fulk Dutton, the mayor of Chester; William Wall, former warden of the Franciscan priory; George Wensloe, the cathedral chancellor; John Chetham, the registrar, and a smattering of priests. Marsh was introduced as 'a scabbed sheep, [weeded out] for corrupting others'.[3] The animosity was unabated throughout; Cotes' belief in the divine origin of the papacy left him vicious in the sight of God. Marsh's serenity, on the other hand, stemmed from his belief in a merciful God who speaks through His eternal, unchangeable and incorruptible Word. Knowing Rome did not want such a God, he harboured no illusions about his own survival. He wouldn't be drawn into attempts at justification or validation. He would only confirm, in remarks recorded by Foxe, that 'in all articles of religion he held none other opinion than was by law most godly established and publicly taught in England at the time of king Edward the Sixth; and in the same religion and doctrine he would, by God's grace, stand, live, and die'.[4] Cotes jabbed his glasses up his nose, drew a sheaf of paper from his robes and began the sentencing. But Wensloe interrupted him: not once but twice. 'Yet, good, my lord', he urged, 'once again [wait]; for if that word be spoken, all is past, no relenting will then serve'. The priests, twittering like linnets, pulled at Marsh's sleeve; Master Pulleyn, a cobbler, whispered 'For shame, man, remember thyself, and recant!'[5] But Cotes' patience was at an end. 'How sayest thou?' he cried. 'Wilt thou recant?' Marsh was calm. He was prepared. In a murmur of perfect peace he replied: 'I would gladly live as you, if in so doing I should not deny my master Christ; and [if] again He should not deny me, before His father in heaven'.

---

1 Foxe, vii. 47.
2 Ibid. 48.
3 Ibid. 50.
4 Ibid. 51.
5 Ibid.

Marsh was pronounced heretic *ex communicate*. In an act of pure spite, masked by the orderliness of the proceedings, the bishop concluded: 'Now I will no more pray for thee, than I will for a dog'.[1] For his part, Marsh assured Cotes that, their differences notwithstanding, he would continue to pray for him. He was then given over to the sheriffs of the city for burning. Outside the great door of the cathedral, tears rolling down his face, stood his former gaoler at Lancaster Castle. As Marsh was bundled away he cried out: 'Farewell, good George!'

Marsh was kept in the infamous gaol at Northgate. A dark and dismal place, raised in sandstone, abutted to the city wall, its dungeons were below ground level. Faintly fetid odours seeped in from the River Dee. A man of field and moor, copse and meadow, Marsh was incarcerated for a month, making stellar virtue of awful reality. He hungered to sleep, faced himself in prayer, praised God and magnified His grace. Occasionally, in the evenings, evangelicals would shout messages of support down the air-chute that ran from the city wall into his cell. Coins would be thrown down, 'ten pence at one time, and two shillings at another time'.[2] Marsh would bellow back the great affirmations of God in Scripture. He knew that by his willingness to imitate Christ by spreading Truth, and dying for it, he offered Chester, as he had Lancaster, an irradiance of feeling, a broader hope, far beyond the reach of papal-Catholicism. As the day assigned for his execution approached, he prayed for 'grace not to faint under the Cross, but patiently bear the same to His glory, and comfort of His church'.[3] His praise of the Saviour was as involuntary as his breath.

On 24 April 1555, George Marsh was shackled and dragged blinking into the light of his last morning. By order of the sheriffs of Chester, he was led to Spital Boughton, outside the walls of the city, flanked by a company of men bearing halberds and pikes. Bystanders sought to press coins on him, to provide, by means of prayers or sung masses, for the hastening of his dead soul's removal to heaven. It was the custom. Marsh's response exemplified a man's doing as he preached. The Word, not custom, was the rule of worship. Like Calvin, like every other Bible-man, he knew that 'the blood of Christ is the only satisfaction, expiation, and cleansing for the sins of believers'.[4]

---

1   Ibid. 52.
2   Ibid.
3   Ibid.
4   *Institutes*, III. v. 6.

All the sins he had ever committed had been dealt with on Calvary. He asked for the coins to be shared among his fellow-prisoners and the poor. For himself, he had a Bible in his hand; it was enough. With each painful step, every scrape of iron on bone, the promises of the Word flooded his heart. Heaven blazed in his head. At the stake itself the deputy chamberlain of Chester displayed an order under a great seal. It stated that if Marsh, even now, accepted transubstantiation as *de fide*,[1] and bent the knee to Rome's religious, judicial and administrative authority, he could return to his family. Marsh didn't hesitate. Such a pardon, he said, would 'pluck him from God'.[2] His burr-like tenacity never, for an instant, loosened its grip on the object he had set for himself: to upraise Christ crucified. He was no victim of ineluctable fate. He was a God-assigned witness to His verity.

With an invincible belief that the Holy Spirit was in him, Marsh turned to the crowd, to talk about Christ as he had found Him. 'George Marsh', roared one of the sheriffs, 'we will have no sermoning now!'[3] Fire-builders were bustling about, discharging the duties that just happened to involve burning a man to death. Marsh was chained to a post, with a firkin—a small cask—of pitch and tar suspended over his head. The faggots at his feet were lit; smoke moved slowly, silently upward. But the fire was ineptly made. Marsh's agonies were prolonged and intense. When the firkin split, and boiling tar streamed down his already blistered flesh, his body was 'so broiled and puffed up'[4] that onlookers could not see the chain securing him to the post. They believed him dead. But God was in him, and about him, and beside him. Suddenly there was movement. Slowly, little by little, his arms spread out, and Marsh called out: 'Father of heaven, have mercy on me!'[5] Seconds later, the rocks and reefs of the present life—its contagion, its destruction, its cruelty—were behind him. There was no more pain, no more sorrow, no more tussling of spirit and flesh. His soul left his body and began its spiritual existence.

Many at Spital Boughton were inspired to hold on to their faith that day. Marsh's steadfastness was taken as a token of superabundant grace. In the light of such a death, the details of his life—each word, each action—

1 Required to be held as article of faith.
2 Foxe, vii. 53.
3 Ibid.
4 Ibid.
5 Ibid.

seemed to pulse and fade, then live again, close and unimpeded. In Chester and Lancaster, in Bolton and Bury, in all the towns where he had preached, or been known, or been seen, he was spoken of as someone apart. He was a martyr all right, they said; he had 'died marvellous patiently and godly'. When reports of this reaction reached the ear of bishop Cotes, he leapt into the pulpit of Chester cathedral to affirm that Marsh 'was a heretic, burnt like a heretic, and was a fire-brand in hell'.[1]

In addition to letters and journals kept at Smithills Hall, a memorial to Marsh—a stone cross with a Saxon base—can be found in the churchyard at St Mary's church in Deane. A window in the church was dedicated to him in 1897. In Chester, a memorial plaque hangs in St John the Baptist church. A granite obelisk was erected in 1888 in Boughton. An inscription reads:

'George Marsh born Co. Lancaster. To the memory of George Marsh martyr who was burned to death near this spot for the truth's sake April 24th 1555'.

---

1   Ibid.

VII

ROBERT FERRAR

In the old market square of Carmarthen a coach party gathers around the statue of General Sir William Nott. A guide circles his charges like a fretful sheep dog. Sir William leans back against the grey morning sky, one hand placed on his hip, the other balanced on the hilt of his sword. The hero of Kabul commands a tightly packed, sloping square of estate agents, travel agents, cafés and charity shops. Over his left shoulder is the Hidden Jewel Tattoo parlour; behind him and to his right a 12th century castle. Some of the coach party dutifully inspect Sir William; a larger group is ushered towards the castle. Two women, having shed their husbands, head off in the direction of Marks and Spencer. No one notices a second memorial, mounted at the base of the general's plinth. Even if they had, it would be no easy task to negotiate the high railings and read an inscription set out in bold relief upon a raised, heavily oxidized, bronze tablet:

> Saturday, March 30th 1555
> Dr ROBERT FERRAR
> BISHOP OF ST DAVID'S

There follows a familiar legend: 'We shall by God's grace light such a candle in England, as shall never be put out'. At the bottom of the tablet, dissected by an open Bible, is a spirited signature line: 'Erected by a Protestant of this town'. At this point the moderately curious visitor to Carmarthen might begin to wonder about this man Ferrar. He might flinch, however, in this multi-faith age, at so bold an avowal of Protestantism. But if he could lay aside his reservations, and look instead into the events that inspired the laying of this tablet, he would discover an interesting story. It might even serve to save his soul.

Robert Ferrar arrived in the diocese of St David's in April 1549. He had

been consecrated bishop on 9 September 1548, following his appointment by
Edward VI. But the settling of his affairs in Yorkshire, and the obligation to
attend several sittings in the House of Lords, had delayed his coming. Ferrar
was the first bishop to be consecrated in accordance with the new English
Ordinal; the psalms and hymns chosen for the service, together with readings
from Paul's epistles and Matthew's Gospel, were conducted in English rather
than Latin. The accompanying service of communion also used an English
wording devised for inclusion in the forthcoming Book of Common Prayer.
The consecration took place in Chertsey, at the house of Thomas Cranmer.
The archbishop was assisted by Nicholas Ridley, recently appointed to the
bishopric of Rochester, and by Henry Holbeach, bishop of Lincoln. Also
in attendance were Thomas Thirlby, bishop of Westminster, and William
May, the dean of St Paul's. The oath repeated by Ferrar throws the timidity
of today's professing church into sharp relief:

> I Robert Ferrar, bachelor of divinity, named by the king's most excellent
> majesty to be bishop of St David's, have now the veil of darkness of the
> usurped power, authority, and jurisdiction of the see and bishop of Rome,
> clearly taken away from mine eyes, do utterly testify and declare in my
> conscience, that neither the see nor the bishop of Rome, nor any foreign
> potentate, hath, nor ought to have, any jurisdiction, power, or authority
> within this realm, neither by God's law, nor by any just law or means.[1]

After his consecration, and before leaving for south-west Wales, Ferrar
preached an audacious sermon at Paul's Cross. Dressed in the garb of an
ordinary churchman he 'spake against all manner of things of the church and
the sacrament of the altar, and vestments, copes, altars, with all other things
…'[2] By laying bare the ostentation of the priests, and the ritualism of the
mass, Ferrar knew he would be marked out, not least in Wales, as a radical
and a troublemaker. But this was just the latest example of a willingness to
act upon the Word of God in a manner guaranteed to incite the hostility
of the world.

He was born, no later than 1505, near Halifax in the county of Yorkshire.
We have no information regarding his childhood. But in the year 1524, when
he was ordained acolyte, sub-deacon and deacon in York, he was living at

---

1   See Andrew J. Brown, *Robert Ferrar* (London, 1997), 87.
2   Ibid. 90.

the Augustinian priory of St Oswald's at Nostell. As such, his daily life would have been regulated by the observance of the Rule of Saint Augustine. St Oswald's was a monastery of so-called Canons Regular, also known as 'black canons' from the black cope and hood that formed the habit. In contrast to the monks, whose vocation was cloistered and contemplative, the canons' role was clerical. They provided a ministry of liturgy and sacraments to local communities. The Rule, writes Philip McNair, 'breathes an evangelical charity wedded to acute psychological insight: the author of the *Confessions* knew the potency of flesh as well as the power of the Spirit'.[1] Ferrar's motivation in these years must remain a matter for conjecture. But an undoubted attraction of the religious life—for clever, quick minds—was the number of good books to be found in the libraries of religious houses.

There is no record of Ferrar being ordained as a priest in 1524, at least not in the diocese of York. Instead, with the priory's financial backing, he was able to pursue successfully his university studies in the following years. This was uncommon. 'From among all the canons of Nostell, in that generation', writes Andrew Brown, 'it seems that [Ferrar] alone was chosen to receive the benefit of a university education and was regarded as the one most suited to these protracted studies'.[2] In all the cathedrals, monasteries and priories in England, only one in every twenty canons was sent to university. The first part of what would be a twelve-year course of study was undertaken at Nostell. Already able to express himself with some precision in Latin, the principles of syntax would have been mastered by making translations of Aesop and Terence, Horace and Ovid. Some attention would have been paid to logic and philosophy, and perhaps to rhetoric. In other words, Ferrar's education was comfortably within the late medieval learned tradition. And then, in late 1524, or early 1525, he left Nostell for the university in the Fens. Cambridge would be his home for the next four years.

Ferrar could not have arrived at a more propitious time. Under the patronage of Lady Margaret Beaufort, grandmother to Henry VIII, Cambridge had become the fulcrum around which Renaissance studies revolved. Desiderius Erasmus, one of the towering figures of European thought, had taught theology and Greek at the university from 1510 to 1515. Under his influence, classical culture—its languages and literature—was put once more into the service of

---

1   *Peter Martyr in Italy* (Oxford, 1967), 71.
2   Brown, 10.

the Christian ideal. But approaches to learning still struggled to keep pace with new ideas. Cambridge had about 2000 inhabitants at this time. All aspects of town life revolved around the university. If, as seems likely, Ferrar was assigned to one of the secular colleges and halls, he would doubtless, soon after his arrival, have been thrust into the debates surrounding the latest views emanating from Wittenberg. And given that Thomas Bilney, Nicholas Shaxton, Robert Barnes and Matthew Parker were all at Cambridge in this period, as was Miles Coverdale, the future Bible translator, it is only a little fanciful to picture the young Augustinian in their midst, wrapped in the fug of the White Horse Inn—'Little Germany', so-called—holding earnest conversations about the nature of true religion. Ferrar's walk with God would take him far from the banks of the Cam. But he would bear the impress of the university for the rest of his life. An intricate network of Reformers grew steadily under Henry VIII and Edward VI, and did much—by prayer, by letter, by tender entreaty—to sustain those imprisoned in the reign of Mary I. This network was built upon friendships forged at Cambridge in the 1520s and early 1530s. Each man, at a critical juncture in the history of these lands, had turned to the Word of God as the foundation for his life and affairs.

The dissemination of Lutheran ideas had been causing the university establishment anxiety ever since the German monk nailed his theses to the doors of the Schlosskirche in 1517. On or around 11 February 1526, John Fisher, the university chancellor and bishop of Rochester, preached at Paul's Cross in the glow of a bonfire of Luther's books. A staunch friend of the Councils of the Church, it is tempting to think that Fisher's horror at the dissemination of forbidden texts stemmed partly from the fact that Erasmus's Latin edition of the New Testament (which also incorporated a Greek text) had been completed during the Dutch humanist's period at Cambridge. Fisher had been instrumental in bringing Erasmus to the university. He had approved his Scriptural investigations. And now, Erasmus' own antagonism towards Luther notwithstanding, many of the ablest students had divined, through the fog of his imperfect translation, the power of the Word of God. It was the spark that ignited the English Reformation. Ferrar and his co-religionists were as men reborn, with a new purpose swirling inside them like a holy storm: to deny the supremacy of the antichrist in Rome, to accord all doctrinal authority to the Bible, and to identify themselves to the end of their days with the great theme of the age: 'A Christian man', wrote Luther, 'is free from all things; he needs no works in order to be justified and saved, but receives these gifts in abundance from his faith alone'. Fisher's own response to these ideas was to start writing the polemical works against Luther on which his reputation now rests.

In 1525 proceedings were instituted against Robert Barnes, the 'usual chairman' of the meetings at the White Horse. As a fellow Augustinian, it is possible that Ferrar attended Barnes' Christmas Eve sermon in St Edward's church. To the horror of the traditionalists—and delight of the Bible-men—the abuses of the clergy in general and of Wolsey in particular were graphically exposed. It was the moment the authorities had been waiting for. Barnes was arrested and sent for trial. The colleges were scoured for heretical books. Barnes was taken to London, then Northampton, where he was confined to the Austin priory before fleeing to Germany. In 1527 Thomas Bilney was charged with heresy, but at this date submitted to the pressure to conform. He later underwent the toils of conscience and burned at the stake in Norwich in 1531. Reflecting on his first reading of Erasmus' New Testament, in the dog days of summer as evening shadows fell across the courts of Trinity Hall, Bilney wrote that 'at last I heard speak of Jesus'.[1]

If the religious and political turbulence that compassed Europe in the 1520s comprised the backdrop against which Robert Ferrar's mature faith was forged, the examples of Barnes and Bilney provided evidence nearer home of the consequences of proclaiming, in Ferrar's own phrase, 'the right honour and glory of God, after his Holy Word'. His later experiences at the university of Oxford, where we find him in or around 1528, must have reinforced his sense of persecution as a seal of adoption into Christ's company. Ferrar had transferred to Oxford on the completion of building work on St Mary's, the monastic college for Augustinian canons. As its statutes make plain, St Mary's demanded the highest standards of personal conduct. Little allowance was made for youthful high spirits in a regimen as disciplined as it was prolonged:

At meal-times one of the students would read aloud a chapter from the Bible. With certain exceptions, all conversation between the students would be in Latin. They were at all times to conduct themselves in a manner befitting the inmates of a monastic institution: they were not to make a practice of visiting taverns or the houses of lay people; they were not to bring women into their rooms, apart from close relatives;

---

1 John Foxe, *Acts & Monuments* (1837), iv. 635.

they were not to go out alone or after dark, and could not leave town or absent themselves from college without permission; they were to refrain from the keeping of hunting dogs, all noisy activities, defamatory talk, quarrels, physical violence, and litigation with fellow canons. Infringement of these regulations rendered the culprit liable to a wide range of financial penalties or, in certain cases, corporal punishment or expulsion.[1]

St Mary's wasn't the only addition to the university. On a far grander scale was the college founded by Thomas Wolsey to reflect his power and munificence. Wolsey believed that Oxford had rested on its laurels in the Renaissance period. He deplored the reluctance of his *alma mater* to embrace humanist subjects as well as classical studies. By filling the new college— named, unabashedly, Cardinal College—with the brightest and best students, not only from the other Oxford Colleges, but from Cambridge as well, he sought to galvanize the curriculum and bolster Oxford's flagging reputation. This suggests one reason for Ferrar's removal from Cambridge. It certainly explains the presence of the great John Frith. But what Wolsey had somehow failed to realize was that the faith common to all the Cambridge migrants had found its home in the religion of the Reformed.

'Printing is the latest of God's gifts and the greatest', declared Luther. 'Through printing God wills to make the cause of true religion known to the whole world, even to the ends of the earth'.[2] Without the rapid production born of the new technology, it is difficult to imagine how, as a pan-European movement, the Reformation could have taken a solid form. The demand for Testaments and tracts, cathechisms and commentaries, increased exponentially through the 1520s. And with the art of printing came the book trade. By the start of the decade there were at least twenty-four printing centres in Europe. Booksellers—and book agents—flourished in England as elsewhere, developing new and ingenious ways of distributing the works of Luther, Tyndale, Melanchthon and others. Bundles of books from the Low Countries were unloaded in the ports of London, King's Lynn and Bristol. Under cover of night the illicit cargo was transported to the universities and larger religious houses. Even a work as controversial as Tyndale's New Testament infiltrated the Cambridge colleges with ease. But John Longland, bishop of Lincoln—and bitter enemy of the 'evangelycall

---

1 See Brown, 13.

2 Quoted in *The Oxford Encyclopedia of the Reformation*, ed. Hillerbrand (New York, 1996), iii. 342.

fraternyte'—swore that the same thing would not happen in Oxford. He had not reckoned with Thomas Garrard.

An early and devoted advocate of Reform, Garrard graduated BA at Oxford in 1518 and became a fellow of Magdalene College in 1519. Having taken his MA in 1524, he went on to Cambridge and was incepted bachelor of theology by 1535. A curate of All Hallows, Honey Lane, London from 1526, he was admitted rector in 1537. On 30 July 1540, along with Robert Barnes and William Jerome, Garrard was burned to death at Smithfield. In the moments before his martyrdom he declared that he had never preached 'against God's holy Word, or contrary to the true faith'.[1] But back in the late 1520s Garrard was the ringleader of a complex book-smuggling operation. He was also a wanted man. Wolsey, in the midst of one of his periodic clampdowns, ordered his arrest in December 1527: at which time Garrard was plying his wares in Oxford, and taking a number of orders from the Greek and Hebrew scholars of Cardinal College.

In the early hours of 22 February 1528, Garrard was found 'lurking' within the university precincts. Thrown into a room at Lincoln College, he managed to pick the lock and make good his escape. In the furore that followed, dozens of students were arrested. As a fuller picture of Garrard's activity began to emerge, the heads of all the colleges were instructed to search students' rooms for all 'impious books'. Those believed to be 'infected with heresy, as they called it, for having such books of God's truth as Garrett [sic] sold unto them'[2] were locked up. John Higdon, the dean, had several men of Cardinal College, including their charismatic leader, John Clarke, thrown into a cellar. This was where salt fish was kept. As salt was a poor preservative, especially in warm weather, the canons breathed in a noxious reek of stinking fish for six months. In mid-August, Clarke, along with Henry Sumner and John Bayly, succumbed to sweating sickness.[3] Wolsey, ever-fearful of creating martyrs, immediately ordered the release of the remaining students. Frith was among them; so were 'two canons of St Mary's College, one of them named Robert Ferrar'.[4] Both took part in a procession of the guilty. As Augustinians their

---

1 Foxe (1838), v. 437.

2 Quoted in Brown, 17.

3 This highly-contagious disease, also called the 'Englishe sweate', reached epidemic proportions in the summer of 1528. Cold shivers, headache and acute pains in the shoulders and neck were closely followed by hot sweats, delirium, intense thirst, heart shakes, exhaustion and death.

4 Foxe, v. 428.

separate status was underlined by their walking 'on the contrary side of the procession bareheaded, and a beadle before them'.[1]

Ferrar's university education lasted another five years. In 1533 he was incorporated bachelor of theology. It should be pointed out that despite being designated 'doctor' in later editions of the *Acts and Monuments*, and on two memorial tablets in Carmarthen (one in Nott Square, the other in St Peter's church), no evidence exists of him crowning his degree with a doctorate. In letters written to him by John Hooper and Laurence Saunders, both preserved by Miles Coverdale, our bishop is always referred to as *master* Ferrar. If Ferrar had indeed been awarded a doctorate, the fact would hardly have gone unnoticed by his friends.

The year of Ferrar's graduation was an historic one. In April, Thomas Cranmer was consecrated archbishop of Canterbury. Three months later, in the wake of his marriage to Anne Boleyn, Henry VIII was excommunicated by pope Clement VII. This was followed in 1534 by the Act of Supremacy. All papal authority was abolished and Henry declared supreme head of the church in England. Still the king wasn't satisfied. With Thomas Cromwell he hatched a plan to export the Reformation to Scotland. To that end a diplomatic mission—called an 'embassy'—would be sent to the court of the Scots' king, James V. It would be led by William Barlow, a protégé of Anne Boleyn. Cromwell and Barlow would play significant roles in the advancement of Robert Ferrar. An Augustinian and zealous advocate of Reform, Barlow saw in Ferrar a kindred spirit. He was duly selected to join the embassy to Scotland. The mission met with limited success. Though he deplored—or so he said—the papal-inspired crusade against Henry, James was not about to risk the disfavour of Catholic France. The embassy did, however, mark Barlow out as a rising star. His organisational flair, and appetite for taking reform to far-flung regions, saw him elevated in January 1536 to the Welsh bishopric of St Asaph. Only three months later he was translated to St David's.

Ferrar's own contribution to the Scottish embassy had not gone unnoticed by Henry's chief minister. The view of Cromwell that still reaches down to us today—the unprincipled schemer and fixer—reached its apotheosis in *A Man for all Seasons*. It is hardly a reliable portrait. The same play, later an Oscar-winning film, takes up the unpromising human material of Thomas More—a torturer and man burner—and virtually deifies him. A skilled practitioner in

---

1 Ibid.

the art of statecraft Cromwell certainly was. Nor was he unaware of where his own interests lay. But his commitment to solid Reformation principles was absolute. Thomas Cranmer ('I loved him as my friend')[1] and John Frith, among others, attested to his kindness, perspicacity and godly zeal. These men knew him, sat with him, talked and corresponded with him. If they regarded Cromwell as a fellow soldier in Christ so might we. For their part Barlow and Cromwell saw in Ferrar a man of unimpeachable integrity: someone who preached the church of God as the congregation of the faithful. Ferrar wanted the Gospel message to permeate the whole of life, and comprise the wellspring from which all policy—social, economic and religious—flowed. Such a man, thought Cromwell, might prove an invaluable ally.

By 1537 we find Ferrar serving as Cromwell's personal emissary in the north. He reported from Northumberland upon the poor state both of law and order and of preaching. He writes with heartfelt dismay that 'as touching the sincere setting forth of God's holy Word and the king his supreme authority and power, I hear of no preacher betwixt Newcastle and Berwick, and few in all Westmoreland, Cumberland, Durhamshire, and the west part of Yorkshire with much of the north parts'.[2] It is clear from this letter and others that Ferrar saw in the absence of private Bible-study and sound preaching the roots of private depravity and public lawlessness. 'He believed', affirms Brown, 'that the spreading of the unadulterated Christian Gospel would bear fruit in the eternal salvation of individual human souls, and also that it would make a vital contribution to social order and stability'.[3] This conviction, at once godly and practical, forms a vital constituent of Ferrar's faith. If we fail to grasp its implications we cannot hope to comprehend the journey that led to the market square in Carmarthen.

In 1538, when Ferrar returned to the monastery of St Oswald's in Nostell, this time as prior, he was still decrying a lack of 'faithful preachers' and 'diligent schoolmasters'.[4] For the Reformers, faith and knowledge were united. The Holy Spirit, working through the Word, disposes the will so that faith is born: a faith that requires no pilgrimages, no tapers or kissing of relics, no mediator between God and man excepting the Lord Jesus Christ. It should be remembered that pluralism was rife; crypto-Roman rectors hardly set foot

---

1   Quoted in Diarmaid MacCulloch, *Thomas Cranmer* (New Haven, 1996), 270.
2   Brown, 43.
3   Ibid. 37.
4   Ibid. 52.

in the parishes for which they were responsible. Their curates were happy to intone the services in Latin. They might choose to exercise a degree of moral authority. But the Bible was, literally and figuratively, a closed book; its life-giving properties had been traded in for priestcraft and formalism. It was as if, in the words of Strasbourg's Wolfgang Capito, 'Christ had been born only for the anointed, as if the people ought to have no business with faith, unless they claim perhaps that you can believe in things of which you are totally ignorant'.[1]

The state of the diocese of Gloucester when John Hooper was appointed bishop in 1551 is described by J.C. Ryle:

> Out of 311 clergy of his diocese, 168 were unable to repeat the Ten Commandments; 31 of the 168 could not state in which part of Scripture they were to be found; 40 could not tell where the Lord's Prayer was written; and 31 of the 40 were ignorant who was the author of the Lord's Prayer![2]

For Ferrar the Englishing of the Word went hand in hand with the revival of learning. Both were needed if the land was to be shaken out of its spiritual slumber. Ferrar felt so strongly about this that he took the unusual step of appointing two preachers—John Best and William Huyck—from outside the monastery. Best and Huyck lectured on Scripture, taught and catechized: not only at St. Oswald's but in the surrounding parishes. Clergy and laity were able to hear, for the first time, the sayings of Christ in their own tongue. Texts were posted in marketplaces, in village squares and on church doors. On Ferrar's watch the doctrine of the Gospel was being taught and faithfully learned. In May 1539 a statute confirming the king's right to all the monasteries was passed.[3] Given the evidence of 'glad hearts desirous to hear and learn [the Word]' at St Oswald's, Ferrar wrote to Cromwell asking that it 'be established a college for the nourishment of youth in virtue and learning, to the increase and advancement of the lively Word of God, diligently, sincerely and truly to be preached to God's people and the king's in these parts, which thanks be to the Lord are right diligent and with glad hearts desirous to hear and learn the same'.[4] Almost inevitably, in this age of

---

1 *The Correspondence of Wolfgang Capito*, ed. Erika Rummel (Toronto, 2005), 226.
2 J. C. Ryle, *Five English Reformers* (Edinburgh, rep. 1999), 38.
3 An Act for Dissolution of Abbeys was passed in May 1539.
4 Quoted in Brown, 71.

tumult, Ferrar's noble venture was stillborn. Nostell Priory, its buildings and lands, were seized in November 1539. Those lands not taken by the crown were sold off to the gentry and nobility, swelling state coffers whilst binding the upper orders to the Act of Supremacy. This was also the year of the Act of Six Articles. Henry VIII, in order to parade his orthodoxy before the Catholic princes of Europe, and to quell religious radicalism at home, was reining back reform in favour of what has been called national Catholicism. The act was championed at an episcopal level by Stephen Gardiner, bishop of Winchester, and on the civil side by Thomas Howard, duke of Norfolk. Howard was the most Catholic of Henry's privy councillors. 'I have never read the Holy Scriptures', declared he, 'and I never will read them. All that I want is that everything should be as it was of old'.[1]

With the passage of the act, anyone denying the doctrine of transubstantiation—in Henry's words that the bread and wine were 'none other substances but the substance of his foresaid natural body'[2]—faced a heretic's death. Other unbiblical accretions—private masses, clerical celibacy, vows of chastity—were backed by the threat of imprisonment and the removal of goods. The articles, writes Peter Ackroyd, 'were essentially the king's declaration of faith. It was a faith shaped by the will of the ruler and by the power of punishment'.[3] The ritualists were back. Many of the Reformed laid low. Some couldn't. Cromwell's distaste for the act, along with his perceived responsibility for Henry's marriage to Anne of Cleves, saw him thrown to the wolves. In the wake of his patron's execution, in July 1540, Robert Ferrar was called to a session of the York Court of Audience. His failure to attend led to his summary excommunication. As for Nostell Priory, it was allowed to fall into ruin. In the eighteenth century its remains were demolished by the Winn family, who built a Palladian mansion in its place.

Aside from one or two phantom sightings, Ferrar disappears for six years. But in 1546 he resurfaces as a farmer, living in a rented house at Revey, near North Bierley in Yorkshire. His landlord is one William Rookes of Royds Hall, Low Moor. Rookes subsequently built him a property called Revey Hall. Consider his journey to this point. The temple bells had guided an Augustinian monk to the shore of biblical humanism. In a spirit of prayer

---

1   Quoted in J. H. Merle d'Aubigné, *The Reformation in England* (Edinburgh, rep. 1963), ii. 385
2   Quoted in Peter Ackroyd, *The History of England* (London, 2012), ii. 142.
3   Ibid.

and supplication he had discovered his voice and his vocation: to testify of Him whom his soul loved. And through abundant grace, as the dawn of Reformation bathed England in its golden light, he had trumpeted the very heart of the Gospel: that we are justified by grace alone through faith alone. But now his preaching days, at least in public, were over. He did not know if they would ever return. He trod the fields of his exile with the enormities of renascent Catholicism pressing in from all sides.

Was he, like the wise virgins, gathering in his vessel the oil of truth: keeping watch, steeling himself for the challenge ahead? He was not one to be morbidly preoccupied with self. He had been presented with a test of trust. Dr Lloyd-Jones reminds us that 'God so deals with us in this life as to bring us to trust him in the dark when we can see no light at all'.[1] Ferrar had already demonstrated physical as well as moral courage. The deaths of Clarke and the others in the salt-fish cellar must have affected him deeply. He was heir to the virtues his friends embodied. And the dying witness of Bilney and Bayfield, both burned to death in 1531, would have thrown the connectedness of Cross and Gospel into sharp relief. Few were as well-girded with the armour of truth. According to Foxe, he was able to commit whole chapters of Scripture to memory. It is a matter of regret that only a handful of his letters have been preserved. Searching these for clues, what emerges is a man of expressive affections; a compound of tender conscience and tenacity. There's a nice crust to him. He seems devoid of malice. Each of these qualities lent its tone to his smallest no less than to his greatest acts. The writing style is sprightly and concise, suggestive of imagination and common sense. And in one detail, from a single letter—one small, indelible human gesture—the essence of Ferrar imprints itself on the memory. At the top of a letter to Cromwell in June 1538 is inscribed the twelfth verse of Psalm 2: *Blessed are all that trust in Him*. The reader might wish at this point to speak that verse out loud; to weigh each word. Because to a remarkable degree this one part of one verse of Scripture seems to both prefigure and determine all that was to follow in the earthly life of Robert Ferrar. It explains more eloquently than a shelf-ful of ecclesiastical history his ultimate triumph in the name of Christ and His true church.

The verse sits scruffily at the top of the letter; it falls over itself, in fact, throwing out the balance of the page. It has been scrawled in as an afterthought.

---

1   D. Martyn Lloyd-Jones, *Spiritual Depression* (London, 1965: rep. 1998), 228.

Ferrar had scrutinized his work, a letter of thanks to the most powerful man in England, and had decided that what was lacking was an acknowledgement that they were both subject to the Lord of Heaven. Before kings or any other earthly master they must bind their concourse to Him. This honesty, this penitent submission to God's will, might explain why Ferrar remained such a favourite of the vicegerent.

With his last breath a corpulent, enfeebled and probably syphilitic Henry VIII whispered 'Monks ... monks ... monks ...' before dying on 28 January 1547. He left monies for masses to be said for his soul. The tyrant was succeeded by his ten-year-old son Edward, in whose reign the cause of Reform in England was to glimpse its sunlit uplands. From an evangelical perspective it is one of the calamities of history that 'the young Josiah'[1] was on the throne for such a short time. By 1549 he had written a 7500-word treatise on the pope as antichrist. An assiduous note-taker, he sat under the preaching ministry of many of the leading Reformers. His theologian of choice, the Strasbourg exile and Regius Professor of Divinity at Cambridge, Martin Bucer, penned this profile of the Bible-loving prodigy:

> The king ... is godly and learned to a miracle: he is well acquainted with Latin, and has a fair knowledge of Greek; he speaks Italian, and is learning French. He is now studying moral philosophy from Cicero and Aristotle: but no study delights him more than that of the Holy Scriptures, of which he daily reads about ten chapters with the greatest attention.[2]

Bucer's last great work, *De Regno Christi* ('On the Kingdom of Christ'), was written for Edward and given to the king as a New Year's gift. An inquiry into the social and ecclesiastical condition of Tudor England, it was a handbook to guide the king in implementing Bucer's vision of a fully fledged Christian commonwealth. In an essay written by Edward after the book's publication, 'Discourse on the Reformation of Abuses', Edward seizes upon Bucer's plan to arrest the growth of unemployment through education and just jurisdiction: more proof that had it not been for the deaths of Bucer in 1551, and of Edward in 1553, Christianity in England would have progressed along markedly different lines. Another example: a proposal in *De Regno*

---

1   Josiah, son of Amon, was the eight-year-old king who *did uprightly in the sight of the Lord* (2 Kings 22:2).

2   Quoted in Constantin Hopf, *Martin Bucer and the English Reformation* (Oxford, 1946), 16.

Christi for regional synods to meet biannually would have steered the church away from diocesan episcopacy towards the kind of presbyterian church order envisaged by Calvin. Under Geneva-style ecclesiastical polity the Geneva Bible (1560)[1] would not have been staunched, the Authorized Version (1611) would not have been launched, and the king's freedom to assert his ideology of kingship would have been kept within bounds. Christians of the 21st century might do well to dust off *De Regno Christi* and consider Bucer's call for the monarch to 'renew, institute, and establish the administration not only of religion but also of all other parts of the common life according to the purpose of Christ our Saviour and supreme King'.[2] And present-day princes might themselves, by grace, by the irresistible desire to get nearer to God, and in solitary self-surrender, heed Edward VI's dying prayer: 'Oh Lord God, defend this realm from papistry, and maintain thy true religion; that I and my people may praise thy holy name, for thy Son Jesus Christ's sake'.[3]

A propitious start to Edward's reign saw Edward Seymour, the duke of Somerset and Lord Protector of England, ordering a Royal Visitation to all the dioceses of England and Wales. Around this time Ferrar was made chaplain to both Somerset and Cranmer. When a party was put together to visit Hereford and Worcester, and the four Welsh dioceses of St Asaph, Bangor, Llandaff and St David's, Ferrar was appointed preacher. In the same group were the registrar George Constantine and a 'preacher in the Welsh tongue', Hugh Rawlins. Both would play significant roles in the future of bishop Ferrar. But in the summer of 1547 the priority of every Reformer was to extirpate papistry from the church. Latin services were ended. An English primer, with the Lord's Prayer, Creed and Commandments in heavy type, replaced the 'book of hours'. Teaching programmes were set in train for children. Stained glass was removed, along with candlesticks, shrines and statuary. After dark, to avoid violence, church walls were whitewashed. The Decalogue was prominently displayed. Roods and their attendant lofts and screens were cut down. Chantries were suppressed. Anything, in fact, considered foreign to the design of the Triune God was expunged. Heady days. On 3 February 1548 the bishop of St David's, Ferrar's old friend William Barlow, was appointed to the see of Bath and Wells. The duke of Somerset

---

1   The New Testament was translated into English in 1575; the complete English version appeared a year later.

2   Martin Bucer, *De Regno Christi* (Louisville, rep. 2006), 384.

3   Foxe, vi. 352.

consulted Barlow on the king's behalf regarding his successor at St David's. The cause of Christ was not finished with Robert Ferrar. *'I will restore to you the years that the swarming locust has eaten'*,[1] says the Lord.

The cathedral church of St David's, seen from its north-eastern aspect, spreads across the fold of a wooded valley on Wales' western seaboard. Overhead, seagulls wheel and plane above the cathedral's square central tower. Torn clouds, whipped by a westerly wind, scud in from St David's Head and pass over the roofs of a sheltering village impersonating a city. Below, the river Alun meanders across curving hillside and damp heathland before running down to the harbour of Porthclais. This westernmost part of Pembrokeshire is a land of purple cliffs pummelled by Atlantic breakers, of rocky coves and pebbled beaches, of feathery tamarisk, shrivelled sea-pinks and scent of gorse. In April 1549 Robert Ferrar, arrived to spread the godly Reformation, beheld the ancient see of St David's for the first time. He was now in his maturity, a strong-looking man of medium height with a thick dark beard. Perhaps, struck by its chill intimacy, he put a hand on one of the cathedral's buttressed walls. And perhaps he uttered a prayer, and tasted the salt tang of the ocean on his lips.

St David's was built on the site of a monastery thought to have been founded by Dewi Sant (St David) in the sixth century. Due in large part to the success of *Buchedd Dewi* ('The Life of David'), an 11th century hagiography by Rhygyfarch of Llanbadarn Fawr, Dewi's status as the embodiment of the Age of the Saints is assured. Though the first stones of the building that bears his name were laid in the last quarter of the 12th century, the cult of Dewi had been sanctioned by pope Calixtus II in the period 1119–24. Before long the cathedral church was recognized as a marvel of medieval Christendom: two pilgrimages to St David's being accounted the equivalent of one to Rome. A vast income accrued through the sale of indulgences[2] and of sung masses for the dead. Another money-spinner was a shrine adjudged to hold the bones of Dewi Sant and his confessor.[3] Pilgrims were also directed to a host of lesser shrines, including that of the holy taper at Haverfordwest. On his translation from St Asaph to St David's in 1536, William Barlow determined to bring an

---

1 Joel 2:25.

2 The remission of penalties for confessed and forgiven sin, to be endured on earth or in purgatory.

3 In the 1920s the present reliquary, a wood and metal concoction, was placed in an arched recess behind the high altar.

end to such unbiblical practices. He called the cathedral 'a delicate daughter of Rome, naturally resembling her mother in shameless confusion and like qualified with other perverse properties of execrable malignity, as ungodly image service, abominable idolatry, and licentious liberty, of dishonest living, popish pilgrimages, deceitful pardons, and feigned indulgences'.[1] In 1534, as prior of the house of Augustinian canons in Haverfordwest, Barlow had observed of the local clergy that 'there is not one that sincerely preacheth God's Word, nor scarce one that heartily favoureth it, but all utter enemies there against'.[2] Such men would not be granted an inch of space in Barlow's mental compass. For him this was a straightforward struggle against heresy and error. Scripture was the rule of truth. If Wales rejected the Gospel message it could not claim to be a holy nation.

Barlow's sense of a cathedral and chapter in thrall to popery and superstition lay at the heart of his most far-reaching proposal: the removal of the see from St David's to Carmarthen. There were good reasons why this might serve the Reformed interest. Wales was both rural and sparsely populated; it also lacked a significant middle-class. It had been in the urban areas, among the merchants and skilled artisans, that the English Reformation had gained a foothold. St David's was difficult to reach and bound by age-old custom. If there was going to be a religious awakening the processes of reform had to infiltrate the larger towns, and be championed by the better-educated laity. Wales had a different language: again, hardly conducive to the propagation of ideas framed in English. To be effective, preaching had to be understood! All these obstacles might be overcome by relocating to Carmarthen—commended by Barlow as 'the best town and in the middle of the diocese'[3]—with its English-speaking population and settled professional class.

A tremendous tussle now ensued between Barlow and his cathedral chapter. Wales was Reformed in name only; the old ways still adhered. 'Mute suffering Wales', wrote O.M. Edwards, 'apathetic while the world around was awakening to a brighter morning'.[4] Only by asserting control over the chapter could Barlow hope to subvert its stubborn attachment to tradition. At the heart of the Reformation was the idea of an equal access to

1   Glanmor Williams, 'The Crisis of the Sixteenth Century' in *St David of Wales,* eds. Evans/Wooding (Woodbridge, 2007), 336.

2   Ibid. 332.

3   Quoted in Glanmor Williams, *The Welsh and their Religion* (Cardiff, 1991), 131.

4   Quoted in Williams' *Welsh Reformation Essays* (Cardiff, 1967), 12.

God through Jesus Christ. But Barlow was attacked for saying that 'where two or three simple persons such as cobblers or weavers were assembled in the name of God, *there* was the true church'.[1] Richard Rawlins (1523–36), the previous bishop, had linked Luther to the devil and the plague. The Reformation itself was understood, by Welshmen who cared enough to think about it at all, in terms of its discontinuity with Wales' past, Wales' identity: an identity wrapped up in a jumble of assumptions about saints and artefacts. In opposing Barlow's authority—in opposing, one senses, the very fact of Barlow—the canons positioned themselves as guardians of that identity first, servants of the Lord second. Their dearest wish was to be left alone. They were quite happy with their Dewi Sant, their relics, their vague undirected mysticism. Barlow, for his part, was headstrong and pointlessly combative. He was tactless. He acted like the governor-general of a backward colony. But first and last he was a Bible-man. And in recruiting and nourishing those who would expound and apply the Word of God he displayed a strength of purpose that was often heroic.

Barlow's plan to relocate the cathedral foundered on the rocks of finding a suitable resting place, other than St David's, for Edmund Tudor, grandfather of Henry VIII. Glanmor Williams comments that 'the decision not to move the cathedral was one for which the Anglican church on balance paid dearly in terms of its own effectiveness in the diocese during the next two or three centuries'.[2] Barlow did, however, win some of the lesser skirmishes. The bishop's residence was moved to Abergwili, adjacent to Carmarthen. Having deplored the fact that 'in the whole diocese is not one grammar school, by reason whereof the clergy is unlearned and the people ignorant',[3] he established a collegiate foundation at Brecon, along with the grammar school which came to be known as Christ College. And in a signal victory over the 'memorial monuments' of Rome's 'puppetry',[4] the relics of St David—in Barlow's words 'two heads of silver plate, enclosing rotten skulls stuffed with purified clouts; two arm bones and a worm-eaten book covered with silver plate'—were sequestered and taken away and the shrine dismantled.

These battles cast long shadows across Ferrar's episcopate. On several occasions he found himself fighting fires ignited in Barlow's time. A man of

---

1 Glanmor Williams, 'The Crisis of the Sixteenth Century' in *St David of Wales*, 334.
2 *The Welsh and their Religion*, 131–132.
3 Ibid. 129.
4 Ibid. 131.

greater spiritual discernment than his predecessor, the new bishop favoured accommodation over conflict. But unlike Barlow, who cleverly appointed his brothers to key positions in the diocese, Ferrar lacked a power base. He cut a lonely figure. This was, perhaps, inevitable given his efforts to weed out the concubinage so ingrained in his diocese, and in Wales generally. A remark directed at bishop Gardiner by John Rogers, at his trial in January 1555, goes to the nub of the matter: 'Ye make yourself highly displeased with the matrimony of priests, but ye maintain their open whoredom, as in Wales, where every priest has his whore openly dwelling with him'.[1] After publicly and privately denouncing immorality of this kind, Ferrar struggled to build alliances. As late as 1536 the clergy of Bangor had petitioned Cromwell, 'knowing our frailty and accustomed liberty',[2] to allow them to go on co-habiting with women. In such an unregenerate atmosphere, Ferrar tried to find his way by degrees, to achieve by persuasion what Barlow had accomplished by force of personality. By nature he trusted too easily. He was an easier proposition all round than Barlow. Nothing, however, outside of the most malign of influences, can explain the antipathy to which he was subjected from the first day he arrived to take up his duties.

George Constantine, the registrar of St David's, Thomas Young the cathedral precentor and Rowland Meyrick, one of the leading canons, had each accepted preferment on the strength of their evangelical sympathies. In their harrying of Ferrar they were to prove themselves dissemblers and hypocrites. All three, in Ferrar's words, had been 'in times past either obstinate enemies to the true bearers of the Cross of Christ, or at least privy lurkers, under pretence of favour toward the Gospel, to sting the poor followers thereof; seeking but their own lucre and pleasure in all their doings'.[3] With Barlow gone they saw an opportunity to bolster their own authority by cutting away the space available to Ferrar. Meyrick and Young also took advantage of the delay between Barlow's vacating of the see and Ferrar's arrival to sell off valuable artefacts. Word of this reached Ferrar in London, where he was involved in important parliamentary debates. His account of his chapter members' activity pulls no punches:

[They had] by their own evil example and winking at the faults of

---

1 Foxe, vi. 603.
2 Quoted in Brown, 93.
3 Foxe, vii. 27.

others, or neglecting to correct the same, left there, amongst priests and others, much detestable whoredom; but had also spoiled the cathedral church of crosses, chalices and censers, with other plate, jewels and ornaments of the church, to the value of five hundred marks or more, for their own private lucre (the church remaining even yet very vile and in great decay).[1]

From his London residence Ferrar made it clear he intended to investigate these crimes with the utmost vigour. The die had been cast. Upon setting foot in the diocese, Ferrar took rooms in Haverfordwest. His first order was to Edmund Farley, his newly-appointed chancellor; Farley was to ride to the cathedral and begin the groundwork for Ferrar's enquiry. But when Farley arrived the canons refused to meet him. No one, they said, outside of the bishop and chapter, was allowed to conduct visitations. A baffled Farley was asked for his commission. In the chapter house, Meyrick's eyes alighted upon the opening line: it made no mention of the king, but ran 'Robert, by divine provision, bishop of St David's ...'[2] Meyrick judged it 'a Romish commission'.[3] This was kite-flying, no more; nothing in law required a commission to acknowledge the Act of Supremacy. But Meyrick's background (he had been the principal official in the consistory court at Wells) gave him an authority in judicial matters to which others routinely deferred. Farley was left high and dry. He was also separated from his commission; this was kept by Young, citing his authority as a justice of the peace. Thus a trivial dispute over terminology was blown up into a major incident. And although he had no way of knowing in advance what a hornets' nest he was entering, a measure of blame must be laid at Farley's door. He had drafted the commission. His use of obsolete language had compromised his bishop and given his enemies the opportunity to present themselves as guardians of the evangelical conscience.

George Constantine now entered the fray, impersonating a man of fine instincts and godly feeling. His object, he said, was 'perpetual amity'[4]. Having positioned himself as an honest broker between bishop and chapter, he and

---

1 Ibid. 9.
2 Quoted in Brown, 94.
3 Ibid.
4 Ibid. 96.

Thomas Huet[1] fashioned a version of events that, according to Huet, led to Ferrar beseeching the two men to 'Be my two hands. Do what you will: kindle the fire or quench it'.[2] If true this was unwise; he had placed his trust in bloodied hands. But we should bear in mind that having accompanied Ferrar on the Royal Visitation of 1547, Constantine was the closest thing to a friend the bishop had in St David's. He was not to know that Constantine was a betrayer: one of the very worst sort. Lies, chicanery and broken faith were his stock-in-trade.

An early convert to Lutheran theology, in 1527 Constantine had recruited one Robert Necton to act as an agent for copies of Tyndale's New Testament. In the spring of 1531 Constantine was seized. Under examination by Thomas More, the lord chancellor, he supplied all the information More needed to arrest Necton and seize a cargo of books. Constantine was not subjected to any kind of physical chastisement. But having started to talk he couldn't stop. In More's own words he 'uttered and disclosed divers of his companions'[3] and revealed the methods by which 'those devilish books which himself and other of his fellows had brought and shipped'.[4] He also divulged the identity of a ship's captain and described the secret marks the Reformed placed on fardels of books. The leader of the book-runners was Richard Bayfield (q.v.). A contemporary of Ferrar's at Cambridge, Bayfield was arrested and burnt 'with excruciating slowness' at Smithfield on 27 November 1531. Peter Ackroyd, More's best modern biographer, then adds that 'Constantine escaped—or, as seems more likely, he was allowed to escape after providing such good service to the old faith'.[5] This was the individual who conciliated between Ferrar and the canons. Almost inevitably the bishop lost out; Farley was dismissed, Thomas Young was installed as chancellor and Meyrick was made commissary in the archdeaconry of Cardigan. Ferrar, not for the last time, had been outmanoeuvred. An actively reforming prelate, his dearest wish was to raise up the Church of Christ by the light of His Word. But all his efforts would come to naught without the support of his diocese. To be caught up, at this preliminary stage, in a tangle of claim and counter claim

---

1   Huet was later appointed precentor. He co-translated a New Testament published in Welsh in 1567.

2   Quoted in Brown, 96.

3   Quoted in Peter Ackroyd, *The Life of Thomas More* (London, 1999), 297.

4   Ibid.

5   Ibid.

regarding the conduct of his cathedral chapter—or, at least, of its two leading lights—would be counterproductive in the short term and might blunt his future effectiveness. In a 'dangerous time of rebellion, then beginning to arise in other places',[1] Ferrar decided to put his duty to offer consolation to uneasy souls ahead of his desire to see guilty men punished. It was the wrong call. He hadn't divined—not yet—the scale of the corruption at the heart of his diocese.

That these were indeed dangerous times is beyond question. In 1548 insurgents in the west country, intent on reviving the old religion, had murdered an archdeacon in Helston. An uprising against the first English Prayer Book in June 1549 was threatening to spread into the Welsh marches. Ferrar was adamant that if what he called 'the grudge of the people'[2] was to be avoided, old forms of religious observance could not be scrapped overnight. New practices had to be introduced gradually, over time, and set alongside the provision of solid preaching. 'We desire first of all', Capito had written, 'to bring all abuses and improper services of God out of the hearts of men through the Word, and then to abolish them outwardly also'.[3] The Bible could not be read in the language of Wales: nor would it be until William Morgan's translation, grounded in the work of William Salesbury, appeared in 1588. In 1551 Salesbury published *Kynniver Llith a Ban* ('Lessons and Verses'), his Welsh rendering of the epistles and gospels in the Book of Common Prayer. The book opens with a letter of address to five bishops: Ferrar of St David's, Kitchen of Llandaff, Bulkeley of Bangor, Parfew of St Asaph and Skip of Hereford. *Kynniver Llith a Ban* was not suppressed—in fact it was well-used—and many copies survived the Marian blood-letting.

In the course of Ferrar's first visitation as bishop, completed in July 1549, every curate was given some biblical text to study. One, Griffith Goch, was considered capable of learning the whole of Matthew's Gospel.[4] Clergy were reminded that under the terms of the royal injunction of 1547, they were obliged to purchase, out of their own pockets, a copy of Erasmus's *Paraphrases*. No one was exempt. Ferrar also (shades of his days at Nostell) enlisted the services of an outside preacher—John Peddar, a fellow of Peterhouse College— to help curates master text in spirit and letter. It is a matter of record that

1 Foxe (1838), vii. 10.
2 Ibid. 12.
3 Quoted in James M. Kittelson, *Wolfgang Capito: From Humanist to Reformer* (Leiden, 1975), 144.
4 See Brown, 101.

Ferrar proposed setting up a school for the poor in the town of St David's. No one could have applied more imagination to the task of establishing his flock in the duties of love. Before long, however, his efforts were overshadowed by a renewal of hostilities between him and his ill-found chapter. Thomas Young, appointed chancellor by Ferrar, repaid his trust by conspiring to protect his right, as he saw it, to admit clergy to vacant benefices. It was customary, in the rotten dioceses of that time, for bribes to be paid in return for preferment. Ferrar gave notice that all appointments would henceforth be subject to his approval. After a short pantomime of injured pride, Young backed down. An uneasy *rapprochement* lasted until July 1550. When Ferrar appointed Henry Goddard, one of his chaplains, to the rectory of Hasguard, he learned that Young, in collusion with Constantine, had instituted his own nominee. Once the issues arising from this affair had been ventilated in the consistory courts, Rowland Meyrick weighed in with another challenge to Ferrar's rights of patronage: this time in respect of the vicarage of Penbryn. In the same period Young married George Constantine's daughter.

Away from the cathedral, Ferrar's attempts to exert a degree of control over ecclesiastical lands drew him into strength-sapping disputes with local gentry. Ferrar was adamant that church property wrested from the pope in Henry's time should be used for the benefit of churches and schools and for poor relief. The enmity of the wealthy landowners was guaranteed. Paul Fagius, newly arrived in Cambridge to advance the Reformation in England, wrote home to Germany that 'I hear that persons in authority are shamefully guilty of seizing on ecclesiastical property; and consequently the churches are miserably destitute of sound pastors'.[1] And Sir William Petre, who accepted high office under Henry VIII, Edward VI, Mary Tudor and Elizabeth I, admitted that 'We, which talk much of Christ' [have left] fishing for men and fish again in the tempestuous seas of this world for gain and wicked mammon'.[2]

So Ferrar was battling on two fronts: against the intransigence and deceit of his cathedral chapter, and against the feudal system and its attendant forms of subordination. In defying this aggregate attempt to marginalize the

---

1   Quoted in MacCulloch, 523. Fagius, together with Martin Bucer, rejected the terms of the Augsburg Interim of 1548, which required Protestants to readopt Roman Catholic beliefs. Their lives in danger, Fagius and Bucer fled Strasbourg under cover of night, arriving in England in April 1549.

2   W. G. Hoskins, *The Age of Plunder* (London, 1976), 131. Quoted by Glanmor Williams in *Renewal and Reformation* (Oxford, 2002), 300.

Reformation in Wales, Ferrar exemplified the ethical and moral commitment that is part of a living faith. It won him few plaudits. He became the scapegoat, the immediate villain, a sponge to absorb all the malice swirling about him. His moral authority was the greater for not being publicly advertised. All his opponents had to offer was their carping inferiority: Meyrick, with his vain regard for his own cleverness; Young, whose only answer to opposition was annihilation; and Constantine, a man of emetic insincerity. Their behaviour towards their bishop proclaims at every turn the fountain of corruption within the human heart.

By September 1550, Ferrar's authority had been so undermined he had no other recourse but to take out a writ of *quo warranto* against his precentor and canons. Had his appeals to civil law proved more successful, this might not have been necessary. But the judges, aware that Ferrar's plans to recover ecclesiastical land struck at their own interests, had often sided with his enemies. The weakness of Ferrar's position was by now an open secret: the stuff of chapter house gossip. The canons, emboldened over time, began citing all kinds of historical precedent in order to act independently of their bishop. His drive to see copies of Erasmus's *Paraphrases* supplied to churches, and clergy examined on their biblical knowledge, was kicked into the long grass; Constantine, meanwhile, stockpiled copies of the *Paraphrases*: the better, Ferrar suspected, to line his own pockets. John Peddar, the preacher imported by Ferrar, was obstructed and discouraged and eventually 'wearied away'.[1] A successor fared no better. Constantine also took it upon himself to pull down the altar in the parish church of St Peter's in Carmarthen. He calculated that Ferrar could not object without exposing himself to accusations of slowing the pace of Reform. Ferrar's plan for a free school in St David's was also undone: Meyrick and Young refused to 'obey the king's godly injunctions, concerning the finding of a school for poor men's children'.[2] With the atmosphere becoming ever more poisonous, and with his canons routinely abusing the power committed to them, Ferrar issued his writ.

Events now took on their own dark momentum. Although Ferrar 'for the respect of unity'[3] elected not to pursue his *quo warranto* case, he wouldn't tolerate Constantine's presence a minute longer. He was dismissed

1 Foxe, vii. 16.
2 Ibid. 14.
3 Ibid. 28.

in November 1550. Young and Meyrick followed in 1551. Ferrar reported that because of their 'covetous respect to their own glory and lucre, not regarding the reformation of sin and specially of shameless whoredom, I was compelled to remove them, sore against their will'.[1] Lest anyone put this down to mud-slinging on Ferrar's part, Matthew Parker, archbishop of Canterbury under Elizabeth I, complained bitterly of Meyrick's reliance, as bishop of Bangor (1559–66), on what Parker called 'pensionary concubinage':[2] allowing parish clergy to keep girls and women in their houses upon the payment of a levy. Although the removals of Meyrick and Young went unchallenged, Constantine's was overturned by the Council in the Marches. Walter Devereaux, viscount Hereford and lord chamberlain of south Wales, was the controlling figure on the council. A scion of the most powerful land-owning family in south-west Wales, Devereaux was visibly and volubly hostile to Ferrar's plans to recover ecclesiastical lands. The march of expediency would not easily be halted.

A succession of petty attacks on all aspects of his episcopal labours, supported by a vicious whispering campaign, eventually culminated in the indictment of Ferrar by his leading canons. This comprised fifty-six articles, presented to the Privy Council in the names of Thomas Lee and Hugh Rawlins. It was heard in the early summer of 1551. Lee, a Carmarthen merchant, was Constantine's brother-in-law. He was described by Ferrar's agents as someone 'who hath sold his ware and spent his money, and now, for want of other business, is become a promoter of the foresaid articles, having his costs and charges borne by the said principal adversaries'. Rawlins, who had accompanied Ferrar and Constantine on the royal visitation, was ostensibly vicar of Tenby. A 'lewd fellow' according to Ferrar, and someone 'willing, and setting his whole delight, to work mischief, both word and deed',[3] Rawlins received income from no less than five benefices. If Ferrar got his way, and a full-time curate was appointed to every congregation, Rawlins faced personal ruin. The canons had chosen well. Ferrar had no doubt that Lee and Rawlins were merely puppets. The indictment, he maintained, had been framed 'after the device of the said George Constantine, and the chanter [Young],

---

1   Ibid.
2   Quoted in Brown, 93.
3   Foxe, vii. 17.

and Rowland Meyrick, the bishop's mortal enemies, and the very devisors and procurers of the informations and bolsterers and bearers ... thereof'.[1]

The fifty-six accusations were marshalled under five headings: abuse of authority, maintenance of superstition, covetousness, wilful negligence and folly. All the gripes and slights that the canons had harboured over three years were dusted off, given a new coat of paint and presented afresh to the eyes of the world. Ferrar faced his ordeal with flintiness and resolution. Not for the first time, nor the last, the quality of his character was revealed in adversity. His replies to the articles are uncluttered and clear, and usually serve to discredit his accusers. The most startling charges were the easiest to refute. That someone who had railed so fiercely against the theocratic ideas of the papacy could be guilty of maintaining superstition was absurd. Ferrar simply believed that in order to avoid civil unrest the pace of change had to be regulated: that parishioners could be weaned off customs such as kneeling, or making the sign of the cross, by the living preaching of the Gospel. The charge that he had dragged his feet on the implementation of new devotional practices was, writes Glanmor Williams, 'a convenient stick with which to belabour [him]'.[2] Ferrar rejected every doctrine and every human tradition that did not rest upon biblical truth. He would not count the pain of death too high a price to pay for that truth.

The abuse of authority charge reads like a frantic attempt to veil the behaviour of a cathedral church sapped of its faith in God. As far as specific allegations are concerned, these relate in large measure to the Farley affair. The foundation of the charge of wilful negligence was the delay between Ferrar's consecration and his arrival in his diocese: this, said the canons, led to 'the great disorder of the king's majesty's subjects, lack of Reformation and ministration of justice'.[3] Ferrar maintained that it was his 'bounden duty to serve the king's highness during the time of the Parliament'.[4] Other articles amount to an elaborate sleight of hand. Ferrar, said Constantine, 'alienated himself from study, that he preacheth indiscreetly, discrediting the office'.[5] Ferrar's piqued reply, that he 'hath been very much hindered both from study

1   Ibid.
2   *The Welsh and their Religion*, 133.
3   Foxe, vii. 8.
4   Ibid. 14.
5   Ibid. 8.

and from preaching by the malicious, crafty and covetous behaviour'[1] of his canons, hints at the kind of pressure he must have been operating under. Constantine also criticized Ferrar's library. The bishop's shelves, he sniffily observed, carried 'only the Bible, and Calvin's *Institutions*, and two or three more'.[2] No doubt Constantine's rooms were overflowing with the right books. But Ferrar didn't share his accusers' tendency to admire themselves by proxy. What fascinates is the idea that after a lifetime of scholarship, Ferrar, when packing for Wales, reached for the Bible and the *Institutes* as the only books he really needed. The choice of Calvin certainly shows where his doctrinal loyalties lay. And one wonders, in the light of all that was to follow, how Calvin's famous dictum that our suffering be seen in the light of God's own self-sacrificial love might have resonated in the heart of Robert Ferrar.

In the articles dealing with Ferrar's alleged covetousness and folly the inanity of the case against him is laid bare. His preference for plain dress, after the Genevan model, had, according to his critics, made him 'a mock to the people'.[3] But Ferrar was no hypocrite. His attack on liturgical vestments at Paul's Cross left no room for compromise. The canons were infuriated by his favourite hat. This was a wide-brimmed affair worn in place of the angled cap favoured by Catholic bishops. No doubt Ferrar was as surprised as anyone to see headgear as a topic for discussion. His response carries a suitably bemused air. In the winter months, he wrote, 'he weareth a hat to bear off rain and snow, and in the summer to shadow him from the sun, without any vow of superstition or offence of the people'.[4] He was mocked for having unvarnished stirrups on his saddle, for his unstudded bridle, for indulging his love of gardening, and for electing to walk rather than ride about his diocese ('not meet for a man in his place').[5] These exchanges loudly proclaim the prejudices of his persecutors. Ferrar himself emerges as a man of settled intuitions, at peace with himself and chary of outward show.

He had whistled to amuse his youngest child. This again awoke in his critics the urge to vilify. Ferrar's riposte, that 'they whistle their horses and dogs, and I am contented; they might also be contented that I whistle my child'[6] pricks

---

1   Ibid. 14.
2   Quoted in Brown, 145.
3   Foxe, vii. 8.
4   Ibid. 15.
5   Ibid. 8.
6   Ibid. 8–9.

their pomposity, but not unkindly. Alas! he was also accused of whistling at a seal in Milford Haven, and of worrying that herring were being overfished. Nor did his domestic affairs escape notice. He is upbraided for preferring to eat downstairs with his servants, rather than upstairs in the dining hall with his social equals. This is submitted as evidence of penny-pinching. As for the tenor of his conversation, this too often, in the opinion of some, leant on 'worldly matters, as baking, brewing, enclosing, ploughing, mining of millstones, discharging of tenants, and suchlike, not only at his table but also most commonly at other places'.[1] Ferrar countered that 'his talk is according to his hearers: that is to say, reverently and truly of faith, love and honest life, according to the Scriptures, to like auditors; and to other irreverent and rash turmoilers of Scriptures and holy doctrine, he doth talk of honest, worldly things with godly intent'.[2] Ferrar, in other words, was embodying what he preached: the great love of God for all mankind. He did not discriminate on the basis of an individual's station in life, or expressions of piety. Knowing that man's natural inclination is to never want God in his heart, he wanted to establish a new order of church and society: an order that truly reflected God's law. And it is God's law, implanted in all creation, that we love our neighbour.[3] For bishop Ferrar, approachability and good manners were not social embellishments, but gifts designed to put other people at ease, that they might 'receive wholesome doctrine of the true fear and love of God'.[4]

That Ferrar continued to ride the length and breadth of his diocese throughout his troubles suggests a remarkable capacity to *cast away everything that presseth down* (Hebrews 12:1). According to Constantine he rode 'from Builth to Kerry and all about the forest of Llanddewibrefi and the mountains in Cardiganshire, to Milford Haven, to Llanddewi in Gower, and diverse other places, little regarding his duty'.[5] This ignores any bishop's duty to oversee his estates, and this particular bishop's wish to raise his understanding of Wales and its people. He was determined to alter the widespread perception of the Reformed religion as *ffydd sayson* ('faith of Saxons'). Having married his wife Elizabeth before moving to Wales, in 1551 he gave his second son the Welsh name of Griffith. In April 1551 he got into hot water with his suggestion, in a

---

1 Ibid. 7.
2 Ibid. 13.
3 Leviticus 19:18; Matthew 5:43.
4 Foxe, vii. 15.
5 Quoted in Brown, 127.

sermon extolling kindness to strangers, that 'the Welshmen were more gentle than the Englishmen were'.[1] Using 1 Peter 2:11 as his text, Ferrar opined that the Welsh 'had received that lesson of loving kindness towards strangers from God's people, and that they were worthy of much commendation for that they kept the same more diligently than other parts of the realm even to this day'.[2] The sermon made a light-hearted reference to some words of Merlin, prophesying the repossession of England by the Welsh. All of this was seized upon by his enemies to portray Ferrar as a divisive influence.

Through the autumn and winter of 1551, and most of 1552, Ferrar attended hearings of the Privy Council. Otherwise he studied and replied to depositions and prepared his defence. This amounted to a criminal squandering of his talents. But he was permitted on occasion to rise above the designs of his enemies. From January to April 1552 he attended the parliamentary session that saw the passing of the second Act of Uniformity. This provided for a revision of the Book of Common Prayer. Words such as 'altar' were expunged; the ordinal was reworked; it was declared that 'as concerning the sacramental bread and wine, they remain in their very natural substances and therefore may not be adored, for that were idolatry, to be abhorred of all faithful Christians'.[3] At the close of the session Ferrar expected to return to St David's. Instead, following a decision of the Privy Council to appoint a commission in Wales to interview witnesses, he entered into a period of extended exile. Foxe records that 'the said bishop was stayed at London, upon the allegation of the said adversaries; which was, that if the said bishop should depart into his diocese he would let them of their proofs'.[4]

Although Ferrar was to embark upon a second visitation of his diocese in July 1552, the efforts of Constantine, Young and Meyrick, aided and abetted by the Welsh nobility, cauterized the growth of biblical Christianity in Wales at a critical juncture. One expositor, surveying the forces arrayed against Ferrar, concluded that 'all and every of the said adversaries are agreed and confederated by all unjust means, both by word and deed, to seek his utter destruction, from the which their wicked purpose the Lord Jesus defend him and deliver him out of trouble, if it be His will'.[5] Ferrar was content to

---

1   Ibid. 172.
2   Quoted in Glanmor Williams, *The Welsh and their Religion*, 135.
3   Quoted in Brown, 195–196.
4   Foxe, vii. 20.
5   Quoted in Brown, 209.

surrender everything—reputation, family, his life if necessary—to that will. Details of how the case against him was concluded are few and far between. Most likely the Privy Council decided there was no case to answer. Perhaps the evidence was so weak the proceedings simply petered out. Before long, the storm clouds that had already begun break over the English Reformation would reduce the internal wrangles of a Welsh diocese to an afterthought. In the April of 1552 Edward VI fell ill with measles and smallpox. Soon after he contracted consumption. The time of blessings was over.

Having overseen the moral and spiritual regeneration of his kingdom, Edward VI died at Greenwich on Thursday July 6th 1553. His sister, the devoutly-Catholic Mary, entered London with her retinue on 3 August. She would be crowned queen on 1 October. One of her first acts was to release Stephen Gardiner from the Tower and appoint him lord chancellor. Events moved quickly thereafter. On 18 August Mary issued a proclamation exhorting her subjects to pay obeisance to Rome. On 29 August John Hooper, the bishop of Gloucester, was interrogated by the Privy Council at Richmond before his despatch to the Fleet prison. Nicholas Ridley, committed to the Tower in late July, was joined in September by Latimer and Cranmer. Ferrar probably received his own letter of summons in the same month. Certainly by 1554 we find him incarcerated in the King's Bench prison along with John Bradford, Rowland Taylor (both q.v.) and John Philpot, the archdeacon of Winchester. Foxe comments:

> Now were come into the churches blind and ignorant mass-mongers, with their Latin babblings and apish ceremonies, who, like cruel wolves, spared not to murder all such, as anything at all but once whispered against their popery. As for all the godly preachers which were in king Edward's time, they were either fled the realm, or else, as the prophets did in king Ahab's days, they were privily kept in corners. As for as many as the papists could lay hold on, they were sent to prison, there as lambs waiting when the butchers would call them to the slaughter.[1]

Ferrar's status as an anathematized and banned priest saw him deprived of his bishopric on 16 March 1554. The records show that he had come to terms with his predicament far in advance of his arrest. On 13 March 1553 he moved to transfer to his wife and three children all interests in his estate

---

1 Foxe, vi. 684.

in Yorkshire. He made out an advowson[1] for the living of Llanddewibrefi
to Samuel, his eldest son. Other papers suggest that 'Pen-y-craig', his home
in Abergwili, was bequeathed to his daughter Sage.[2] Several of the Bible-
men fled abroad. Gardiner believed the threat of execution would persuade
the rest to recant and receive a pardon. Relatively few actually did. History
records, however, that one whose views were judged acceptable by the new
regime was William Barlow. After a brief period of imprisonment he was
permitted to leave the country. The greater man had, after all, been cloaked
in the less dominating personality. For Ferrar the claims of conscience would
always prevail. Knowing this, he had quietly set his affairs in order.

On 30 November 1554 cardinal Reginald Pole, sent by Rome as papal
legate, absolved the realm from its supposed sin of heresy and schism and
reconciled it to the Roman Catholic Church. Parliament revived three
heresy acts and repealed eighteen acts enacted under Henry VIII and Edward
VI. The centrepiece of this legislative programme was the act entitled *De
Haeretico Comburendo*, allowing bishops at their own discretion to examine
suspected heretics and give them over to the secular authorities for burning.
The promulgators of these laws were thereby complicit in the murders of
seventy-one Protestants in 1555, eighty-nine in 1556, eighty-eight in 1557
and forty in 1558. John Hooper, bishop of Gloucester, and John Rogers,
the biblical scholar and translator, became on 29 January 1555 the first to be
condemned by these acts. The previous week Ferrar had been taken from
the King's Bench to appear before a commission of bishops and lawyers.
This took place at the bishop's house near the church of St Mary Overy's in
Southwark. In attendance were Cuthbert Tunstall, bishop of Durham, Sir
John Bourne, secretary of state, Nicholas Heath, bishop of Worcester, and
the same Thirlby, bishop of Ely, who had attended Ferrar's consecration.
The presiding officer was Stephen Gardiner, bishop of Winchester and lord
chancellor.

If Ferrar's appearances before the commission were marked by anxiety, the
eye-witness accounts hardly reflect it. Perhaps Ferrar had already set his mind
and body beyond this world. He certainly wasn't impressed by Gardiner's
assurance that 'her majesty will be good unto you if you will return to the

---

1   An appointment to a vacant benefice.
2   Archive of George Eyre Evans, National Library of Wales, Aberystwyth.

Catholic church'.[1] But this, we should remember, was Gardiner's priority: not to burn the Reformers, but to bring them to heel. All his energies were exercised with this object in mind. Hence Nicholas Ridley's concern, in the letter that was his last farewell, to warn the brethren that 'the whore of Babylon may make you so drunk with the wines of her filthy stews and whoredom (as with her dispensations and promises of pardon *a paena et culpa*) that for drunkenness and blindness ye may think yourselves safe'.[2] The clearness of Ferrar's sight is apparent in the record of the hearing held on 22 January. The opening exchanges also reveal, not unamusingly, the muddled nature of the commission's attack:

Bourne: You went from St David's to Scotland.

Ferrar: That did I not.

Bourne: You did.

Ferrar: That I never, but I went from York into Scotland.

Bourne: Ah! So said I: you went with Barlow.

Ferrar: That is true, but never from St David's.

Bourne: You carried books out of Oxford to the archbishop of York, Lord Lee.

Ferrar: That did I not.

Bourne: You did.

Ferrar: I did not, but I carried old books from St Oswald's to the bishop of York.[3]

Ferrar appears unfrightened and unfazed. He is never less than courteous. Gardiner interprets his consistency as stubbornness, his refusal to admit his guilt as malice. When he rolls a belligerent eye and calls the Reformer 'a false knave', Ferrar rises to his feet: 'No my lord! I am a true man: I thank God for it! I was born under king Henry VII; I served king Henry the Eighth and king Edward the Sixth truly; and have served the queen's majesty, that

1 Foxe, vii. 22.

2 *The Letters of the Martyrs,* ed. Coverdale (London, rep. 1837), 76.

3 Foxe, vii. 22.

now is, truly with my poor heart and word: more could I not do; and I was never false, nor shall be, by the grace of God'. Gardiner insists that he took an oath 'to live without a wife'. Ferrar replies: 'I made a profession to live chaste—not without a wife'. He then turns the tables on Gardiner by referring to an oath, made at his consecration, and 'which your lordship made before me', to resist Rome's blasphemy. After a hurried consultation the lord chancellor 'did ring a little bell'. John Bradford was brought forward; Ferrar sent back to the King's Bench. Despite appearing before Gardiner on at least two other occasions, the causes of Ferrar's arrest and imprisonment would only be alluded to in the final act. This, in accordance with Gardiner's wishes, would be played out in Wales. On 14 February 1555, Robert Ferrar, one-time bishop of St David's, was removed to Carmarthen, the main town of that diocese.

There was no pretence of fairness in the court session convened at St Peter's church in Carmarthen. By this time John Rogers (4 February, Smithfield), Laurence Saunders (8 February, Coventry), John Hooper (9 February, Gloucester) and Rowland Taylor (9 February, Hadleigh) had all gone to glory. Every attempt to pervert Ferrar to the cause of papal-Catholicism having failed, there was no chance of a reprieve. No correction in a court of appeal was possible because there would be no appeal. The trial was presided over by Ferrar's successor at St David's, Henry Morgan. In his place at the registrar's desk sat none other than George Constantine. With the prevailing wind now blowing from Rome, Constantine had shed every scrap of radicalism. He was now the willing instrument of men who would imprison and kill Reformers. In that familiar setting, and among such company, Ferrar's ordeal must have been doubly distressing.

The first session opened on 26 February. Ferrar appeared again on 28 February. It seems likely that he would have anticipated the main thrust of their attack: his refusal to allow that, at the priestly words of consecration, the elements of bread and wine are converted into the substance of the body and blood of Christ. This dogma constituted the first cause of Ferrar's martyrdom. It should be pointed out, however, that Ferrar's affirmation that 'in the eucharist or the sacrament of the altar, together with the body and blood of Christ there remains the substance of bread and wine'[1] is much more in line with Lutheran than with Zwinglian or Calvinist opinion. Other

---

1   Quoted in Brown, 242.

replies reflect a religious use of the material world. In 1551 Ferrar, attending a wedding at Abermarlais, allowed the newly-weds, Elinor Jones and Griffith Rees, to abstain from the Lord's Supper on the grounds that he, Ferrar, 'had travelled fourteen long Welsh miles' and was 'not able to celebrate the holy communion fasting'.[1] Such behaviour would have been frowned upon by more radical brethren. On the Continent, Zwingli had even promoted a sausage-eating binge during the season of Lent.

In both sessions, articles relating to the doctrine of transubstantiation and clerical celibacy were 'ministered unto' Ferrar. Initially he refused to recognize the authority of the court. But on 4 March he 'gently required that the copy of the articles, and a competent term to be assigned unto him to answer for himself'.[2] When his voice rose above the hate-filled throng, it was to repudiate the worship practices of a degenerate faith. Foxe records that 'to these articles thus objected to him, he refused to subscribe, affirming that they were invented and excogitated by man'.[3] On 11 March, Constantine exhibited Ferrar's written replies. Though these have not been preserved, and were most likely destroyed by Morgan, we know that Ferrar believed, 'in equity and justice'[4] that he was still the bishop of St David's. He had not deserted his flock. But the jurisprudential mugging was over. All that remained was the formality of degradation and sentencing.

Griffith Leyson, sheriff of Carmarthenshire, escorted Ferrar to St Peter's church for the last time on 13 March 1555. With the eyes of the diocese upon him, Morgan was determined to wring every drop of advantage from the occasion. Ferrar was pronounced guilty of holding 'heresies and false opinions, opposite, contrary and repugnant to divine law and the decision of the catholic, universal and apostolic church'.[5] On account of his 'manifest contumacy and obstinacy',[6] he was deemed 'unworthy of priestly and ecclesiastical office'.[7] An epic of sanctimony preceded the ritual of degradation. Morgan's men dressed Ferrar in his episcopal garments, then ceremonially, layer by layer, plucked them off. His joy at being unburdened

1 Foxe, vii. 19.
2 Ibid. 24.
3 Ibid.
4 Ibid. 25.
5 Foxe, quoted in Brown, 243.
6 Ibid.
7 Ibid. 244.

of 'the rags and relics of Rome'[1] was unfeigned. Our Christian identity is often found in the things that seek to damage us. Yet again he was called upon to accept transubstantiation as a *de fide* doctrine of the church. The rancour that greeted his rejection of this and other articles was subsumed into the sentence of condemnation.

He was then given back to Leyson to await execution.

As Ferrar prepared to pass from death to life, one incident is so revealing of his walk with God that it must be assigned a place in this narrative. Shortly before his execution, possibly in the course of his last evening, Thomas Young and George Constantine visited Ferrar to beg his forgiveness. Along with Rowland Meyrick, these men had conspired against Ferrar from the very start. They had dissembled and deceived and employed every foul means imaginable to subvert his authority and advance their own interests. In the words of Foxe they had 'hunted after his bishopric'[2] and brought him to the very edge of despair. Ferrar forgave them. He *forgave* them. This was verified by a close acquaintance of the Ferrar family, Richard Pratt. The one-time prebendary of Llanddarog told Foxe that '[Ferrar] forgave them, so that they were in brotherly love'.[3]

No more details have been passed down to us. But we know that Ferrar was a man who loved and understood his Bible. He was about to enter the flames for biblical truth. And we need only return to the indictment against him, to the notorious fifty-six articles, to confirm that Ferrar's forgiveness would have been contingent upon his canons' repentance. In the forty-third article, opprobrium is heaped upon him for teaching that 'a man was not bound to forgive'.[4] The article refers to a sermon preached in St David's cathedral on 13 September 1551. In that sermon Ferrar recited the third and fourth verses from the seventeenth chapter of Luke: *Take heed to yourselves: if thy brother trespass against thee, rebuke him: and if he repent, forgive him. And*

---

1   Ibid. 243.

2   Foxe, vii. 21.

3   Quoted in Brown, 248. The fortunes of Meyrick, Young and Constantine rose sharply in the period of the Elizabethan Settlement. Rowland Meyrick was consecrated bishop of Bangor in 1559. Thomas Young fared even better, being elected archbishop of York in 1561. His time in office was 'notable for an absence of crusading zeal'. He died in 1568 and was buried with great pomp and splendour in York Minster. George Constantine became archdeacon of Brecon. He was about to be offered a bishopric when he died in 1561.

4   Foxe, vii. 8.

though he sin against thee seven times in a day, and seven times in a day turn again to thee, saying, it repenteth me, thou shalt forgive him. Ferrar commented that it 'appeareth by this place of Scripture that we are not bound (except he repent) to forgive him, but we are bound to pray to God to forgive him and to give him grace to repent, that we may forgive him'.[1] The mere existence of a door marked 'repentance' is not enough: forgiveness can't extend to those who show no interest in going through it. Ferrar's charity must be seen in this context, and not interpreted foolishly, as a variation on 'let bygones be bygones'. At this juncture, with his heart already raised to heaven, no words would have left his lips in any way contrary or injurious to the Gospel.

On 30 March 1555, Robert Ferrar was led to the market square in Carmarthen. At that time of the year the sky in south-west Wales can be filled with a fusion of pink and gold and grey. On the hopelessly constricted stage of the market square, it would have taken an age for Ferrar to reach 'the south side of the market-cross':[2] the spot selected for his execution. Onlookers, their feet sinking in the miry ground, would have swelled forward, pressing in and closing behind him, a seething shifting mass. Others would be thronging up the hill, some clambering upon roofs and the boughs of trees to gain a better vantage point. Always visible is the stake, ribbed by early sunlight, pointing to the sky like an accusing finger.

Foxe tells us that Leyson, the sheriff, 'would not suffer bishop Ferrar, when he was at the stake to be burnt, to speak his mind'.[3] It is known, however, that Ferrar exchanged some remarks with Richard Jones, the son of Sir Thomas Jones. Obviously affected by his expressions of pity, but safe in the knowledge that *he that endureth to the end, he shall be saved* (Matthew 24:13), Ferrar told the young man 'that if he saw him once to stir in the pains of his burning, he should then give no credit to his doctrine'.[4] The faggots (bundles of sticks) are set ablaze. A murmur of voices, a thread of smoke, a sickening crackle; tongues of flame lap and curl around Ferrar's legs, then shoot upward. A gasp from the crowd; a choked-off cry; amidst 'the torments and passion of the fire'[5] Ferrar submits his soul to the care of God who is all around him.

---

1   Ibid. 15.
2   Ibid. 26.
3   Foxe, vi. 712.
4   Foxe, vii. 26.
5   Ibid.

John Foxe wrote with something like wonder: 'And so he said, so he right well performed the same, for so patiently he stood that he never moved, but even as he stood (holding up his stumps), so still he continued'. Richard Gravell, a soldier, was sufficiently moved by this display of Christian fortitude that 'with a staff [he] dashed him upon the head', and so brought to an end the sufferings of Robert Ferrar: Cambridge scholar, Reformer in Wales and true servant of the living God.

> Out of his mouth, fire like a glory broke,
> And smoke burned his sermons into the skies.[1]

---

1 'The Martyrdom of Bishop Ferrar' by Ted Hughes. With the kind consent of Messrs. Faber & Faber Ltd. The stone that supported Ferrar's stake now forms the apex or finial of the spire of Abergwili church.

VIII

JOHN BRADFORD

John Bradford was born in Blackley, near Manchester, around 1510. He attended Manchester Grammar School. Little is known of his early years, but he appears to have been a studious, introspective youth, devoted to his parents and his three sisters. He never married and would guard his sisters' spiritual welfare all his life. In 1544 family connections—and his proficiency in Latin and arithmetic—brought him to the attention of Sir John Harrington, vice-treasurer of the army in France. Bradford would serve as Harrington's assistant for nearly three years. He shared his friendships, his partial loyalties, his scraps of honour. His duties included acting as army paymaster and keeping watch over the king's property and buildings in Boulogne. Harrington, reports Foxe, 'trusted Bradford in such sort, that above all others he used his faithful service'.[1]

Such dependability and diligence masked the fact that Bradford struggled to find military affairs in any way congenial. His higher thoughts were cloistered in an unquiet mind. In April 1547, not long after the accession of Edward VI, he enrolled in the Inner Temple as a student of common law. By the end of his first term he saw with a golden clearness that Scripture partook of the nature of God Himself. Thomas Sampson, a fellow student, tells us that 'such was his love of Christ and zeal to the promoting of His glorious Gospel, that he changed not only the course of his former life, as the woman did (Luke 7), but even his former study, as Paul did change his former profession and study'.[2] He bundled up his law books, added them to 'his chains, rings, brooches and jewels of gold, which before he used to wear',[3] sold the lot and distributed the proceeds among the poor. The Lord

---

1   John Foxe, *Acts & Monuments* (1838), vii. 143.
2   *The Writings of John Bradford* (Edinburgh, rep. 1979), ii. p. xiii.
3   Ibid.

having opened his eyes, he saw no reason to look back. On 12 May 1548 he
told John Traves that 'I am minded afore midsummer to leave London to go
to my book at Cambridge, and, if God shall give me grace, to be a minister
of His Word'.[1] A short time later he gained admission to St Catharine's
College. Foxe records that 'he departed from the Temple at London, where
the temporal law is studied, and went to the university of Cambridge, to
learn by God's law how to further the building of the Lord's temple'.[2]

Sometimes the Word of God becomes so clarified in a Christian's mind that
it sees into his or her heart and leaves them no room for moral evasion. So it
was with Bradford. Sampson relates that having heard Hugh Latimer preach
of 'restitution to be made of things falsely gotten',[3] a fraud perpetrated in
France was awoken in Bradford's memory. He admitted his part in concealing
it, and 'could never be quiet till by the advice of the same Master Latimer
a restitution was made'.[4] He wrote directly to Harrington, demanding that
he return the embezzled funds. Albeit reluctantly, Harrington agreed. In the
summer of 1548 Bradford was able to write that 'it has pleased God to bring
it to this end, that I have a bill of my master's hand, wherein he is bound
to pay the sum afore Candlemas next coming'.[5] At Cambridge, Bradford
'[learned] by God's law how to further the building of God's Temple'.[6] He
became himself, in a concentrated form; in the power of God he saw the
beginning and end of all love. Every phase of the rest of his life would be
marked by a determination to see morality united with conduct.

Bradford needed the thorn in the flesh. Sampson attests that every bedtime
he wrote in a journal, so that 'whatsoever he did hear or see, he did so pen
it that a man might see in that book the signs of his smitten heart. For, if he
did see or hear any good in any man, by that sight he found and noted the
want thereof in himself, and added a short prayer, craving mercy and grace
to amend. If he did hear or see any plague or misery, he noted it as a thing
procured by his own sins, and still added *Domine miserere mei*, "Lord, have
mercy upon me"'.[7] In the company of friends he would often fall silent,

---

1   Ibid. p. xvii.
2   Foxe, vii. 143.
3   Apparently, Bradford heard Latimer preach at court in 1548 on Matthew 22:21.
4   *Writings*, ii. p. xiv.
5   *Writings*, ii. p. xv.
6   Foxe, vii. 143.
7   *Writings*, ii. pp. xix-xx.

overcome by the sheer privilege of knowing Christ. And on these occasions, writes Sampson, 'I perceived that sometimes his tears trickled out of his eyes as well as for joy as for sorrow'.[1]

On 19 October 1549, only a year into his university career, Bradford was awarded his MA. He was thirty-seven years old. The following month he was elected a fellow of Pembroke, a college 'noted from the very dawn of the Reformation for scripturists and encouragers of gospel learning'.[2] Such rapid progress testifies to Bradford's 'diligence in study, and profiting in knowledge and godly conversation'.[3] It also shows how keen Nicholas Ridley was to secure his services. In a letter to Traves, Bradford refers to a spat 'betwixt the Master of Catharine's Hall [Edwin Sandys] and the bishop of Rochester [Ridley], Master of Pembroke Hall, whether should have me'.[4] Bradford blossomed at Cambridge. He was a star scholar: highly-regarded and popular, tutor to one future archbishop, John Whitgift, and friend to another, Edmund Grindal. The most ardent radical spirits of his day knocked on Bradford's door: the translators, exiles and martyrs who would come to define the English Reformation. But the mainspring of Bradford's personal theology was Martin Bucer: the greatest foreign divine to teach at Cambridge since Erasmus. Following his refusal to ratify on behalf of the Strasbourg churches the text of the Interim of Augsberg (1548),[5] Bucer, along with his friend Paul Fagius, a noted Hebraist, had landed in England in April 1549. Until his death on 28 February 1551 he would occupy the regius chair of divinity at Cambridge. He actually took up his post in January 1550, expounding on Paul's epistle to the Ephesians before hundreds of wide-eyed students. Every lecture was prefaced by the same prayer:

> Eternal God, most kindly Father, it is thy will that we should unite in thy name and hold godly assemblies and that also academies ('scholas') should exist among thine own by which should be preserved and set forth thy law and doctrine; to those of us assembled here in thy name grant thine aid so that whatever we say or do will serve to show forth

---

1 Ibid. p. xxix.
2 Ibid. p. xvii.
3 Foxe, vii. 143.
4 *Writings*, ii. p. xxvii.
5 The Interim effectively mandated the re-Catholicization of Germany.

thy glory and renew thy church, through thy Son our Lord Jesus Christ
who lives and reigns in the unity of the Holy Spirit, for ever. Amen.[1]

It would be easy, and wrong, to overstate Bucer's impact upon the English
Reformation. Claims that he and Fagius 'laid the foundation of the exegetical
and historical science of the Church of England'[2] are untenable. Always more
of a pastoral theologian than a systematic one, Bucer's plan for an English
church based on a biblical—and apostolic—pattern died with Edward VI. But
Bucer would, in this last great phase of his career, exert a decisive influence
on many Reformers, and patrons of Reform. Under that influence, opines
Diarmaid MacCulloch, Thomas Cranmer 'moved to the final phase of his
eucharistic belief'.[3] Bucer acted as mentor and guide to Matthew Parker,
Roger Ascham, Thomas Horton, Thomas Sampson, Edwin Sandys and
Edmund Grindal. Both Lady Jane Grey and Catherine Willoughby, duchess
of Suffolk, would routinely seek his advice on doctrinal and liturgical matters.
Bucer did not cease, wrote Lady Jane, 'to supply me with all the necessary
instructions and directions for my conduct in life; and who by his excellent
advice promoted and encouraged my progress and advancement in all virtue,
godliness and learning'.[4] The sum of these relationships gave Bucer his
remarkable insight into the religious and social condition of England. That
insight, as much as his own practical visions, would dictate the shape and
form of De Regno Christi, his blueprint for reforms in church and state.

But of all those within Bucer's circle, it was John Bradford, says David
Wright, who was 'more closely fashioned by Bucer's distinctive theological
opinions than any other Reformer'.[5] The convictions, goals and personality
of the one he called 'my father in the Lord'[6] are as unmissible in Bradford's
sermons, and treatises, as they are in his prison letters. It was to Bucer that
Bradford turned when he doubted his ability to preach. 'If thou have not
fine manchet-bread',[7] advised Bucer, 'yet give the poor people barley-bread,

---

1   Quoted in Basil Hall, 'Martin Bucer in England', *Martin Bucer: Reforming Church & Community*,
ed. D. F. Wright (Cambridge, 1994), 149.

2   C. G. McCrie, *Beza's Icones...* (London, 1906), 85.

3   *Thomas Cranmer* (New Haven, 1996), 392.

4   Quoted in Eric Ives, *Lady Jane Grey* (Malden, 2009), 73.

5   David Wright, *Common Places of Martin Bucer* (Appleford, 1972), 25.

6   *Writings*, i. 355.

7   A high-quality wheaten bread.

or whatsoever else the Lord hath committed unto thee'.[1] The German was not happy in England. He was constantly ill and homesick. In a letter of January, 1550 he bewailed 'the weather, the language, the food, the customs, the housing, and just about everything else'.[2] As one illness abated, another flared up: kidney stones, rheumatism, leg ulcers, vomiting. After the death of Paul Fagius, who succumbed to plague in November 1549, Bucer leant more and more upon Bradford, his 'bosom friend':[3] the one 'most dear unto him'.[4] Bradford was with him on his last journey to Oxford in July 1550. Seven months later Bradford prayed at his deathbed. As he contemplated his own death, in gaol in 1555, Bradford turned to Bucer's *Commentary on Romans*.[5] And shortly before his martyrdom, in his heartbreaking 'Farewell to the University and Town of Cambridge', he would exhort all 'that love the Lord Jesus' to 'remember the readings and preachings of God's prophet and true preacher, Martin Bucer'.[6]

On 10 August 1550, Nicholas Ridley, bishop of London, appointed Bradford one of his chaplains. The following summer he was collated to the prebend of Kentish Town in London: Ridley speaking of him as 'a man by whom (as I am assuredly informed) God hath and doth work wonders'.[7] The energy that marked Bradford's proclamation of Christ won more recognition in December 1551. Along with Grindal, John Knox, John Harley, Andrew Perne and William Bill, he was appointed to an élite corps of chaplains in ordinary to Edward VI: 'to be itineraries, to preach sound doctrine in all the remotest parts of the kingdom, for the instruction of the ignorant in right religion to God, and obedience to the king'.[8] Much of Bradford's time was spent in the north of England, preaching mainly in Manchester but extending to Liverpool, Bolton and Stockport. He drew large crowds and attracted a number of converts. But his labours also stirred up opposition among the local gentry.

1   Foxe, vii. 143.
2   Quoted in Constantin Hopf, *Martin Bucer and the English Reformation* (Oxford, 1946), 255.
3   Patrick Collinson, *Archbishop Grindal: 1519–1583: The Struggle for a Reformed Church* (London, 1979), 57.
4   Foxe, vii. 143.
5   *Writings*, i. 351–364.
6   Ibid. 445.
7   Ibid. p. xxv.
8   Ibid.

The household of faith, declared Bradford, was open to all. But he was never afraid to question the reality and depth of our Christian profession. He was content to be unpopular in his determination to be faithful. 'If you look for the truth', wrote C.S. Lewis, 'you may find comfort in the end: if you look for comfort you will get neither comfort or truth—only soft soap and wishful thinking and despair'.[1] Bradford would doubtless have approved such sentiments. In Manchester in 1552 he preached on Noah's flood, and warned of plagues to come. At Blackley on Boxing Day his text was Matthew 23:34–39. Full of plain speaking and lively illustrations, the sermon closed with a prayer that the Gospel be preached until the end of time. There were no gimmicks, no rhetorical flourishes, just a desire to speak what God had spoken. In the Lenten season of 1553 he launched a crusade against sin in high places. His chief target was the king's maternal uncle, the erratic Edward Seymour, duke of Somerset, who had governed the country as Lord Protector. John Knox gives this gripping account of Bradford preaching before the court of Edward VI:

> Master Bradford (whom God for Christ's His Son sake comfort to the end) spared not the proudest; but boldly declared that God's vengeance shortly should strike those that then were in authority, because they loathed and abhorred the true Word of the everlasting God; and amongst many other willed them to take ensample [example] by the late duke of Somerset, who became so cold in hearing God's Word, that, the year before his last apprehension, he would go to visit his masons, and would not dingy [trouble] himself from his gallery to go to his hall for hearing of a sermon.

> 'God punished him', said that godly preacher, 'and that suddenly: and shall he spare you that be double more wicked? No, he shall not. Will ye or will ye not, ye shall drink the cup of the Lord's wrath. The judgement of the Lord, the judgement of the Lord!' lamentably cried he with a lamentable voice and weeping tears.[2]

For Bradford, the restoration of sound doctrine had magnified and raised the obligations of rulers. His ecclesiology—his sense of the *corpus christianum*[3]—led

---

1 *Mere Christianity* (London, 1952; rep. 2002), 32.
2 *Writings*, i. 111.
3 The body of the church, the community of all Christians.

him to envisage a church and state united in the Lord and fully committed to His rule. All of life, he said, belongs to God.[1] Nothing lies outside His sphere of interest. Nowhere in Bradford do we find a conception of faith as a purely private matter. And by his justice towards men, and dependence on God alone, the consummately unthreatening behaviour of the modern church is revealed as little more than moral cowardice. The Word, maintained Bradford, 'alloweth not unity, except it be in verity'.[2]

On 6 July 1553, Edward VI died 'towards night' at Greenwich. On the 9th, Nicholas Ridley preached at Paul's Cross that Mary and Elizabeth were illegitimate, thereby aligning himself with the royal claims of Lady Jane Grey, daughter-in-law of the duke of Northumberland, the head of government. On Edward's death a document was produced excluding his half-sisters from the throne and vesting the succession directly in Jane. For nine days this 'good and innocent'[3] girl reigned as queen. But Northumberland's fellow privy councillors, seeing the roll-call of Marian loyalists gathering in East Anglia, abandoned Jane and fell over themselves to pay obeisance to her rival. Northumberland surrendered in Cambridge on 23 July. Jane was executed in February 1554. Bradford had distanced himself from Northumberland early on. For him, the death of Edward and the accession of Mary were wholly marks of God's judgement. From various pulpits, in what Sampson termed a 'mighty and prophetical spirit', he had condemned England's shunning of the Word and identified several auguries of God's wrath, including a dog at Ludgate carrying a piece of a dead child in its mouth. He never believed that Edward's reign represented some kind of golden age. When the bishop of Durham declared that 'the doctrine taught in King Edward's days was God's pure religion', Bradford shot back: 'What religion mean you in king Edward's days? What year of his reign?'[4] So speaks Bucer's protégé. In contrast to the optimism that had marked his first weeks in England, by the winter of 1549/50 Bucer was certain that he and his fellow exiles were being ignored: 'although we have not ceased to lobby our patron [Cranmer] face to face and in writing about a true and firmly grounded restoration of the kingdom of Christ'.[5] His letters to Calvin in this period are part witness, part polemic.

---

1 See *Writings*, i. 194–195.
2 *Godly Letters of the Martyrs,* ed. Coverdale (London, 1837), 267.
3 *Writings*, i. 283.
4 Quoted in Peter Ackroyd, *The History of England* (London, 2012), ii. 186–187.
5 A letter to Guillaume Farel, quoted in MacCulloch, 470.

He talks of unlettered clergy, of congregations yet to hear a sermon preached, of professors 'who, as far as they are able, entice young people to come to their lectures and imbue them with hatred for sound Christian teaching and discipline'.[1] In an unhappy land where 'something of the old leaven is retained',[2] nobles and gentry grow fat on seized ecclesiastical property. 'It is greatly to be feared', concluded Bucer, 'that the dreadful wrath of God will very shortly blaze forth against this kingdom also'.[3]

Bradford's own frustration mounted in the weeks following Bucer's death in February 1551. He feared that the English Reformed, though zealous and godly, with much to say about the responsibilities of individual believers, lacked the vision and determination—and perhaps the will—to rebuild the community of the church. Edward's untimely end was evidence of 'God's anger thus kindled against us'.[4] The Reformation in England, for the want of effective preachers, had failed in its primary duty: to draw the people into a careful consideration of the Word. Mary's reclamation of the crown was God's judgement on an impenitent nation. 'We have deserved it', confirmed Bradford in 1553. 'For three years, O Lord, yes, and three before that, you came to look for fruit: but you found none, only leaves. Not even that, Lord, no leaves did you find: for our wickedness is so manifest that all nations see now our shame, that we never received your Gospel but to cloak our covetousness, ambition and carnality'.[5] And in his immortal *Sermon on Repentance* he wrote: 'I pray you, my good brethren, know that God's anger for our sin towards us cannot but be great, yea, too fell, in that we see it was so great that our good king could not bear it. What followed Jewry after the death of Josias? God save England, and give us repentance!'[6]

Mary, resplendent in purple velvet and satin, entered the capital with her retinue on 3 August 1553. Images of the virgin had been placed overnight in windows as a sign of 'the inestimable joys and rejoicing of the people'. Within days the structure of hierarchy, with its attendant forms of subordination, was resting again upon a papal foundation. The mass was celebrated throughout the city, even though the Act of Uniformity of 1552 had deemed it illegal.

1   Quoted in Greschat, 239.
2   Quoted in MacCulloch, 470.
3   Quoted in Greschat, 239.
4   *Writings*, i. 20.
5   Ibid. 21.
6   Ibid. 62.

It is worth recording that under the minority of Edward VI, all innovations in respect of worship were forbidden until sanctioned by Parliament. Mary's failure to act in the same way was an affront to the legally constituted authority of the state. Far from punishing Romanists who broke the law, Mary sought pretexts for arresting Reformers. In the light of the storm which was about to be unleashed, certain remarks of John Calvin, in a letter to Bullinger in September 1553, seem uncannily prescient:

> We have good reason to feel anxiety—yea, even torment—regarding that nation. What is to become of so great a multitude of pious men, who have betaken themselves to voluntary exile in that country? There is a danger, also, that we shall hear very sad news ere long, of the many native English who have already embraced Christ, if the Lord do not in His mercy send help to them from heaven ... Moreover, as I have always heard that she [Mary] is a very haughty animal who succeeds to the crown, and cruel withal, there sometimes steals over me a prophetic conjecture, that her audacity will carry her all lengths. You are aware of the rash daring peculiar to her family. She will prove troublesome to almost all parties in the long run. Should she make a weak attempt to alter the existing constitution, she will find opponents not a few. Meanwhile the church of God will be in a manner buffeted by manifold tempests. Let us, therefore, as you say, commend this very troubled state of affairs to God.[1]

In the wake of Edward's burial in Westminster Abbey, Gilbert Bourne, the bishop of Bath, was told to preach at Paul's Cross before Bonner, the bishop of London. Behind him, alongside John Rogers (q.v.), stood Bradford. In an atmosphere laden with tension, the preening prelate 'made a seditious sermon',[2] fawning on Bonner while 'openly railing against king Edward'.[3] Rumbles of discontent primed shouts and threatenings; soon every word was lost in a cacophony of protest. The mayor's attempts at restoring order seemed only to fan the flames; the people, according to Foxe, 'being almost ready to pull [Bourne] out of the pulpit'.[4] Bourne, immobilized by fear, and

---

1 *Gleanings of a Few Scattered Ears,* ed. George Cornelius Gorham (London, 1857), 302.
2 Foxe, vii. 144.
3 Ibid. 145.
4 Ibid. 144.

thinking 'he should there end his wretched life',[1] turned to Bradford. With every sign of a riot present, the Reformer stepped forward. As he entered the pulpit a dagger, thrown at Bourne, grazed his own sleeve. He didn't hesitate. With simplicity and reverence, he preached obedience as the source of all knowledge of God. He outlined the characteristics of a well-ordered church. He upheld the doctrine of law. The threat of violence dissolved like mist on a summer's morning. Soon the crowd was dispersing in cheerful groups, crying with a single voice 'Bradford, Bradford, God save thy life Bradford!'[2]

Bourne, his nerves shredded by the dagger-attack, was cowering at the back of platform. Eventually the mayor and sheriffs coaxed him as far as a schoolmaster's house. Bradford, we are told, 'went at his back shadowing him from the people with his gown, and so to set him safe'.[3] Chaos had been subdued and disaster averted. But Bradford's magnanimity did not win unanimous approval. One elderly gentleman was heard to remark, "Ah Bradford, Bradford, thou savest him that will help burn thee ..."[4] This Reformer, however, would do nothing merely to please, unless it was to please God. New birth, and new life, had sprung from bitter experience; he would no longer tolerate what the Lord found intolerable. All the vulgar externals of ambition were absent in Bradford. After saving the life of bishop Bourne, he preached at Bow church in Cheapside. He might have called attention to his derring-do at Paul's Cross. Instead, despite being warned that 'you shall never come down alive if you do', he 'reproved the people sharply for their seditious demeanour'.[5] Under the Spirit they were expected to gain control of themselves, not lose it. Any self-righteousness on their part was a denial of the Cross.

The sermons, letters, treatises and declarations of this modest, self-denying man are a sustained invitation to enter the battleground of faith. Upon that ground, however, modesty and self-denial will not be enough. They will not, insists Bradford, save your life. No, the aching need of every age is for sound doctrine: for, maintains Calvin, 'whosoever applies his mind to the study of truth, can never be deceived'.[6] Furthermore, says Bradford, those

---

1   Ibid.
2   Ibid.
3   Ibid.
4   Ibid. 145.
5   *Writings,* i. p. xxxii.
6   *Calvin's Wisdom,* ed. Graham Miller (Edinburgh, 1992), 363.

who cleave to that truth, and regard it as a principle of belief *and* action, can never—will never—be defeated:

> Never shall the enemies be able to burn it, to prison it, and keep it in bonds. Us they may prison, they may bind, and burn, as they do, and will do so long as shall please the Lord: but our cause, religion, and doctrine, which we confess, they shall never be able to vanquish and put away. Their idolatry and popish religion shall never be built in the consciences of men that love God's truth. As for those that love not God's truth, that have no pleasure to walk in the ways of the Lord, in those, I say, the devil will prevail; for 'God will give them strong illusion to believe lies'. [1]

When reports of the happenings at Paul's Cross reached the ear of Stephen Gardiner, the new lord chancellor, Bradford was seized at a private house in Fleetstreet. Along with Rogers he was summonsed before the Privy Council and charged with sedition and inciting a riot. This was patently absurd. But it served Gardiner's purposes to depict Bradford's action in quelling the violence as proof of him being the orchestrator of it. He wouldn't know another day of freedom this side of heaven. In the words of Foxe, 'he was committed first to the Tower, then unto other prisons, out of which neither his innocency, godliness, nor charitable dealing could purchase to him liberty of body, till by death (which he suffered for Christ's cause) he obtained the heavenly liberty, of which neither pope nor papist shall ever deprive him'. [2]

Imprisoned in the Tower, Bradford was held in solitary confinement, seeing 'no man but my keeper'. In a letter to a friend, he describes his cell as being below ground: 'which is an example and memorial of my earthly affections (which God I trust will mortify) and of my sepulchre, whereunto I trust my Lord God will bring me in peace in His good time'. [3] Later on he was moved to more comfortable quarters in an annexe of the Tower known as the 'Nun's Bower'. With him was Edwin Sandys, master of Catharine Hall. In a charming episode related by Foxe, Bradford and Sandys converted their guard, John Bowler, 'a very perverse papist', to Christ's cause. He became 'their son begotten in bonds', and knelt down with his eminent charges to receive the Lord's Supper. [4] From the start of his lord chancellorship,

---

1 *Writings*, i. 457.
2 Foxe, vii. 145.
3 *Godly Letters of the Martyrs*, 234.
4 *Writings*, ii. p. xxxii.

Gardiner's policy was to unsettle Reformers by moving them from prison
to prison. On 6 February 1554, in the wake of Wyatt's Rebellion,[1] Sandys
was transferred to the Marshalsea. Bradford was heartsick. By God's grace,
however, he was soon sharing a cell with Latimer, Ridley and Cranmer.
'We four', wrote Latimer, 'were thrust into one chamber, as men not to be
accounted of, but, God be thanked, to our great joy and comfort—there
did we together read over the New Testament with great deliberation and
painful study'.[2] Such fellowship in the Gospel, and the inward peace it
inspired, would sustain him over the difficult days ahead. On the 11th or
12th of March 1554, Cranmer, Latimer and Ridley were taken to Oxford.
On the 24th Bradford left for Southwark and the King's Bench prison. The
path was not easy, but the end to all conflict and difficulty was in sight. He
wrote to a friend in the Fleet prison that 'we both be going in the high way
to heaven, for by many afflictions must we enter in thither; whither God
bring us, for His mercies' sake. Amen, amen'.[3]

In the company of Robert Ferrar, bishop of St David's, Rowland Taylor
of Hadleigh, a close ally of Cranmer, and John Philpot, the archdeacon of
Winchester, Bradford spent ten months at the King's Bench. The sheer
volume of tracts and treatises and general correspondence that flowed from
his pen indicates a humane regime, and a plentiful supply of paper and ink.
The prisoners were mostly unchained. On a site that extended about a
hundred yards from the street to a perimeter trench, they were allowed to use
a walled garden. Bradford's gift for gaining sympathy while fortifying souls
was much in evidence. Sir William FitzWilliam, the knight-marshall, gave
him leave to preach twice daily, and to administer the sacraments. In every
theological discussion within the King's Bench, Bradford's was *the* governing
voice. On the very day of his arrival he managed to dissuade a vacillating
Robert Ferrar from participating in the rite of communion 'in one kind':
a Catholic form of the sacrament that entailed receiving the bread without
the cup. Bradford was 'such an instrument', reflects Foxe, 'that few or none
there were that knew him, but esteemed him as a precious jewel and God's
true messenger'.[4]

The most potent threat to evangelical unity in the King's Bench came not

---

1   A popular uprising driven by a desire to stop the marriage of Mary I to Philip of Spain.
2   *Writings*, ii. p. xxxiii.
3   *Godly Letters of the Martyrs*, 273.
4   Foxe, vii. 146.

from papal-Catholicism, but from a group of radical sectaries from Kent. Freewillers, or 'Free-will men', under the charismatic leadership of Henry Harte, had been condemned by Ridley and threatened with imprisonment by Cranmer. Usually defined in terms of their violent opposition to the predestinarian formulas of Calvin, Freewillers might more accurately be described as revivers of the Pelagian heresy; Harte, in a series of confessional articles, argued that man is capable, unaided by the dispensation of God's grace, to take the first steps on the road to salvation by himself. At the King's Bench, but also in the Marshalsea, Comptor in Poultry, the Clink, and White Lion, Harte's ideas primed heated discussion. For Bradford, Freewillers were 'plain papists, yea, Pelagians, and ye know that a little leaven corrupteth the whole lump'.[1] He resolved to retard the growth of this ideology both inside the gaol—among men like John Trew and Richard Harmon—and outside. Two Kentish conventiclers, Robert Cole of Faversham and John Ledley of Ashford, were well-known visitors to the King's Bench. Both were converted to Bradford's demanding vision. Both went on to serve as envoys between the prisoners and brethren who had fled to the Continent. Bradford was tireless; his pastoral ministry had never felt so vital, so effective! He fired off letters of admonition, composed a *Defence of Election* and *Treatise on Predestination*, and addressed his opponents directly in *To a Free-Willer* and *To Certain Free-Willers*. The *Defence* was sent to Cranmer, Ridley and Latimer in Oxford. Bradford attached 'a writing of Harry Hart's own hand':

> Whereby ye may see how Christ's glory and grace is like to lose much light, if that your sheep quondam [former sheep] be not holpen [helped] by them which love God, and are able to prove that all good is to be attributed only and wholly to God's grace and mercy in Christ, without other respect of worthiness in Christ's merits. The effects of salvation they so mingle and confound with the cause, that if it be not seen to, more hurt will come by them, than ever came by the papists.[2]

On the substantive issue, Brian Cummings writes that 'whereas Harte made free will the opposite of justification, so that acts of virtue are operations of deliberate choice, Bradford's reading of Paul follows Bucer's in drawing

---

1 *Writings*, i. 171.
2 *Writings*, i. 170.

back any good will to the will of God'.[1] Our own free will, maintains Bucer, 'is of no avail for the appropriation of the things that belong to true godliness, but only for their refusal and rejection'.[2] This is consistent with Buceran—and Calvinist—thought generally, which holds that believers, the elect, are bound to behave in accordance with how God originally disposed His creation. The best works of unbelievers remain sin. At the same time Bucer reconciled particular predestination and a universal Gospel by saying that although Christ died for the elect alone, the Gospel calls on every man to believe in his election: that Christ died for him. His pupil takes up the same point. '[The] promises of the Gospel', wrote Bradford, 'depend and hang upon God's truth; that, as God is true, so they cannot but be performed to all them which lay hold on them by faith ... They are universal, offered to all; all I say, which are not so stubborn as to keep still their hands, whereby they should receive this almesse [alms] in their bosoms, by unbelief'.[3]

At the King's Bench prison, and later in the Clink and at the Compter in Poultry, Bradford produced many of the treatises, declarations and letters that comprise his literary remains. All are immensely readable; the letters, in particular, display an ability to translate complex truths into beautifully weighted prose. 'No one', affirms John Knott, 'wrote more or better letters to individual Christians than John Bradford'.[4] His effusive rhetoric of self-denial sets the pulse racing. And his deeply devotional 'Farewells', to the city of London, to Lancashire and Cheshire, to the town of Walden, and, most affecting of all, 'To the University and Town of Cambridge', have been stirring souls—and awakening consciences—for over four hundred years:

> Thou, my mother, the university, hast not only had the truth of God's word plainly manifested unto thee by reading, disputing and preaching, publicly and privately; but now (to make thee altogether excuseless, and as it were almost to sin against the Holy Ghost if thou put to thy helping hand to the Romish rout to suppress the verity, and set out the contrary) thou hast my life and blood as a seal to confirm thee, if thou wilt be confirmed, or else to confound thee and bear witness against thee, if thou wilt take part with the prelates and clergy; which now 'fill up the

---

1 *The Literary Culture of the Reformation* (Oxford, 2007), 244.
2 Wright, 148.
3 *Writings*, i. 66.
4 *Discourses of Martyrdom in English Literature* (Cambridge, 1993), 93.

measure of their fathers which slew the prophets' and apostles, 'that all the righteous blood from Abel' to Bradford 'shed upon the earth' may be required at their hands.[1]

Later on he says: 'Oh, what is honour and life here, but plain bubbles? What is glory in this world, and of this world, but plain shame?'[2] The diversity of Bradford's concerns is striking. When one considers the nature of prison life, and the fact that he was surviving on four hours sleep a night, his achievements are incomprehensible outside his own persuasion of God's mercy towards him. Letters to Bradford came thick and fast. His replies demonstrate how 'tenderly he comforted the heavy-hearted, how faithfully he confirmed those whom he taught'.[3] So unquestioned was his integrity, he was even, on occasion, given leave to visit the sick. His promise to return was all that was needed. Once a week he would tour the prison itself, talking to pickpockets and other criminals, exhorting them to amend their ways. He would give them money 'for their comfort'.[4] This tenderness, this sympathy for those on the margins of society, was typical of Bradford. We are told that 'when he saw any drunk or heard any swear [he] would railingly complain, "Lord, I have a drunken head; Lord, I have a swearing heart"'.[5] And his comment, upon seeing some criminals led to the scaffold, that 'There goes John Bradford, but for the grace of God', has become a popular expression of compassion. In directing his own readers to Bradford, J.C. Ryle commends the letters for their 'peculiar fire, unction, warmth and directness':[6] qualities equally observable in the man. His submission to the will of God was absolute. One friend's offer to campaign for his acquittal was met with something like indifference. He didn't care, records Foxe, 'whether he went out or no'.[7]

On 20 November 1554, Reginald Pole returned to England as papal legate after a twenty-year absence. On the 30th he reconciled the realm to Rome. Parliament revived three heresy acts. Reformers were deprived of their bishoprics and replaced by Roman Catholics. One of Mary's first acts

1 *Writings*, i. 442.
2 Ibid. 443.
3 Foxe, vii. 196.
4 Ibid. 146.
5 *Writings*, ii. p. xliii.
6 *Five English Reformers* (Edinburgh, rep. 1999), 132.
7 Foxe, vii. 146.

as queen had been to prohibit married priests from officiating at church services. As a result, one in five was evicted from his living.

The English Reformation can appear, from an evangelical perspective, like an aircraft moving massively down a runway, loaded with godly intent, rising once or twice but never really taking off. The loss of one who might have been its chief pilot, Martin Bucer, was, perhaps, more significant than has been generally allowed. A shrinking of horizons, resulting from a failure to supply qualified preachers in sufficient numbers, or to properly resolve disputes over clerical vestments and the so-called 'Stranger' churches (q.v.), can be dated from 1550/1551, the period of Bucer's last illness. Shortly before his death, Bucer wrote home to Strasbourg that 'of those devoted to the service of religion [in England] only a small number have as yet addicted themselves entirely to the kingdom of Christ'.[1] Two years later his 'most loyal English disciple'[2] gave his own damning verdict. No other nation, said Bradford, had so 'horribly abused [Christ's] Gospel and contemned this as we have done. Yea, alas Lord! Presently we do it: so that righteous art thou if thou take it away, and give it to a nation that will bring forth the fruits of it'.[3]

On 22 January 1555, and again on the 29th, Bradford was interrogated by Stephen Gardiner at Southwark. Bonner was on hand to give his account of the Bourne affair: 'I saw him with my own eyes', he said. 'He took upon him to rule and lead the people malapertly; thereby declaring that he was the author of the sedition'.[4] It was suggested that Bradford's silence on certain issues, notably on the Lord's Supper, signalled a reluctance to defend the views propounded in Edward's reign. To this he replied that 'that which I have written and spoken I will never deny … saving my oath, ask me what you will, and I will plainly make you answer, by God's grace, although I now see my life lieth thereon'.[5] By this stage the lord chancellor had wrung sufficient concessions out of William Barlow, the bishop of Bath and Wells, to allow him to take refuge abroad. Cardmaker (q.v.) had also won a reprieve. But Bradford was a greater prize, the beating heart of the godly company, a man 'of whose worth the papists themselves were so sensible, that they took more

---

1   Quoted in Peter Ackroyd, *The History of England* (London, 2012), ii. 212.
2   *De Regno Christi*, ed. Wilhelm Pauck (Louisville, rep, 2006), 161.
3   *Writings*, i. 21.
4   Foxe, vii. 149.
5   Ibid. 156.

pains to bring him off from the profession of religion than any other type'.[1]
At one point we find Gardiner virtually cooing with empathetic feeling: 'It
was not my doing', he says, 'although some there may be, that think this to
be the best way. I, for my part, have been challenged for being too gentle
oftentimes'.[2] Bradford's reply doesn't stint on irony. 'My lord', he murmurs,
'I pray you stretch out your gentleness, that I may feel it; for hitherto I never
felt it'.[3] Other answers combine solid argument with genuine concern for the
souls of his enemies. Eventually, his every attempt to procure a recantation
having failed, Gardiner set Bradford's death-witness in motion:

> *Gardiner:* Well, yesterday thou didst maintain false heresy concerning
> the blessed sacrament; and therefore we gave thee respite till this day to
> deliberate.

> *Bradford:* My lord, as I said at the first, I spake nothing of the sacrament,
> but that which you allowed; and therefore you reproved it not, nor gave
> me any time to deliberate.

> *Gardiner:* Why! didst thou not deny Christ's presence in the sacrament?

> *Bradford:* No, I never denied nor taught, but that to faith, whole Christ,
> body and blood, was as present as bread and wine to the due receiver.

> *Gardiner:* Yea, but dost thou not believe that Christ's body naturally
> and really is there, under the form of bread and wine?

> *Bradford:* My lord, I believe Christ is present there to the faith of the
> due receiver: as for transubstantiation, I plainly and flatly tell you, I
> believe it not.[4]

When asked whether an evil man can receive the body of Christ, Bradford
replied that 'the receiving maketh not the presence, as your lordship would
affirm; but God's grace, truth and power, is the cause of the presence, the which
the wicked that lacketh faith cannot receive'.[5] His sentence was pronounced
with frigid gravity on 31 September 1555. Hearing it, Bradford fell to his

---

1   Strype, 3/1.363–4.
2   Foxe, vii. 157.
3   Ibid.
4   Ibid. 162–163.
5   Ibid. 163.

knees in the certain knowledge, he declared, that God 'will give His blessing where you curse'.[1] Given over to the secular power, he was taken first to the Clink, then to the Comptor in Poultry. His books were confiscated, along with his paper and ink. He was kept in solitary confinement. But inflexible hierarchy wasn't finished with Bradford, not by a long chalk.

The original plan, as Bradford himself had understood it, was for him to be taken back to Manchester and burned as a warning to the local populace. That was abandoned in favour of an unprecedented effort, over the next five months, to break him out of his faith. Among those beating a purposeful path to the Compter in Poultry were Willerton, Bonner's chaplain; Harding, chaplain to the bishop of Lincoln; Heath, the archbishop of York, and George Day, bishop of Chichester. Two Spanish divines, Alfonso de Castro and Bartolomé Carranza, were also enlisted to the cause. When Willerton asked him how he thought his sisters would feel, seeing him burn, Bradford replied that he had 'learned to forsake father, mother, brother, sisters, friends, and all that I ever have, and mine own self; or else I cannot be Christ's disciple'.[2] With Harding, Bradford repaid haughty aspersion with loftier scorn. 'Seeing him altogether given up into popery', he wrote, '[I] bade him farewell'.[3] To Heath and Day's comment that he 'make[s] too much of the church before Christ's coming', a criticism often levelled at Bucer, Bradford responded that 'I do but as Peter teacheth (2 Peter 2) and Paul very often'.[4] He also tells the archbishop and bishop that 'full well may a man doubt of the Roman church; for she obeyeth not Christ's voice, as Christ's true church doth'.[5]

Bradford's account of his interview with de Castro and Carranza does not omit its farcical element. De Castro was 'wonderfully chafed, and spake, as often he had done before, so that the whole house did ring again with an echo. He hath a great name of learning; but surely he hath little patience. If I had been anything hot, one house would not have kept us both'.[6] These histrionics were met with reserve and courtesy; Bradford's mind was in the hand of God, and the Spaniards' case was easily dismantled. The hapless de Castro quickly reached his boiling point: 'Lord God', writes Bradford, 'how

---

1   *Writings*, i. 492.
2   Ibid. 499.
3   Ibid. 501.
4   Ibid. 526.
5   Ibid. 527.
6   Ibid. 534.

angry he now was, and said that he came not to learn at me ... for he was
very testy and hasty: and here he dispraised Bucer and all that praised him,
with much other talk'.[1] Bradford was accounted Bucer's protégé: Bucer's
theology was the ground upon which his opponents chose to attack him.
But every attempt to entice or bludgeon him into other ways of thinking
failed. His heart and mind were encased in the Word of God.

As a summer moon sailed over the Comptor, Bradford wrote to his mother:
'Forgive them that kill me; pray for them, "for they know not what they do".
Commit my cause to God our Father. Be mindful of both your daughters,
to help them as you can'.[2] He also told her 'to look for no more letters':

> For if it were known that I have pen and ink, and did write, then
> should I want all the foresaid commodities I have spoken of concerning
> my body, and be cast into some dungeon in fetters of iron: which thing
> I know would grieve you. And therefore, for God's sake, see that these
> be burned ... and look for no more, sweet mother, till either God shall
> deliver me, and send me out, or you and I shall meet together in heaven,
> where we shall never part asunder. Amen. I require you, Elizabeth and
> Margaret my sisters, that you will fear God, use prayer, love your husbands,
> be obedient unto them, as God willeth you; bring up your children in
> God's fear, and be good housewives.[3]

On 30 June 1555, as Bradford took a walk in the late afternoon, he was
waylaid by the gaoler's wife. In incoherent spurts she told him that 'tomorrow
you must be burned, and your chain is now a-buying, and soon you must
be off to Newgate!' Bradford replied gently that 'I have looked for the same
a long time'.[4] He returned to his cell to pray. He set aside the writings he
wished preserved. His remaining money he gave to the Comptor's staff, with
an exhortation that they renounce evil and own Jesus Christ as their only
righteousness. He put on a shirt made for him by one of his supporters.

Bradford was taken by cart to Newgate around midnight. Even at that
hour the evangelical community was out in force, 'gently [bidding] him
farewell, praying for him with most lamentable and pitiful tears'.[5] Though

---

1   Ibid. 537.
2   *Writings*, ii. 250.
3   Ibid. 265.
4   Ibid. p. xxxix.
5   Ibid. p. xl.

his burning was scheduled for four in the morning, Bradford did not reach Smithfield until nine. By that time the largest crowd to witness an execution in England had gathered. Men and women, boys and girls, flowed down the streets and alleys like a giant sea rolling against a distant shore. On 'every corner of Smithfield', wrote Foxe, 'there were some, besides those which stood about the stake'.[1] Mary Honywood, a correspondent of Bradford's, and a great sustainer of the Reformed generally, had her shoes trodden off in the crush. She walked in her stockinged feet as far as St Martin's.

The bedlam that attended Bradford's final journey might take some imagining; the brutality of his guards is a matter of record. For the crime of gripping Bradford's hand, Roger Beswick, his brother-in-law, was dealt such a blow on the head by the sheriff of London, David Woodroffe, that blood gushed from an open wound. Manhandled away from the stricken Beswick, Bradford 'bade his brother farewell, willing [him] to commend him to his mother … and to get him to some surgeon betimes'.[2] At the stake, Bradford and John Leaf, a nineteen-year-old apprenticed to a candle-maker, prostrated themselves in prayer. But another of the sheriffs, mindful of an edge to the crowd's restlessness, begged Bradford 'Arise, and make an end; for the press of the people is great'.[3] At this, Bradford picked up one of the faggots that awaited the flame, kissed it, and kissed the stake. He asked if his tunic might be given to his servant, 'for I have nothing else to give him'.[4] He lifted his eyes skyward: 'England, England', he cried out, 'repent thee of thy sins, repent thee of thy sins. Beware of idolatry, beware of false antichrists; take heed they do not deceive you'.[5] Woodroffe threatened to bind his hands. 'Oh, master sheriff', said Bradford, 'I am quiet: God forgive you master sheriff'. Nor was he spared the derision of the fire-builders, men hired for their strength and easy cruelty. 'If you have no better learning than that', said one, 'you are but a fool, and were best to hold your peace'.

Once chained to the post, and girdled by reeds, Bradford called out with a gladsome heart to John Leaf: 'Be of good comfort, brother; for we shall have a merry supper with the Lord this night'. As the flames rose Bradford intoned quietly, determinedly: 'Strait is the way, and narrow is the gate, that

---

1 Foxe, vii. 148.
2 Ibid.
3 Ibid. 194.
4 Ibid.
5 Ibid.

leadeth to eternal salvation and few there be that find it'.[1] Thomas Fuller, the churchman and historian, wrote that Bradford 'endured the flame as a fresh gale of wind in a hot summer's day, without any reluctance; confirming by his death the truth of that doctrine, which he so diligently and powerfully preached during his life'.[2]

---

1   Ibid.
2   Ibid. p. xlii.

IX

LAURENCE SAUNDERS,
ROBERT GLOVER,
JOHN HULLIER

In 1440 Eton College—'The King's College of Our Lady of Eton beside Windsor'—was founded by Henry VI as a charity school. Seventy 'poor boys' were to be equipped with a free education before being sent on to The King's College of Our Lady and St Nicholas, a constituent college of the University of Cambridge. The affiliation was formalized in the *Amicabilis Concordia* of 1444.[1] Eton was showered with funds, being designed as a corporation of priests and clerks who would intercede for the king's soul in a chapel larger than Salisbury Cathedral. Among the relics on display were fragments of the purported True Cross and Crown of Thorns. Eton was also allowed, following an appeal to the pope, to grant indulgences on the Feast of the Assumption: an entitlement unique in England. The College itself was to consist of 'a Provost, 70 poor Scholars, 10 Priest-Fellows, 10 Chaplains, 10 Clerks, 16 Choristers, a Head-Master, an Usher and 13 poor infirm men'.[2] At its inception, writes Richard Ollard 'the thrust was clearly devotional and charitable, with a strong secondary impulse toward education'. At the start of the sixteenth century that education was entirely classical.

In the Tudor period, Eton scholars would be awakened at five o' clock. While dressing they would chant Latin psalms. Each boy would sweep under his bed and deposit the dust in the middle of the dormitory; four juniors would then gather the dust and remove it. Washing was done at the 'children's pump'. An usher would be reading prayers in the school-room

---

1 A similar arrangement was recognized between Winchester College and New College Oxford.
2 From the original statutes.

by six; in the first hour each boy was inspected for personal cleanliness. After breakfast at nine, boys would be recalled to school and further prayers. Dinner was at eleven; work resumed at midday and lasted until three. An hour of recreation was followed by more work. At five, boys left for supper in double-file. Hereafter work was monitored by older boys. A meal of beer and bread was made available around seven. The boys went to bed at eight, again chanting prayers. On Friday—always a fast day—the week's misdeeds were recounted and the guilty punished. On Friday and Saturday boys were tested on their classwork. The curriculum, all in Latin, included Cato, Aesop's Fables, Cicero's *Epistles*, Thomas More, Ovid's *Metamorphoses* and Virgil.

When a vacancy arose at King's, the top scholar at Eton had to leave for Cambridge or lose his place. Other boys, to be aged not less than fifteen but no more than twenty, were tested in grammar, morals and general fitness in July or August. A selection panel comprised the provost and two fellows of King's, and the provost, vice-provost and headmaster of Eton. At both Eton and King's, selection was weighted in favour of boys born in Cambridgeshire or Buckinghamshire. After three years of probation, those approved by the provost and a majority of graduate fellows were admitted as 'true and perpetual fellows' of the college. Given King's prestige, and lavish amenities—it boasted one of the finest Gothic chapels in Europe—such awards were highly prized: not least by those seeking to join the administrative class of church and state. A rule exempting the college from all external authority, including that of the chancellor, was repealed through the efforts of other members of the university. But despite discontinuities within developing Christian traditions, many of its statutes were still in place by the mid-1800s.[1]

Such was the shared experience of John Frith (q.v.), Robert Glover, John Hullier and Laurence Saunders. As the last three were near-contemporaries at Eton, any discussion of early influences must take into account the enlightened provostship of Roger Lupton (1504–1535) and Richard Cox's tenure (1528–1534) as headmaster. An Etonian and King's scholar himself, Cox 'was from the first a warm adherent of the Lutheran party in the church, and he probably imbued some of his pupils with his own views'.[2] In 1533 he appears as the author of an ode to Anne Boleyn. In 1540, or thereabouts, he was appointed

---

1   For information on Eton and King's in the sixteenth century I am indebted to H. Maxwell Lyte's *History of Eton College* (London, 1875) and to Mrs P. Hatfield and Elizabeth Ennion, archivists of Eton College and King's respectively.

2   Lyte, 110.

senior tutor to the young prince Edward. Much of Edward's commitment to reformist ideas seems to have sprung from Cox's teaching. Imprisoned in the Marshalsea on Mary's accession, Cox escaped to the Continent with Edwin Sandys, the future archbishop. Once settled in Frankfurt, Cox vigorously defended the 1552 Prayer Book against the Genevan form of the service adopted by John Knox. His fellow exiles were soon segregating along Knoxian and Coxian lines. According to Calvin the cause of Reform in the city was ill-served by Cox's 'immoderate fervour for meddling'.[1] On the accession of Elizabeth, Cox returned to England and was elected to the senior bishopric of Ely, succeeding Thomas Thirlby. He remained at Ely for twenty-one years.

Of the three Etonians martyred by Bloody Mary in the period 1555/6, the best-known is probably Laurence Saunders. The son of Thomas and Margaret Saunders of Sibbertoft, Northants, Saunders had five brothers, including Edward, judge and chief justice under Elizabeth, and three sisters. After graduating BA in 1541, his early career was spent in commerce. Saunders, however, 'not liking that kind of trade of life', and being 'ravished with the love of learning',[2] was persuaded by Sir William Chester, the merchant to whom he was apprenticed, to resume his studies at Cambridge. There he remained, proceeding MA in 1544 and adding Greek and Hebrew to his knowledge of Latin. And there he submitted in faith to the Word of God inscripturated. Though tormented by temptation and mental strife, Saunders found glorious counsel in his Saviour, and 'was able to comfort others who were in any affliction, by the consolation wherewith the Lord did comfort him'.[3] At the beginning of the reign of Edward VI he was ordained and married, and found a position lecturing in divinity in Fotheringhay. When his college was dissolved he settled in Lichfield with Joanna, his young wife, and their son Samuel. His reputation for godliness was enhanced as a reader at the cathedral. His next appointment was to the living of Church Langton in Leicestershire. He 'taught diligently', we are told, 'and kept a liberal house'.[4] Saunders' last removal was to All Hallows in Bread Street: a hotbed of religious radicalism. But on hearing that the priests had presented one of their own to Church Langton, Saunders withdrew his resignation. He would manage both livings; he would split his time between countryside and metropolis,

---

1 Quoted in *Oxford Encyclopedia of the Reformation*, ed. Hillerbrand (New York, 1996), i. 447.
2 John Foxe, *Acts & Monuments* (1838), vi. 612–13.
3 Ibid. 613.
4 Ibid.

to the detriment of his health and certain benefit of his flock. Upon the death of Edward, and with Romanism resurgent, Saunders intensified the work of salvation. Foxe records him preaching at Northampton, 'nothing meddling with the state, but boldly uttering his conscience against popish doctrine and antichrist's damnable errors'.[1]

In a few short weeks in July 1553, Mary Tudor, Edward's half-sister, was able to rally support for her claim to the throne. The resistance of those aligned to Lady Jane Grey collapsed. In August Mary entered London amidst scenes of frenzied acclamation. In a proclamation of 18 August, any preaching not authorized by the state was forbidden. A blind eye was turned to the—as yet—illegal celebration of the Latin mass. Nicholas Ridley, the bishop of London, and Hugh Latimer, the court preacher, were seized in mid-September. They were soon joined by Cranmer. On 30 September, Mary was crowned and anointed in Westminster Abbey as a representative of the true faith. When her first parliament assembled on 5 October, the mass was legalized and legislation asserting royal supremacy over the church repealed.

With a Catholic tide threatening to engulf the Bible-men, friends begged Saunders to go into exile. He refused. On 14 October, hurrying to Bread Street, he was waylaid by Sir John Mordant, one of Mary's councillors. Mordant advised him to leave London. 'How shall I then be discharged toward God', replied Saunders, 'if any should slip into error, and receive false doctrine?'[2] Having heard Saunders preach at Bread Street once before, Mordant was invited to 'hear me again in the same place: where I will confirm, by the authority of God's Word, all that I said then'.[3] The next day Saunders preached on *I have prepared you for one husband, to present you as a pure virgin to Christ: But I fear lest as the serpent beguiled Eve through his subtlety, so your minds should be corrupt from the simplicity that is in Christ* (2 Corinthians 11:2–3). The wiles of the serpent are identified with the idolatry of Rome; the one, said Saunders, had found a breeding ground in the other. Church services in English under Edward VI are compared and contrasted to the Latin mass. The former was good 'because it was according to the Word of God'. The latter was wholly evil: its aesthetic appeal was 'as a little honey or milk mingled with a great deal of poison, to make them drink all up'.[4]

---

1   Ibid.
2   Ibid. 614.
3   Ibid.
4   Ibid. 615.

In the evening, as he neared the pulpit, Saunders was seized by the agents of Edmund Bonner, bishop of London.[1] They had been tipped-off. In Fulham Palace, before Bonner himself, Saunders was accused of treason, for violating the conditions of Mary's decree, and of heresy for the content of his sermons. Alongside the bishop sat Sir John Mordant, Saunders' betrayer. When Bonner demanded his opinion on transubstantiation, Saunders supplied a written answer. 'My lord', it ran, 'ye do seek my blood, and ye shall have it. I pray God that ye may be so baptized in it, that ye may thereafter loathe blood-sucking, and become a better man'.[2]

'As Annas sent Christ to Caiaphas',[3] writes Foxe, so Bonner sent Saunders to Stephen Gardiner. After a short, spiky interview, the lord chancellor had him committed to the Marshalsea, a notorious prison in Southwark, just south of the river. It would be Saunders' home for the next fifteen months. Unlike the nearby King's Bench, or Comptor in Poultry, the Marshalsea was overcrowded and insanitary; gaol fever and other diseases were rife. The cells were airless in summer and raw in winter; the stench of faecal sludge and rotting food was unremitting. By a grate in the wall, his wife Joanna would linger, and call down to him, despite his fears for her safety. But as his letters make plain, he did not bewail the sadness of his case for a second. Day and night, in worship pure and agreeable to His Word, he sought the fatherly favour of God: he also 'look[ed] for battles, which the root of unfaithfulness, the which I feel in me, will most eagerly give unto my conscience when we come once to the combat'.[4] A euphoric sense of blessing so filled his heart it couldn't be stifled. Christ was all: every shadow had been swallowed up by His light. 'I resign myself wholly unto my Christ', he told Joanna, 'in whom I know I shall be strong as He seeth needful'.[5]

In the same period, another scholar of Eton and King's was acting in ways equally vexing to the new regime. Robert Glover was one of four sons born to a prominent Warwickshire family. The youngest, William, wrote a well-known

---

1   Bonner took personal responsibility for flogging prisoners in the orchard at Fulham Palace. In the course of examining Thomas Tompkins, he held Tompkins' hand over the flame of a candle to make him realize the pain he would suffer if sent to the stake. Tompkins was martyred on 16 March 1555.

2   Foxe, vi. 615.

3   Ibid.

4   *The Letters of the Martyrs*, ed. Coverdale (London, rep. 1837), 148.

5   Ibid. 152.

panegyric to Anne Boleyn. Outside of the fact that he settled in Ashford in Kent, nothing is known about Thomas Glover. But John, the eldest, is described as being 'like one placed in heaven already, and dead in this world'. In word and deed, says Foxe, he 'led a life altogether celestial, abhorring in his mind all profane things'.[1] Shortly after his conversion, John was brought to a state of anguished introspection by his reading of Hebrews 6:4–6. For five years he suffered the 'sharp temptations and strong buffetings of Satan'.[2] He lived a life of uncompromising asceticism: refusing to eat meat, hardly sleeping, eschewing all forms of physical comfort. But the Lord preserved him, and he was reborn in a kind of ecstasy, having at last comprehended his justification by the innocent death of Christ. His separation from the world brought him unprecedented acceptance and respect; he became the bonding agency of the West Country Reformed. The eldest son and therefore heir to his father's fortune, he exhibited an extraordinary generosity. Most of his lands were given over to his evangelical brethren; anything remaining was committed 'to the guiding of his servants and officers, whereby the more quietly he might give himself in godly study'.[3]

John was a gentleman farmer. The academic of the family was Robert. A pupil of Richard Cox at Eton, at King's he immersed himself in the *via antiqua*: he read medieval texts, classical Greek and Roman literature and philosophy. There is little evidence to support his own claim to be 'but basely learned'. He incepted BA in 1538 and was MA by 1541. He held a fellowship until 1542/3. A strapping, genial young man, Robert's marriage to Mary, Latimer's favourite niece, placed him at the hub of an ideological revolution. Most Bible-men, however, John Foxe among them, held John Glover in far greater esteem. 'In those things which appertained to heavenliness and good conscience', wrote Foxe, '[John] was far more exercised'.[4] In a lethal aside, Foxe tells his readers that although Robert 'was better seen in the literature which doth polish and bring a man to eloquence, John less feared peril'.[5] The bookish younger brother was suspected of laying claim to certainties he didn't hold; his motivation was seen as temperamental and pragmatic rather than doctrinal.

---

1   Foxe, vii. 386.
2   Ibid. 385.
3   Ibid. 386.
4   Ibid. 391.
5   Ibid.

By the mid-1540s, Robert and Mary were settled in conjugal bliss in Baxterley in Warwickshire, not far from Mancetter, where John lived with his wife Agnes. The Glovers soon had a young family to support, as well as a large household and lands to maintain. Mary's practicality and intelligence were widely recognized and admired, not least by her husband. The daughter of one of Latimer's six sisters, she had kept house for her famous uncle until her marriage. It has been suggested that Latimer fostered Mary after the death of her parents. What is certain is that Latimer provided the greater part of her dowry.

Due, perhaps, to the constant presence of Latimer at Baxterley, the Glovers' hospitality was enjoyed by many evangelicals, including John Bradford—a great favourite of Latimer—and Laurence Saunders, known to Robert from King's, and probably Eton. In a letter written to the Glovers on the day he was executed, Saunders referred to Robert and John as 'my dear brethren, whom I love in the Lord, being loved by you also in the Lord'.[1] Another regular visitor was John Careless. A weaver of humble origins and slight schooling, Careless confounded a succession of learned interrogators before dying in prison in July 1556. Throughout his incarceration, first in Coventry, then at the King's Bench in London, he kept up a constant stream of letters to all the Reformed leaders. If his furious polemicism knew no bounds, he was also capable of great compassion. After the burnings of Latimer and her husband, Careless counselled Mary Glover to 'think sweetly of the Lord and of His goodness, and thank Him most heartily that ever He would vouch you worthy to sustain the loss of your chiefest treasures in earth for His sake … and make you worthy, strong and able to suffer the loss of your own life for the testimony of the truth; which (as your good uncle said to me once, and your dear husband full often) is the greatest promotion and dignity that God can bring us in this life'.[2]

In the wake of the Act of Six Articles (1539), unfriendly eyes appraised the Glovers' proximity to Latimer and prominence within the Reformed camp generally. The Articles, corrected and revised by Henry himself, restored the sacramental machinery of the Catholic church to full working order. The key tenets of Reformed belief, including a denial of the mass as a real sacrifice of Christ, were declared heretical. In July Latimer resigned the see

---

1   *The Letters of the Martyrs*, 159.
2   Ibid. 481.

of Worcester. As for Robert, he was cast into a wilderness of silence and disapproval for six years. In the only report we have on him in this period, his home was turned upside down in a search for banned texts. Latimer was imprisoned twice, latterly in the Tower. But in 1547, having ridden out the 'dangerous tempests of king Henry's time', the Reformers were stabled in 'the mild and halcyon days of king Edward VI'.[1] Latimer, a hero to the new anti-papal regime, was released from the Tower and offered a bishopric. He declined, but accepted the role of preacher to Edward's court.

In July 1547, the duke of Somerset, Edward's maternal uncle and Lord Protector of England, ordered a royal visitation to all the dioceses of England and Wales. No less a figure than John Calvin had written to Somerset, urging him to pray that Almighty God 'may approve you as a repairer of His temple, so that the times of the king your nephew may be compared to those of Josiah'.[2] At last the Reformers were able to put into effect the changes required if the church was to embody the Gospel it preached. The use of candles, palms and ashes during Lent was prohibited; Easter practices such as creeping to the Cross on Good Friday also ceased. By the end of 1549 clerical marriage had been sanctioned and the service of the Latin mass, the so-called 'book of hours', replaced by a Book of Common Prayer written in English. Church walls were whitewashed, rood screens cut down, and shrines removed. The Ten Commandments were proudly displayed. The light of God's truth was shining in darkened hearts. But with the death of Edward in 1553, the forces of disintegration began to reassemble. In hindsight, the Christmas sermon preached by firelight at Baxterley Hall in 1552, in which Latimer—surrounded by the Glovers, their children, servants and friends—attacked the whole hierarchical system of bishops and monastic orders, was a kind of swansong for the English Reformation. In a few short months a campaign of virulent antagonism would be loosed.

Dr Ralph Baines, a graduate of St John's College, Cambridge, and a former rector of Hardwick, left England in 1549 to become a professor of Hebrew in Paris. On Mary's accession he returned to England and was appointed to the see of Coventry and Lichfield. A joyless, periodically vicious figure within the clerical establishment, he is only remembered today as the persecutor of Joan Waste. Joan was a 22-year-old blind girl from

---

1   Foxe, v. 697.
2   Quoted in R. Tudur Jones, *The Great Reformation* (Bridgend, rep. 1997), 157.

Derby, uneducated, but a skilled rope maker like her father. After her father's death she was looked after by her brother, Roger, who would lead her by the hand around the town. In the reign of Edward VI, brother and sister started to attend Reformed services. Filled with a spirit of prayer, and eager to learn the Bible, Joan saved up her rope making money to buy a copy of Tyndale's New Testament. For this, and for the crime of asking her friends to read it aloud to her, Joan was gaoled on the accession of Mary. Brought before Baines and Anthony Draycot, his chancellor, Joan spoke with modest, serious discrimination against transubstantiation. She went to her execution on 1 August 1556, having, in the words of Foxe, 'said such prayers as she had learned, and cried upon Christ to have mercy upon her'.[1] As Draycot fell into a drunken stupor outside a local inn, Roger Waste led his sister to Windmill Pit on the outskirts of Derby. Having let go of her hand, Roger stood next to the stake calling out to her until she lost consciousness. Amidst the smoke and flame, a single word—'Jesus'—was seen to form on her lips.

In an attempt to reverse six years of West Country reform in one fell swoop, Baines ordered the mayor of Coventry to arrest John and William Glover on a charge of heresy. But the birds had flown. Upon their arrival at Mancetter, the mayor's men found only the servants and Robert, pale and feverish in an upper chamber. The grounds for Robert's arrest were slight; the authorities, he remonstrated, had 'no commandment concerning me, but [only] for my elder brother'.[2] Perhaps, as the legend says, he really was mistaken for John. But it seems more likely that the mayor's men thought that any arrest was better than none. Or perhaps their frustration made them vindictive. What is certain is that the least troublesome Glover was bundled out of bed and borne away to the common gaol in Coventry. To his dank cell, 'never called to my answer of the masters, contrary to the laws of the realm',[3] he was abandoned for ten days, awaiting the bishop's pleasure. But the path of divine providence was about to take another turn. A change overcame Robert. He 'wept for joy and gladness', praying 'Oh, Lord, who am I, on whom thou shouldest bestow this thy great mercy, to be numbered among the saints that suffer for thy Gospel's sake?'[4] In spite of earth and

---

1 Foxe, viii. 250.
2 Foxe, vii. 390.
3 Ibid.
4 Ibid. 389.

hell, he would, he was sure, have strength for all his trials, and find glorious rest at last.

In his sharply perceptive, well-organized, and often moving letters to his wife Mary, Robert's chief object was to present Christ as the only head of the church of God: that very Christ Jesus papal-Catholicism had rejected, choosing instead 'the man of sin, the son of perdition, enemy to Christ, the devil's deputy and lieutenant, the pope'.[1] In an especially affecting passage he makes clear his intention—in spite of illness, and 'never [being] called to be a preacher or minister'—to forgo his possessions ('above the common sort of men'),[2] marriage, even his children, in order to help overthrow 'the whorish abomination of the Roman antichrist'.[3] This is strong meat: too strong for modern tastes. But we must unflaggingly remind ourselves that for the Bible-men detachment in defence of truth was no virtue. There was no Swiftian coolness of observation: no attempt to forestall reprimand, no space for empty rhetoric. The tone is one of ringing sincerity. And if we flinch from it, what, exactly, are we flinching from? Faith for the Glovers, as for Latimer, did not exist in a state of daring privacy. In their keen-sighted, unclouded truthfulness, we hear an invincible certainty: both of their own conversion and of their high purpose as awe-struck auditors of Christ.

That certainty formed the core of Robert's dialogue with bishop Baines. Censured for not attending Catholic rites, he avowed he would never 'come to their church as long as their mass was used there to save (if I had them) five hundred lives'. He challenged Baines 'to show me one jot or tittle in the Scriptures for the proof and defence of the mass'. And in his response to the prelate's cry of 'Who shall judge the Word?', we discern that obedience which is the source of all right knowledge of God: 'Christ was content', said Robert, 'that the people should judge his doctrine by searching the Scriptures, and so was Paul: I think you should claim no further privilege nor pre-eminence than they had'.[4] The tenor of his deposition—its clarity, astringency and good sense—shows him certain and secure, and expanding with spiritual joy. In the course of several interviews, Robert exposes as a fiction the bishop's idea of a church growing in grace and wisdom. Far from revealing God's truth, Romanism had persistently obscured it. Robert declares

---

1   Ibid. 388.
2   Ibid. 389.
3   Ibid. 390.
4   Ibid. 394.

himself content that 'the primitive church, next to the apostles' time, should judge between the bishop and him'.[1]

In the summer of 1555, Robert Glover saw himself as an instrument of God's providential purpose. That much is certain. But he was also, as he told the mayor of Coventry, 'a man subject to a very great sickness, and have been by the space of seven years and more'.[2] When another prisoner took him aside and whispered that there was a plan afoot to transfer him to Lichfield, he deplored his own quaking spirits: what he later called 'this infidelity in myself': 'What make I of God?' he asked himself, head in hands: 'Is not His power as great in Lichfield as in Coventry?':

> So long as we place our trust in Him, we shall neither be destitute of His help, neither in prison, neither in sickness or in health, neither in life nor in death; neither before kings, nor before bishops, nor in the devil himself … With such like meditations I waxed cheerful, of good consolation and comfort; so that, hearing one say that they could not provide horses enough for us, I said: 'Let them carry us in a dung-cart if they wish. For my part I am well content'.[3]

From the common gaol in Coventry he was taken to Lichfield by a body of constables, arriving at dawn. Until his condemnation he was to languish in an unidentified prison 'very cold, with small light', being allowed 'a bundle of straw instead of my bed, without chair, form, or any other thing else to ease myself withal'.[4] But he had his Latin New Testament. He had a Prayer Book. He lowered his head to the storm, and clung, often blindly, but not despairingly, to the Word. After two days he was visited by Anthony Draycot, Baines' chancellor. Historical distance might make Draycot bearable; nothing could lend him enchantment. Robert's purest thoughts, his dearest longings, were heard in a hush of calm contempt. He was mocked as a hopeless sinner incapable of applying his mind to the study of truth: even less capable of expressing it. 'What then', retorted Robert: 'Must I deny His Word, because I am not worthy to profess it? What bring I to pass in so doing, but add sin to sin? What is greater sin than to deny the truth of Christ's gospel?'[5]

---

1   Ibid.
2   Ibid. 395.
3   Ibid. 394–395.
4   Ibid. 395.
5   Ibid. 397.

Some days later, in an anteroom off the main prison, he was interrogated
by Baines. His replies articulated a theology of suffering that reached back
to apostolic times. The church of which he was a member 'hath been from
the beginning, though it bears no glorious show before the world, being
ever, for the most part, under the Cross and affliction, condemned, despised,
and persecuted'.[1] His testimony overflowed with silent hymns of gratitude.
All Baines had to offer was his sullen ferocity. Accused of heresy, and of
arrogance in the face of God, Robert begged the bishop to support his claims
with 'some Scriptures and good learning'.[2] Nor did he think it seemly that
the cause of Reform—a cause for which he was happy to die—should be
judged by a minor bishop in a squalid ante-room. His ordained brethren had
appeared before panels of privy councillors. Several were seen by the lord
chancellor. His friend Bradford had been questioned by an archbishop, two
bishops and two leading Spanish divines. Robert did not demand the same
handling. But he still wanted his witness preserved: ongoing work for the
kingdom of Christ should not be hidden 'in corners'. Baines could hardly
contain his irritation. Unless Robert cooperated, he would have 'neither
meat nor drink'.[3] Foxe confirms that Robert did, eventually, face Baines and
Draycot in open court. But so promptly was the writ for burning expedited,
no record of the trial was preserved.

In the last days, Robert's confidence and consolation all but deserted
him. When he raised his heart to heaven, it sank into the dust. How could
he, a miserable sinner, be the recipient of God's mercy? He felt wretched.
He felt alone. Oh, that he might be found worthy to bear the cross of the
martyr! He shuddered at the thought of disgracing the cause of Christ in
such a public setting. His one visitor, the minister Austen Bernher, could
only counsel him to bear the pains of privation willingly; Robert should
await the Lord's pleasure, and trust that by the power of the Spirit he would
receive a sense of personal summons. But dawn broke on 19 September 1555
with Robert still destitute of hope or comfort. A night of profitless prayer
had left his limbs weary; his mind sluggish. His burning, bursting heart had
striven in vain to pour forth its agony. But God, by His own good grace,
opens the eyes of the mind. In the shadow of the stake, Robert looked to

---

1 Ibid.
2 Ibid.
3 Ibid.

the clouds, to the treetops, to every living thing around him, and knew that their God was his God. From fear of hell he saw a glorious view of heaven. The kingdom of Christ was at hand; the Lord Jesus was leading him on! So long thirsty, so long famished, he was 'mightily replenished with God's holy comfort and heavenly joys'.[1] He began to furiously clap his hands, and blink away tears of joy: 'Austen, Austen!' he cried out, 'He is come, He is come!'[2] As the sheriff's men secured him to the stake, Robert Glover comprehended, with all his heart, the greatness of God. He pitied his oppressors' failings, excused their offences and finished his course as bright and true a Christian as England ever saw. 'Such was the change', says Foxe, 'of the marvellous working of the Lord's hand upon that good man'.[3]

Robert certainly had the best of it. In the aftermath of his brother's death, John Glover was ridden with guilt. Believing that Robert had perished in his place, he sank into a deep depression. When Baines realized he was still at liberty, officers were sent to Mancetter to arrest him. This time John was at home, but managed to slip away and take refuge in some nearby woods. After several weeks of living on roots and berries, he caught pneumonia and died a protracted death. He was buried in the local churchyard. But when Draycot heard of this, he ordered that the body be 'taken up, and cast over the wall into the highway'.[4] A local cleric told him this was impossible, for the body had entered its state of decomposition. 'Well then', said the chancellor, 'take this bill, and pronounce him in the pulpit a damned soul, and a twelvemonth later take up his bones, and cast them over a wall, that carts and horses may tread upon them'.[5]

In a melancholy coda to the Glovers' story, Agnes, John's wife, was bullied into an abjuration. As for William, the youngest brother, he seems to have died of natural causes in Wem in Shropshire. But due to the actions of a malign curate, his body was not allowed a proper burial. He was roughly interred in a scrub-field.

Having languished in the Marshalsea for a year and three months, Laurence Saunders was finally summonsed, on 30 January 1555, to appear before a panel of bishops and privy councillors at the church of St Mary Overy's in

---

1   Ibid. 398.
2   Ibid.
3   Ibid. 399.
4   Ibid. 400.
5   Ibid. 401.

Southwark. In the chair was the lord chancellor, Stephen Gardiner. Despite Gardiner's initial cordiality and assurances that 'if you will show yourself conformable, and come home again, mercy is ready',[1] Saunders refused to derogate from the authority of the Word or qualify human depravity. His confinement, like Glover's, had ennobled his witness; his testimony, from first to last, runs like a flame through stubble. When charged with pride and arrogance for denying the sacrificial mass, Saunders admitted to loving both life and liberty 'if I could enjoy them without hurt to my conscience'.[2] But, he added, 'I may not buy liberty at such a price'.[3] He went on to upbraid the bishops for their failure to abide by an oath, voluntarily given, never to consent to papal jurisdiction: 'But you, the whole sort of you', he observed, 'have agreed to cut off the supremacy of the bishop of Rome, whom now you will have to be the head of your church again!'[4] He also jogged Gardiner's memory regarding *De vera obedientia*, a tract of 1535 in which the lord chancellor upheld the royal supremacy and approved the executions of John Fisher and Thomas More. This brought the interview to a crashing halt. Gardiner declared Saunders unfit to live: 'and that you shall understand within these seven days. And now away with him!'[5] Out of sight of the commission, and while awaiting the return of Rowland Taylor and John Bradford from their examinations, Saunders set forth God's inestimable forgiveness to a crowd gathered outside St Mary Overy's. He spoke freely, we are told, 'exhorting them by repentance to rise again, and to embrace Christ with stronger faith, to confess Him to the end in defiance of the antichrist, sin, death and the devil'.[6]

The following week Edmund Bonner passed through the gates of the Compter gaol in Bread Street, a stone's throw from the church where his men had first arrested Saunders. The bishop had arrived to formally degrade Saunders prior to his burning under the revived act *De Haeretico Comburendo*. Bonner, being Bonner, shouted loudly and listened jubilantly to the echo. At the ritual's end Saunders was heard to comment: 'I thank God I am not of

---

1   Foxe, vi. 625.
2   Ibid. 626.
3   Ibid.
4   Ibid.
5   Ibid.
6   Ibid. 627.

your church'.[1] The following day, escorted by a troop of the queen's guard, he embarked upon his last journey: to the Midlands town of Coventry. As with others of the godly company, Saunders' burning would be carried out in the region where his labours had borne most fruit. Such objectified ignominy, it was hoped, would resonate among local populations, and act as a brake on evangelical impulses. Shortly before leaving the Comptor, Saunders penned these words, addressed to his wife and friends:

> I now suffer among [my flock] for Christ's Gospel's sake, bidding them to beware of the Roman antichristian religion and kingdom, requiring and charging them to abide in the truth of Christ, which is shortly to be sealed with the blood of their pastor; who though he be unworthy of such a ministry, yet Christ their high pastor is to be regarded. That the truth has been taught to them by me, is witnessed by my chains, and by His power by my death also. Be not careful, good wife, cast your care on the Lord, and commend me unto Him in repentant prayer, as I do you and our Samuel, who even at the stake I will offer, as myself, unto God. Fare ye well all in Christ, in hope to be joined with you in joy everlasting. This hope is laid up in my bosom. Amen, Amen; Pray, Pray![2]

On 8 February 1555, a chill and ominously damp day, a great press of people gathered in a park on the outskirts of Coventry. In the mid-morning, Laurence Saunders, wearing an old gown and bare-footed, was led out between the sheriff and his officers to a place set aside for executions. Again he was asked to put off his heresies; again he refused, declaring 'I hold no heresies, but the doctrine of God and the blessed gospel of Christ. That hold I, that believe I, that I will never revoke'. And then, turning to the stake as if to a dear friend, he embraced and kissed it, saying 'Welcome the cross of Christ, welcome everlasting life!'[3] The sheriff's men, having fastened Saunders to the wooden post, banked up faggots and bales of straw all around it. The jockeying crowd, some murmuring and praying, others catcalling and whistling, fell silent as the smoke billowed. The wood was green!—it burned, but with excruciating slowness. Soon the faces of onlookers were masked in wood ash. But in all the drawn-out torment of his martyrdom,

---

1   Ibid.
2   *The Letters of the Martyrs*, 156–157.
3   Foxe, vi. 628.

Saunders was never less than serene, binding every scrap of agony to the plan
and purpose of God. He stood erect, steady and unflinching, falling asleep,
we are told, 'full sweetly in the Lord'.[1]

John Hullier was admitted to King's College from Eton around 1534.
How old he was is not recorded, but he is likely to have been about sixteen.
Once there he distinguished himself as a scholar but chose not to complete
his studies, being appointed a chaplain of the college in 1539. Having learnt
to sanctify the Lord in his heart, he was filled with an irresistible urge to see
the Gospel encompass all of society. To that end, in 1549, he accepted the
curacy of Babraham near Cambridge. It was an auspicious year for reform.
Parliament approved clerical marriage and agreed to an Act of Uniformity
that brought in a Book of Common Prayer written in English. Edmund
Bonner, the bishop of London, was removed from his see after being tried by
Cranmer in a spiritual court. And the theologians of Strasbourg, Paul Fagius
and Martin Bucer, arrived to take up positions at Cambridge University. Parish
records reveal an especially strong link between Babraham and the university.
As early as 1504, Margaret, countess of Richmond, had provided funds for
a preaching scholar from Cambridge to give annual sermons in the church.

When next we hear of Hullier, Mary is on the throne and he is up to his
neck in what Foxe calls 'divers conflicts with the papists'.[2] In addition to
pastoring his flock in Babraham, he is preaching all over East Anglia. Not for
Hullier expressions of queasy piety. He spoke of justification by faith in the
merits of Christ: of sins forgiven and eternal life bestowed. There is a choice
to be made, he said, in respect of our Christian education. One can attend
'the wicked and whorish schoolhouse'[3] of antichrist, and be subject to the
devices of our own guilty souls. Or we can opt for the tutelage of Christ,
'that at length we may be inheritors with Him of everlasting joy'.[4] There is
no pulling of punches. Hullier had identified the 'great trouble in hand, as
here in England'.[5] The faint-hearted, who might favour some kind of mixed
syllabus, are told that 'it is manifestly declared in the Revelation of St John
[that] the fearful shall have their part with the unbelieving and abominable,

1   Ibid.
2   Foxe, viii. 378.
3   *The Letters of the Martyrs*, 398.
4   Ibid. 399.
5   Ibid. 397.

in the lake that burneth with fire and brimstone'.[1] In his sermons and letters Hullier never flinched from portraying the terrors of the second death. In the fires of hell the unregenerate would find no God, no mediator to plead their cause, no hand to give them comfort.

As events under Mary assumed their blood-stained course, and given the incendiary nature of his preaching, one wonders how long Hullier expected to remain at liberty. Towards the end of 1555 he was finally arrested by authority of Thomas Thirlby, bishop of Ely, and brought to the city in the Fens. This was the same Thirlby who, as a student, had roomed below Thomas Bilney at Trinity Hall. When the strains of Thirlby's recorder drifted up through the floorboards, a scandalized Bilney would sink to his knees in prayer. Thirlby was no sadist like Bonner; nor an emotionally vacant narcissist like Gardiner. He was, in fact, an inglorious example of a breed far more common in the Tudor age: the ecclesiastical hack. Thirlby rose without trace and maintained his position by aligning his prejudices to those of his political masters. In this way he served four monarchs, each with a markedly different conception of the national church. With no regard paid to ability and merit, power will always be granted to those willing to pay homage to hierarchic authority. Bonners and Gardiners are mercifully rare, but Thirlbys are ubiquitous: then as now. It is the Thirlbys that win preferment, the Thirlbys that endure. And with the religious current flowing in the direction of Rome, it proved *politique* for this Thirlby to pitch Hullier first into Cambridge castle, and afterward to have him 'conveyed to the town prison, commonly called the Tolbooth, lying there almost a quarter of the year'.[2]

When he emerged at last from that dank, forbidding place it was to face a commission of bishops, lawyers and academics at Great St Mary's, the university church. The commission was led by Nicholas Shaxton, the former bishop of Salisbury. Once an almoner of Anne Boleyn, Shaxton had recanted his evangelical views in favour of a feeble and tepid self-interest. He was now working his passage back to the papal fold. Thirlby's droll biographer notes that his subject was 'in sympathy with Shaxton's uncertain outlook';[3] a rapport underlined by Thirlby's selection of Shaxton as his suffragen. Shaxton's chief deputies on the commission were John Young and Thomas

---

1   Ibid. 401.
2   Foxe, viii. 378.
3   T.F. Shirley, *Thomas Thirlby: Tudor Bishop* (London, 1964), 162.

Sedgwick. In June 1550, in a disputation held before royal visitors, Young and Sedgwick had opposed Martin Bucer's teaching on justification by faith and on the sufficiency of Scripture. With Mary on the throne, Young was appointed master of Pembroke. He also took over the prebend of Ely from Matthew Parker, one of Bucer's protégés.

Hullier's condemnation, and sentence of death, were pronounced by Thirlby's chancellor—and soon-to-be master of Jesus College—John Fuller. A typical degradation, 'after their popish manner',[1] followed. Hullier was dressed in a mocked-up version of his priest's vestments prior to its solemn stripping away. The crown of his head was scraped with a knife. So were his palms and fingertips.[2] The ritual completed, a bloodied Hullier declared 'this [the] joyfullest day I ever saw, and I thank you all, that you have delivered and lightened me of all this paltry'.[3] A Catholic onlooker, unnerved by this display of high spirits, tore Hullier's New Testament from his hand and hurled it across the floor. The mayor, master Brasey, ordered the removal of all books and writing materials from his cell. But letters were still smuggled out. Hullier urged his flock to confront their own, albeit lesser, forms of suffering; to regard them as a means to spiritual growth. With God's help they would '[taste] of the Word of God, and the power of the world to come'.[4] Church history and current events were presented as the struggle of fleshly and spiritual churches:

> Now choose you which way you will take: either the narrow way that leadeth into life, which Christ Himself and His faithful followers have gone through before; or else the broad pathway that leadeth to destruction, which the wicked worldlings take their pleasure in for a while. I, for my part, have now written this short admonition unto you of good will (as God be my witness) to exhort you to that way which you yourselves should prove and find to be best, yea, and rejoice thereof. And I do not only write this, but I will also (with the assistance of God's grace) ratify, confirm, and seal the same with the effusion of my blood, when the full time shall be expired that He hath appointed; which (so far forth as I may judge) must needs be within these few days. Therefore I

---

1   Foxe, viii. 378.
2   This in order to remove all traces of the holy oil with which he had been anointed.
3   Foxe, viii. 378–379.
4   *The Letters of the Martyrs*, 403.

now bid you all most heartily farewell in the Lord; whose grace be with your spirit. Amen. Watch and pray, watch and pray. Pray, pray. So be it.[1]

On Maundy Thursday 1556 Hullier was led to Jesus Green, 'not far from Jesus College'.[2] According to Foxe's correspondent it was a fine, warm day. After uttering a prayer that his words be pleasing in the sight of God, the Reformer begged the crowd to pray for him. 'The Lord strengthen thee!' someone roared. Master Brisley, the sergeant-at-arms, told the well-wisher to 'hold his tongue, or he should repent it'.[3] While undressing for the stake, Hullier exhorted all to bear witness that he 'died in the right faith, and that he would seal it with his blood ... and that there was no other rock but Jesus Christ to build upon, under whose banner he had fought, and whose soldier he was'.[4] From an embankment above the stake, three men surveyed the scene with mounting ire. George Boyes, Henry Barley and Master Gray were Trinity Hall men; Boyes, significantly, was also a proctor[5] of the university. 'Master Proctor', muttered Gray, 'what blasphemy this fellow talks. Surely it is evil done to suffer him?' The implied criticism stoked Boyes' fury to bursting point. 'Master mayor!' he cried, seeing Brasey standing nearby, 'what are you doing? If you allow him to talk freely, I tell you that the council shall hear of it, and we shall not take you to be the queen's friend. He is a pernicious person, and may do more harm than you know!'[6] Hullier, meanwhile, turned to the stake as if it were a bed of roses. He was bound with chains and lifted bodily into a pitch-barrel. In an odd silence the sergeant applied a torch to the reeds and wood, stepping backward at the first wisp of smoke. The fire was set. The clamour was pitiless. A nagging breeze wafted the flame to Hullier's back; the pouches of gunpowder around his neck failed to ignite. As the torments inflicted upon his body grew ever more grievous, Hullier prayed ever more fervently. His friends induced the sergeants to light the woodpile windward of his face. That done, busy hands cast a number of books into the flames. By God's providential purpose what Foxe terms 'a communion-book'[7] landed in Hullier's hands. This he read with great joy until blinded

---

1 Ibid. 404.
2 Foxe, viii. 380.
3 Ibid. 379.
4 Ibid.
5 An officer of the university having disciplinary functions.
6 Foxe, viii. 379.
7 Ibid.

by the fire. Holding the text against his heart, he thanked the Lord for His great gift. When all thought him dead he roused himself a final time: 'Lord Jesus', he breathed, 'receive my spirit'.[1] The sole Cambridge martyr to burn in Cambridge departed this earth as he lived: bold in witness, bold in prayer, compelled without fear of men to fulfil God's holy will and pleasure.

In the aftermath of Hullier's martyrdom, many people began to weep and pray around the margins of the fire. Boyes and his friends, having ogled the burning itself with naked gusto, were horrified. From the top of the bank they cried 'that he was not to be prayed for; and being a damned man it could profit him nothing'.[2] Even Hullier's blackened remains seemed to mock their claims to victory; his bones, says Foxe, stood upright in the pitch-barrel 'even as if they had been alive'.[3] A pack of souvenir hunters descended upon the scene. Several pieces of bone were taken; 'one had his heart, the which was distributed as far as it would go; one took the scalp, and looked for the tongue, but it was consumed except the very root'.[4] Such coveting of relics reflects the stubborn persistence of Catholic habits and practices well into the Reformation age.

Hullier left behind two letters. Both are fervent in doctrine, discipline and all that assists salvation. He also bequeathed a prayer of singular simplicity and warmth. It is a humbling experience to read Hullier's words seated on a wooden bench on Jesus Green, a stone's throw from where he counted the cost his faith demanded. In the gathering, vaporous dusk, the Gothic red brick and stone facings of Jesus College are seen but dimly, like the past itself. But Hullier's prayer comes alive with a pristine freshness, its sentiments full of the seed of spiritual life, his love of Christ as tangible as the bells ringing out from Great St Mary's:

> Wherefore I now wholly submit myself to you, O God, having trust and confidence in none other but in you, O heavenly Father, and in the Cross, passion, bloodshedding of your Son Jesus Christ, whereby the world is crucified in me, O Lord, and I to the world; hungering and thirsting for nothing else but the health and salvation of my soul,

---

1   Ibid. 380.
2   Ibid.
3   Ibid.
4   Ibid.

and to live with Christ, who is my life, my joy, my hope, and my whole delight, solace and treasure ...

Now, O most merciful Lord, according to your most faithful and loving promise made therein, let your great power and exceeding virtue be made perfect through my infirmity and weakness, that I may this day most quietly, meekly and steadfastly suffer death, and with a constant and perfect faith give a strong witness to the world, even as my Christian brethren have done before me, for your Word's sake, and for the most true and infallible testimony of your dear Son Jesus Christ.[1]

A plaque affixed to the bench on Jesus Green records Hullier's martyrdom in a manner consistent with the dignity of the religion for which he strove. There is also a tablet to his memory in the church at Babraham.

---

[1]   Ibid. 136–137.

X

NICHOLAS RIDLEY,
HUGH LATIMER

It is generally allowed that of all the English Reformers, Nicholas Ridley was the ablest theologian. We should be wary of proceeding to such judgements. Frith 'displayed the finest mind'[1] and wrote English prose as scintillating as More's. Barnes' gifts, from which sprang 'the nearest thing to a work of systematic theology that the Henrician Reformers produced',[2] might have been better used. Cranmer's liturgical genius still dictates the shape and form of traditional Anglican worship. Bradford's literary legacy, says J.C. Ryle, 'entitles him to a very high rank among Christian authors'.[3] But the untimely death of Martin Bucer deprived the English Reformation of the one figure capable, temperamentally and intellectually, of steering it through a multiplicity of truths to a point where every aspect of life was in subjection to the rule of Christ. *De Regno Christi*, Bucer's great theological and political reform text, was completed in October 1550. Four months later the ailing émigré was dead. His plan to construct a Christian society which sees the Bible as the centre of civil as well as religious thought was stillborn. Peter Martyr Vermigli, Bucer's equal as a theologian, but not as a churchman, returned to Strasbourg in 1553. These were significant losses. No English Reformer made theological contributions of a kind likely to leave much trace. Their work is mostly derivative. With regard to Ridley's place in the history of the English church, however, no one would disagree with Marcus Loane that 'the weight of his learning, the force of his judgement,

---

1   William Clebsch, *England's Earliest Protestants* (Westport, 1964), 78.
2   Carl Trueman, *Luther's Legacy, Salvation & the English Reformers 1525–1556* (Oxford, 1994), 3.
3   *Five English Reformers* (Edinburgh, rep.1999), 132.

his resolute spirit, his moderate conduct, all served to mark him out as a leading figure'.[1]

He was born, in 1502 or thereabouts, to a Northumberland gentry family in Willimoteswick, a fortified dwelling at the confluence of the rivers Allen and South Tyne, quite near Hadrian's Wall. One of his uncles was Robert Ridley, fellow of Queen's College, doctor of divinity in Paris and friend of Erasmus. Cuthbert Tunstall, the Henrician and Marian bishop,[2] and unflagging enemy of the Bible in English, was another relative. After a conventional schooling in Newcastle-upon-Tyne, Robert Ridley secured a place for his nephew at Pembroke Hall. This was in 1518. In his 'Farewell Letter', written shortly before his execution, Ridley would refer to Cambridge as 'my loving mother and tender nurse'.[3] He recalled memorizing, within the walls of the orchard at Pembroke, most of the epistles of Paul: 'Of which study, although in time a great part did depart from me, yet the sweet smell thereof, I trust, I shall carry with me into heaven: for the profit thereof I think I have felt in all my life-time ever after'.[4] His progress was remarkable. He graduated BA in 1522 and took his MA three years later. He was incepted BTh in 1537 and DTh in 1541. In 1524 he became a fellow of Pembroke, and by 1531 had been offered the chaplaincy of the university. Given the demands of an academic life in this period, the rapidity of Ridley's rise suggests an exceptional mind. By way of comparison, Thomas Cranmer took eight years just to graduate BA.

At the urging of Robert Ridley, Nicholas is also reckoned—although no reliable evidence can be found of this—to have studied at Paris and Louvain in the years 1527–1530. We do know that he held a professorship in Greek at Cambridge from 1535 to 1538, and that by 1540 he had been elected to the mastership of Pembroke Hall: this despite the fact that he had ceased to reside in it. In 1537 archbishop Cranmer made him one of his chaplains. Shortly afterward he was instituted to the 'worshipful and wealthy' living of Herne in Kent, 'the first cure whereunto I was called to preach God's Word'.[5] It had been fully twenty years since Martin Luther had posted his ninety-five theses on the door of the castle church in Wittenberg. The assumption that

---

1   Marcus Loane, *Masters of the English Reformation* (London, rep. 1956), 147.
2   Tunstall became bishop of London in 1522; he was transferred to Durham in 1530.
3   John Foxe, *Acts & Monuments* (1838), vii. 557.
4   Ibid.
5   Ibid. 558.

the dogmas of the church were something apart and irrefutable was being openly questioned. Popes and councils, wrote Wolfgang Capito, 'may err and have often erred, and conciliar and papal law does not bind us any further than God binds us through His Holy Word'.[1] If the church and its hierarchy could be wrong, said the Reformers, the sole principle to stand firmly upon was the certainty of the Bible.

At Herne, and before his elevation to the see of Rochester in 1547, Ridley strove to fulfil his ministry 'not after the popish trade, but after Christ's Gospel'.[2] He promoted the singing of the Te Deum in English rather than Latin. He preached against 'the rulers of the darkness of this world',[3] and took delight in observable proofs of piety among his parishioners. These were testing years for the friends of Reform. The Six Articles (q.v.) were instituted a year after Ridley's appearance at Herne; Thomas Cromwell fell a year after that. But for Ridley it was a joyous and formative period. Once settled into his Kentish idyll, far from the political brawling of court or university, Ridley was able to pursue, relatively unhindered, the foundation of a biblical theology. Simply refuting the ideas of the traditionalists was not enough. His mind was set upon the plan of ages; upon understanding his own relation to the eternal. To that end, for a short time, he was happy to ruminate in the cloister of his own heart.

The flow of reforming ideas in which Ridley swam was deep and wide. Among the books he studied was one on the Lord's Supper by Ratramnus, a ninth-century monk of the House of Corbie, in the French region of Amiens. Ridley had arrived in Herne an orthodox believer in transubstantiation. As such, he held that the bread and wine of the eucharist, upon consecration, retain all outward appearances but are transformed into the actual body and blood of Christ. But from the mid-1540s onward he would talk of himself as Herne's 'debtor for the doctrine of the Lord's Supper; which at that time, I acknowledge, God had not revealed to me'.[4] In a disputation held at Oxford in April 1554, Ridley credited Ratramnus as 'the first that pulled me by the ear, and that brought me from the common error of the Romish church, and called me to search more diligently and exactly both the Scriptures and the

---

1   Quoted in James M. Kittelson, *Wolfgang Capito: From Humanist to Reformer* (Leiden, 1975), 167.
2   Foxe, vii. 558.
3   Ibid. 556.
4   Ibid. 558.

writings of the old ecclesiastical fathers in this matter'.[1] There was, however, no suggestion of equivalency between those two sources. The mature Ridley, typifying the Reform movement as a whole, regarded the canon of Holy Scripture as the sole reflection of the God who speaks through it. The Word was authoritative in itself. All human opinion, philosophical and theological, was derivative and subordinate.

What Ridley had taken from Ratramnus is summarized in an address written by the French divine to the duke of Burgundy: 'The bread called the body of Christ is a figure, because it is a mystery. The body proper is no figure; it is the manifestation of the Thing itself'.[2] Such sentiments fired Ridley's imagination one moment—and lay uneasily on his conscience the next. But by the end of 1545 we find him openly declaring that 'Of Christ's body we say, He is true God, Son of the Father before the worlds; true man, Son of His mother in the end of the world. But this cannot be said of the Body which in mystery we celebrate!'[3] But Ratramnus only took Ridley so far. The next—and overwhelmingly most important—component in Ridley's developed thought arrived with Peter Martyr Vermigli, the great Florentine humanist and theologian. Vermigli had been persuaded by Cranmer to leave the Strasbourg School and become regius professor of divinity at Oxford. For several weeks after his landing in England on 20 December 1547, Vermigli stayed with Cranmer at Lambeth Palace. In his satchel was a letter, dated 28 November 1547, from Bucer (called by Vermigli 'my closest friend'),[4] expounding the Strasbourg position on the Lord's Supper. 'We acknowledge', writes Bucer, 'that the bread and wine do not change in their nature, but that they become signs ... by which signs [Christ] indeed with His own benefits and gifts may be offered to everyone. We do not consider that Christ descends from heaven, nor that He is joined with the symbols, nor that He is included in them'.[5] Vermigli also presented his host with a Latin version of *Ad Caesarium monachum*, an epistle to Caesarius the monk attributed to Chrysostom (*c.* 347–407), and copied by Vermigli from a manuscript kept in the library of S. Marco in Florence. This formed the basis of a celebrated conference, involving Vermigli, Cranmer and Ridley, which, we are told,

1   *A Brief Declaration of the Lord's Supper,* ed. H.G.C. Moule (London, 1895), 11.
2   Quoted in Loane, 143.
3   Ibid. 145.
4   *Vermigli: Life, Letters and Sermons,* ed. Donnelly (Kirksville, 1999), 115.
5   Quoted in Diarmaid MacCulloch (New Haven, 1996), 381–382.

'did not a little confirm'[1] Ridley in his conversion. The complementarity of Ratramnus and Chrysostom, writes MacCulloch, 'much excited Cranmer and Ridley':[2] especially Ridley it seems. He was still drawing upon the Chrysostom letter in his *A Brief Declaration of the Lord's Supper*, written in gaol in Oxford in 1554:

> Before the bread (says Chrysostom) be hallowed, we call it bread, but the grace of God sanctifying it by the means of the priest, it is delivered now from the name of the bread, and esteemed worthy to be called Christ's body, although the nature of the bread abides in it still.[3]

'Wherein I pray you', implores Ridley, 'what can be said or thought more plain against the error of transubstantiation?'[4] So the bread remains bread. But Ridley uses the Chrysostom letter to affirm ('delivered now from the name of the bread') the view of Vermigli, Bucer and Calvin that the bread and wine upon consecration become—Calvin here—'something which they were not before'.[5] He spoke of a real spiritual feeding on Christ. At the Lord's Table there was 'an operation of divinity' at work, nothing less than a transformation, wherein 'the common bread before, it is made a divine influence'.[6]

Although his evangelical leanings were well in evidence at the time of the Act of Six Articles, Ridley was still, in the early 1540s, commending auricular confession as 'a godly mean' to bring sinners to Christ. By the end of Henry's reign, however, albeit with degrees of equivocation, he appears to have absorbed the shape and spirit of the major reforming doctrines.[7] His intimidating intellect, tactful nature and affinity with Cranmer had helped to deflect much of the opprobrium heaped upon less distinguished Gospellers.

By the winter of 1546 the conservative faction under bishops Gardiner

---

1   Foxe, vii. 409.

2   MacCulloch, 382.

3   Moule, 155.

4   Ibid.

5   Quoted in *The Oxford Encyclopedia of the Reformation*, ed. Hans J. Hillerbrand (New York, 1996), i. 238.

6   *The Great Parliamentary Debate in 1548 on the Lord's Supper*, ed. J. T. Tomlinson (London, n.d.), 49–50.

7   In *Archbishop Grindal, 1519–1583: The Struggle for a Reformed Church* (Berkeley, 1979), Patrick Collinson also alludes to the 'cautious evolution of [Ridley's] own opinions over three decades' at p. 38.

and Bonner was in headlong retreat. Gardiner's name was excised from the list of councillors due to govern the country during the minority of Edward VI. On 19 February 1547, the nine–year-old king rode on horseback to his coronation in Westminster Palace. He passed pageants proclaiming his scholarliness, royal lineage and, most particularly, his devotion to the Word of God. Any need for subterfuge was removed; the peak of the Reformation project was in sight and its major figures were stepping forward. In June Ridley preached the funeral sermon of Francis I, king of France. Already designated bishop of Rochester, he was consecrated on 5 September with the imposition of hands and the medieval ritual of chrism. After Edmund Bonner was deprived of his bishopric by Cranmer in an ecclesiastical court, Ridley was translated to the see of London in February 1550.

As bishop of London Ridley was able to present the hope of God's call, and the religious and ethical principles of the Word, and make them the basis for genuine moral conduct. In the opinion of Patrick Collinson, Ridley, following Bucer's lead, '[did] not expect Reformation to come from the suppression of the old religion alone, but from the proper deployment of reliable and learned preachers'.[1] As if to draw a line under the anxiety of the Henrician years, Ridley appointed as chaplains three other Pembroke College men: John Bradford, Edmund Grindal and John Rogers. Each saw justification by faith as the glory of Christ, and the only hope of salvation. Each, reported the bishop, was equipped 'both in life and learning to set forth God's word in London'.[2] Ridley immediately set about testing the biblical knowledge of his parish clergy. Any who did not pass muster were summarily dismissed. His Gospel interests could not be separated from his practical pursuits. Before his consecration as bishop, he had written of his desire to rid his diocese of altars. By the end of his first year every church had a communion table. It was an exciting, productive and optimistic period.

Ridley, Grindal and Bradford had become disciples of Bucer during the German's two-year exile in England. For each, Bucer was the very model of what a Reformer, churchman and true servant of God should be. Grindal called him 'our common instructor';[3] 'As Master Bucer used to say'[4] was his customary argument-clincher. For Ridley, busily reshaping the diocesan

1   Collinson, 57.
2   *The Writings of John Bradford* (Edinburgh, 1979), ii. p. xxv.
3   Quoted in Collinson, 51.
4   Ibid.

and parochial life of London, Bucer's conception of Christian discipline and pastoral care working together in a manner commanded by God operated as some kind of guiding principle.[1] Ridley was especially exercised, as Bucer had been, by the evils that attend an unthinking and uncaring attitude to the poor: unemployment, idleness and homelessness. In March 1553 the bishop preached a sermon on practical charity before the king at Whitehall. As a result, Greyfriars church in Newgate, together with its income, was put to the service of 'the innocently helpless'. Similar arrangements were set up for the sick and disabled at St Bartholomew's, and at Bridewell for the correction of criminals. On his deathbed Edward underwrote 4,000 marks a year for these charities.

Like every holder of his post, Ridley resided at Fulham Palace. Foxe provides a delightful portrait of his daily routine. 'Duly every morning', we are told, 'so soon as his apparel was done upon him, he went forthwith to his bedchamber, and there upon his knees he prayed the space of half-an-hour; which being done, immediately he went to his study (if there came no other business to interrupt him) where he continued until ten of the clock, and then came to the common prayer, daily used in his house. The prayers being done, he went to dinner, where he used little talk, except otherwise occasion by some had been ministered, and then it was sober, discreet and wise, and sometimes merry, as cause required'.[2] When his day of work and study was done, Ridley might relax with chess and conversation. By eleven o'clock he would be by his bed 'saying his prayers upon his knees, as in the morning when he rose'.[3] A singular aspect of Ridley's tenure at Fulham Palace was the presence at his table of Edmund Bonner's mother. In the reign of Mary, Bonner would send seventy-five Reformers to the stake. But knowing that Mrs Bonner was living in straitened circumstances in the wake of her son's deprivation, Ridley insisted she be given her dinner and supper in Fulham Palace, being 'ever placed in the chair at the table's end, being so gently entreated, welcomed, and taken, as though [Ridley] had been born of her own body, never being displaced'.[4]

Alongside his campaign to rid his diocese of formalism and idolatry, two

1 Readers are directed to Amy Nelson Burnett, *The Yoke of Christ: Martin Bucer and Christian Discipline* (Kirksville, 1994).

2 Foxe, vii. 408.

3 Ibid.

4 Ibid.

other issues were to direct the course of Ridley's episcopate. As well as
defining, in large part, his contribution to the national church, both exposed
fault lines in Ridley's relationship with more radical brethren, hinting at the
limits of his—and Cranmer's—vision for reform. The first of these related to
London's two 'stranger' churches, founded early in Edward's reign to meet
the needs of immigrants, including religious refugees, from France and the
Low Countries. Many were of Dutch origin, predominantly well-educated
merchants and skilled artisans. All sought the same root-and-branch reform
being enacted in Switzerland and Germany. Under the leadership of Jan
Laski, an intimate of Calvin and Bullinger, the so-called Stranger Church
moved quickly to a Geneva-inspired version of ecclesiastical polity. A self-
governing, semi-autonomous role was envisioned and constituted: 'We
have nothing to do with bishops!' was the cry. Office-bearers were elected.
Laski preached the Word as the true foundation of church order; anything
that smacked of Catholic hierarchy would be resisted. So would suffocating
entanglements with princely courts. Ridley was immediately suspicious.
He had spent a lifetime being esteemed, first as the scion of a prominent
family, latterly as an academic and master of Pembroke. His goodness and
grace notwithstanding, there was something of the grandee about Ridley.
By an almost involuntary principle of behaviour he became, writes Patrick
Collinson, 'a most monarchical bishop'.[1] James Brooks, bishop of Gloucester,
famously said of him that 'Latimer leaneth to Cranmer, Cranmer to Ridley,
and Ridley to the singularity of his own wit'.[2] To such a personage, the
advance of a church inside his diocese, but outside his control, set off all
kinds of warning bells.

   At a much more basic level, however, the Stranger Churches—French
as well as Dutch—represented for Ridley, as for Cranmer, a Reformed
bridge too far. Despite their attachment to the biblical Gospel, and sincere
belief in its primacy, both men were wary of a movement born on the
Continent that placed confessionalization and clear doctrinal unity above
the commands of the king. They wished to proceed by degrees, levelling
differences between factions as they went. Such pragmatism was bound to
yield something at odds with a Calvinist—or Buceran—vision of an entire
society acting in conformity with the Word of God. Writes MacCulloch

---

1   Collinson, 57.
2   Quoted in Moule, p. x.

of the Stranger Churches: 'There is no doubt of the importance of these thoroughly reformed congregations in the midst of a national church which was half-reformed; they were a signpost to one version of the future'. It was a version from which Ridley instinctively recoiled. The émigrés' attempts to bind their churches as tightly as possible to the European Reformation plunged the bishop into a state of thwarted watchfulness. He 'considered them a nuisance and did his best, as newly appointed bishop of London, to harass their independent establishment'.[1]

One result of congregational democracy, a provision for the Lord's Supper to be taken seated, rather than kneeling, was as badly received in Lambeth as in Fulham. The 1549 Prayer Book required that any believers 'minded' to partake of the Supper should be 'kneeling humbly on their knees'. In an exchange of letters with the archbishop, Laski articulated the view, drawn from Leviticus 10, that to kneel at the Lord's Table was to infect the sacramental body with idolatry. His misgivings about the Prayer Book, and frustration at the pace of change, placed Laski firmly in the camp of John Hooper, the soon-to-be bishop of Gloucester. In a Lenten sermon of February 1550, Hooper had taken some spirited side-swipes at the revised ordinal. The copes, chasubles and other vestments associated with medieval tradition were 'rather the habit and vesture of Aaron and the gentiles, than of the ministers of Christ'.[2] In this matter, Hooper demonstrated, not for the first time, or the last, his fidelity to Zwingli. As early as 1523 the Swiss Reformer had made his position on clerical clothing abundantly clear:

> You papists wear gowns, the tonsure and signs. Tell me, do you wear these to please God or people? You will undoubtedly answer, 'To please God'. But how does that go? Could you not please Him without such signs? Why did not He Himself indicate the need of such? Or do you think that He might not recognize your worship unless you wear one of these disguises? He is not blind just because He is old. He does not look upon your outward worship; rather, He looks into the heart. But you make so much ado over your gowns and insignia that He does not have any need of the heart. He sees well by your clothing who you are, namely, mummers and hypocrites.[3]

---

1 MacCulloch, 477.
2 Quoted in MacCulloch, 471.
3 *Huldrych Zwingli: Writings*, trans. Furcha/Pipkin (Eugene, 1984), i. 204.

In October 1550 Hooper sent a statement of his position to Bucer and to
Peter Martyr Vermigli. Although Vermigli advised Hooper 'not to become
an obstacle to yourself by your immoderate and excessively bitter sermons',
and told him that 'it is advantageous to put up with [vestments] for a time',
he nonetheless allowed that 'I do not suffer in good part being torn from
that pure and simple custom which, as you know, we all used for a long
time at Strasbourg, where distinctive clothing for sacred ceremonies had
been abolished. I, most of all, always approved that custom as more pure and
extremely redolent of the Church of the Apostles'.[1] Hooper had lived on
the Continent for nine years, first at Strasbourg, then at Basel, and finally in
Zürich, where a lasting friendship with Bullinger, Zwingli's chief disciple,
was forged. In the same sermon which criticized the wearing of vestments,
Hooper 'did not a little wonder'[2] why, in Cranmer's ordinal, the invocation
of saints in the oath of supremacy hadn't been withdrawn. In his *Sixty-Seven
Articles*, an exposition of his evangelical principles, Zwingli had spoken of
the theft of human freedom represented by ideas and actions that have no
Scriptural warrant:

> Hence, in whomever a person puts his trust, the same then is his god.
> If you put your confidence in one of the saints, you have made him a god
> to all intents and purposes; for 'God' is the good in which we put our
> trust so that it may afford us the good which we need. If you consider
> them to be your comfort, you have made them your God.[3]

Having identified their common purpose, Hooper and Laski began to
operate in the manner of a two-edged sword. Any aspect of worship, doctrine
or belief that interfered with God's truth had to be cut away. The sin of
man was absolved by Christ's broken body and shed blood, not by ritual, by
prescribed prayers, or by accretions of scholastic interpretation. For Hooper,
the Stranger Church represented a model for an aspirant Church of England
to follow. Any influence he could muster was used to shield it from Ridley's
interference and prevent curbs on its freedom. Laski, in turn, proved a vocal
ally in the quarrel over vestments, even writing a memorandum to Cranmer
echoing Hooper's views and setting out his own congregation's independency

---

1 Donnelly, 102–103.
2 Quoted in MacCulloch, 471.
3 *Writings*, i. 172–173.

on the issue. By such means did the two proto-Puritans open up the first crack in the edifice of the Edwardian Reformation. Traditional, conventional or princely ways of doing things must yield to the certainty of the pure Bible text: to the revelation of Him who is Truth Himself. This struck at the heart of accepted episcopal prerogatives. For the Continental Reformed, 'bishop' was a name of office of service, not of authority; he was, in fact, a simple 'overseer'. Christ alone could teach with authority.

Not least of the issues faced by the English Reformed, as they observed the disputes between Cranmer and Ridley, Laski and Hooper, was to determine, as individuals and as a movement, what, exactly, constituted 'the church'. For Hooper, the English Züricher, it was the united assembly of those led by the Word and Spirit, and known to God alone. No assembly or council of bishops could act or speak for it. In Zürich, writes G.R. Potter, 'Christ alone was High Priest, and any attempt or claim or assume the honour and the power that is His alone, any claim to be His representative, lieutenant, "statthalter" (steward), was vain; any one displacing Christ was himself antichrist'.[1] Worship was to be wiped clean of human pride; the best form of prayer was personal and silent, at home or in church, untainted by outward show. The Second Commandment, as re-emphasized in the New Testament, was inviolable: 'Even the crucifix was unacceptable', comments Potter. 'Nothing [was] allowed to distract attention from the worship of God'.[2] As for magistrates, the earthly welfare of the citizenry remained their responsibility. But it was also the job of rulers and regulators to monitor religious observance. In short, civic commune and church community were to work together in accordance with the divine order of being which Christ Himself had instituted. Any instruction from prince or Parliament deemed offensive to that order was to be disobeyed.

On 15 May 1550, despite the finger-wagging that had followed his Lenten sermon, Hooper was nominated to the diocese of Gloucester. The novelty of his reaction still takes one's breath away. With the backing of Laski, he gave notice he would not be consecrated in white rochet, black chimere or any other 'papistical remnant'. He would not answer to 'my lord'. His apostle-length beard, already deemed unfitting by the church hierarchy, would not be shaved off. For a heady period Hooper appeared to have won the day. The

1 G. R. Potter, *Zwingli* (Cambridge, 1976; rep. 2008), 108.
2 Ibid. 115.

Privy Council fashioned a compromise deal out of the issue of adiaphorism: the distinction between 'things indifferent' (*Res Indifferentes*) and serious articles of faith. Hooper, they said, did not have to wear the despised robes, so long as he conceded that others were free to do so. Cranmer and Ridley were advised that in respect of the 'saints' part of the oath of supremacy, Hooper could not be charged 'with an oath burdensome to his conscience'. The last concession was soon academic. The Bible-loving Edward VI, in an act of righteous indignation, crossed out the offending clause with his own pen.

The response of Ridley and Cranmer to the ruling of the Council is instructive. They ignored it. Ridley was relaxed about the idea of vestments being indifferent. What he wouldn't tolerate—even in non-essential matters— were slights, real or perceived, against the king's majesty. He shifted the ground of the argument. He would fight Hooper on the importance of obeying the king's commands: not, directly, on the issue of vestments. Order and authority were at stake. In backrooms and corridors he began to portray Hooper as a maverick propagating foreign ideas in an English setting. For his part, Hooper went on preaching the reborn Christ as the only guide for thought and action. He cited Romans 14:23 to prove that a thing indifferent was not harmless—or even neutral—in its effects: even priestly clothing required a mandate outside of tradition, and Ridley would struggle to find one in Scripture. But Ridley wasn't reading Scripture. He was conversing with privy councillors. At the conclusion of his appeal, Hooper committed a tactical error. He asked for the civil jurisdiction to be excluded from all decisions surrounding the dispute. To ears primed by the sagacious Ridley to suspect Hooper of desiring some sort of separation of church and state, this sounded like the anarchy of the anabaptists. Hooper had been bested, in politics if not in theology. With a portmanteau charge of defying the command of authority hanging over his head, Hooper was placed under house arrest. On 13 January 1551 the Privy Council gave him over to Cranmer's custody at Lambeth. A fortnight later he was confined to the Fleet prison.

On 15 February 1551 John Hooper wrote to Cranmer begging 'the judgement of your clemency'.[1] He would not obstruct plans for a piecemeal reformation of the church. It was a very English outcome. In Geneva, Calvin had built his Reformed church around four kinds of ministers: pastors who preached the Word, professors who taught the Word, elders who maintained

---

1   Quoted in MacCulloch, 482.

Christian discipline, and a deaconate who collected funds for the poor. In the end, this public and collective idea of the Christian society, wherein equals and peers (*collegae et socii*) 'serve the church for salvation',[1] proved insufficiently alluring to the leaders of the English church. By voice and pen, Cranmer and Ridley approved the doctrinal basis of the Reformation. Yet in their public careers neither was able to shake off a paralysing sense of protocol. Neither solved—or even properly addressed—the problem of how to marry the plan and purpose of God to direct action without treading on the antiquarian privileges of the Crown. The Hooper affair provides a rare example, in a period suffused with a renewed sense of God's presence, of high-mindedness and low politics, in extremely elevated concentrations, pushing against one another.

The capitulation of Hooper, once called, by a Dutch pastor in London, 'the future Zwingli of England',[2] was soon complete. He was consecrated as bishop of Gloucester and preached before the king in the very garments he despised. Laski disappeared from the English scene on the accession of Mary. Hooper was without doubt the most radical of all the bishops appointed under Edward. No one was more assiduous in pressing the moral demands of the Christian faith. In the words of Foxe, he laboured 'to leave neither pains untaken, nor ways unsought, how to train up the flock of Christ in the true Word of Salvation, continually labouring in the same'.[3] The Cross was never absent from his witness. The account of his martyrdom under Mary provides evidence aplenty of his personal courage, of his devotion to stout Reformation principles, of his abiding distrust of ecumenicity. But in the vestments controversy of 1550–1551, and in the parallel disputes over the Stranger Churches, the Reformation in England arrived at a fork in the road. Something was lost then, and there was no going back. A bishop of a later century, J.C. Ryle, concluded 'after carefully weighing the whole affair, that Hooper was most likely in the right, and Cranmer and Ridley were most likely in the wrong'.[4] From an evangelical standpoint that seems fair. As does MacCulloch's assessment, that the kind of Anglicanism we live with today

---

1 Quoted in Hillerbrand, i. 238.
2 Quoted in Collinson, 129.
3 Foxe, vi. 643.
4 *Five English Reformers* (Edinburgh, rep. 1999), 48.

'became a possibility at the moment when Hooper reluctantly reached for his pen to write to Cranmer, admitting the game was up'.[1]

On 2 April 1552 Edward VI contracted measles and smallpox. He rallied quickly; by early May his condition was 'much amended'. But during his convalescence at Greenwich he fell victim to consumption: what we would call tuberculosis. By Christmas he was feverish with cold. Never physically robust, the boy king was sinking fast. In September, Ridley and Edmund Grindal had visited Mary, Edward's half-sister, at Hunsdon in Hertfordshire. As Mary was a Catholic and heir to the throne, it seems certain that the visit was an elaborate scouting trip to see how tractable she might be in matters of religion. The initial exchanges augured well. The princess thanked Ridley for his solicitude. She warmly recalled a sermon he had preached before her father Henry VIII. Following dinner with her retinue, Ridley was escorted into the royal presence. After another exchange of commonplaces, Mary's still-pleasant demeanour encouraged Ridley to offer to preach before her 'on Sunday next, if it will please you to hear me'. Mary's countenance darkened. She eyed him solidly for a while. Eventually she spoke: 'My lord, as for this last matter I pray you make the answer for it yourself'. Ridley reaffirmed his duty to preach the Word. The princess set her lips. 'If there be no remedy but I must make answer', she said; 'the door of the parish church adjoining shall be open for you if you come, and ye may preach if you list; but neither I, nor any of mine shall hear you'. 'Madame', murmured Ridley, 'I trust you will not refuse God's Word?' Mary's reply was savage in its intensity: 'I cannot tell what ye call God's Word: that is not God's Word now that was God's Word in my father's days'. The bishop was a picture of immutable gravity. 'God's Word is all one in all times', he told her, 'but hath been better understood and practised in some ages than in others'. Mary next contrasted Ridley's defence of Roman orthodoxy under her father with his recent authorship of Reformed texts: 'I thank God I never read any of them', she cried, 'I never did, nor ever will do!' Much venom was loosed before the interview was ended. The princess, through gritted teeth one imagines, thanked him for his visit: 'but for your offering to preach before me, I thank you never a whit'.[2] Away from the royal gaze, Ridley burned with self-recrimination. 'I have drunk in that place', he told a confidant, 'where God's Word offered

---

1   MacCulloch, 484.

2   Foxe, vi. 354.

hath been refused. Whereas, had I remembered my duty, I ought to have departed immediately, and to have shaken off the dust of my shoes for a testimony against this house'. The bishop's conviction of having ill-served his Saviour was so fierce, records Foxe, that 'some of the hearers afterwards confessed their hair to stand upright on their heads'.[1]

By 1552–53 Edward, according to at least one authority, was 'beginning to rule'.[2] In the remaining months of his life he became convinced that if Mary inherited the throne, all his efforts to reform the English church would come to naught. By early June 1553 he was in a state of physical collapse. One report of the previous month had it that 'he does not sleep except when he be stuffed with drugs, which doctors call opiates … The sputum which he brings up is black, fetid and full of carbon; it smells beyond measure'.[3] In this period he redrafted, in his own hand, his 'devise for succession'. This named his cousin, the evangelical Lady Jane Grey, his rightful heir. Twenty-six peers approved Edward's 'devise'. The superior claims of Mary and Elizabeth, Edward's half-sisters, were overridden on the basis that both were illegitimate, and likely to marry foreign Catholics. Ridley was the only bishop to offer Lady Jane his unequivocal support.

On 9 July 1553, having already signed the letters patent giving the throne to Lady Jane, Ridley preached a sermon at Paul's Cross. The reaction of the crowd planted an ominous hint of all that was to follow. Ridley's assertion that Mary and Elizabeth were bastards brought boos and catcalls. His encomium to his own efforts to secure London for the Gospel was met with silence. The state-directed character of England's Reformation, and its failure, despite good intentions, to renew and transform the whole realm—secular as well as spiritual—was laid bare. The biblical underpinning was too weak to support much beyond the organization of a church. On 10 July, four days after the death of Edward, the 'prettily shaped and graceful'[4] figure of Jane Grey climbed the steps of the wharf at the Tower of London. She had been browbeaten into accepting the crown by the united efforts of her father, husband and father-in-law. 'The crown', she confided, 'is not my right and pleases me

1 Ibid. 355.

2 W. K. Jordan. Quoted in Eric Ives, *Lady Jane Grey* (Malden, 2009), 134.

3 Quoted in Peter Ackroyd, *The History of England* (London, 2012), ii. 236.

4 Eyewitness report, 10 July 1553; cited in Susan Doran, *The Tudor Chronicles 1485–1603* (London, 2008), 237.

not'.[1] Two months before, Jane had been hastily married to Guildford Dudley, the son of the duke of Northumberland: president of the king's council and the most powerful man in England. She travelled by state barge, radiant in a green robe and jewelled coronet. The spectators on the river bank 'were very silent ... Not a single shout of welcome was raised'.[2] Once inside the Tower she was received as monarch. When the proclamation was repeated at Paul's Cross, a boy raised a cheer for Mary. He promptly had his ears nailed to a pillory. The portents were not auspicious. In the days ahead, despite physical illness, along with 'infinite grief and trouble of heart',[3] Jane carried out her duties with diligence and good sense. She also managed to enrage her in-laws by her refusal to appoint her husband as king consort. Jane argued that no such provision had been made in Edward's 'devise'.

The clamour for Mary and the old religion was not easily quelled. The rallying cry of her followers, *Vox populi vox Dei* ('The voice of the people is the voice of God'), already scrawled on walls all over London, was raised in towns and villages. Mary, fearing a Janeite plot to seize her, avoided London and fled from Hunsdon to her East Anglian estates. From Kenninghall she wrote to the Privy Council ordering her proclamation as queen. By 12 July 1553, a military force of ten thousand provided by the legitimist élites of East Anglia and the Thames Valley had gathered at Framlingham Castle. There Mary was joined by 'innumerable companies of the common people'.[4] Over the next week, the Privy Council, taken aback by the force of the uprising, defected en masse to Mary. She was proclaimed the rightful queen in London on 19 July. Like every other notable of the Janeite regime, Ridley judged it expedient to recast the opinions he had expressed so vividly a few days earlier. With Jane effectively a prisoner in the Tower, Ridley hotfooted it to Framlingham to implore Mary's pardon. But the reports of his sermon at Paul's Cross were fresh in the queen's memory. He was arrested en route and sent back to London on a lame horse. Once arrived he was committed to the Tower on a charge of treason.

We might spare a thought at this point for the enigmatic Lady Jane herself. The tendency of historians to treat her life as an adjunct to the lives of others

---

1   Quoted in Helen Castor, *She-Wolves: The Women Who Ruled England before Elizabeth* (London, 2011), 406.

2   Contemporary report; cited in R. J. Minney, *The Tower of London* (London, 1970), 156.

3   Quoted in Castor, 407.

4   Charles Wriothesley, *A Chronicle of England during the reigns of the Tudors* (London, 1875–7), ii. 87.

hardly does her justice. This was one of the most remarkable girls of the age, a Latin and Greek scholar who spoke fluent French and Italian, and some Spanish. John Aylmer,[1] her tutor, believed her cleverer than Edward VI; Roger Ascham, the humanist and English prose pioneer, admitted that her ability eclipsed that of his own charge, the princess Elizabeth. A skilled proponent of evangelical thought, she had begun to lay the foundation of a knowledge of Hebrew, Chaldaic and Aramaic, that she might more expertly direct others to what she called 'the sweet consolations and promises of the Scriptures'.[2] This fascination with early texts was, at least in part, the result of her devotion to the person and ideas of Martin Bucer. Bucer and Jane are likely to have met in 1550, in the holiday month of July, at the home of Catherine Brandon, duchess of Suffolk. Jane also corresponded with others of the Continental Reformed, notably Heinrich Bullinger. In one letter to the Swiss divine she compares reading his latest work to gathering 'as out of a most beautiful garden, the sweetest flowers'.[3] Her biographer comments that 'Despite her youth, Jane Grey really had been accepted as a recruit to the fellowship of European Reformist scholars'.[4] But it was her convictions, even more than her affiliations, that invited the wrath of Mary. She abominated the Catholic mass. One day, passing through a chapel with Anne Wharton, a Catholic favourite of Mary's, she saw a consecrated wafer over the altar. As Anne approached it, she made a curtsey. 'Why do you do so?' enquired Jane. 'Is the Lady Mary in the chapel?' Anne replied: 'No, Madam, I make my curtsey to Him that made us all'. Jane said: 'Why? How can he be there that made us all, and the baker made him?'[5] Her remarks were immediately reported to Mary.

The best candidate for a definitive likeness of Jane is an engraving by Willem de Passe and his sister Magdelena. This is the only portrait of Jane that is actually identified as being of her. It shows a flaxen- or red?- haired girl with a long oval face, slender neck and high cheekbones. The sharp discrimination and reserve within the sitter's gaze are striking. It is the face of a high-born young girl caught in the web of Tudor politics. Jane eschewed ostentation. Much to her mother's chagrin, she cast aside her fashionable

---

1   Aylmer (c.1521–94), the leading Greek scholar of his day, was later appointed bishop of London.
2   Foxe, vi. 421.
3   Quoted n Leanda de Lisle, *The Sisters Who Would Be Queen* (London, 2008), 72.
4   Eric Ives, *Jane Grey* (Malden, 2009), 67.
5   Quoted in Ives, 77.

clothes and jewellery in favour of sober, modest garments of black or white. She wrote finely-wrought poetry. Not for Jane the intrigues of court or the gaiety of hunting parties: 'Whatsoever I do else learning', she acknowledged, 'is full of grief, trouble and fear, and wholly misliking unto me'.[1] Roger Ascham, upon visiting Bradgate Park, the Grey's residence in Leicestershire, found Jane alone in her chamber, immersed in Plato's *Phaedo*. Ascham asked her why she was not out hunting with the rest of the household. 'I think', she replied, 'all their sport in the park is but a shade to the pleasure I find in Plato'.[2] Having never sought the crown, Jane was greatly relieved when it was taken from her. She looked forward to returning to her solitary pursuits, to her Bible-reading and other studies, far from the public gaze. But the actions of those closest to her, along with their fellow-travellers, ensured she would never leave the Tower.

On 12 February 1554, a frosty, misty morning, Jane Grey stood upon the scaffold on Tower Green and recited the fifty-first Psalm in English. Guildford Dudley, her hapless young husband, had been beheaded on Tower Hill earlier that day. Jane had had to resist a number of attempts to break her out of her faith. On 10 February, Mary had sent her own chaplain, John Feckenham, to try and 'reduce [Jane] from the doctrine of Christ to queen Mary's religion'.[3] Jane refused to recant, accounting her travails 'a more manifest declaration of God's favour toward me, than any He showed me at any time before'.[4] Every attempt by Feckenham to trip her up on matters of doctrine was ably and gracefully dealt with. As he took his leave, the former monk was overwhelmed by the thought 'that we two shall never again meet'. Her intellectual integrity, as much as her sweet nature, had won his respect. Jane answered evenly, not unkindly, 'that we shall never meet, except God turn your heart; for I am assured, unless you repent and turn to God, you are in an evil case'.[5]

Jane wore a simple black gown under a black furred cape and hood. Even the embroidered edge of the hood was of jet. Trying not to shiver too much in the chill air, she handed her prayer book to the deputy lieutenant of the Tower, Thomas Brydges. Along with farewell messages, she had copied out

1   Quoted in Hillerbrand, ii. 194.
2   Quoted in Ives, 51.
3   Foxe, vi. 415.
4   Ibid. 416.
5   Ibid. 417.

A time to be born, and a time to die (Ecclesiastes 3:2). In her last moments, Jane was determined to uphold the Word as the sword of the Spirit. To that end, she asked the small crowd to help her with their prayers 'while I am alive':[1] a pointed repudiation of Catholic prayers for the dead. The executioner, a giant man in a black hood, knelt down before her. He begged her forgiveness. This was freely given; Jane's only request was that he work speedily. One of Jane's ladies-in-waiting took her cape. Another blindfolded her with a white linen handkerchief. This sent Jane into a paroxysm of panic. She knelt down and began to grope around for the block: 'What shall I do?' she cried, 'Where is it, where is it?'[2] Someone, most likely Brydges, took her hands and directed them to the sides of the block. Jane quickly composed herself. She placed her head upon the block, tossing her hair forward. She stretched out her small frame. The last words of the nine-day queen were those of our Lord as recorded by Luke: 'Father, into thine hands I commend my spirit!'

The axe fell, and the earthly life of Jane Grey was ended. She was not quite seventeen years old. The letters and the effectual prayer painstakingly constructed in the Tower comprise a written legacy consistent with one who chose 'to die, and gloriously with honour reign with Christ, in whom even death is life'.[3] One historian called her 'a woman of the most rare and incomparable perfections';[4] bishop Burnet referred to a 'mind wonderfully raised above the world … the wonder of her age. She had a sweetness of temper as well as a strength of mind that charmed all who saw her'.[5] Even John Calvin, that enemy of empty rhetoric, celebrated her as 'a lady whose example is worthy of everlasting remembrance'.[6] Jane's place in the Reformed pantheon is assured. But this was a Christian girl, not a paragon, and personality is better grasped in small acts rather than grand gestures. The sixty-one-year-old lieutenant of the Tower, John Brydges, the brother of Thomas, asked Jane if she would leave him a message in her prayer book. He had grown fond of his young charge. Jane promised him she would.

---

1   Quoted in Ives, 277.
2   Foxe, vi. 424.
3   Ibid. 419.
4   John Hayward, *Life & Raigne of King Edward the Sixth* (Ohio, 1993). Quoted in Ives, 281.
5   Gilbert Burnet, *The History of the Reformation of the Church of England* (London, 1880). Quoted in Ives, 281–282.
6   Quoted in Ives, 288.

Here are the words discovered by Brydges in one of the lower margins of Jane's prayer book:

> Forasmuch as you have desired so simple a woman to write in so worthy a book (good)… therefore I shall as a friend desire you, and as a Christian require you, to call upon God to incline your heart to His laws, to quicken you in His way, and not to take the word of truth utterly out of your mouth.[1]

Nicholas Ridley was brought by boat to the Tower of London sometime in July 1553. He was followed in September by Latimer and Cranmer. As they reached the oaken wicket of Traitors' Gate, shadowed by the lofty immensity of the Tower, none would have doubted, in the words of Ridley, that they 'should have been the first to have been called to the stake'.[2] The illustrious trio remained in the Tower for nine months. Due to overcrowding, they and John Bradford were placed in the same chambers. From early morning they read the Bible. Of the four friends, it was Latimer, the oldest of the first generation of Reformers, who took longest to break free of tradition. Several times he yielded to pressure to rein in his Reformist instincts. As late as 1550 he could still be found remembering the dead in prayer. Looking back in a sermon of 1552, he declared himself to have been, up to the age of thirty, 'as obstinate a papist as any was in England'.[3]

Hugh Latimer was born in Thurcaston, Leicestershire, around 1485. The only boy in the family to survive infancy, he had several sisters, perhaps as many as six. His father, wrote Latimer, 'was a yeoman, and had no lands of his own, only he had a farm of three or four pound a year'.[4] This experience of rural poverty would inform many of his sermons. Even in the gilded period 1549–50, as Edward VI's court preacher, he didn't hesitate to declaim against the grabbing of church lands and evicting of tenant farmers. In 1506, at a conspicuously late age, Latimer entered Clare Hall, Cambridge. His 'ready, prompt and sharp wit'[5] marked him out. By 1510 he had graduated BA and been elected a fellow of the college. He completed his MA in 1514. When Henry VIII visited Cambridge in 1522, it was Latimer who bore the silver cross

---

1   Held at the British Library. Quoted in Doran, 242–243.
2   Quoted in Loane, 157.
3   *Sermons,* George Elwes Corrie (Cambridge, 1844; rep. Lewes, 1987), 334.
4   Ibid. 101.
5   Foxe, vii. 437.

of the university. The bestowal of such an honour is a strong indicator of his standing among the Catholic élite; he was a kindred spirit, one whose faith, like theirs, evinced an awed respect for the Councils of the Church. In 1517, Martin Luther had ignited the Reformation. His teaching made rapid inroads across a Scripturally-starved Europe. In Cambridge, theological conservatives under the leadership of John Fisher, bishop of Rochester, struggled to staunch the flow of Lutheran books. Was there a more exhilarating time to be a young scholar? But Latimer was not young. His opinions were settled, and prey to the putative conservativeness of middle-age. He became, in the words of Foxe, 'a very enemy of Christ's Gospel'.[1] His bitterest gibes were reserved for George Stafford. A reader in divinity loved as much for his kindliness as for his erudition, Stafford had begun to examine Scriptural material using Greek and Hebrew texts. His aim was to lay the foundation for a new era of theological understanding. But Latimer saw only pestilential Lutheranism. He began 'most spitefully railing against [Stafford], and willing the youth of Cambridge in no wise to believe him'.[2] Later in life he confessed that his bachelor of divinity degree was won on the back of an oration that 'went against Philip Melanchthon and against his opinions'.[3]

Latimer's conversion to the Reformed religion began when he was brought under the influence of Thomas Bilney. This was in the spring or summer of 1524. Despite a somewhat complicated personal theology, 'Little Bilney' would be the inspiration for many who would go on to play leading roles in the Edwardian church. A sensitive soul, and an instinctive preacher, he was able to spot, where others had not, something counterfeit in Latimer's die-hard formalism. Bilney was 'stricken with a brotherly pity towards him, and bethought by what means he might best win this zealous ignorant brother to the true knowledge of Christ'.[4] He knocked on Latimer's door. No details of their discussion have been passed down. But in those moments, or minutes, or hours, by the mighty workings of grace, Hugh Latimer, the bitter opposer of Luther, turned his back on priestcraft and embraced the practice and example of Christ. In his own words he 'began to smell the Word of God, and forsook the school doctors and such fooleries'.[5] The Scriptural mandate

---

1   Ibid.
2   Ibid.
3   Corrie, 334.
4   Foxe, vii. 438.
5   Corrie, 334–5.

to be salt and light awoke in him an overwhelming sense of moral obligation. He began to visit the sick and witness to those in prison. For the next three years his days were spent 'partly in the Latin tongue among the learned, and partly amongst the simple people in his natural and vulgar tongue'.[1] These were years of fluctuating fortune for the Bible-men, as Henry VIII weighed the threat to the established church against his own self-interest. The likes of Barnes, Bilney and Arthur were imprisoned and cited before Wolsey, the unchallenged master of the English church. In 1525/6 Latimer was prohibited from preaching in any of the university pulpits.

In July 1529 the Second Legatine Court refused to expedite the annulment of Henry VIII's marriage to Catherine of Aragon. In his Christmas sermons of that year, in the church of St Edward King and Martyr, Latimer preached regeneration by faith, by means of God's Word. The Bible was the eternal and infallible rule of His holy truth: a truth, said Latimer, graspable by every human being. This drew him into rancorous debates with 'whole swarms of friars and doctors [who] flocked against him on every side, almost through the whole university, preaching likewise and barking against him'.[2] With all of Cambridge agog, Latimer was warned by the vice-chancellor 'to touch no such things in the pulpit as had been in controversy between him and others' and 'to be circumspect and discreet in his sermons'.[3] The cloud of excommunication hung over him. It is a measure of those volatile times that a short time later, in March 1530, as a result of his support for Henry's matrimonial position, Latimer was appointed a royal chaplain and preached for the first time before the king at Windsor.

In 1531 Latimer received his first benefice at West Kington, near Chippenham in Cheshire. By 1535, when he was promoted to the bishopric of Worcester, he was regarded as England's finest preacher. His clearness of style and earnest simplicity amplified the grace of the Spirit. 'I have an ear for other preachers', said the Cambridge fellow Sir John Cheke, 'but I have a heart for Latimer'.[4] The king's brutal rejection of Anne Boleyn cast Latimer into a season of soul-searching. A friend to the Reform-minded queen, he was a witness to her self-incriminating candour. She happily allowed him to pass judgement on her girlish indiscretions. 'You do me much good', she would

---

1   Foxe, vii. 438.
2   Foxe, vii. 451.
3   Quoted in Loane, 99.
4   Ibid. 98.

whisper, 'Pray never pass over a single fault'.[1] We know from his sermons that the seizure of monastic revenues by the nobility brought him close to despair. With the notorious Act of Six Articles of 1539 he was left with no other option but to resign his see. 'At what time', writes Foxe, 'he first put off his rochet in his chamber among his friends, suddenly he gave a skip on the floor for joy, feeling his shoulder so light and being discharged as he said of such a heavy burden'.[2] For the next six years we find Latimer moving about the country, staying in the homes of his friends, being looked after by his favourite niece, and labouring in private to comprehend a fuller measure of God's truth. His unparalleled status as a preacher, however, and custom of taking 'so little ease and care of sparing himself, to do the people good'[3] ensured he would not be forgotten by friend or foe. In 1546 he returned to London to assist his old comrade Edward Crome, in hot water for speaking out against the formularies of Catholic belief. Crome recanted, not for the last time, and was pardoned after doing penance. But in Latimer the clerical party had captured a bigger fish, and decided to hang on to him. On 13 May 1546, facing the hastily worked-up charge of having 'counselled and devised with Crome',[4] Latimer was examined at Greenwich and 'at length was cast into the Tower; where he continually remained prisoner till the time that blessed king Edward entered his crown'.[5]

In the wake of Edward's coronation on 19 February 1547, it was assumed that Latimer would be restored to the bishopric of Worcester. But the ageing Reformer had had his fill of diocesan politics. In the days left to him his wish was to preach Christ's inheritance to all who 'wholly express the charity of God, tending only to the union and love of us all, to the profit and salvation of our souls'.[6] Cranmer's idea that he reside at Lambeth Palace was picked up with alacrity, and he embarked upon an arduous schedule of study and preaching. With Cranmer's vast library at his disposal, and opportunities to converse with house-guests like Bucer and Vermigli, Latimer examined afresh the ideas that had shaped his thinking. Much of his attention was concentrated on the Lord's Supper. He listened to the judgements of the Continental

---

1   Quoted in J. H. Merle d'Aubigné, *The Reformation in England* (London, rep. 1963), ii. 266.
2   Foxe, vii. 463.
3   Ibid. 46.
4   Quoted in Corrie, p. xii.
5   Foxe, vii. 463.
6   Ibid. 491.

masters 'as one who is beyond measure desirous that the whole truth may be laid open to him, and even that he may be thoroughly convinced'.[1]

Along with every other Bible-man Latimer deemed it 'an abominable presumption'[2] to believe that in conducting mass the priest offered up the sacrifice of Christ. Though never a Lutheran in the strict sense, the 1530s Latimer did embrace a Lutheran view of the Supper: namely, that the actual body and blood of Christ are conveyed with, through or under the bread and wine. In the autumn of 1548, however, we find Bartholomew Traherne reporting to Bullinger, the chief arbiter of Swiss doctrine, that Latimer, along with Cranmer, 'has come over to our opinion respecting the true doctrine of the eucharist'.[3] That opinion recast the Lord's Supper as a memorial celebration: the presence of Christ is purely symbolic. So: was Traherne right?—was Latimer a new recruit? Certainly he had broken free of Luther. But a case, a decidedly strong one, can be made for the Englishman leaning more towards Bucer and Calvin than to Zwingli and Bullinger. One sees no trace in his writing of any Swiss-sounding talk of the bread and wine commemorating, rather than presenting, an absent Christ. Latimer upholds Christ's 'spiritual kingdom', and Christ Himself as a 'spiritual judge',[4] but avers 'that in the sacrament, by spirit and grace, is the very body and blood of Christ, because that every man, be receiving bodily that bread and wine, spiritually receiveth the body and blood of Christ, and is made partaker thereby of the merits of Christ's passion'.[5] The sacrament, then, does more than testify to grace. It is an instrument for our salvation. There is, says Latimer—like Calvin, like Bucer, unlike Bullinger—'a change in the bread and wine, and such a change as no power but the omnipotency of God can make, in that that which before was bread should now have the dignity to exhibit Christ's body; and yet the bread is still bread, and the wine still wine'.[6] The Latin verb 'exhibere' had been employed by Martin Bucer since about 1536 to embrace the figurative and actual offering of Christ's body. Its adoption here by Latimer may indicate an indebtedness to the German. But compelling proof is elusive.

---

1 Letter from Bartholomew Traheron to Bullinger, quoted in Loane, 121.
2 Corrie, 275.
3 Quoted in MacCulloch, 392.
4 Corrie, 276.
5 Foxe, vii. 533.
6 Ibid.

What we do know is that Latimer was thoroughly disheartened at the sluggish course of the English Reformation. Along with John Hales, William Turner, Robert Crowley, Thomas Becon, John Hooper and others, he spoke tirelessly on the theme of the nation's moral, spiritual and material want. This affiliation of like-minded individuals—later given the title 'Men of the Commonwealth'—shared the same vision of a Christian commonwealth that inspired Bucer to write *De Regno Christi*. Unlike Bucer, however, the group stopped short of submitting ideas for the reform of church and state. According to Martin Greschat, 'They had much to say about moral decay, divine wrath, and the responsibility of the Christian, but were at a loss when it came to proposing concrete political and social measures'.[1]

By the end of the decade, age and failing health had begun to catch up with Latimer. With a heavy heart he decided, at the close of the Lenten season of 1550, to relinquish the position of court preacher. Until the reign of Mary he served the duchess of Suffolk, doyenne of the Reformed, in various capacities. He preached a famous series of sermons at Grimsthorpe Castle. He revelled afresh in his pastoral labours. Otherwise, his days were spent at Baxterley, the Warwickshire home of Robert and Mary Glover. Robert's elder brother, John Glover, whose self-denying faith was an inspiration to West Country evangelicals, also lived nearby. In this period, surrounded by those whose aim was exalt, honour and live out the truth of Scripture, Latimer seems to have slipped into the role of evangelical éminence grise. As such, writes Foxe, he 'admonished such as then were in authority of their duty, and assisted them with his godly counsel'.[2] In 1553 Latimer, unlike Ridley, refused to support efforts to have the succession vested in Lady Jane Grey. But his reputation as the magnetic north of moral truth, and unrivalled ability, as Loane puts it, 'to arouse the conscience of England',[3] made his arrest and persecution under Mary an inevitability.

On her entry into London on 3 August 1553, Mary's first act was to release the cleric-politician Stephen Gardiner from the Tower. A deeply unabided figure, even by many on his own side, Gardiner had been deprived of the bishopric of Winchester for opposing ecclesiastical and civil reform. The duchess of Suffolk reflected the general view when she commented: 'It

---

1 *Martin Bucer: A Reformer & His Times* (Louisville, 2004), 231.
2 Foxe, vii. 463.
3 Loane, 118.

was merry with the lambs when the wolf was shut up'.[1] A prolific writer of papal theology, promoter of the Act of Six Articles, favourite of Henry VIII and vanquisher of Thomas Cromwell: only Gardiner was capable, felt Mary, of championing her cause and rallying the English church around the miracle of the mass. She appointed him lord chancellor. On 4 September 1553 a summons from the Privy Council, now controlled by Gardiner, was delivered to Latimer by hand. He assured the herald that 'you be a welcome messenger to me: and be it known unto you and all the world that I go as willingly to London at this present, being called by my Prince to render a reckoning of my doctrine, as ever I was at any place in the world'.[2] That 'reckoning' would be not be heard until Latimer, along with Ridley and Cranmer, was removed from the Tower in March 1554 and taken to the Bocardo ('a filthy and stinking prison'), by the north gate of Oxford. Between 14 and 20 April, first in the university church, then in the divinity school, the Reformers debated the doctrine of transubstantiation and the sacrifice of the mass with a group of hand-picked theologians from the universities. The part-trial, part-disputation was rigged from the start. 'The school of divines', writes Peter Ackroyd, 'resembled a beargarden'.[3] Ridley himself maintained he 'never in all my life saw or heard anything done or handled more vainly or tumultuously':

> And surely I could never have thought that it had been possible to have found any within this realm, being of any knowledge, learning and ancient degree of school, so brazen-faced and so shameless as to behave themselves so vainly and so like stage-players as they did in that disputation.[4]

There was no doubt about the outcome of this state-directed travesty; Gardiner had stated in advance that 'he would have the axe laid at the root of the tree: the bishops and most powerful preachers ought certainly to die'.[5] On the final day the three Reformers were hauled before an assembly of divines at St Mary the Virgin church to be formally condemned. Cranmer first, then Ridley, finally Latimer, were asked whether 'they would turn or

1   Quoted in Anthony Martienssen, *Queen Katherine Parr* (New York, 1973).
2   Foxe, vii. 464.
3   *The History of England* (London, 2012), ii. 263.
4   Quoted in Loane, 163.
5   Quoted in Ryle, *Five English Reformers* (Edinburgh, rep. 1999), 103.

no'.[1] Each stood fast in the Gospel way. Latimer thanked God 'most heartily that He hath prolonged my life to this end that I may in this case glorify God by that kind of death'. Ridley avouched that 'Although I be not of your company, yet doubt I not but my name is written in another place, whither this sentence will send us sooner than we should by the course of nature have come'.[2] The following morning they were forced to witness the parade of the sacrament through the streets of Oxford. Latimer, brought from the house of a local bailiff, imagined he was being taken to the stake. His heart bursting to honour Christ, he badgered one of his captors to 'make a quick fire'. But at the first sight of the sacrament, records Foxe, 'he ran as fast as his old bones would carry him, to one Spenser's shop, and would not look towards it'.[3]

The length of time the three men remained in custody in Oxford after their condemnation—eighteen months in the case of Latimer and Ridley—is explained, at least in part, by the obligation placed upon Parliament to re-enact the statutes for burning heretics repealed at the peak of reform under Edward. The fact that Cranmer had been consecrated before the break with Rome was another complicating factor. But for Ridley and Latimer there was no room for dejection. The former was secured in the house of an alderman called Edmund Irish. Mrs Irish, an inveterate lover of ritual, was described by Ridley, with characteristic insight, as 'a little old lady, peevish and very superstitious, who prides herself on being reported to guard me closely, and with the utmost care'. If nothing else, Ridley's proximity to Mr and Mrs Irish confirmed him in the single state. 'I seem to see', he reflected, 'in some measure how great a calamity and how intolerable a yoke it is to be married to an evil wife'.[4] Despite the close attentions of Mrs Irish, Ridley managed to improvise writing instruments (for example, a piece of lead from a window), gather together bits and pieces of paper (including toilet paper), and smuggle out the letters and theological tracts that 'portray him as one of the most noble saints and servants of our English story'.[5] If Latimer was a little less productive, it was because the years of confinement had all but ruined his health.

---

1 Foxe, vii. 534.
2 Ibid.
3 Ibid.
4 Quoted in Moule, 54.
5 Loane, 167.

In the late summer of 1555, Reginald Pole—cardinal and papal *legate a latere*—sent three episcopal commissioners—the bishops of Lincoln, Bristol and Gloucester—to Oxford to officiate at a new trial. On 30 September Latimer and Ridley were brought to the divinity school. Ridley, who was to be examined first, recognized the authority of the court by removing his cap. He replaced it when Pole's name was mentioned. The bishop of Lincoln, grimly lauding the cardinal as 'a man worthy to be reverenced with all humility', demanded that Ridley uncover his head 'at the nomination, as well of the said cardinal, as of the pope's holiness'. But Ridley refused to play the hypocrite. He would give 'no obeisance or honour' to any lackey of the pope, 'whose usurped supremacy, and abused authority, I utterly refuse and renounce'.[1] After two more appeals to doff his cap were ignored, one of the beadles—officers of the court—was told to forcibly remove it. As the atmosphere grew ever more febrile, Ridley was charged with being 'a setter-forth of that devilish and seditious doctrine which in these latter days was preached among us'.[2] He was reminded that 'you were once one of us':[3] that he had praised the pope's holiness and expounded with great skill the doctrine of transubstantiation. Ridley did not deny any of this. He agreed that 'I was once of the same religion which you are of. The truth is, I cannot but confess the same. Yet so was Paul a persecutor of Christ'.[4] In the afternoon it was Latimer's turn. Due to his worsening condition—hardly helped by 'gazing upon the cold walls'[5] all morning—he was allowed to sit down. He was urged by Lincoln 'to consider your estate; remember you are a learned man; you have taken degrees in the school, borne the office of a bishop; remember you are an old man'.[6] Latimer's reply bore the fleeting echo of satire: 'Lo', he murmured, 'you look for learning at my hands, which have gone so long to the school of Oblivion, making the bare walls my library; keeping me so long in prison, without book, or pen and ink'.[7] No less an observer than Ryle deemed Latimer's conduct in adversity 'wiser

1   Foxe, vii. 519.
2   Ibid. 520.
3   Ibid.
4   Ibid. 522.
5   Ibid. 529.
6   Ibid. 530.
7   Ibid. 532.

and better than that of the other martyrs'.[1] Such comparisons are invidious. But we do get a firm sense of the heavenly life being uppermost in Latimer's mind; of his closer relation to love. Unlike Ridley, he fought shy of lengthy exchanges. He had outgrown his accusers' arguments. But when articles relating to transubstantiation were raised he affirmed with plainness and authority that in the Lord's Supper the visible elements retain the substance of bread and wine. 'Christ', he concluded, in his reply to the third article, 'made one perfect sacrifice for the whole world, neither can any man offer him again, neither can the priest offer up Christ again for the sins of man, which He took away by offering Himself once for all upon the Cross; neither is there any propitiation for our sins, except His Cross only'.[2]

The following day a restive crowd squeezed itself into the church of St Mary the Virgin 'to see the end of these two persons'.[3] The bishops sat in thrones trimmed with silk. Below them, at a framed table 'a good space from the bishops' feet',[4] Ridley drew a sheaf of papers from the folds of his cloak and began to read. This was a detailed setting forth of his rejection of the customs and claims of papal hierarchy. The papers were snatched from his fingers, inspected and pronounced evil and blasphemous. He was granted forty words to defend his sacramental theology *extempore*; the crowd, egged on by Lincoln, counted to forty and Ridley was silenced. Afterward Lincoln rose to pronounce the formal condemnation. Ridley was told 'he did affirm, maintain and stubbornly defend certain opinions and assertions contrary to the Word of God'. He was declared heretic and given over to the mercy of the secular power. He was also excommunicated 'by great excommunication'.[5] Latimer, leaning on a staff, spectacles hanging from a cord at his breast, was next in line. He had to fight his way through a crush at the entrance, being jolted and pressed in from all sides. When he reached the bishops he begged them to 'set a better order at your entrance: for I am an old man, and have a very evil back, so that the press of the multitude does me much harm'.[6] Lincoln apologized, and with real emotion urged

1   Ryle, 103.
2   Foxe, vii. 533.
3   Ibid. 434.
4   Ibid.
5   Ibid. 540.
6   Ibid.

Latimer to 'recant, revoke your errors and turn to the Catholic church'.[1]
Latimer dealt first with terminology. There was indeed a catholic church
to which he would happily submit: but 'not the church which you call
Catholic, which sooner might be termed diabolic'.[2] Lincoln, stoney-faced,
retreated behind his Articles of Inquiry. The rest of Latimer's replies were
brief and unfussy, and consistent with his previous testimony. 'Christ made
one oblation and sacrifice for the sins of the whole world', he insisted, 'and
that a perfect sacrifice. Neither needeth there to be any other, neither can
there be any other, propitiatory sacrifice'.[3]

They had reached the end of the road. Latimer was convicted of heresy
as a matter of course and told by the bishop 'that now he could not hear
him, neither ought to talk with him'. An agitated silence was broken by the
darkest of utterances: 'Now he is your prisoner, master mayor'.[4]

In a two-week hiatus between his condemnation and execution, Ridley
penned his immortal 'Farewells': to Tyneside, to his parishes and sees, to
the nation; most touchingly of all to Cambridge, his 'loving mother and
tender nurse'. He wrote of fellowship, of long walks reading the epistles of
Paul, of kindnesses shown, honours received, and of his affection for the
'right worshipful college' of Pembroke: 'and I pray God', he wrote, 'that
His laws, and the sincere Gospel of Christ, may ever be truly taught and
faithfully learned in thee'.[5] But reminiscence isn't allowed to predominate.
The Catholic bishops are warned to 'repent, if ye will be happy, and love
your own souls' health: repent, I say, or else without all doubt, ye shall never
escape the hands of the living Lord, for the guilt of your perjury, and breach
of your oath'.[6] In a muscular dissection of sin and its dominion, Ridley
begs his readers choose 'rather in respect of that which is to come, with
the chosen members of Christ, to bear Christ's Cross, than for this short
lifetime to enjoy all the riches, honours and pleasures of the broad world.
Why should we Christians fear death? Can death deprive us of Christ, who

---

1 Ibid.
2 Ibid. 541.
3 Ibid.
4 Ibid. 542.
5 Ibid. 557.
6 Ibid. 563.

is all our comfort, our joy, and our life?'[1] The series of short farewells with which Ridley ends his testimony is both a hymn of praise and a call to arms:

Farewell. Christ's dearly beloved spouse here wandering in this world, as in a strange land, far from thine own country, and compassed about on every hand with deadly enemies, which cease not to assault thee, ever seeking thy destruction!

Farewell, farewell, O ye the whole and universal congregation of the chosen of God, here living upon earth, the true church militant of Christ, the true mystical body, the very household and family of God, and the sacred temple of the Holy Ghost, farewell!

Farewell, O thou little flock of the high heavenly pastors of Christ; for to thee it hath pleased the Heavenly Father to give an everlasting and eternal kingdom. Farewell!

Farewell, thou spiritual house of God, thou holy and royal priesthood, thou chosen generation, thou holy nation, thou won spouse. Farewell! Farewell![2]

Early in the morning of 15 October, a delegation led by James Brooks, bishop of Gloucester, descended upon the home of alderman Irish. Ridley was asked again to 'recant this your fantastical and devilish opinion'. His refusal was met by Gloucester's declaration that 'we take you for no bishop, and therefore we will the sooner have done with you'.[3] This was the signal for Ridley's degradation, wherein the outward symbols of his clerical status were to be stripped from him. For a Tudor degradation to work—to fulfil its purpose, not to be ridiculous—a modicum of cooperation was required from the degradee. At the very least, he had to allow himself to be dressed. Ridley offered no cooperation whatsoever. 'Put off your cap, master Ridley', ordered Gloucester, 'and put upon you this surplice'. Ridley ignored the surplice. 'Not I, truly', he said. 'But you must', said Gloucester. 'I will not',[4] said Ridley, and 'did earnestly inveigh against the Romish bishop and all

---

1   Ibid. 566.
2   Ibid. 567.
3   Ibid. 543.
4   Ibid.

that foolish apparel'.[1] Master Edridge, an attendant, called out: 'he should be gagged: therefore let him be gagged!' With Ridley immovable, and Gloucester splenetic, the messiest degradation on record lurched to a close. Only then was a poignant note struck. Ridley begged for his dependents, now homeless and in penury, to be granted some measure of charity by the queen. As his sister's name left his lips he began to sob. 'This is nature that moveth me', he said, 'but I have now done'.[2]

On his last evening Ridley washed his beard. He ate a supper of mutton and pork, cheese and pears. As they rose from the table, George Shipside, his brother-in-law, offered to stay with him; Ridley, he assumed, would struggle to sleep. He might prefer to sit up and talk of great matters. But Ridley was having none of it. 'No, no, that you shall not', he told Shipside. 'For I mind (God willing) to go to bed, and to sleep as quietly tonight, as ever I did in my life'.[3] As for Latimer, there is no reason to suppose that on his last night on earth he would have set aside his custom of reading his Bible until two o'clock in the morning. 'The wise men of the world', he wrote in an undated letter, 'can find shifts to avoid the Cross … but the simple servant of Christ doth look for no other but oppression in the world. And then is there the most glory, when they be under the Cross of their Master Christ'.[4]

A stake was erected 'in the ditch over against Balliol-college',[5] outside the northern wall of the city. Ridley, flanked by the alderman and the mayor, wore an expensive furred gown and slippers, with a velvet tippet and night-cap. No formless terrors had haunted his sleep; he looked every inch the master of Pembroke. Far behind him trailed Latimer, a cap buttoned under his chin, a threadbare frock hanging from his frame, apostolic simplicity made manifest. Ridley turned and called out affably: 'Oh, be ye there?' Latimer paused, and raised his eyes. 'Yes', he cried out, 'as fast as I can follow'.[6] Once arrived at the stake Ridley clasped his hands together and gazed heavenward, before greeting Latimer with an embrace and a kiss. 'Be of good heart, brother', he said, 'for God will either assuage the fury of the flame, or else will strengthen us to abide it'. Kneeling side by side, they prayed. After preaching a sermon

---

1 Ibid.
2 Ibid.
3 Ibid.
4 Quoted in R. Tudur Jones, *The Great Reformation* (Bridgend rep. 1997), 162.
5 Foxe, vii. 547.
6 Ibid. 548.

brimming with hatred, Richard Smith, a local clergyman, called on the crowd to beware the Bible-men: 'for they were heretics, and died out of the church'. These were not martyrs, he said, but suicides: as Judas was, as 'the woman in Oxford that of late hanged herself'[1] had been. Ridley tried to respond, to combat the design of idolatrous minds, but was manhandled into silence. If he abjured, he would be heard. 'Not otherwise?' asked Ridley. 'Well, so long as the breath is in my body, I will never deny my Lord Christ and His known truth; God's will be done in me'. He was perfectly composed. 'Well then', he cried, with an air of finality, 'I commit our cause to Almighty God which shall indifferently judge all'.[2]

Amidst roars of talk and restless silence, Ridley began to disrobe. His outer clothing was given to onlookers; 'happy was he', records Foxe, 'that might get any rag of him'.[3] He also handed out a few mementoes, including a silver coin and some nutmegs. As Latimer undressed to his shirt, Ridley reached a hand to the sky. He knew with an all-embracing certainty what lay ahead. But he did not forget the ruin he was leaving behind. He implored the Lord Jesus Christ to 'take mercy unto this realm of England, and deliver the same from all her enemies'.[4] It was his last gift. Only the mechanics of judicial murder remained. A blacksmith was called to chain the two men together, back to back. Pouches of gunpowder were laced around their necks. When the faggots were lit, Latimer turned to Ridley and spoke those words that reverberate still in the hearts of Christian men and women, as fresh and inspiring as on the day they were minted: 'Be of good comfort, Master Ridley, and play the man. We shall this day light such a candle, by God's grace, in England, as I trust shall never be put out'.[5] His release came quickly. As the blaze wrapped itself around him, Latimer held out his hands as if to wash them. The words 'O Father of heaven, receive my soul' fell from his lips, and this most eloquent herald of the glory of God passed into His heavenly kingdom 'with very little pain or none'.[6]

The same could not be said of Ridley. The fire was ill-made; the oaken faggots were mossy and so tightly packed on Ridley's side that the whirl of

---

1   Ibid.
2   Ibid. 549.
3   Ibid.
4   Ibid. 550.
5   Ibid.
6   Ibid.

flame only covered his feet and legs. His agonized cry of 'I cannot burn!' caused his brother-in-law to panic. As smoke billowed all around, Shipside thickened the pile until Ridley was virtually up to his neck in green wood. This had the effect of further suffocating the fire. To the horror of onlookers—including Cranmer, watching from the roof of the Bocardo—the Reformer's legs were burned off, leaving the rest of him untouched. 'For God's sake', he shrieked, 'let the fire come to me! I cannot burn! Lord have mercy on me!'[1] One of the soldiers, more clear-headed than the rest, tore away some of the wood, allowing the flames to shoot through. Somehow, in a physical effort quite unfathomable outside the grace of God, Ridley managed to arch his torso forward. The gunpowder around his neck ignited. The struggles of this holy and mortified man then ceased, and he dropped over the chains at Latimer's feet.

> But the precious blood shed by martyrs
> That it might be as a testimony rendered to its God
> Will in the church of God serve as seed
> From which children will come forth, filled with understanding.[2]

---

1 Ibid. 551.

2 John Calvin, *Song of Victory* (1541); composed in Latin, translated from the French. See J. Graham Miller, *Calvin's Wisdom* (Edinburgh, 1992), 241.

XI

THOMAS CRANMER

On 1 October 1553, surrounded by the Catholic nobility, Mary Tudor was crowned at Westminster Abbey. To mark the return to Roman Obedience the new queen was anointed with specially consecrated oil sent from abroad. Her accession was lauded all across Catholic Europe; Mary herself saw it as part of a sacred dispensation. Her first Parliament assembled on 5 October. Five weeks later Thomas Cranmer was convicted of treason. He wasn't pardoned, but was allowed to live so that his opinions might be tested at Oxford in April 1554. In the autumn of 1555 he was tried for heresy; Henry Machyn, a citizen and merchant-tailor of London, reported that a comet 'did shoot out fire, to great wonder and marvel to the people, and continued certain nights'.[1] His trial provided the formal evidence for a condemnation by Rome in December 1555. On 21 March 1556 Cranmer was martyred in Oxford. His passivity and patience, personal contradictions and 'dignified presence, adorned with a semblance of goodness'[2] had directed the whole course of the Reformation in England.

Cranmer was born in 1489. The second son of a Nottinghamshire gentry family, he excelled at grammar school, being subject to 'a marvellous severe and cruel schoolmaster'.[3] In 1503 he was admitted to Jesus College, Cambridge. A diligent rather than especially talented scholar, Cranmer, cast among the finest minds of his generation, began to tread water. No less than eight years would pass before he graduated BA. Four years later, in 1515, he gained his MA; around the same time he fell in love with Joan, the niece of the mistress

---

1 Machyn online 1556, quoted in Susan Doran, *The Tudor Chronicles 1485–1603* (London, 2008), 250.

2 A. F. Pollard, *Henry VIII* (New Edition, 1934), 20. Quoted in Marcus Loane, *Masters of the English Reformation* (London, rep. 1956), 218.

3 *Narratives of the Days of the Reformation,* ed. J. G. Nichols (London, 1854), 218.

of the Dolphin Inn, where the *collegii pueri* (college boys) routinely gathered. By marrying Joan, Cranmer automatically relinquished a fellowship. He also lost his residence, and was forced to accept a position as a 'common reader' at Buckingham: the Benedictine university college later re-founded as Magdalene. Cranmer's young wife died in childbirth. Nor did the child survive. Cranmer regained the Jesus fellowship and by 1520 had been ordained priest. It is a tantalizing thought that had Joan or her offspring lived, holy orders could not have been conferred on Thomas. With no ordination—and no archbishopric—a Cranmer-less Reformation might have produced a markedly different Church of England.

The next decade saw Cranmer pursuing his academic interests while sheltering from winds of change. Around midday on October 31, 1517, Martin Luther had pinned his ninety-five theses to the north door of the castle church in Wittenberg. 'My conscience', he declared at Worms in 1521, 'is captive to the Word of God'. All over western Europe nascent reform movements were emerging. If some failed to understand or appropriate every aspect of Luther's doctrine, all were at one on the primacy of *Schriftprinzip*: the text of Holy Writ. In Cambridge, minds more receptive than Cranmer's, drawn in by Erasmus' Graeco-Latin New Testament, had rejected the idea of merit acquired by good works. Personal actions, in other words, however strenuous, virtuous or good, were of no avail without faith. Men of brilliance such as Thomas Bilney and Robert Barnes were embarked upon a purer method of theological enquiry. As such, both were attendees, along with Lambert, Parker, Coverdale and others, of reformist gatherings at the White Horse Inn. Cranmer, meanwhile, his conservative instincts well to the fore, applauded the backlash to criticisms of popes and councils. In the marginalia of his copy of John Fisher's refutation of Luther, *Assertionis Lutheranae Confutatio*, he condemns in black ink 'the arrogance of a most wicked man'.[1]

In the summer of 1529, due to an outbreak of plague, Cranmer was forced to flee Cambridge. He took lodgings in Waltham and mulled over the possibility of tutoring the sons of a female relation.[2] He was still there when Henry VIII came to visit Waltham Abbey. The king was accompanied by Stephen Gardiner, master of Trinity Hall, presently acting as the king's secretary, and by Edward Foxe, provost of King's College. Both lodged with

---

1   Quoted in Diarmaid MacCulloch, *Thomas Cranmer* (New Haven, 1996), 27.
2   A relation married into the Cressy family.

Cranmer. Over supper on 2 August 1529 the three dons fell into a lengthy discussion of the king's 'Great Matter': the Royal Divorce: Henry's scheme to rid himself of Catherine of Aragon and marry Anne Boleyn. The king had married Catherine, his brother's widow, by papal dispensation in 1509. By October 1528 he was insisting that his marriage was unlawful and that 'an angel descending from heaven would be unable to convince him otherwise'. When appealed to by his guests for an opinion on how to take the matter forward, Cranmer, by guttering candlelight, argued that canon law was a cul-de-sac. 'There is but one truth in it', he said, 'which the Scripture will soon declare, make open and manifest, being by learned men well handled, and that may be as well done in England in the universities here, as at Rome or elsewhere in any foreign nation'.[1] The king should bypass the pope and go directly to the professors of theology: 'whose sentence may be soon known and brought so to pass with little industry and charges ... And then his majesty in conscience quieted may determine with himself that which shall seem good before God, and let these tumultuary processes give place unto a certain truth'.[2] Had he foreseen the far-reaching effects of his words, might Cranmer have held his tongue? Gardiner and Foxe had assumed the issue could only be resolved in Rome. Their evening with Thomas Cranmer had thrown up an intriguing alternative.

Events were now hectically telescoped, and did not fall in a manner at all agreeable to Cranmer. Gardiner and Foxe reported his remarks to Henry, who demanded that Cranmer be brought to him. 'If I had known this device but two years ago', said the reliably boorish monarch, 'it would have saved me a great deal of money, and rid me of much disquiet'.[3] Cranmer had already left Waltham for Cambridge, afterwards travelling to Nottingham. The king's dispatch eventually caught up with him in London. Cranmer felt ambushed, and horribly exposed. He complained bitterly to Gardiner and Foxe about what he saw as a betrayal of confidence. He desired only to resume his studies in Cambridge, and implored Gardiner to free him from the web of the 'king's question'.[4] It was a vain hope. Within days he was delivered to the king and told he had 'the right scope of this matter'.[5] The poet Thomas Gray

1 John Foxe, *Acts & Monuments* (1839), viii. 7.
2 Quoted in Eric Ives, *The Life and Death of Anne Boleyn* (Malden, 2004), 132.
3 Foxe, viii. 7.
4 Ibid. 9.
5 Ibid. 8.

wrote that Henry saw the light of the Gospel dawn first in the eyes of Anne Boleyn. A less whimsical soul has observed that 'whatever light Henry saw in those eyes we may be sure had little to do with the gospel'.[1] But whatever his motives, Henry would brook no challenge to his right, as he saw it, to do whatever he wished. Cranmer, in an unguarded moment, had furnished him with a means of satisfying those wishes. 'I charge and command you', said Henry, 'all your other business and affairs set apart, to take some pains to see this my cause to be furthered according to your device, as much as it may lie in you, so that I may shortly understand whereunto I may trust'.[2] Cranmer had painted himself into a corner. He was instructed to lodge with the earl of Wiltshire, the father of Anne Boleyn, until the task of committing his thoughts to paper was completed.

Cranmer's case for the annulment of Henry's marriage, carefully ordered and transcribed, was used by Gardiner and Edward Foxe to gather opinions favourable to the king in Oxford and Cambridge. The majority of university divines fell into line; Henry's marriage, they concluded, having violated certain injunctions in Scripture,[3] was invalid. This was in February and March 1530, by which time Cranmer had joined an embassy to Charles V at Bologna. He stayed in Rome until September, eliciting favourable views on the annulment from within Italy. Upon his return to England in October, he collated the *Censurae academiarum (Determinations of the universities)*, the purpose of which was to present historical and theological evidence for Henry's right, as he saw it, to exercise supreme jurisdiction, spiritual as well as civil, within the realm. By January 1532 Cranmer had been appointed a royal chaplain. Before the end of the month he was back on the Continent, travelling through the Low Countries, following Charles V along the Rhine to Worms and Speyer before decamping at Nuremberg. During his stay he met several of the Lutheran leaders; he also married Margaret, his second wife, the niece of Andreas Osiander. It cannot be considered immaterial that Osiander was the only important Lutheran to endorse the theological basis of Henry's annulment. Even William Tyndale had declared himself opposed to the divorce.

If Cranmer's rejection of his vow of celibacy was a Reformist act, it was

---

1   William Eddison, *Epping Forest: Literary & Historical Associations* (London, 1946), 11.

2   Foxe, viii. 8.

3   Leviticus 18:16; 20:21. These verses, it was claimed, prohibited sexual congress between a man and his brother's wife.

still one he desired to keep under wraps. In England Margaret enjoyed 'so low a profile as to be invisible'.[1] Such triangulations proved sadly typical of Cranmer. A joke told in ecclesiastical circles had Thomas transporting Mrs Cranmer around in a wooden box drilled with breathing holes. It's not a bad joke. But the marriage does provide evidence of a shifting theological stance we can trace back to 1531 and Cranmer's contact with Martin Bucer of Strasbourg and Simon Grynaeus.[2]

Cranmer returned to England upon the death of William Warham, the archbishop of Canterbury since 1503. A former lord chancellor, Warham had passively dissented over the annulment and had opposed any extension of Henry's authority. Warham it was who contrived the limiting clause 'as far as the law of Christ allows' in the clergy's otherwise complete caving in to the principle of royal supremacy. His death on 22 August 1532 is thought to have removed an important obstacle to Henry's breach with Rome. On 25 January 1533, without telling Cranmer—his archbishop-in-waiting—Henry married Anne Boleyn in a private ceremony. His pursuit of Anne had begun in 1526: yet the grounds for believing that Anne remained a virgin until the autumn or winter of 1532 are strong. Shortly after the marriage a bill of appeals declared that the authority of any foreign court would no longer be recognized in England. Cranmer, by all accounts reluctantly, was provided to the see of Canterbury on 21 February. He was consecrated the following month. On 5 April, Henry's marriage to Catherine was declared invalid by Convocation. On Easter Saturday Anne was proclaimed queen at Greenwich. All that remained was the formality of an ecclesiastical court. On 23 May, at a priory in Dunstable, at the end of a turgid two-week process, Cranmer pronounced the marriage to Catherine void. On the 31st, almost six months pregnant, resplendent in white, her dark hair falling loosely, Anne Boleyn processed through a silent, resentful crowd from the Tower of London to Whitehall Palace. The following morning, Whit Sunday, she was crowned at Westminster Abbey.

Cranmer was in thrall to the magic of monarchy. In private he might yearn for a return to pure, apostolic Christianity; in public he submitted his conscience to the king's every impulse, no matter how tyrannical or

---

1 MacCulloch, 250.

2 Grynaeus (1493–1541) became the leader of the Reformed church in Basel after the death of Johannes Oecolampadius in 1531.

WHITHER GOD BRINGS US

base. Henry, says one commentator, 'played with his timorous archbishop, like a big cat with a mouse'.[1] His behaviour in respect of Anne Boleyn was especially abject. In April 1536, with Anne recovering from a miscarriage, Henry had his mistress, Jane Seymour, lodged in rooms in Greenwich. The next month Anne was arrested on a charge of incest with her brother George. Four other men were accused of illicit sexual behaviour with the queen, behaviour then associated with witchcraft. None of the dates of her supposed assignations chimed with the record of her actual whereabouts. Anne and George were tried on 15 May 1536. At the Tower of London, in the King's Hall, in front of 2,000 people, the queen gave 'wise discreet answers to all things laid against her'.[2] It counted for naught. Once the evidences have been weighed, the truth of Anne's fall, for serious historians, is uniform and staggeringly clear. She 'could simply not have behaved as alleged'.[3] The king's men 'contrived or connived at cold-blooded murder'.[4] Yet the fiction of Anne's promiscuity endures, especially among novelists. They find it modern and exciting; a welcome diversion from the complex of factions and statecraft at the royal court. And a woman of faith, 'a zealous defender of Christ's Gospel',[5] viewed through a 21st century prism, seems more distant, less knowable—less, ultimately, deserving of respect—than a sexually incontinent arriviste, clawing her way through the tissues of Tudor politics.

It must be born in mind that Anne Boleyn was not only Cranmer's great friend, but a benefactress of the Reformed generally. This was a clever young woman. Her knowledge of the art of the Renaissance—of architecture and painting, of costume and fabric, of illuminated manuscripts, of music and dance—was far in advance of her contemporaries. But her deepest reading was in theology. Educated at Malines and Paris, she was an avid collector of French Reformist texts. 'The absolute conviction which drove Anne', claims her best biographer, 'was the importance of the Bible'.[6] After she became

---

1 David Starkey, *Six Wives* (London, rep. 2004), 724.

2 Charles Wriothesley, *A Chronicle of England during the Reigns of the Tudors*, ed. W. D. Hamilton (London, 1875–77), i. 37. See also Doran, 168–169.

3 Eric Ives, *The Life and Death of Anne Boleyn* (Malden, 2004), 348.

4 Ives, 'Faction at the Court of Henry VIII: The Fall of Anne Boleyn', *The Journal of the Historical Association*, LVII (June 1972), 190.

5 John Foxe, quoted in Ives, 260.

6 Ives, 268.

queen she encouraged the trade in Bibles between England and the Low Countries. In her rooms a vernacular Bible was kept open on a lectern, for anyone—man or woman—to read. Having asked for a copy of Tyndale's *The Obedience of a Christian Man*, she passed it on to Henry, marking passages for him to read. She also gave him a pamphlet that referred to priests as 'ravenous wolves'.[1] Henry 'kept the booke in his bosom 3 or 4 dayes'.[2] Those she helped through royal patronage included William Barlow, Edward Crome, Matthew Parker and Nicholas Shaxton. Her evangelical allegiance, according to Eric Ives, 'laid the foundation blocks of Protestant England'.[3] But after her arrest Cranmer didn't lift a finger to save her. At Lambeth Palace on 17 May he declared Anne's marriage to Henry void. No reasons were offered. Diarmaid MacCulloch describes this judgement as 'a stain on Cranmer's reputation, the unacceptable face of his loyalty to the Supreme Head'.[4] The night before her execution Cranmer heard Anne's confession. Her whole body trembling, but with the utmost conviction, she restated her innocence before God.

At eight o'clock on 19 May, a fine, bright morning, Anne Boleyn, queen of England for a thousand days—'a thousand days of support for Reform from the throne itself'[5]—climbed the steps of her scaffold clutching a small prayer book. After absolving the king of any blame for her death, she knelt down and said: 'To Jesus Christ I commend my soul'.[6] A bandage was placed over her eyes. A skilled executioner, brought over at Henry's expense from Calais, slipped off his shoes and reached under some straw for his sword. A single stroke severed Anne's head from her body. Meanwhile, a tearful Thomas Cranmer paced the gardens of Lambeth Palace. A Scottish visitor was told by the distraught archbishop that 'she who has been the queen of England on earth will today become a queen in heaven'.[7] MacCulloch witheringly concludes that 'he had much to cry about: both for his own soiled integrity,

---

1 *A Supplication for the Beggars* by Simon Fish.
2 Quoted in Peter Ackroyd, *The Life of Thomas More* (London, rep. 1998), 277.
3 Ives, p. xv.
4 MacCulloch, 158.
5 Ives, 260–261.
6 Quoted in Doran, 169.
7 Quoted in MacCulloch, 159.

and for the uncertain future of the evangelical cause'.[1] The next morning Henry was secretly betrothed to Jane Seymour.

In 1539 a dry-eyed Cranmer raised no public objection to the passage of the Act of Six Articles—the 'whip with six strings'—which defined as heresy the Reformers' core beliefs, and effectively brought the Henrician part of the English Reformation to an end. The revilers of the Bible-men were back in the driving seat. Under the civil leadership of Thomas Howard, duke of Norfolk, and submitting to the theological bias of Stephen Gardiner, they sought an immediate return to the formularies of Catholic belief. Cranmer proved eminently steerable. He was 'an almost powerless puppet', writes MacCulloch, 'swept along in events beyond his control and directly contrary to his hopes and plans'.[2] The conservatives exploited the king's suspicion of religious radicalism; the installation of national Catholicism appealed as much to his orthodoxy as to his self-regard. At the same time Henry was desperate to appease the Catholic princes of Europe and banish from their minds any thought of an invasion of England: a distinct possibility in 1538/9. All of this played into the hands of those who determined the final shape of the Six Articles. A heretic's death was decreed for all who denied transubstantiation. Auricular confession was restored, along with vows of chastity, private masses and clerical celibacy. The reactions of Hugh Latimer, bishop of Worcester, and Cranmer to this sudden reverse are instructive. Latimer resigned his see and accepted the consequences. The married archbishop kept silent and arranged to have his invisible wife sent abroad.

Already, in the autumn of 1538, Cranmer had conducted the show-trial of the Reformer John Lambert (q.v.), charged with denying Christ's corporeal presence in the bread and wine of the mass. Lambert was burned at the stake in Smithfield on 22 November. With Lambert's 'burning and blood', writes Foxe, '[Cranmer's] hands had been before anything polluted'.[3]

Until Henry's death in January 1547, Cranmer clung to the authority of the crown, confounded attempts by Gardiner to smear his reputation[4] and survived all the infighting that marked the reign's inglorious conclusion. His opportunity—the greatest ever afforded an English churchman—to establish

---

1   MacCulloch, 159.

2   Ibid. 237.

3   Foxe, viii. 90.

4   As bishop of Winchester, Gardiner attempted to fasten a charge of heresy on Cranmer for contravening the Six Articles.

the true pattern and perfect rule of the Word of God arrived under the minority[1] of Henry's long-awaited male heir, Edward VI. The reign of 'the young Josiah' embraced moral regeneration, significant amounts of liturgical reform, the relief of poverty and disease and the provision of schools. He was the best educated monarch England has ever had. He spoke four languages. He was an accomplished musician. John Cheke and Roger Ascham taught him the liberal sciences and moral philosophy; his theological training was entrusted first to Richard Coxe and Nicholas Ridley, later to Martin Bucer. By 1551 he had already begun to formulate aspects of royal policy. His hand was on the tiller of rule.

A kind of divine confluence, comprising the death of Henry, the accession of Edward, the flowering of true doctrine and the arrival upon our shores of such notable figures as Bucer, Fagius and Vermigli, had instilled in the minds of many the idea of reshaping England as a Reformed Utopia. It was an idea that died aborning. In his dotage, Richard Cox,[2] Edward's earliest tutor, recalled his young charge with an old man's nostalgia, believing him to have embodied 'an age of gold, beside which the Marian years were an age of iron, and Elizabeth's an age of brass'.[3] In the midst of that age, however, the great Martin Bucer looked all around and saw, as he himself expressed it, 'fallow ground, such as the devastation of the antichrist is wont to leave'.[4] Bucer's verdict, set down in letters to Calvin and others, was that the English Reformation had foundered on the rock of Cranmer's congenital hesitancy. Though he and his fellow exiles had 'not ceased to lobby our patron [Cranmer] face to face and in writing',[5] a consistent and complete plan for reform had yet to emerge. Instead, in the universities and colleges, unbibled professors grew old 'in impious ease, and pre-empting the place and opportunity of younger men who wish to dedicate themselves to true theology and the ministries of the churches'.[6] It was from these colleges—

---

1   Edward's reign witnessed the governance of England by a regency council. The council was led first (1547–1549) by Edward Seymour, Duke of Somerset, and then (until 1551) by John Dudley, Duke of Northumberland.

2   Bishop of Ely after Elizabeth's succession.

3   Quoted in Patrick Collinson, *Archbishop Grindal: 1519–1583: The Struggle for a Reformed Church* (London, 1979), 48.

4   Ibid.

5   From a letter to Guillaume Farel, quoted in MacCulloch, 470.

6   *De Regno Christi*, ed. Pauck (Louiseville, 2006), 274.

wrote Bucer to Calvin—that 'swarms of faithful ministers ought to have
been sent forth from time to time'.[1] The renewal of the church, for Bucer,
was inextricably linked to the theological condition of the universities. His
sense of an intellectual class failing to act upon this link brought him close
to despair. In his sermon at Bucer's funeral, Matthew Parker represented
his friend's death as God's judgement on Cambridge for its negligence in
providing adequately prepared clergy.

Bucer had fled his homeland for the Gospel's sake. For him, as for the
other émigrés, faith was a matter of allegiance as well as self-denying trust: it
was always active, never passive. Cranmer had spared no effort in recruiting
these Continental masters. He had drunk deeply of their biblical scholarship,
had accumulated vast amounts of knowledge relating to their European
ministries—and now seemed reluctant to apply it. *De Regno Christi* (1550),
'The Kingdom of Christ', was Bucer's audacious bid, in the face of Cranmer's
inertia, to reboot the processes of religious transformation. A fragmented and
chaotic masterpiece, Bucer's book called upon Parliament to enact fourteen
laws covering both civil and ecclesiastical matters. At its heart was the idea
of a self-determining Christian commonwealth, wherein associations of
believers, supported by civil magistrates, assemble for catechetical instruction,
to publicly confess their faith and to submit to the authority and admonition
of the church. *De Regno Christi* found favour with the young king. But
Cranmer was instinctively suspicious of anything that might dissipate the
authority of the Crown. Under his stewardship, writes Wilhelm Pauck,
the Reformation 'had not sufficiently progressed to allow its sponsors to
attempt such steps as [Bucer] had recommended'.[2] A failure of nerve, or an
acceptance of comfort: at any rate, a disappointment.

When Edward died in July 1553, his sister Mary set about restoring the
dominion of Rome. Cranmer's tacit support for the attempt to place Lady Jane
Grey on the throne left him exposed. He managed to remain at liberty until
September 1553. By then his refusal to authorize the use of the sacramental
mass in Canterbury had become known. Having stood first before the Star
Chamber, at his Guildhall trial in November 1553 Cranmer was found guilty
of treason. He was tried again, this time for heresy, in September 1555. At
his degradation the following February he knelt before bishop Bonner, who

---

1   Quoted in Constantin Hopf, *Martin Bucer and the English Reformation* (Oxford, 1946), 104.
2   *Melanchthon and Bucer,* ed. Wilhelm Pauck (Louisville, 1969), 170.

personally, and with great relish, desecrated the fingers that had administered extreme unction. 'Now', said Bonner, 'you are lord no longer'.[1] As each vestment was stripped away, Bonner supplied a running commentary. 'This is the man', he said, 'that despised the pope, and is now judged by him. This is the man who pulled down churches, and is now judged in a church. This is the man that condemned the sacrament, and is now condemned before it'.[2] Cranmer's conduct in this period, during which he fashioned no fewer than six grovelling recantations, has drawn blushes from Protestants ever since. His denial of Christ's carnal and real presence in the eucharist, he wrote, 'bitterly tortures my soul'.[3] He upheld masses for the dead. He begged the pope for forgiveness, and the queen for pardon. Shame hardened on him like a crust. Even Foxe, that most sympathetic—and severally partial—observer of the godly company, deplores the fact that 'in him should appear an example of man's weak imbecility'.[4] Only when he realized that no amount of compliance would save him did Cranmer begin, at last, to embody his best instincts. At his burning at Oxford on 21 March 1556, he famously thrust the hand used to sign his recantations into the flames, crying out 'This hand hath offended'.[5] At the very end, by the grace of God, his wretchedness was eclipsed by spiritual vitality. But if what Marcus Loane calls 'the moral grandeur'[6] of his martyrdom cannot be gainsaid, what might be called his moral status provides endless scope for discussion. Lives, it might be pointed out, are more instructive than deaths.

All this is significant on a number of counts. Cranmer was, after all, the beating heart of ecclesiastical policy throughout the reigns of Henry VIII and Edward VI. But his own witness for reform was riven with ambiguity. To one historian he was 'a man of piety rather than of principle; he was as much an ecclesiastical lawyer as a divine who saw his way forward through compromise and conciliation'.[7] Yet this most reluctant of martyrs, this tool of tyranny, so willing to set aside the moral obligations of faith to please his king, was the architect of the Church of England in its doctrinal and liturgical

1 Foxe, viii. 79.
2 Ibid. 72–73.
3 Quoted in MacCulloch, 599.
4 Foxe, viii. 82.
5 Strype, iii. 254. Quoted in Loane, 240.
6 Loane, 241.
7 Peter Ackroyd, *The History of England* (London, 2012), ii. 468.

aspects. The first English eucharistic liturgy (1548), the two versions of the *Book of Common Prayer*, and the ordinal of 1550 are wonders of English prose directly attributable to Cranmer. In addition he oversaw the construction of the Forty-Two Articles and the publication of *The Book of Homilies* (1547). 'It is impossible', writes MacCulloch, 'to disentangle Cranmer's career from the confused manoeuvres which led to the birth of one strand of world Christianity, the Anglican Communion'.[1] That career—that confusion—ensured that the national church would never achieve a solid form. An authentic, Bible-based Reformation, built upon the uncomfortable talents of men like Barnes and Frith, Hooper and Bradford, Lambert and Ferrar, was jettisoned in favour of a weary *via media* between Protestantism and Roman Catholicism.

Cranmer's personality and methods, his advances and retreats, affected far too many people for his influence to cease with his death. The Elizabethan Settlement recovered his work and refashioned it. Richard Hooker (c. 1554–1600), the foremost apologist of the age, maintained that a reformed Church of England stood in continuity with the Church of Rome. He also held that the reasonable person of faith—Catholic, Lutheran or Reformed—does not delve too deeply into the nature of Christ's presence in the eucharist. If that is right, then the majority of our martyrs are rendered *un*reasonable persons of faith, for each had looked into the subject unflinchingly: sifting, studying and defending the rule of truth line by line. None counted the agonies of the stake too high a price to pay for that truth. Hooker's opinions are wholly exhibitive of the sclerosis affecting evangelicalism by the time of the Settlement, and of the queen's determination to temporize at all costs between Protestants and Catholics. The dog's breakfast of antithetical elements that resulted was, writes Ackroyd, 'as alien to the pure spirit of Protestantism, adumbrated in Zürich or Geneva, as it was to the doctrines of Rome'.[2] The coming men, however—men like Hooker—could be trusted never to push the truth of any doctrine beyond the bounds of *politesse*. Thus, to the horror of the faithful, the theology that knew no law but Scripture and no Master but Christ, was sidelined in favour of a flabby inclusivity. No attempt was made to resolve, or even properly address, the tensions that had governed the relationships between many of the leading Henrician and Edwardian

---

1   MacCulloch, I.
2   Peter Ackroyd, *The History of England* (London, 2012), ii. 468.

Reformers. Alister McGrath, reviewing the liturgical changes made under Elizabeth, argues that the 1559 *Book of Common Prayer* synthesizes the two earlier versions 'without attempting any form of theological resolution. Both Lutheran and Zwinglian found something which they could approve, and there, it seems, it was hoped the matter would rest'.[1] How very Cranmerian. A disinclination, or inability, to set out the fundamentals of faith is now an identifying characteristic of the Church of England. When a recent archbishop of Canterbury published a book of essays called *Anglican Identities*, one reviewer remarked that 'reading them was like trying to grab hold of jelly in a bath'.[2] The truths of revelation have long been cast aside; the 'values' of the *bien-pensant* ushered in. What counts is how you feel. Cranmer would, no doubt, be appalled. But it is nonetheless striking how, in the centuries since his death, the state religion, out of a desire to build consensus, accept human contradiction, proceed cautiously and harm no one—along with a number of less attractive traits, like sycophancy, vacillation and cowardice— has continued to reflect the character and approach of Henry VIII's 'most principal minister of our spiritual jurisdiction'.[3]

---

1 McGrath, 259.
2 Christopher Howse, *Sacred Mysteries* (London, 2007), 139.
3 Henry VIII, quoted in MacCulloch, 91.

XII

JOHN BLAND

In 1525 Dr Roger Lupton, provost of Eton—and chaplain to both Henry VII and Henry VIII—began to gather monies for the founding of a school in Sedburgh, his birthplace. At sixty-nine, he was weighing his legacy. He felt that however defective the works of believers might be, a chantry school, properly resourced, would direct young minds towards the right worship of God. Two years later he established six scholarships to St John's College, Cambridge, to be held in perpetuity for Sedburgh's most gifted pupils. In 1535 two more were added, along with a provision for two fellowships. The best-known beneficiary of Lupton's philanthropy was John Bland. Of north Yorkshire gentry stock, Bland incepted BA at St John's in 1536 and became a fellow. Among his pupils were Edwin Sandys and Edmund Grindal, both future archbishops of York. At St John's, Bland's reading of Tyndale's New Testament kindled in his heart a brighter flame of faith than had ever yet arisen. He set himself before God's tribunal and submitted to His Word; he became, in Foxe's words, 'inflamed with an incredible desire to profit the congregation'.[1] He began to associate with a number of radical groupings, in particular the Kentish Freewillers. A loose alliance of lay-led congregations, Freewillers opposed the doctrine of predestination: the idea that certain persons are infallibly guided to eternal life. Henry Harte of Pluckley, their leader, took his stand on the liberty of the human will and its cooperation with God. He stressed a reciprocal element in salvation: a link between God's gracious acceptation and our own commitment to right living. 'If you put to a willing mind', he argued, 'you shall find the Lord ready with His grace at your hand'.[2] To Freewillers, Luther's notion of *servum arbitrium*, of the unfree will, was an inducement to moral laxity. The devotees of such

---

1   John Foxe (1838), vii. 288.
2   Quoted in D. Andrew Penny, *Freewill or Predestination* (Woodbridge, 1990), 81.

thinking, wrote Harte in 1548, wrapped themselves 'in a foolish cloak of necessity, saying in themselves it cannot otherwise be; when indeed they strive not at all to make resistance but do let the fleshly mind run where it lusteth'.[1] In common with other separatists, the Freewillers organized illegal meetings, called conventicles, to read the Bible among themselves and discuss its teachings.

Bland also consorted with the circle around Joan Bocher, known as Joan of Kent. Bocher was condemned to death in 1549 for espousing the doctrine of Christ's celestial flesh. This heresy, taught by the sometime Lutheran, then anabaptist, Melchior Hoffman (1495?–1543), explained Jesus' sinlessness by saying He brought His flesh with Him from heaven; He did not derive it, in other words, from Mary. As early as 1539 another contact of Bocher's, one Thomas Dawby, had written that 'Our Lady was no better than another woman': she was 'but a sack to put Christ in'.[2] John Foxe attended Bocher's trial. So convinced was he that she should not be burned that he visited the Reformer John Rogers (q.v.), one of her examiners, to beg for leniency. His appeals fell on deaf ears. After a long wait in prison, Bocher was finally put to death on 2 May, 1550.

The lack of discrimination that marked his religious radicalism has blighted Bland's reputation. His theology was a distinctly idiosyncratic brew. He argued, in Canterbury and elsewhere, that 'in the christening of children, priests be murderers'.[3] He also believed, and indeed stated in his own church (18 March 1542) that 'the image of the Trinity is not to be suffered': the term 'Trinitas' being an invention of Athanasius, and not in the least Scriptural.[4] Such comments lend weight to George Williams' idea that 'the relationship between anti-Trinitarianism and anabaptism may have been closer in England than anywhere else in Europe except Poland'.[5] It may have been, but we must attend to terminology. The name 'anabaptist' was applied to a gamut of sectarian beliefs in mid-Tudor England. Bland himself seems to have belonged to a group of what have been called 'halfway anabaptists'.[6] These were men of Essex and the Kentish towns who took their beliefs from the

---

1 Quoted in M. T. Pearse, *Between Known Men and Visible Saints* (Cranbury, 1994), 27.
2 Ibid. 57.
3 Ibid. 88.
4 Quoted in Penny, 43.
5 *The Radical Reformation* (Philadelphia, 1962), 778–782.
6 M. M. Knappen, *Tudor Puritanism* (Gloucester, Mass., 1963), 149–150.

Bible alone. But there is no hard evidence of this group—or, indeed, any other 'anabaptists'—authorizing or performing the rebaptizing of adults. Home-grown sectaries, writes M.M. Knappen, 'denounced the doctrine of predestination, and refused to have their children baptized by Roman Catholic clergy, though they did not object to infant baptism as such, or hold many of the other anabaptist principles of which they were accused'.[1] It was the involvement of 'priests' (ie. Catholic clerics) in the sacrament that was objected to by Bland, not infant baptism *per se*. In respect of his anti-Trinitarianism, mitigating factors are harder to find. There is no outright rejection of the doctrine of the Holy Spirit. But his remarks are undoubtedly suggestive of a radically altered biblicism.

The beginning of anabaptism is usually traced to instances of adult baptism in Zürich in 1525. By the end of the decade, wildly different strains had emerged in north, south, and central Germany, and in the Low Countries. Anabaptism was where you found it. Belief and practice were not shaped by clerical, educational or political elites, but by the personalities of leading figures like, say, Hoffman in north Germany or Hans Denck (1500?–1527) in the south. Most insisted that regenerated Christians should have no truck with institutions—the magistracy, for example—that were in and of the world. As for theology, writes James Stayer, that 'was rudimentary and differences of religious ideas were secondary to differences of practice, which were more widely understood'.[2] But a new model for dissident Christologies did appear in the 1530s. Miguel Servetus (1509?–1553) had studied anatomy and medicine in Paris before becoming an editor of Scriptural texts. In July 1531 he produced his first composition rejecting the belief of the Trinity, using rabbinic sources to assert that God is solitary in Himself but various in His manifestations. Though he never denied the divinity of Christ, Servetus argued against His personal pre-existence. Christ was generated at the moment of conception, wrote Servetus, when God's Spirit entered the womb of Mary: 'and because His Spirit was wholly God, He is called God, and He is called man on account of His flesh'.[3] For this reason Servetus referred to Christ as 'the Son of the eternal God' rather than 'the eternal Son of God'.[4] He is the light of the world, said Servetus, emanating from the One Light; He is

---

1   Quoted in Penny, 3.
2   *The Oxford Encyclopedia of the Reformation,* ed. Hans Hillerbrand (New York, 1996), i. 33.
3   *De Trinitatis Erroribus* (1531), 59b.
4   Ibid. Book 7.

God's supreme act of self-disclosure, the ultimate dispensation of His grace, the measure of His divine immanence:

> The kingdom of Christ is a thousand times called eternal. Yet in the consummation of the ages He shall restore it to God. Not that the glory of Christ is thereby diminished, for it is His highest glory to have ruled all things well, even to the end, and to have subjected them all as He intended to the Father. This is to have delivered up the kingdom to God, just as the general of the universal army renders up the palm of victory to the emperor. In the same way, inasmuch as all reason for ruling will then end, all power and authority shall be abolished, every ministry of the Holy Spirit shall cease, since we shall no longer need an advocate or mediator because God will be All-in all. Then, also, the Trinity of dispensation will terminate.[1]

Servetus found a publisher for *De Trinitatis Erroribus* ('On the Errors of the Trinity') in Hagenau, a village near Strasbourg. In the city itself he consorted with well-known personalities. That Martin Bucer and Wolfgang Capito, co-architects of the Strasbourg church, declined to hand Servetus over to the civil authorities has been ascribed to the compassion each felt for one headed inevitably to the stake.[2] Both men, however, were horrified by his views. Bucer denounced antitrinitarianism in a series of public lectures, Capito in a petition to the senate. Servetus was eventually ordered to leave Strasbourg by the *Magistrat*, the city government. In August 1553, *en route* for Italy, he stopped off in Geneva. Thinking he'd look less conspicuous inside a church, he went to hear Calvin preach. The records of the Geneva Consistory state that 'he was recognized by certain brothers and it seemed good to make him a prisoner'.[3] At his trial Servetus was examined on his publications, on his doctrine, on his biblical exegesis—what Calvin called his 'futile trifles and impious ravings'.[4] Rumours of sexual misconduct were also investigated. He was said to have joked that there were enough girls in the world without marrying. Servetus did not recall the joke, but admitted he might have used levity to mask the real reason for his single state: his

---

1   Ibid. 81b-82a; cf. I Cor. 24–28. See Roland H. Bainton, *Hunted Heretic* (Rhode Island, 1953; rev., 2005), 31.

2   See Miriam Usher Chrisman, *Strasbourg and the Reform* (New Haven, 1967), 199–200.

3   Quoted in Bainton, 115.

4   Quoted in Bainton, 127.

impotence, the result of a rupture. The divines attempted to link Servetus to Judaism (easy because of his Hebraic erudition) as well as to Islam. Servetus admitted to reading the Qur'an, which he declared 'a bad book, but he had used only the good. He would no more aid Muhammad than the devil'.[1] The trial proved a sensation, and achieved a national profile. The magistrates and ministers of the Swiss cantons stepped forward as one man to condemn the heretic. Much energy was expended, and spleen vented, in styling him 'a cancer to despoil the members of Christ' and 'an excited snake [that] hisses curses and contumely against Calvin, that most sincere servant of God'.[2]

On 27 October 1553, at Champel, just outside Geneva, Servetus was burned to death with what was thought to be the last copy of his magnum opus, the *Christianisme Restitutio*, tied to his leg. 'I will burn', said Servetus, 'but this is a mere event. We will continue our discussion in eternity'. At the stake Servetus was sprinkled with sulphur and crowned with straw and leaves. A thick rope was twisted around his neck. The wood pile was heaped with 'green oaken faggots, still in leaf'.[3] The fractious, self-willed, yet oddly guileless theologian took half-an-hour to die. A few months later Servetus was again executed, this time in effigy, by the Catholic Inquisition in France. Servetus exerts a peculiar kind of influence even to the present day. His legacy is claimed by Unitarians and Jehovah's Witnesses and a certain type of Pentecostalism. He has also been appropriated by secularists and militant atheists, who like to adorn their agenda with his suffering. The burning of one of Europe's leading intellectuals threw into sharp relief the whole question of religious liberty within the church. A year after the ignoble event Sébastien Castellion encapsulated the thoughts of many: 'To kill a man', he wrote, 'is not to defend a doctrine. It is to kill a man'.

His doctrinal novelties notwithstanding, John Bland played a crucial role in the furtherance of Reform in Kent. In 1537 he had been presented to the living of Ospringe, which was in the gift of St John's College. In 1542/3 he stripped the church of stained-glass, rood loft and screen, candlesticks and shrines. At Faversham he denounced images, fast days, invocations to saints and other interferences with Christ's gospel. At Staple he complained that men were having their heads broken 'for speaking of the truth'.[4] Always

---

1   See Bainton, 129.
2   Quoted in Bainton, 138.
3   From *Historia Mortis Serveti* (1554). See Bainton, 152.
4   Quoted in Penny, 43.

close to Thomas Cranmer, and shielded by him, Bland was a prime target in the notorious Prebendaries' Plot of 1543: an attempt by five canons of Canterbury cathedral to oust Cranmer and damage the evangelical faction at court. Due in large part to the efforts of Christopher Nevinson, Cranmer's commissary, Bland secured the much sought-after living of Adisham, close to Cranmer's palace at Bekesbourne. He also acquired some sort of role in his administration. On 27 September 1543, in the wake of a Palm Sunday sermon at Adisham, in which he inveighed against the hallowing of palms and other superstitious practices, Bland was indicted for heresy. The case against him foundered on the rock of Henry VIII's revitalized confidence in Cranmer.

With the accession of Mary Tudor in July 1553, Kentish evangelicals braced themselves for a backlash. Cranmer was arrested in mid-September. The following month, cousins John and Thomas Austen, both churchwardens at Adisham, demanded that the communion table be removed and the stone altar rebuilt. They also wanted the rood screen restored. Richard Austen, the brother of Thomas, accused Bland of being 'against the queen's proceedings; for you say there are abominable uses and devilishness in the mass'. Bland didn't flinch. 'Goodman Austen', he replied, 'if so I said, I will say it again; and, God willing, stand to the proof of it'.[1] On 28 December, the Austens procured a priest from nearby Stodmarsh to celebrate the mass at Adisham. In a remarkable act of faith, not to mention physical courage, Bland burst into a packed church to declaim against the false ministering of the sacraments. In a trice, reported Bland, the churchwarden and his son-in-law 'violently came upon me, and took my book from me, and pulled me down, and thrust me into the chancel with an exceeding roar and cry'.[2] When the initial frenzy had abated, Bland begged to be allowed to wait in the churchyard until mass was ended. But the churchwarden, convinced that he would flee and seek shelter among the conventiclers, had him locked in a side chapel. After mass, the Austens encircled him again. He was searched; his dagger confiscated. With hard looks and wild words he was berated for having 'married against God's law and the queen's'. Bland was nothing daunted. 'Ye lie, goodman Austen',[3] he said. Along with Laurence Ramsey, a Freewiller friend, Bland

---

1   Foxe, vii. 289.
2   Ibid. 291.
3   Ibid.

was arrested and led to the general sessions in Canterbury by no fewer than eighteen armed guards. Both he and Ramsey were later bailed.

Due to the machinations of Sir Thomas Moyle, a leader of the Prebendaries' Plot and Speaker of the House of Commons, Bland was shuttled back and forth between the religious and civil authorities from February 1554 until his execution in July 1555. For most of that time he was held at Canterbury castle. His interrogators, over the seven or eight examinations to which he was subjected, included two other prebendary plotters: Cyriac Pettit in the spiritual court, and Sir John Baker[1] in the county sessions. In the chapter house, the largest of its kind in England, he also appeared before Nicholas Harpsfield, archdeacon of Canterbury. A fervent advocate of heresy trials, Harpsfield was described by Foxe as 'the sorest and of least compassion' of all the archdeacons involved in the Marian bloodletting. He was assisted by Robert Collins, the recently-appointed commissary, and one Dr Faucet, a former pupil of Bland's. About Faucet, Bland commented drily: 'I was once his tutor, but I was never able to do him any good'.[2] Asked whether he believed that 'after the consecration of the blessed sacrament of the altar, there remaineth no substance of bread, but the substance of Jesus Christ, both God and man', Bland affirmed that 'no, I do not believe: for the Scriptures do not teach me that there should remain the flesh of Christ, to eat as a man should eat man's flesh'.[3] Later, to a priest of Christ's Church in Canterbury, Bland scorned the idea of the wine being transformed. Why, if that were so, 'it follows that a man might be drunken by miracle!'[4] The rest of Bland's answers are forceful, yet curiously detached; perhaps he'd sensed a sham aspect to the proceedings. The last thing his enemies wanted was to expedite his case quickly. Legislation approving the burning of heretics had yet to be enacted.

In the winter of 1554/5 Parliament passed the Revival of Heresy Acts, and Bland, after a year in the cells, was brought before Sir John Baker for the last time. The nature of the justice on offer can be gauged by Baker's concluding remarks. As he passed Bland back to the spiritual jurisdiction, he pledged to personally donate six faggots (bunches of sticks) towards the Reformer's burning. From that point onward, Richard Thornden, bishop

---

1 Baker was a Justice of the Peace and a Privy Councillor.
2 Foxe, vii. 301.
3 Ibid. 299.
4 Ibid. 302.

of Dover, was Bland's tormentor-in-chief. A former friend of Cranmer, and promoted by him, Thornden had betrayed the archbishop in the course of the Prebendaries' Plot. As a protégé of Cranmer, Bland could expect little mercy. On 25 June, standing before Thornden in the chapter house of the cathedral, he 'boldly withstood the authority of the pope',[1] declaiming in tones of fearless sincerity the infallibility of the Bible and the Lordship of Jesus Christ. He was condemned for his 'damnable opinions and heresies' alongside three others: John Frankesh, vicar of Rolvenden near Tenterden; Nicholas Sheterden, a Freewiller once detained under Edward VI; and Humphrey Middleton, a conventicler from Ashford. Middleton had told the Faversham conventicle that 'all men being in Adam's loins were predestinate to be saved, and that there were no reprobates'.[2] Another man, named Thacker, won his freedom upon recanting and agreeing to do penance.

On 12 July 1555, Bland, Sheterden, Frankesh and Middleton were brought to a field adjacent to the walls of the town. And there, in one fire, at two stakes, they yielded their souls into the hands of Almighty God. All four, wrote Foxe, 'like true soldiers in Christ, gave a constant testimony to the truth of His Holy Gospel'.[3] Before dying, Bland pleaded with God the Father to 'accept this burnt offering and sacrifice O Lord, not for the sacrifice itself, but for thy dear Son's sake my Saviour; for whose testimony I offer this free-will offering with all my heart and all my soul'.[4] The day was sunny and clear. Kentish summers rise from the ground in a dizzying array of scents: wild parsley, burnt sap, baked nettles. A nineteenth-century writer recalled the 'rich masses of clustering trees' surrounding the site of the martyrs' pit: the 'fields of golden corn, and many a cottage home dotting the pleasant landscape, as it lies, now in shade and now in sunshine, beneath the deep blue heavens, while the shadows of the rolling clouds pass swiftly over it'.[5] Not the worst place, then, to end your troubles and find a better rest in the kingdom of Christ, the complete justifier.

It is a matter of record that more burnings took place in Kent than in any other region of England: sixty-one in all. About one in five of the Marian martyrs was, by birth or adoption, Kentish. A martyrs' memorial—a grey

1   Ibid. 305.
2   Quoted in Pearse, 27.
3   Foxe, vii. 312.
4   Ibid. 305–306. The reference to 'free-will' is surely significant.
5   C. B. Tayler, *The Memorials of the English Martyrs* (London, 1853).

stone obelisk surmounted by a cross—publicly funded at a cost of £600, was erected in 1899 near Wincheap Street in Canterbury. The inscription reads: 'In Memory of the Forty-One Kentish Martyrs who were Burnt at the Stake on this Spot in the Reign of Queen Mary'. All forty-one names are listed on two side-faces. Among them is John Bland, the rector of Adisham. The chain of dark circumstance under Mary I would not be broken for three years after Bland's death. Though several persons tried to dissuade her from it, Mary remained committed to her policy of man-burning until the end of her reign. In Canterbury itself, the last of the martyrs, a group including John Corneford and Christopher Browne, would go to glory only seven days before the tyrant's death early in the morning of 17 November 1558.

XIII

ROWLAND TAYLOR,
Richard Yeoman

The market town of Hadleigh, situated between Sudbury and Ipswich, seems an unlikely barometer of the religious condition of England; Suffolk has long been a prosperous, conservatively-inclined county, remote from the kind of forces that make for innovation. Hadleigh's own prosperity was built in the fifteenth century upon its trade in wool and cloth; its timber-framed Guildhall, red-brick deanery tower and pargeted, half-timber houses proclaim a well-fed serenity. Even into the nineteenth century the town existed as a still-life portrait of a vanished age,[1] in which landowner and tenant, priest and peasant, existed co-operatively against a background of benevolent despotism and maudlin sodality. But on the accession of Mary Tudor in 1553, as the beast of Catholic recidivism began to bite, many acts of violent persecution, even unto death, were recorded at Hadleigh. The most notorious of these acts, the burning of Dr Rowland Taylor, is depicted in stained-glass in the south chapel of St Mary's church. At Aldham Common, just north of Hadleigh, a rough-hewn stone bears the inscription: *1555 D. Taylor in defending that was good at this plas left his blode.* An obelisk was erected by public subscription in 1819.

Rowland Taylor was born in Rothbury, roughly twenty-five miles due north of Newcastle upon Tyne, around 1510. An able scholar, he studied civil law at Cambridge, possibly at Pembroke. He incorporated BCL in 1530; he learnt his Aristotelian texts, repeated exercises and argued in a scholastic fashion. Four years later he was awarded a DCL. By that time he

---

[1]   See Hugh Pigot, Rector of Hadleigh, *Hadleigh, the town, the church and the great men who have been connected with the parish* (1854), a paper published by the Proceedings of the Suffolk Institute of Archaeology (Michigan, 2010), iii. 1–129.

had already taken the unusual step of becoming warden of Borden, a hostel for law students. A strand of conjecture, not proven, dates Taylor's marriage from the award of his doctorate, which might explain the curious career path. The marriage, to Margaret, begat four sons and four daughters. They also adopted another daughter, Elizabeth. The undergraduates of Borden would typically rise at four in the morning. The first hour was spent on devotions. From six o'clock they would privately study or attend lectures. A dinner was eaten around ten. More study, more lectures, until five. After a supper of manchet-bread[1] and beer they might socialize until bedtime at nine or ten o'clock. While at the hostel Taylor is known to have lectured on Justinian I (483–565), whose writings on civil law aided the advancement of canon law. But Taylor was unsuited to the life of a warden/teacher. His lectures were sparsely attended and listlessly received.

In these years, although we find Taylor serving the archdeacon of Ely in some minor capacity, no preferments came his way. For a scholar of his calibre, ordained exorcist and acolyte as early as 1528, this failure to make headway suggests that Taylor was already ruffling feathers. An incipient humanism was sparked, in all likelihood, by his reading of the two-volume *Unio Dissidentium*, published in Antwerp in 1527. A collection of quotations from the church fathers, all weighted in favour of the New Learning, these volumes were instantly popular among the more radically-inclined students. Given its Strasbourg-inflected theology, and the verbosity of some of the articles, the editorship of *Unio Dissidentium* is usually laid at the door of Martin Bucer.

Dr William Turner,[2] an intimate of Nicholas Ridley and a fellow of Pembroke from 1530, is credited with leading Taylor, his fellow Northumbrian, to the preaching of Hugh Latimer. Like John Cardmaker in the same period, it was the force of Latimer-inspired evangelicalism that led Taylor to renounce the papal-Catholic tradition he had been trained in. The rule of the popes, he now declared, was an offence to Christian liberty. Henceforth he would argue for a new city of God: for inner prayer over conciliar decree, for faith against works, for the full and perfect redemption wrought on the Cross against the dogma of transubstantiation. The Word of God had given him evidences he couldn't ignore; or resist. He bound himself heart and mind to the cause of Reform. When Latimer was promoted to the bishopric of

---

1   Wheaten bread.
2   Dean of Bath & Wells, and Edward VI's personal doctor. He also pioneered the study of botany.

Worcester in 1535, Taylor accompanied him as commissary general and preaching chaplain. In addition to a cathedral chapter strongly conservative in its bent they found a diocese devitalized by forty years of Italian absentee bishops. Latimer's immediate predecessors were Silvestro de' Gigli (1498–1521) and Girolamo Ghinucci (1522–1535). On the death of the former, and before the latter's consecration, Guilio di Giuliano de' Medici served as apostolic administrator. In 1523 he was elected pope Clement VII. Each man was on permanent leave of absence, milking English temporalities from Rome while local gentry, aided and abetted by the cathedral chapter, enclosed common land and leased parish tithes. Pluralism[1] was entrenched. Biblically-illiterate curates would scuttle to and from communion services like poultry farmers collecting eggs. It was rare to find a communicant who could recite the Lord's Prayer. This indifference to the spiritual condition of the realm went hand in hand with moral laxity. Concubinage was rife, with priests betraying their vows of celibacy with housekeepers or maids.

Latimer and Taylor, and other chaplains drafted in by Latimer such as John Joseph,[2] immediately set about transforming the diocese through the power of the Word preached. An intense campaign of pulpiteering sought to reach every village. Latimer also confronted the grosser forms of superstition. In one famous episode he and Henry Holbeach, his newly-appointed prior, caused Our Lady of Worcester, an image of the virgin in the cathedral, to be stripped of its jewels and ornaments. In a letter to Thomas Cromwell of 1536, Latimer wrote that 'our great Sibyl[3] hath been the devil's instrument, I fear, to bring many to eternal fire; now she herself with her older sister of Walsingham, her younger sister of Ipswich, with her two other sisters of Doncaster and Penrhys, will make a jolly muster in Smithfield. They would not be all day in burning'.[4] Taylor's own knight-errantry led him down paths and tracks worn down by the packhorses of a dozen generations. From heathy ridge to downland village, from mercantile towns to grassy upland, from rabbit-cropped hill to a church nestling in the fold of a valley, he rode all over Worcestershire, into Gloucestershire and as far south as Bristol. It was a far cry from the scholarly hush of Pembroke library, or the hurly-burly of the *collegii pueri* (college boys). But Taylor was evangelical in the best sense. If the

---

1 The practice of holding more than one benefice at a time.
2 A Franciscan warden in Worcester. He joined Latimer's preaching team in July 1536.
3 A name given to sundry prophetesses in the Greek and Roman worlds.
4 *Sermons and Remains* (Cambridge, 1884), 395.

Lord desired that *every knee shall bow to me, and all tongues shall confess unto God* (Romans 14:11) so did he. To that goal he brought not only his robustness, temperamental as well as physical, but that combination of doctrinal clarity and involved emotion which produces the best kind of preacher.

Already, by 1538, when Taylor embarked upon another diocesan tour, the possibility of setting up Christ's rule in England was looking increasingly remote. In November Henry VIII presided in person at the show-trial of the 'sacramentary' John Lambert (q.v.). In the same month Lambert was taken to Smithfield and burned to death. The Bishops' Book, a statement of doctrine drawn up by the English bishops and clergy,[1] was given a series of rhetorical cudgellings; Henry thought it too Lutheran, and with breathtaking presumption listed 250-odd revisions. Innovation was ended, a cycle of reaction begun. But Latimer and his men drew strength from oppression. On horseback in Kidderminster Taylor laid bare the hierarchy of priests; the church of Rome was 'the purpled spiritual whore, the golden gilded harridan drab'.[2] God's glory was connected indissolubly to our justification by grace alone, through faith in Christ alone. His demotic assault on the whole medieval order was too much for some. A local tailor fumed at the 'folysshe sermonde of the new lernynge', and dearly wished the Reformer's horse had 'wynsyd [winced] and broken his necke'.[3]

The year 1539 saw the passage through Parliament of the Six Articles: the so-called 'whip with six strings'. Transubstantiation was reaffirmed, as were clerical celibacy, private masses and auricular confession. Henry's role in the formulation of the Act was crucial. The articles, Cranmer wrote later, were 'in some things so enforced by the evil counsel of certain papists against the truth and common judgement both of divines and lawyers, that if the king's majesty himself had not come personally into the parliament house, these laws had never passed'.[4] Two bishops resigned on account of the Act: Shaxton of Salisbury and Latimer of Worcester. It also marked the beginning of the end for Thomas Cromwell, champion of the Bible-men.

In the wake of Latimer's house arrest,[5] Taylor moved sideways into the

1   It expounded the sacraments, the Commandments, Lord's Prayer and Ave Maria.
2   J. S. Craig, *The Marginalia of Dr Rowland Taylor*, Historical Research 64 (1991), 411–20.
3   National Archives: PRO, SP 1/134, fols. 298r-300r.
4   Quoted in J. H. Merle d'Aubigné, *The Reformation in England* (London, rep. 1963), ii 387.
5   In the aftermath of the Six Articles, Henry ordered Latimer to be held at the bishop of Chichester's house in London.

chaplaincy team of Thomas Cranmer. For five years he lived with Cranmer in Lambeth and Canterbury, and at Bekesbourne in the Kentish weald. In an administration awash with talent, typified in men like Thomas Bacon and John Poyet,[1] Taylor's sturdy common sense set him apart. He was given the role of Cranmer's chief troubleshooter. As such, along with Richard Cox, the king's chaplain, he was charged with investigating the so-called Prebendaries' Plot: a bid by Stephen Gardiner, the perennially rivalrous bishop of Winchester, to oust Cranmer. The reconstitution (under royal charter) of Canterbury's cathedral chapter had seen the installation, in April 1542, of a core of conservative canons. Gardiner's control over the canons, and influence among the local gentry, delivered him a gilt-edged opportunity to reduce Cranmer's authority, increase his own and strike a blow for Catholic orthodoxy. But Gardiner hadn't taken account of Henry's unshakable belief in his archbishop. The king, forewarned of the heresy charge brought against Cranmer, summoned him to Greenwich to give him his personal ring: the supreme symbol of royal favour. According to one source 'Nevermore after no man durst spurn [Cranmer] during the King Henry's life'.[2] Cranmer was vindicated; Gardiner and his cohorts, lay and clerical alike, routed. As a result of the intelligence sifted by Cox and Taylor, and the menaces of Thomas Legh, an enforcer from the north, nearly 300 people—including cathedral canons, local curates and Kentish gentlemen—were implicated in the plot.

At this point Cranmer's fatal propensity for half measures took over. Only a handful of the conspirators were punished[3] or even censured. At Bekesbourne the double-dealing of Richard Thornden, his once-trusted aide, and John Barber, the principal of the archdiocese, was swept aside 'with gentle and comfortable words, in such sort that never appeared in his countenance or words any remembrance thereof'.[4] Two years later Cranmer appointed Thornden his suffragen bishop. Cranmer's eye for integrity was ever rose-tinted, and glass. How else to explain his love for that monstrous

---

1   Poyet was appointed bishop of Rochester in 1550; he left England on the accession of Mary. In *A Shorte Treatise of Politike Power* (1556), he dismissed the idea that kings are ordained by God to rule His church on earth.

2   *Narratives of the Reformation*, ed. J. G. Nichols (C. S. 1st ser. 77, 1859), 254–258. Quoted in Diarmaid MacCulloch, *Thomas Cranmer* (New Haven, 1996), 321.

3   These included Germain Gardiner, bishop Gardiner's nephew, executed for treason in February 1544.

4   John Foxe, *Acts & Monuments* (1839), viii. 30.

narcissist Henry? Thornden, in the reign of Mary Tudor, became a 'bitter persecutor against God's servants'.[1] An echo of the Prebendaries' Plot was heard in 1554 at the trial of John Bland (q.v.), rector of Adisham and a close associate of Cranmer. Over the course of seven or eight examinations, Bland was interrogated by no less than three leaders of the Plot: Sir Thomas Moyle, Sir John Baker, and Cyriac Pettit. In the spring of 1555, after languishing more than a year in the undercroft of Canterbury castle, Bland was sentenced to burn by none other than Richard Thornden, bishop of Dover.

In the wake of the Prebendaries' Plot, Taylor's faithfulness in discharging the duties entrusted to him was rewarded. Cranmer presented him to the living of Hadleigh: 'a notorious haunt of evangelicals'.[2] The chance he had longed for had arrived. Across his Cambridge years, and especially under the wing of Latimer, a vision of the kingdom of Christ had imprinted itself on Taylor's mind. Here was a chance to forge that vision within a specific community. Among the clothiers of Suffolk the Reformation ideal of earthly welfare and eternal salvation might be realized, and at the same time deepened, through a Gospel-infused understanding of faith. To these ends Taylor did not, in the manner of his predecessors, form cosy arrangements with the local gentry or draft in unbibled curates. As 'a good shepherd, abiding and dwelling among his sheep',[3] he left Cranmer's side and moved his family into the parsonage at Hadleigh. There his domestic life was marked by the depth and frequency of his Bible-reading. The Word, unchangeable and incorruptible, was where Taylor's courage, physical as well as moral, inhered. Every preacher, he said, 'must be bold and not milk-mouthed'.[4]

In 1546 Taylor got caught up in a battle, savage in temper, relentless in prosecution, around the king's church policy. The traditionalist party, under Gardiner's direction, convinced many at court that the king's long wished-for alliance with Charles V, king of Spain and Holy Roman Emperor, was being undermined by religious reform. This sparked a purge of evangelicals, 'legally bizarre and clearly desperate',[5] that began in March with the arrest of Anne Askew (q.v.). It culminated in her burning to death on 16 July. It was no coincidence that Edward, Anne's brother, was in Cranmer's employ.

---

1   Foxe, vi. 297.
2   MacCulloch, 110.
3   Foxe, vi. 677.
4   Craig, 420.
5   MacCulloch, 354.

The conservatives' *modus operandi* was to lobby for the arrests of low- and middle-ranking evangelicals in order to destabilize the higher-ups. Anyone with a strong link to Cranmer was a prime target. With Henry enfeebled by syphilis, tormented by ulcerated legs, and needing every drop of energy to make plans for government under Edward, the 'evangelycall fraternyte' was left unprotected. In the months between Anne's arrest and burning, Richard Turner ('a noisy evangelical in Kent'),[1] John Cardmaker, Edward Crome, Nicholas Shaxton and Rowland Taylor were all summonsed before the Council in Greenwich to answer charges of heresy. Latimer, on the strength of his friendship with Crome, was seized on a visit to London, taken to Greenwich and 'molested and troubled of the bishops'.[2] Both he and Turner were sent to the Tower. The rest, threatened with rackings and death, adopted a strategy of non-compliance. When that proved impractical, each man devised a form of abjuration he could live with. Only Shaxton, the former bishop of Salisbury, was broken by his accusers. Still active as a curate in Hadleigh, Shaxton signed a thirteen-article recantation, affirming his devotion to the Old Faith. This was published with a fawning epistle to Henry, thanking him for his mercy. Cowed into a different kind of bondage, Shaxton became the worst kind of enemy: the disloyal friend. He tried and failed to persuade Anne Askew to betray her contacts at Court. She told him that it would have been better if he had never been born. Weeks later he presided at Anne's burning. After that he made something of a specialty of persuading others to recant. Under Mary he became suffragen to Thirlby, bishop of Ely, and was instrumental in the burning of three more evangelicals.[3] As his self-exculpation reached new levels of refinement, his friendship with Taylor congealed into seething enmity. In the margin of Taylor's Latin Bible, preserved in Bury St Edmunds, Shaxton is styled 'tonshax': *Tonsure/Shaxton*.

With the death of Henry on 28 January 1547 'a new face of things began now to appear, as it were in a stage new players coming in, the old being thrust out'.[4] After the run of burnings, beheadings and persecutions under Henry, no one in the six years of Edward's reign would be executed, or tortured, for their religious views. This breadth of toleration, unexampled in the sixteenth century, was Scripturally-led and born of an appetite to import into England

---

1 Ibid. 303.
2 Foxe, vii. 463.
3 William Wolsey and Robert Pygot (the 'Ely Martyrs'), and John Hullier (q.v.).
4 Foxe, ix. 1320.

the spirit and principles of the European Reformation. On 31 January 1547 the executors of Henry's will, including Cranmer, nominated Edward Seymour, duke of Somerset, as lord protector. In May, Seymour announced a general visitation of all the dioceses of England and Wales. The nation was divided into six circuits. Each one was criss-crossed by evangelical activists, administrators as well as preachers, armed with thirty-six royal injunctions. Taylor and Ferrar were the most active of the Cambridge Reformers. As well as preaching the Word, their rôle was to instruct, question and guide officeholders. Curates and churchwardens were ordered to use an English litany and to buy paraphrases of the Gospels. With hired masses forbidden, chantry priests began new lives as schoolmasters. Shrines were destroyed. Every parish was inspected for 'misused images … clothes, stones, shoes, offerings, kissings, candlesticks, trindles of wax and such like'.[1] Alongside the injunctions were seventy-five articles devoted to the moral conduct of parishioners. For the Bible-men, discipline belonged with the Word and the sacraments as constitutive marks of the church of Christ. Nothing—no aspect of the parishioners' behaviour—was considered unimportant, or a purely private affair. Personal freedom, deeply rooted in the Reformers' understanding of faith, found its limit at any point where the well-being of the fellowship was imperilled. Thus adulterers, soothsayers and committers of incest were to be identified and admonished—but so were sowers of discord and gossiping women. For the makers of the Reformation the use of admonition not only prevented sin, but fostered the virtues of humility and obedience. This wasn't playing at piety. It was a concerted attempt, in the words of Martin Bucer, to 'establish the administration not only of religion but also of the other parts of the common life according to the purpose of Christ our Saviour and supreme King'.[2]

In the year of the visitation Taylor was made a canon of Rochester cathedral. In 1548 he was nominated archdeacon of Bury St Edmunds, and in 1552 archdeacon of Cornwall. In between Cranmer asked him to join the college of Six Preachers of Canterbury cathedral. Back in Hadleigh his charitable yet pragmatic spirit perpetuated the influence of Latimer. Daily visits to the sick and bedridden were a natural expression of a life lived in the light of God's presence. To the poor he gave 'an honest portion' of his stipend. As the peak

---

1   Quoted in Peter Ackroyd, *The History of England* (London, 2012), ii. 191.
2   Martin Bucer, *De Regno Christi*, ed. Pauck (Louisville, 1969), 384.

of the English Reformation hove into view, reports Foxe, 'the whole town seemed rather a university of the learned, than a town of cloth-making or labouring people: and (what most is to be commended) they were for the more part faithful followers of God's Word in their living'.[1] At the same time, battle was joined with those elements whose attitude to religious reform was determined more by self-interest than by real faith. Under Henry VIII what Taylor termed 'nobl ritch gentlemens'[2] had profited immeasurably through the buying up of monastic property. In the first years of Edward's reign the same pockets were filled by the enclosure of common land and the reckless alienation of advowson rights. These were the same 'rent-raisers' and 'step-lords' of whom Latimer had written: 'you have for your possessions too much ... thus is caused such dearth that poor men which live of their labour cannot with the sweat of their faces have a living'.[3] A rural exodus ensued, along with an explosion in poverty. In Suffolk, Taylor's ire was directed at both sides of the governing élite: the older landowning class, and the newly-rich clothiers, who saw in the use of land a way of cementing their status. Influential men were labelled 'proud, envious, slothful, covetous, gluttonous, lecherous, carnal and worldly, beastly, epicures, oppressors, defamers, receivers, tyrants, hypocrites, idolaters'.[4]

This frankness, verging on recklessness, granted him little room for manoeuvre when events took a new and envenomed twist. On the evening of 6 July 1553 Edward VI, stricken by 'the disease of the lungs',[5] coughed away the last of his life in Greenwich. In the swirl of religious strife and political positioning that followed, Taylor sided with the succession claims of the king's cousin, the evangelical Lady Jane Grey. On 19 July, Mary Tudor was proclaimed queen. Six days later the Privy Council ordered Taylor's arrest.

Although he was released in November, the return to Catholic Obedience under Mary ensured Taylor would not know freedom this side of heaven. The almost identical circumstances surrounding the arrest of John Bland

---

1   Foxe, vi. 677.

2   Craig, 415.

3   *Selected Sermons of Hugh Latimer,* ed. Allan G. Chester (New York, 1978), 65.

4   Craig, 415.

5   The king's surgeon, quoted in Chris Skidmore, *Edward VI: The Lost King of England* (London, 2007), 207. Most histories state that the king died of tuberculosis, following a bout of measles and smallpox. Some recent scholarship suggests he may have contracted a pulmonary infection, leading to pneumonia.

(q.v.) in December 1553, and Taylor's rearrest in March 1554, are emblematic of the inundation of superstition and death that began to assault the English church. The Reformers' insistence on the Word as an external, objective authority, one easily understood by ordinary people—without the mediation of clerics, without recourse to an ecclesiastical tradition—had removed the painted veil, the 'partial shelter'.[1] That was why Mary was so pitiless in her dealings with the Reformers: not because she was a sadist (she was not), but because of her belief, sincerely held, that those 'as by learning would seem to deceive the simple'.[2] At the heart of that doctrine of contempt sat the mass,[3] called by Taylor 'one of the antichrist's youngest daughters, in the which the devil is rather present and received, than our Saviour, the second person in the Trinity, God and man'. Hadleigh, he went on to say, must never 'defile itself with the cake-god'.[4] So when two churchwardens, Foster and Clark, emboldened by Mary's overturning of religious law, procured a priest to celebrate the mass in Hadleigh church, a collision course that would lead to the stake was set.

On the Tuesday after Palm Sunday, John Averth of Aldham, the priest in question, was smuggled into Hadleigh on the back of a cart. At the church gate he was met not only by Messrs Foster and Clark, but by an armed guard, thoughtfully provided 'less any man should disturb him in his missal sacrifice'.[5] By his fireside in the parsonage Taylor was engrossed in his Bible. Only when he heard the pealing of bells did he venture out. The west door of the church was shut and barred. As reported to Foxe, Taylor eventually found a way in through the south chancel door. The scene that met his eyes struck him with all the force of a physical blow. A tonsured priest hovering over an altar stone was the embodiment—and in Taylor's own church—of everything he had abandoned in favour of Christ and now detested: worship in Latin, praying for souls departed, auricular confession, transubstantiation, 'and other unchristianity thereunto belonging'.[6] In the face of popish pageant, in the bitter attrition of feeling and care, the Reformer's anger spilled over.

---

1   T. S. Eliot, *Murder in the Cathedral* (a verse drama), part one.

2   Quoted in *Oxford Encyclopedia of the Reformation,* ed. Hillerbrand (New York, 1996), iii. 31.

3   According to the Catechism of the Catholic Church (1324–1327), the holy eucharist is 'the source and summit of the Christian life'.

4   *The Letters of the Martyrs,* ed. Coverdale (London, 1837), 393–397.

5   Foxe, vi. 678.

6   Coverdale, 496.

'Thou devil!' he shouted. 'Who made you so bold to enter into this church of Christ and defile it with this abominable idolatry?'[1] In the near-riot that followed, Taylor was called heretic and traitor. When he refused to withdraw, both he and his wife, who had fallen to her knees to deplore 'this injury [to] the blood of Christ',[2] were manhandled out of the church. Two days later Foster and Clark gleefully reported the matter to Stephen Gardiner, the new lord chancellor.

A herald arrived in Hadleigh, summonsing Taylor to appear before the Privy Council. All the Reformer's friends begged him to take refuge abroad. He had plenty of time to do so, and a choice of escape routes. Even Gardiner would have been glad to see him go. Some 800 of those sympathetic to reform would flee during Mary's reign, including such luminaries as William Barlow, bishop of Bath & Wells, Richard Cox, senior tutor to Edward VI, and Miles Coverdale, the Bible translator. But Taylor would not be one of them. 'Verbum Dei [the Word of God]', he wrote later, 'made us go to London'.[3] In another place he declared 'my cause to be so good and righteous, and the truth so strong upon my side, that I will, by God's grace, go and appear before them, and to their beards resist their false doing'.[4]

In his first interview with bishop Gardiner, Taylor recalled the oath, once sworn by Gardiner at his own consecration, to reject papal jurisdiction. A flushed and ruffled lord chancellor declared it 'Herod's oath, unlawful, and therefore worthy to be broken'.[5] Gardiner's discomfiture was obvious. But Taylor's quarrel was God's quarrel. In this way the Bible formed not just the background to his thought, but the framework within which, and through which, he judged every action. Gardiner might have been released from his oath by the pope, but, said Taylor, 'you shall not so be discharged before Christ'.[6] When an enraged Gardiner called him 'an arrogant knave, and a very fool',[7] and accused him of 'resist[ing] the queen's proceedings' in Hadleigh, Taylor asserted his right, as the minister in that town, to oppose any and all who would 'presume to infect the flock committed unto me, with venom

1 Foxe, vi. 679.
2 Ibid.
3 Craig, 414.
4 Foxe, vi. 680.
5 Ibid. 682.
6 Ibid.
7 Ibid.

of the popish idolatrous mass'.[1] The eucharist, he maintained, was not a real sacrifice of the body and blood of Christ, but 'only memorative, in the remembrance of Christ's death and passion'.[2] Gardiner had heard enough; he ordered Taylor's immediate incarceration in the King's Bench prison. In a petulant coda he told his men to 'charge the keeper he be straitly kept'.[3]

By the spring of 1554 the main London prisons—Newgate, the Tower, Marshalsea, Comptor and King's Bench—were becoming like Reformed seminaries. At the King's Bench, Robert Ferrar, the bishop of St David's, and John Philpot, archdeacon of Winchester, had been joined by the great John Bradford: the authorities, in a move to relieve overcrowding, had transferred him from the Tower. At the beginning of April, a matter of days after Taylor's arrest, Nicholas Ridley was already writing to Bradford from the Bocardo in Oxford, where he languished with Latimer and Cranmer. Ridley relates how 'joyful it was unto all of us to hear the report of Dr Taylor and his godly confession [before Gardiner], I ensure you it is hard for me to express. Blessed be God which was, and is, the Giver of that and of all godly strength and stomach in the time of adversity'.[4]

That the news of Taylor's rearguard action in Greenwich had already permeated the walls of an Oxford prison speaks volumes for the evangelical grapevine. There was no lack of observers able to tell what they knew. But Ridley's reaction also brings home the shared nature of their resistance. Like flowers in a well-tended garden they stood upright before God. They helped each other to grow. Within that garden the rector of Hadleigh was valued as one whose robustness was entirely rooted in Scripture. Taylor was all truth. There was nothing he said he did not believe. Bradford called him 'trusty Taylor',[5] and 'thanked God that He had provided him such a comfortable prison-fellow'.[6] In the days left to them, the two friends were content to work out, for themselves and for each other, the weight of eternal glory:

> And so they both together lauded God, and continued in prayer, reading, and exhorting one the other; insomuch that Dr Taylor told his

---

1   Ibid. 683.

2   Ibid.

3   Ibid.

4   *The Writings of John Bradford*, ed. Aubrey Townsend (Cambridge, 1853; rep. Edinburgh, 1979), ii. 82–83.

5   *Writings*, ii. 190.

6   Foxe, vi. 684.

friends that came to visit him, that God had most graciously provided for him, to send him to that prison where he found such an angel of God, to be in his company to comfort him.[1]

In the ten months or so that Taylor spent at the King's Bench he was brought before Gardiner three times. His final examination, at Southwark on 22 January 1555, was as persuasively civilised a sham as the Marian state could devise. Alongside the lord chancellor sat Cuthbert Tunstall, bishop of Durham, and Nicholas Heath, bishop of Worcester. Also in attendance were Sir Robert Rochester, comptroller of the royal household; Sir Richard Southwell, a privy councillor; and John Bourne, secretary of state. Several Reformers were interrogated that day, including the bishops Robert Ferrar and John Hooper, and John Rogers, a canon of St Paul's. Each session was dominated by debates over clerical marriage and the Lord's Supper. Taylor's defence of Reformed doctrine, set alongside his letters from the King's Bench and (later) Comptor, imparts a real sense of his moral armature. In an atmosphere of general execration, with the threat of violence never far away, he wouldn't be cowed. He told the bishops that 'the religion set out in king Edward's days was according to holy Scripture, which contained fully all the rules of our Christian religion'.[2] He argued that the present threat to the church, and to the laws and constitution of England, came from one source: papal-Catholicism. He was severe and simple, impassioned and engaged. All his rhetorical skills came to the fore. Like his friend Bradford he embraced persecution as 'the true touchstone, which trieth the true church-children from hypocrites, as the wind doth the wheat from the chaff'.[3] Like Bradford, Marsh, Saunders and several others, he identifies himself as a prisoner of Christ, 'in bonds' for Him. The Pauline wording is key: it fortifies all the Reformers' letters. 'Pray for me'; writes Bradford, 'and I, by God's grace, will do the same for you'.[4] 'For God's sake', implores Taylor, 'pray for us, for we fail not daily to pray for you'.[5]

In another letter to the Bocardo, Taylor enjoins Ridley, Latimer and Cranmer to praise God 'again and again' for this 'most excellent promotion

1 Ibid.
2 Ibid. 685.
3 Quoted in Knott, 96.
4 Coverdale, 283.
5 Ibid. 130.

which you are called unto at this present: that is, that you are counted worthy
to be allowed amongst the number of Christ's records and witnesses'. Their
present state is, he says, 'another manner of nobility'.[1] There is no hint, in
any of these letters, of the displaced form of self-therapy that mars some
puritan autobiography. What emerges is a deep and tranquil affection for
one another, a spiritual kinship, 'a holy community', according to John
Knott, wherein individual acts 'appear as part of a collective expression of
faith'.[2] That faith was shaped and penetrated by the Bible. They did not
draw heavy black lines between church and state or between the individual
and society. Because clerical celibacy lifted human legislation above divine
institution, Taylor styled it 'the doctrine of devils, against natural law, civil
law, canon law, general councils, canons of the apostles, ancient doctors, and
God's laws'.[3] Such views, voiced in a modern context, would be thought
wincingly inappropriate. But Taylor wasn't improvising themes on the
honour of religion; he was proclaiming *the whole will of God* (Acts 20:27). His
battleground was the threshold of faith, where 'not only one or two of our
dear Redeemer's strongholds are besieged, but all his chief castles, ordained
for our safeguard, are treacherously impugned'.[4] On one side stood Christ
and His Gospel, promised and expected from the beginning of the world.
On the other were ranged the numberless fictions—what Calvin calls 'big
words and bombast'[5]—of the Roman Church. In his letters Taylor adopts
the apostolic model to erect a wall of disparity between the gardens of the
Lord and the deserts of Babylon: 'all we in the world', Taylor tells his wife,
'pertain to two princes, either to the Father of light and truth, or else to
the prince of darkness and lies'.[6] The gulf is fixed, the sentence irrevocable.

At the end of January, again in Southwark, Taylor, along with Laurence
Saunders and John Bradford, was formally condemned. 'God be praised',
he said, 'even from the bottom of my heart. I am immovably settled upon
the rock, nothing doubting that my dear God will perform and finish the
work, that He hath begun in me and others. To Him be all honour both

---

1   Ibid. 129–130.
2   *Discourses of Martyrdom in English Literature 1563–1694* (Cambridge, 1993), 84–85.
3   Coverdale, 131.
4   Ibid. 130.
5   *Calvin's Wisdom,* ed. Graham Miller (Edinburgh, 1992), 314.
6   Coverdale, 493. See Romans 13:12; 1 Cor. 4:5; 2 Cor. 4:6, 6:14.

now and forever, through Christ our only Saviour'.[1] He was taken first to the Clink, where an excited crowd gathered at the prison gates. 'God be praised good people', he cried, 'I am come away from them undefiled, and will confirm the truth with my blood'.[2] A few hours later, 'toward night', he was taken to the Comptor in the Poultry, a small prison in Cheapside. And there, on 4 February, he was conducted into the unlovely presence of Edmund Bonner, bishop of London. Bonner had arrived to carry out the ritual of degradation: the tearing away piecemeal of his canonical dress. In the face of high-handed rebukes and brutal threats, Taylor showed the kind of courage it is apt to call grace under pressure. When offered his freedom if only he would conform, he counselled Bonner to turn to Christ. 'As for me', he declared, 'I will not turn to antichrist'.[3] He refused to dress himself in the vestures of his rank. These were pulled onto him bodily by Bonner's henchmen, from the innermost layers of benet and colet, representing the orders of exorcist and acolyte, to the frocks of high office. Once, in Foxe's memorable phrase, 'thoroughly furnished', Taylor opted for satire, parading himself before an enraged Bonner. 'How say you, my lord?', cried the well-built, bearded man of action, 'am I not a godly fool? If I were in Cheap[side], would not all the boys laugh at these apish toys, and toying trumpery?'[4] Having failed so abjectly to inflict mental anguish, Bonner drew a knife. He scraped the crown of Taylor's head and the tips of his fingers until they were bloody.[5] But Taylor was undaunted. As Bonner prepared to hit him with his crosier-staff his chaplain spotted a chilly glint in Taylor's eye. 'My lord', he breathed, 'strike him not, for he will surely strike you'. The lineaments of sweet reason were etched onto the Reformer's face. But toughness was there too. 'Yes, by Peter I will', he said. 'The cause is Christ's, and I were no good Christian if I would not fight in my Master's quarrel!'[6]

Bonner, his pretensions to dignity fading, judged discretion the better part of valour. He contented himself with the laying on of a curse: the design of which placed the prisoner in the hands of the secular power. This cut no ice

---

1 Foxe, vi. 688.

2 Ibid. 691.

3 Ibid.

4 Ibid.

5 A common, though not compulsory, part of the ritual was to remove every trace of holy oil (extreme unction) with which a priest had been anointed, and had anointed others.

6 Foxe, vi. 691.

with Taylor. 'Though you curse me', he said, 'yet God doth bless me. I have the witness of my conscience, that you have done me wrong and violence: and yet I pray God, if it be His will, to forgive you. But from the tyranny of the bishop of Rome, and his detestable enormities, good Lord deliver us'.[1] Taylor had little instinct for introspection, even less for ingratiation. At no time, from the moment of his arrest onward, does he appear to have taken a backward step. Even as he was being escorted back to the cell he shared with Bradford, he was calling out to Bonner: 'God deliver me from you! God deliver me from you!'[2] The bishop had foundered on the rock of Taylor's delight in loving Christ. Once reunited with Bradford, he expatiated, with great relish, upon his ordeal. 'His chaplain told him not to strike me with his crosier-staff', he chuckled, 'saying I would strike him again'. He leaned forward, rubbing his hands: 'In truth, I made him believe I would indeed do so!'[3]

In the days remaining Taylor rested on the promises of the merciful God: that death itself had been overthrown, and *the dead which die in the Lord, are fully blessed* (Revelation 14:13). At the Comptor he was allowed to spend a last evening with his wife Margaret, his son Thomas, and John Hill, his devoted servant. Before supper, in the mustiness of his cell, they sank to their knees and prayed. After supper, as wood-smoke drifted across from the Poultry fires, Taylor thanked God for the privileges of faith and hardship, knowing that *unto you it is given for Christ, that not only ye should believe in Him, but also suffer for His sake* (Philippians 1:29). Turning to his son, he urged him to live a life wholly unto God and for God. As God cannot be separated from His Word, the boy should learn his Bible; he should serve the Lord with prayer, remember the poor and destitute, and look after his mother in her old age. He was adamant that Margaret should remarry. Once condemned, Taylor had forfeited all his moveable goods at the queen's mercy. So there were practical reasons why Margaret should seek another husband. Added to which, absolute devotion to any human being—even to a wife or husband—was, to the Bible-men, a form of sinful servitude.

Taylor's final plea was his most heartfelt: that Margaret bring up their children 'in the fear of God, and in learning, to the uttermost of your power,

---

1   Ibid. 691–692.
2   Ibid. 692.
3   Ibid.

and keep them from this Romish idolatry'.[1] This farewell was, perhaps, the hardest suffering of his imprisonment. When the rap on the door came, they wept and prayed, and kissed each other. Taylor thrust his prayer book into Margaret's hand, and a work in Latin by Bede,[2] telling the history of the Christian church in England, into Thomas's. The inscription inside the back cover could easily stand as an encomium on the principles that governed Taylor's life, and that he wished to see reflected in the lives of his family and the Hadleigh congregation. 'Beware of the sin against the Holy Spirit', it ran, 'now after such a light opened so plainly and simply, truly, thoroughly, and generally to all England'. And to his wife he wrote: 'Count me not dead, for I shall certainly live, and never die. I go before, and you shall follow after, to our long home'.[3]

At two o'clock the next morning Taylor was awoken, stiff and disorientated. In the courtyard below the sheriff of London was waiting with a company of men to take him to Aldgate. Even then his good-humour did not desert him. He reached up and swung his considerable bulk from a beam that separated his bed from Bradford's. 'Oh, master Bradford', he said, 'what a notable sway I should give if I were hanged!'[4] Outside it was raining, cold, pitch black; torches fizzled and guttered. Down deserted roads, through the boding echoes of a city at slumber, the sheriff 'without any light led [Taylor] to the Woolsack, an inn without Aldgate'.[5] Also in Aldgate, following a tip-off, were Margaret, their daughter Mary, and their adopted daughter Elizabeth. All three had spent the night huddled in the porch of St Botolph's church. Elizabeth was first to hear the clangour of shod hoofs; she ran out, crying 'Here is my father, led away!'[6] Margaret's eyes were not as sharp; the horsemen rose as phantom shapes against the streak of dawn. 'Rowland, Rowland, where art thou?' she cried. 'Dear wife, I am here',[7] said Taylor. The sheriff held his men back as Taylor, with young Mary in his arms, knelt down to say the Lord's Prayer. As they kissed and embraced, Taylor told Margaret he was 'quiet in my conscience'. To Mary he said 'God bless thee,

---

1 Ibid.
2 *Ecclesiastica Historia.*
3 Foxe, vi. 693.
4 Ibid. 700.
5 Ibid. 693.
6 Ibid. 694.
7 Ibid.

and make thee His servant'. Last of all, kissing little Elizabeth, he prayed that
'you all stand strong and steadfast unto Christ and His Word, and keep you
from idolatry'.[1] The sheriff, not unmoved, offered Margaret lodgings for
the night. As she let go of her husband's hand, she summoned the courage
that is God's special gift. 'God be with thee, dear Rowland', she said. 'I will,
with God's grace, meet thee at Hadleigh'.[2] 'Trusty' Taylor was embarked
upon his last journey: the longest, the best.

   At eleven o'clock Taylor was handed over to the sheriff of Essex, his escort
as far as Chelmsford. By then, outside the Woolsack, knots of well-wishers
were pushing against hastily constructed rails. As the sheriff's party emerged,
and Taylor was spotted, a cheer went up. Thomas, Taylor's son, was borne
aloft in the arms of John Hill. 'Good people', announced a joyful Taylor,
'this is mine own son, begotten of my body in lawful matrimony; and God
be blessed for lawful matrimony!' And he set his hat onto his little boy's head
and blessed him; then grasping Hill by the hand said: 'Farewell, John Hill,
the faithfullest servant that ever man had'.[3] This note of hectic vitality, of
holy joy, would persist all the way to Hadleigh. But his self-dedication to
Christ's cause would not allow it to entirely predominate. Everything was
immanent now; everything was close. God must be heard! Even the unborn
souls of his adversaries might be stirred by his witness! Among the Calibans
of Queen Mary, Taylor was a Prospero. In Brentwood he was forced to wear
a hood, with slits for the mouth and eyes, lest the sight of him prove too
decisive a spur to Gospel living.

   In Chelmsford, at supper, in a shadowy inn lined with high-backed benches,
caressing voices called him 'well beloved of all men'.[4] Also invoked were his
'great learning and wisdom'.[5] His table companions—the sheriffs of Essex
and Suffolk, and four yeomen of the guard—volunteered as 'suitors for his
pardon'[6] should he decide, even at this late stage, to recant. They filled his
cup. And waited. The Reformer's reply, when it came, set pulses racing. 'I
have been deceived myself', he remarked. 'And I am about to deceive a great

---

1   Ibid.
2   Ibid.
3   Ibid.
4   Ibid. 695.
5   Ibid.
6   Ibid.

many in Hadleigh of their expectation'.[1] The sheriff of Essex was vivid with excitement. 'O yes, good master doctor!' he cried, 'God's blessing on your heart!'[2] But Taylor was teasing them. He had expected to die in his bed, and had, in that respect, been deceived; but also deceived, since he was to be burned, not buried, were 'a great number of worms in Hadleigh churchyard, which should have had a jolly feeding upon this carrion, which they have looked for, for many a day'.[3] It is easy to imagine a predatory stillness falling on the scene. Taylor's love of the Saviour, and its relation to truth and beauty, were beyond the sheriffs' comprehension. All they had was their bitterness, their pride, their impregnable consensus.

There were other attempts, on the road to Hadleigh, to break Taylor out of his faith. The enmity of one of his guards, called Holmes, unfolded in a particularly loutish fashion: Holmes, writes Foxe, 'used him very homely, unkindly and churlishly'.[4] In Lavenham, on the western bank of the river Brett, he was subjected, over two days, to the futile hovering of a succession of priests. A pardon was waved in front of him; he was even offered, by nod and wink, a bishopric. But Taylor's house was not *builded upon sand* (Matthew 7:26) but upon the rock that is Christ Jesus. By this stage Taylor was so far outside the compass of conventional piety, of extrinsic values, that he hardly seems to have been breathing the same air as his captors. The substance of salvation had overtaken him; he embraced the end of life as its deepest fulfilment. Two miles short of Hadleigh he leapt off his horse 'and set a frisk or two, such as men commonly do in dancing'.[5] When he entered the town he found the streets lined with well-wishers. Most of these, he told the sheriff of Suffolk, he had 'most heartily loved, and truly taught'. Several were weeping. But Taylor did not weep. A little thinner now, a little frailer now, he continued to meet the pathos of human need with the message of God's mercy in Christ. 'I have preached to you God's Word', he announced, 'and am come this day to seal it with my blood'.[6]

Taylor is taken to Aldham Common, a little way north of Hadleigh. A great crowd is assembled. The Reformer, hooded throughout his ride, uses

1 Ibid. 696.
2 Ibid.
3 Ibid.
4 Ibid. 695.
5 Ibid. 697.
6 Ibid.

both hands to rip off the hood. Gasps of disbelief; shouts of protest: Taylor is barely recognizable. His beard is white and unkempt, his scalp—after Bonner's knife-play—matted with blood. Taylor attempts to speak, to console his flock, but the metal tip of a staff is jammed into his mouth. The sheriff of Suffolk, Sir John Shelton, reminds him of an oath, made to Council, to still his tongue, lest it be cut out. 'Well', murmurs Taylor, 'promise must be kept'.[1] He undresses, gives his boots away, then his shirt. He attempts to say some words of farewell, but Holmes, with predictable ill-grace, swipes him across the head with a broken pot. His face, foul and snarling, is thrust next to Taylor's: 'Is that the keeping of thy promise, heretic?' A weak sun stains the thin, drifting clouds; the earth is a sodden reek of mud and branches. Taylor kisses the stake and is lifted bodily into a pitch-barrel. A local butcher is told to gather dry bunches of twigs, called faggots, for the fire. He refuses. Even when threatened with gaol he shakes his head. But four others step forward: Mulleine, Soyce, King and Warwick. Such persons, belonging to all ages and civilisations, are ubiquitous. They yearn to pay homage to the public power, and accept—as a dogma, a postulate—its right to humiliate its victims. They are the external auxiliaries of every totalitarian state.

The fire is built. As a sop to the savagery of the mob, Warwick hurls a faggot at Taylor's head, lacerating his face; a sordid, callow little indecency, in some ways more shocking than the burning itself. As blood trickles down his cheek the Reformer is heard to say: 'Oh friend, I have harm enough; what needed that?'[2] The fire is lit; the faggots damply crackle. Taylor begins to recite the Miserere, the fifty-first psalm, in English: 'Have mercy upon me, O God, after thy great goodness: according to the multitude of thy mercies, do away mine offences'. Standing nearby, boiling with distaste, is Sir John Shelton. He strikes Taylor across the mouth. 'Ye knave', he hisses, 'speak Latin: I will make thee!'[3] But Taylor has transcended the hierarchies of the world. He is reaching into eternity. At the same time he is part of all he has touched and has touched him. The flames rise, his beating heart storms through; he roars and cries out, though there is no despair in him: 'Merciful Father of heaven, for Jesus Christ my Saviour's sake, receive my soul into your hands!'[4] The low tempestuous night is over; the high glorious morning has

---

1   Ibid. 698.
2   Ibid. 699.
3   Ibid. 700.
4   Ibid.

arrived. Taylor folds his hands. He is calm, readied. The man Soyce, a local drunkard, picks up a halbert—part spear, part axe—and crushes his skull with a single blow. There is no more movement, no more sound. The dark world of men lies stricken beneath a listless sun. 'Thus', writes J.C. Ryle, 'died one of the best and bravest of the English martyrs'.[1]

When Dr Taylor was summonsed by the Privy Council, Richard Yeoman, his seventy-year-old curate, dutifully assumed the role of surrogate rector. The fugitive data on Yeoman cannot be pushed very far. It is usually stated that he was a graduate of Cambridge University. But Oxford is just as likely. His virtues were of the quiet sort; any drama in his life was confined to the realm of ideas, not circumstances. Even then he was learned without being especially profound. He was no theologian. His preaching drew few plaudits. But in the fierce crosswinds of religious change, he clung to the Word as the absolute measure of who we are and what we might become. He spoke openly against the cultish worship of the saints and the virgin. And among the faithful of Hadleigh he was loved for the kind of goodness that puts ambition out of countenance.

Yeoman's stewardship of the parish was short-lived. One by one the leading Reformers were being imprisoned and burned to death. In London bishop Bonner went about his work with especial relish. 'Yes, yes', he said, 'there is a brotherhood of you, but I will break it, I warrant you!'[2] In Hadleigh the traditionalist faction, visible and belligerent, preached Mary's accession as part of a sacred dispensation. A proclamation was enforced, stemming from the queen herself, which 'willed all men to embrace that religion she had of long time observed, and meant, God willing, to continue the same'.[3] The mass was chanted in Latin; images and altars, candlesticks and crucifixes, were dusted off and brought up from the cellars. And in a direct attack on the doctrine of the Word, no one was allowed 'under pretext of sermons or lessons either in Church, publicly or privately, [to] interpret the Scriptures, or teach anything pertaining to religion, except it be in the Schools of the university'.[4] Any stumbling block to conformity was crushed or badgered out of existence; or, in the case of Richard Yeoman, banished from the town. In the infirmity of old age, impoverished and newly destitute, he embarked on

---

1   *Five English Reformers* (Edinburgh, rep. 1999), 82.
2   Quoted in Ackroyd, 247.
3   *The Chronicle of Queen Jane* (London, 1850), 24.
4   Quoted in Ackroyd, 246.

the life of a wandering evangelist. He travelled from village to village, town to town, preaching outdoors and at illegal meetings, 'moving and exhorting all men to stand faithfully by God's Word'.[1] In suffering adversity with the Gospel, Yeoman directed more souls heavenward than at any time in his career. His enemies—chief among them a priest called Newall—could not ignore the defiance. A plot was concocted to entrap and imprison him. We know nothing of the details of this plot, nor of how Yeoman came to hear of it. But he bundled up his meagre belongings and, wife and children in tow, fled into Kent. There, according to Foxe, he earned a mean living selling pins and scraps of lace door to door.

Kent was a hotbed of religious dissent: revivals of Pelagian and Celestinian errors rubbed along with incarnational peculiarities and Lollard ideas. At this time every radical grouping was labelled 'anabaptist[ic]': John Hooper, the bishop and martyr, writing to his friend Heinrich Bullinger in 1550, described Kent as being 'troubled with the frenzy of the anabaptists more than any other part of the kingdom'.[2] Given his reverence for the magisterial Reformers,[3] it seems unlikely that Yeoman would have found the company of separatists in any way agreeable. There is no mention of him preaching anywhere in the county. When he was recognized, arrested and put in the stocks for a day and a night by Sir Thomas Moyle, one of the leaders of the Prebendaries' Plot (q.v.), no charges were brought against him: a solid indictor that he had settled for silence and obscurity. The following morning he was released.

Were it not for the clear teaching of the Bible, examined and adduced by Yeoman and his co-religionists, that *the trial of your faith, being much more precious than gold that perisheth (though it be tried with fire) might be found unto your praise, and honour and glory at the appearing of Jesus Christ* (1 Peter 1:7), his next decision might seem very odd indeed. He headed back to Hadleigh: to the one place where, for him, capture and martyrdom were virtual certainties. But we should recall his age, and the physical demands latterly placed upon him. At the end of his life he wanted to be still; to look within and prepare his soul for eternity. And where better to effect that great transition than in Hadleigh, where his plain declaration of the Gospel had borne so much fruit.

---

1   Foxe, viii. 487.

2   Quoted in M. T. Pearse, *Between Known Men and Visible Saints* (Toronto, 1994), 24.

3   Men like Luther, Calvin, Bucer and Zwingli, who argued for the interdependence of church and civil authority.

His wife, whose name is not recorded, took lodgings in the town in her own name. For over a year she hid Richard in the attic of the local Guildhall. How she acted and reacted in extremis is a story no less remarkable than her husband's. She would go early into the streets to beg for bread and meat for her family. Her nights were spent spinning wool into yarn. The raw wool would often be carded by Richard. Otherwise he devoted himself entirely to the Book of Life, filling whole days, and whole nights, with Scripture-reading and prayer, advancing in his faith, imitating loftier things, imitating, most of all, our Lord Jesus Christ, who went alone into the desert to pray. Plunged into shadow, he saw Christ with greater clarity than ever before; the day-long, unmoving silence was infused with meaning. Fear and depression were overcome by the sheer vitality of his imagination.

A lot of care, planning and ingenuity were required to keep Yeoman safe. Anyone who knew the secret, even if they harboured only good intent, could endanger him. Did rumours grow? Was he betrayed? Was a candle seen, were voices heard? One night, as Yeoman slept, a noise broke on the cobbles below. Door jambs splintered. Shouts reverberated. Boots thudded on the oaken staircase. Light leeched across the floor. All this happened as a consecutive whole, as Newall, Rowland Taylor's successor, 'brake up five doors upon Yeoman, whom he found in bed with his wife and children'.[1] It made for a piteous spectacle. As Yeoman and his family cowered in one another's arms, Newall stood framed in the doorway, his men behind him, a lantern raised in front of his face. Light flooded the chamber; every detail stood out hard and clear. Newall took a pace forward. 'I thought I should find a harlot and a whore together!' he cried, and attempted to pull off the bedclothes. But Yeoman dragged them back, and with an overmastering dignity told his wife to dress herself. 'Nay parson', he corrected Newall, 'no harlot, nor whore, but a married man and his wife, according unto God's ordinance; and blessed be to God for lawful matrimony. I thank God for this great grace, and I defy the pope and all his popery'.[2]

Yeoman was wrenched from his family, led to the town gaol, and set in stocks alongside John Dale, a weaver. Dale was forty-six years old, a good age for an artisan, and despite his lack of formal education could read and write and hold his own in debate. An impulsive, ardent, and keenly sensitive

---

1   Foxe, viii. 487.
2   Ibid.

evangelical, the force of faith had carried him far beyond the palliatives of silent resistance. In Hadleigh church, in the middle of Newall's celebration of the mass, he had risen from his knees to rail against the pretensions of baronial popery. 'Oh miserable and blind guides', he shouted, 'will ye always be blind leaders of the blind? Will ye never amend? Will ye never see the truth of God's Word; will neither God's threats nor promises enter your hearts? Will the blood of the martyrs nothing mollify your stone stomach?'[1] The priest demanded Dale's arrest. When Yeoman was brought to the gaol, Dale had been in the stocks for three days. For both men a sense of the inevitable was ominously defined. In a world pregnant with threat, they gave thanks for being forgiven men and endeavoured to be holy men. When the Justice of the Peace, Sir Henry Doyle, loftily pronounced them 'persons of no reputation', and asked Newall to consider Yeoman's age and Dale's 'poor estate',[2] and let them go after a day or two, it did seem, after all, that they might be returned to their families. But Newall's thirst for retribution had not been slaked: not remotely. He tore into Doyle, exhorting him 'in a great rage' to 'defend holy church, and help to suppress these sects of heresies, which are false to God, and thus boldly set themselves, to the evil example of others, against the queen's gracious proceedings'.[3] His words were well chosen. Mary's devotion to the Old Faith had left the magistracy 'afraid of every shaven crown'.[4] Doyle, Pilate-like, wriggled awhile, then plumped for self-preservation over justice or mercy. He issued a prerogative writ, defining the actions of Yeoman and Dale as unspeakable heresies contrary to the queen's majesty.

The Bible-men, their hands bound, their legs tied under their horses' bellies, were brought to Bury St Edmunds: to a gaol built in the shadow of the Benedictine abbey. To the defenders of tradition, heresy was the unholy offspring of *superbia* and *pertinacia*, that is, arrogance and stubbornness. As Yeoman and Dale could not be reached by reason, or persuaded by theology, chastisement and coercion were necessary to divert their minds from error. Accordingly they were ill-treated on route, fettered on arrival and thrown into the deepest dungeon. How long they lingered there is not known. Unlike other Reformers in these accounts, Yeoman had no retinue of admirers to

---

1 Ibid. 487–488.
2 Ibid. 488.
3 Ibid.
4 Ibid.

record the dates of his arrests or arraignments. But we know that Dale, the indomitable weaver-scholar, 'through sickness of prison and evil-keeping',[1] died in July 1558 in a delirium of fever. His body was thrown onto a cart, taken outside the walls of the town and buried in rough ground. Yeoman was removed to Norwich. Given its role in civic affairs, Yeoman was probably detained in the city's fifteenth-century Guildhall. If so, he might have spent his last night in the same undercroft as Thomas Bilney, twenty-seven years earlier. Unlike Bilney, whose trial was a national event, no one thought to preserve the documentation on Yeoman's trial. But when asked to submit himself to the power and prestige of the pope, Yeoman replied: 'I defy him, and all his detestable abominations. I will in no wise have [anything] to do with him, nor anything that appertaineth to him'.[2]

On the 10th of July, Richard Yeoman was taken by river to Lollards' Pit in Norwich. His death by burning, as reported by an eyewitness, was inexpertly handled. He suffered indescribable agonies. Wrote Foxe: 'So ended he his poor and miserable life, and entered into the blessed bosom of Abraham, enjoying with Lazarus the comfortable quietness that God hath prepared for his elect saints'.[3] In life Yeoman did not make a single claim to importance of any kind; in death he was soon forgotten. Reasons for this are not hard to find. He was no churchman in the mould of Cranmer, moving easily between Convocation and Royal Court. Nor was he a famous preacher like Latimer, audacious book runner like Garrard, scholar/author like Frith or princely theologian like Ridley. Unlike, say, Barnes, he did not travel widely. His story lacks the kind of grandeur that adheres to those of Rowland Taylor or Robert Ferrar. He did not share Bilney's social gift. Nothing he did, including his dying, caused many ripples. No memorials were constructed; either in Hadleigh or Norwich. But he suffered as the others suffered, looking beyond time and place to remind his countrymen—as he reminds us still—that Christian freedom is, in every particular, a spiritual matter. In the teeth of the Marian holocaust, assailed by arbitrary cruelties, he clung to the certainty of the pure Bible text. He rejected the man-made Councils of the Church. He loved his wife and children, but the Saviour most of all.

---

1 Ibid.
2 Ibid. 488–489.
3 Ibid. 489.

He lived a brave, simple and truthful life. It would be difficult to exhaust the significance of his example.

APPENDIX I

BUCER, VERMIGLI AND THE ANGLO-ZÜRICHERS

In England, as elsewhere in Europe, the doctrine of the Lord's Supper was the central issue of the Reformation, setting the agenda on every side of the debate. This was the time of diets and colloquies, all aimed at establishing confessional consensus between the theologians of Wittenberg and those of south Germany and Switzerland. At stake was the unitive ideal on which the success of the Reformation depended. Shortly after his arrival in England in 1549, Martin Bucer, *de facto* leader of the south Germans, was thrust into draining disputes over Zürich-inspired doctrine and practice. John Hooper, the most vocal of the Anglo-Zürichers, had told Bucer in June 1548 that the Swiss divines opposed his view of the Supper: 'as I do myself'. Bucer ignored the slight. He did, however, beg Hooper to temper his criticism of John Calvin. Hooper yielded, but confessed that Calvin's commentaries on 1 Corinthians 'displeased me exceedingly'. In April 1549 Hooper sent word to Heinrich Bullinger that Bucer 'would leave no stone unturned to obtain a footing'[1] for his sacramental expatiations. According to Martin Greschat 'many of Bullinger's supporters not only openly opposed Bucer but even felt unmitigated hatred toward him'.[2] Bullinger himself did little to restrain their impulses. He wrote to the cloth merchant John Burcher: 'How is Bucer conducting himself in England, I beg you to let me know'.[3] Burcher had written to him in May 1549, expressing the wish that Bucer 'may not pervert' Cranmer's view of the Supper 'or make him worse'.[4] By 1550, this distrust had curdled into the belief that, in the glad event of Bucer's

---

1   Quoted in Basil Hall, 'Martin Bucer in England' (essay), *Reforming Church & Community*, ed. D. F. Wright (Cambridge, 2002), 149.

2   *A Reformer & His Times* (Louisville, 2004), 234.

3   Quoted in Hall (essay), 149.

4   Ibid. 150.

ill-health leading to death, 'England will be happy and more favoured than all the other countries in having been delivered in the same year from two men of the most pernicious talent':[1] Bucer and Fagius.[2]

In the same period, Peter Martyr Vermigli, Bucer's fellow émigré, was caught up in a disputation on the eucharist at Oxford. Against this background, Vermigli's conclusion to his Oxford *Treatise* (1549) strikes poignant and prophetic notes:

> I have observed so far that the eucharist (with which we are dealing) has been so overwhelmed, buried and deformed by lies, devices and superstitions that it could be reckoned anything besides what the Lord instituted in the Supper. To prevent its easily being purged, the devil (the greatest enemy of all peace and truth) has sown so many opinions, controversies, disagreements, heresies and battles, although without blood, that scarcely any consent worthy of Christians can be hoped for by human reason. Alas! We have not endured these things without harm, for we have dealt double injury to the sacrament: in part because we have erected an accursed idol instead of the excellent and special gift in Christ; in part because we have abused these special mysteries, without sincere faith, with conscience defiled by grave sins, scorning a proper examination of our own hearts.[3]

The Florentine's high exegetical approach, wedded to a reluctance to dismiss an idea until he had first fully grasped it, makes him the ideal expositor of a Reformed understanding of the Supper. This much was allowed by Calvin, otherwise the greatest systematic thinker of them all. The whole doctrine of the eucharist, stated Calvin, 'was crowned by Peter Martyr, who left nothing more to be done'.[4] One should not forget, however, that Vermigli's rejection of Romanist, Lutheran, and Zwinglian opinion, in favour of a conception of the eucharist as a vehicle for spiritual union with Christ, is rooted in the mediating theology developed in Strasbourg under Bucer. Vermigli, like Calvin, spent formative years in south Germany as a colleague of Bucer;

---

1   Ibid.

2   Paul Fagius, the noted Hebraist and Bucer's friend and companion from Strasbourg, died in Cambridge on 13 November, 1549.

3   *The Oxford Treatise and Disputation on the Eucharist,* ed. Joseph C. McClelland (Kirksville, 2000), 125.

4   Ibid. p. xxxi n.

Calvin, insists Joseph McClelland, is Vermigli's natural ally. But all three—
Bucer, Calvin and Vermigli—'must be considered as holding an essentially
identical doctrine of the Eucharist'.[1]

According to Willem van 't Spijker, the deep and abiding friendship
between Bucer and Calvin 'can be accounted for by the strong theological
and religious affinity which enabled each to influence the other'.[2] Calvin
had a much higher opinion of Luther than of Zwingli, whose position on
the Lord's Supper he judged 'profane'.[3] But Bucer, he told Simon Grynaeus,
'remains unsurpassed today by anyone'.[4] As for Bullinger, *Antistes* of the
Zürich church since 1531, Calvin resented his refusal to teach the sacrament as
an instrument of divine grace, bridging the gulf between earth and heaven.[5]
Bullinger regarded it as a testimony of previous grace: nothing more. But
why, persisted Calvin, 'would the Lord put the symbol of His body in your
hands unless to assure you of a true participation in it?'[6] For Calvin, the
Zürich view was a reproach on the name of Christ. He was sure that 'in
His sacred Supper [Christ] bids me to take, eat, and drink of His body and
blood under the symbols of bread and wine. I have no doubt that He truly
proffers them, and that I receive them'.[7] The visible elements, autographed
by God's Word, become something (and this is key) 'which they were not
before':[8] Christ in fact 'condescends to us both in the outward symbol as
well as in His Spirit'.[9] Nor does His ascension to heaven preclude His being
wholly in the sacrament, for 'dwelling in us by His Spirit, He so raises us to
Himself into heaven, that He transfuses into us the life-giving vigour of His
flesh'.[10] It is hard work making this compatible with Swiss-style theology.
And although by the time of the Second Helvetic Confession (1566) it was

1   Quoted by Peter Opitz in *A Companion to Peter Martyr Vermigli,* ed. Kirby, Campi, James (Leiden, 2009), 387.
2   'Bucer's Influence on Calvin' (essay) in *Martin Bucer: Reforming Church & Community,* ed. D. F. Wright (Cambridge, 2002), 32.
3   *The Oxford Encyclopedia of the Reformation,* ed. Hillerbrand (New York, 1996), ii. 79.
4   Quoted in Greschat, 148.
5   See Calvin's letter to Bullinger in *Gleanings of a Few Scattered Ears during the Period of the Reformation in England,* ed. Gorham (London, 1857), 49.
6   *Institutes,* IV. xvii. 10. See Hillerbrand, ii. 76.
7   Inst. IV. xvii. 32.
8   Quoted in Hillerbrand, i. 238.
9   Ibid.
10 Calvin's 'Exposition of the Heads of the Zürich Consent' reproduced in Gorham, 333.

expedient for Bullinger to reconsider and redraft the view, contained in the Zürich Confession (1545), that recalling 'is the real chief part and purpose' of the Supper, his later presentation, says Brian Gerrish, still 'lacks the use of instrumental expressions; the outward event does not convey or cause or give rise to the inward event, but merely indicates what is going on'.[1]

Calvin based his Geneva liturgy of 1540 upon the service of word and sacrament first enacted by Bucer in Strasbourg in 1524: 'a clear token', says Gerrish, 'of theological affinity'.[2] McClelland develops the same theme, but goes further. Not Zürich, not Wittenberg, 'but the Strasbourg of Bucer, from which both Calvin and Martyr went forward to a massive and powerful theology' is the place where had 'emerged a positive theology which was in a profound sense the true gravitational centre of the Reformation'.[3] This was the theology, in the persons of Vermigli, Bucer and Paul Fagius, that arrived in England in the reign of Edward VI.

In July 1548 Jan Laski, the Polish émigré, and soon-to-be superintendent of London's Stranger Churches, wrote from Emden that 'the Sacramentarian Controversy is begun to be agitated in [England] among some persons; and a public disputation has been appointed in that matter, to which I am called by the earnest prayer of many. Bucer is expected; our Thomas Dryander is already there; and there are many whispers about Calvin, but he is a Frenchman'.[4] John Bradford, Bucer's 'most loyal English disciple',[5] was lamenting 'the evil which is now-a-days most to be feared concerning the sacrament'.[6] Along with Nicholas Ridley, Bradford stood four-square behind Bucer's mature eucharistic opinion; as, for a while at least, did Cranmer. A striking aspect of Bradford's *Sermon on the Lord's Supper* is its indebtedness not only to the ideas of Bucer, but to his language. Like Bucer, Bradford makes free use of 'exhibit' and 'exhibition' to describe the offering of Christ's body; he also adopts one of Bucer's favourite illustrations, seen especially in his work on Matthew's Gospel, in which the analogy of the sun and its rays is used to explain how, despite Christ's body being locally in heaven, believers are able

1   B. A. Gerrish, *Theology Today*, vol. 23, no. 2 (July 1966), 234.
2   Hillerbrand, ii. 77.
3   Quoted by Peter Opitz in *A Companion to Peter Martyr Vermigli,* ed. Kirby, Campi, James (Leiden, 2009), 387.
4   From a letter in Gorham, 52.
5   *De Regno Christi,* ed. Wilhelm Pauck (Louisville, 2006), 161.
6   *Writings* (Edinburgh, rep. 1979), i. 96.

to participate in its substance. Also present is the idea, synonymous with Bucer and Vermigli—though actually picked up from Augustine—of Christ offering Himself sacramentally in visible words:

> Not that Christ is not so much present in His Word preached, as He is in or with His sacrament; but because there are in the perception of the sacrament more windows open for Christ to enter into us, than by His Word preached or heard. For there (I mean in the Word) He hath an entrance into our hearts, but only by the ears through the voice and sound of the words; but here in the sacrament He hath an entrance by our senses, by our eyes, by our nose, by our taste, and by our handling also: and therefore the sacrament full well may be called seeable, sensible, tasteable, and touchable words.[1]

For the Anglo-Zürich group, this loaded the sacrament with too much meaning. Yes, said Hooper and Laski, we can consider Christ's perfection, remember His sacrifice and give thanks, but the words *this is my body* (Matthew 26:26) were to be understood in a purely symbolic sense. The outward signs cannot present the absent Christ; what happens at the Lord's table is predominantly psychological. For Laski too, adds Ian Hazlett, the Supper was 'understood passively as the fellowship between Christ and believers, whereas Bucer, even if he does take passive communion for granted, pleads for an active communion as well—which requires a positive distribution, with the aid of a minister, of the body of Christ and its benefits'.[2] Little wonder, then, that Laski objected to Bucer's preference for 'Given and Partaken' ('percipi') to describe our reception of Christ, over his own 'sealed' ('obsignari').[3] From the day of his arrival in England, what Basil Hall describes as 'a powerful company of energetic promoters of Zürich theology'[4] sought to subvert Bucer's efforts to plant his ideas in English soil. This faction was alarmed by his influence over Cranmer, whom they deemed—not unreasonably, given his doctrinal wanderings—biddable. Hooper even went so far as to spread a rumour, quite unfounded, that Bucer taught the ubiquity of Christ's body. On his part, Bucer was never slow to condemn those who 'seclude Christ

---

1   Ibid. 101.

2   'Eucharistic communion: impulses and directions in Martin Bucer's Thought' (essay) in *Martin Bucer: Reforming Church & Community*, 80.

3   See Gorham, 30.

4   'Martin Bucer in England' (essay) in *Martin Bucer: Reforming Church and Community*, 149.

our Saviour from our sacraments and holy assemblies, and confine Him to His place in heaven'.[1] In a letter to Calvin of August 1549, Bucer deemed the Swiss view 'a feeble way of speaking of the sacraments': wherever memorialism was taught 'there will be found a vast number of persons, now-a-days, who never partake of the Lord's Supper'.[2] In their mania to distance themselves from sacramental-sacrificial, papal-Catholic dogma, Zwingli—and more especially his followers—had turned the Supper into a devotional exercise. Peter Martyr Vermigli, writing from Oxford, summarized the position he and Bucer were facing in England: 'Transubstantiation, I think, is now exploded, and difficulty respecting the presence is at this time the most prominent point of dispute'.[3]

Matters came to some kind of head with the appearance of *The Book of Common Prayer* (1549). At the request of Goodrich, bishop of Ely, Bucer provided a detailed evaluation of the book. The *Censura* (critique) contained fifty-eight examples of how the text might be made less susceptible to Romanist bias. His propositions included a pared-down liturgy, fewer holidays, fewer ceremonies, less frequent bell-ringing, and even less concentration on vestments, extreme unction, and on the actions of piety, such as crossing oneself and consecrating objects. The influence of Bucer's *Censura* pervades *The Second Book of Common Prayer* (1552). But still: his impression of the first prayer book was overwhelmingly positive. If some of the old practices persisted, he wrote, these were 'only to be retained for a time, lest the people, not having yet learned Christ, should be deterred by too extensive innovations from embracing His religion, and that rather they may be won over'.[4] So far as the communion service was concerned, he was little short of jubilant. 'Transubstantiation', he wrote, 'is not affirmed … at the Lord's Supper, a true exhibition of the Body and Blood of Christ is expressed in words exceedingly clear and weighty'.[5] He gave 'utmost thanks to God, who has given it to be so pure, and so scrupulously faithful to the Word of God, especially in light of the time in which this was done. For excepting a very few words and signs I perceive nothing in it at all which may not be

---

1   Quoted in Constantin Hopf, *Martin Bucer & the English Reformation* (Oxford, 1946), 50.
2   From a letter in Gorham, 104.
3   *The Oxford Treatise & Disputation on the Eucharist* (1549), p. xix.
4   Quoted in Hopf, 56.
5   See Hall (essay) in *Martin Bucer: Reforming Church & Community*, 151.

drawn out of the Holy Scriptures'.[1] He went out of his way to advocate the retention of the phrases 'so as to eat the flesh of thy dear Son Jesus Christ'[2] in the Prayer of Humble Access, and 'may worthily receive the most precious body and bloude of thy sonne Jesus Christe'[3] in the prayer after the Prayer of Consecration. This was Hooper's cue to begin a full-scale attack on the Prayer Book. In a letter to Bullinger he fulminated that 'I am so much offended with that book and that not without abundant reason that if it be not corrected, I can nor will communicate with the church in the administration of the Supper'.[4]

These are still contentious matters, so one or two points need to be clarified. Bucer spoke not against the sacrament itself, but against the papal-Catholic dogma of the mass, according to which Christ's once-and-for-all sacrifice on the Cross is endlessly re-enacted. He also condemned transubstantiation: the idea that the bread and wine of the eucharist, after consecration by a priest, are transformed into Christ's actual body and blood. Such teaching undermined the unique efficacy of His atoning work; a priest standing in front of an altar was a clear indication to the faithful that he was performing a sacrifice on their behalf. But what Bucer called this 'utterly detestable bread-worship of the antichrists'[5] in no way impaired his own sense of how Christ is given and received in the sacred Supper. In his *Confession of the Eucharist* (1550)—'which Dr Martin Bucer left, written and signed in his own hand, shortly before he fell asleep in Christ, in England'[6]—we see the great Reformer tightening the nuts and bolts of his sacramental doctrine:

But if I am asked about the use here of bread and wine, my reply is that they are presenting *(exhibitiva)* signs whereby the Lord presents and imparts Himself as bread from heaven, the bread of eternal life, in exactly the same way as He bestowed the Holy Spirit on the disciples by the sign of the bread of His mouth, and as He conferred healing of body and mind on many by the touch of His hand, and sight by clay made

1   Quoted in Hopf, 57.
2   Ibid. 79.
3   Ibid. 80.
4   Quoted in Hall (essay), 151–152.
5   *Common Places of Martin Bucer,* ed. D. F. Wright (Appleford, 1972), 392.
6   Ibid. 381.

from spittle, and circumcision of heart by circumcision of the flesh, and regeneration by baptism.[1]

Every benefit of our union with Christ is, so to speak, sacramentally available. But Bucer was anxious to fend off any conception of a sacrament that worked *apart* from the action of faith. Unbelievers were excluded from a true, definitive form of spiritual eating: 'for the body of the Lord as such can neither be reached nor understood by reason, but faith must rather be active here'.[2] As the mouth eats the bread, so the mouth of faith partakes of the body of Christ: anyone taking hold of the signs 'to eat and drink without living faith in Christ, so far from receiving any nourishment the Lord here bestows on His own, takes hold instead of death and damnation for himself'.[3] Nor does the body of Christ have to alter its location in heaven in order to be with the sacrament, for 'we apprehend Him present by faith only, without any idea of place':[4]

As the sun is truly placed determinately in one place of the visible heaven, and yet is truly and substantially present by means of his beams elsewhere in the world abroad, so our Lord, although He be comprehended in one place of the secret and divine heaven, that is to say, the glory of His Father, yet nevertheless by His word and holy tokens He is exhibit present truly whole God and man, and therefore in substance in His holy supper.[5]

This put Bucer at loggerheads with Luther and Melanchthon. Nothing, however, would deter the Anglo-Zürich faction from presenting him as an incorrigible Lutheran. Given his expressed 'grief on account of the ruin of our churches in Germany',[6] the emergence of an unbalanced attitude towards the externals of worship in his new homeland must have hit Bucer hard. His spirits were already weighed down by ill-health. In a letter to William Farel he expressed his frustration with 'the weather, the language, the food, the customs, the housing, and just about everything else'[7] in England. At this

---

1 Ibid. 395.
2 Quoted in Greschat, 135.
3 *Common Places of Martin Bucer*, 396.
4 Letter in Gorham, 92.
5 From Bucer's commentary on Matthew; see Jeanes, 159.
6 Letter in Gorham, 84.
7 Quoted in Greschat, 245.

time, says Diarmaid MacCulloch, John Calvin and the Geneva leadership 'represented [for Bucer] the only reliable confidential counsellors in an unsympathetic world'.[1]

With the Italian Inquisition snapping at his heels, Peter Martyr Vermigli crossed the Alps into Protestantism in August 1542. A one-time Augustinian monk, Vermigli's reading of Bucer's commentaries on the Gospels and the Psalms comprised his pathway into Reformed thought. After fleeing first to Zürich, then Basel, Vermigli arrived in the evangelically-disposed city of Strasbourg in October. He settled quickly, falling under the influence of the circle around Bucer, and teaching, alongside Paul Fagius, Caspar Hedio and others, at the Haute-Ecole, the so-called Senior School. Both in England and later in Zürich, Vermigli would remain beholden to the exegetical tradition established on the Upper Rhine. As for Bucer himself, Vermigli would forever regard him as 'the most excellent divine of our age'.[2] A house-guest of Bucer's for a while after his arrival, the Florentine depicted the Bucer home as 'a hospice for those forced into pilgrimage for the sake of Christ and the Gospel'.[3] Vermigli observed the great man's working habits at close hand. 'I have never seen Bucer inactive', he wrote. 'He spends his time either preaching or looking after the order and leadership of the church ... After having done this kind of work all day, he devotes his nights to study and prayer. Seldom did I wake up and not find him awake as well'.[4] Bucer, on his part, enthused to Calvin about a scholar 'quite learned in Greek, Hebrew and Latin, and splendidly versed in Scripture, forty-four years of age, of sober morals and sharp judgement, Peter Martyr by name'.[5] The friendship of Bucer and Vermigli, forged over five years of religious superintendency in Strasbourg, would be maintained in England by a superabundance of correspondence.

On the death of Wolfgang Capito, Fagius, his brilliant protégé, was expected to take over as lecturer in Hebrew Bible at Strasbourg. But Fagius, absorbed in the translation of Hebraica in Isny, was in no hurry to return to teaching. Bucer recommended that the position be offered to Vermigli. The Florentine had first studied Hebrew in the 1530s, in Bologna, with the celebrated Jewish

1   MacCulloch, 470.
2   Quoted in Patrick Collinson, *Archbishop Grindal 1519–1583* (London, 1979), 49.
3   Quoted in Kirby, Campi, James, 38.
4   Quoted in Greschat, 203.
5   Quoted in Kirby, Campi, James, 39.

physician Isaac. In common with every major Reformer, Vermigli deemed
a working knowledge of Hebrew a prerequisite to understanding the Bible.
'Let us go back, I beg you', he implored his students, 'let us go back to the
first sources of the Scriptures'.[1] Capito himself had been arguing from the
mid-1520s onward that 'unless the historical, with the aid of the Spirit, have
faithfully laid the foundation, whatever reflection is built on them will collapse
in ruins, wandering about in unsure passages, making itself a laughing stock
with its allegories'.[2] Vermigli had joined a cadre of scholars willing and able
to challenge the power and prestige of the established order. Each sought to
shift the focus of authority from the church to Scripture: Scripture being
defined by Vermigli as 'a certain expression of God's wisdom, breathed by
the Holy Spirit into religious men, then sealed for attestation by written
memorials'.[3] If misunderstandings of Scripture occur, said Vermigli, it is for
want of prayer in the first place, and of hard study in the second.

His first lectures at the Senior School featured the minor prophets. A
series on the Book of Lamentations followed. Vermigli's commentary on
Lamentations is a masterwork to set alongside his better-known eucharistic
writings. There is no uncertainty of purpose, no desire to hide behind
allegorical exegesis or poetic imaginings; the aim is to grasp the objective
truth of whatever is being said. The prose crackles with salvific intent.
Jerusalem is destroyed: what is worse, *The Lord hath forsaken His altar: He
hath abhorred His sanctuary* (2:7). Only the prophet's recollection of God's
covenant love keeps despair at bay. 'While some people admire its elegance',
writes Vermigli about the book's alphabet poetry, 'I for my part think that it
was done either for the purpose of memorization or because a custom had
evolved to compose public hymns along this principle'.[4] Equally enlivening
is Vermigli's willingness to read across from the fall of Jerusalem to events of
his own day. In this way, as there is nothing new in human affairs, he traces
the shape of our own discontent. One example: he allows for the possibility
that Islam, as an agent of God's judgement, might overrun a spiritually
indolent Western Europe:

---

1   *Commentary on the Lamentations of the Prophet Jeremiah,* ed. Daniel Shute (Kirksville, 2002),
p. xxxvi.

2   See Jerome Friedman, *The Most Ancient Testimony: Sixteenth-Century Christian Hebraica in the
Age of Renaissance Nostalgia* (Ohio, 1983), 127.

3   *Commentary on Lamentations,* p. xlix.

4   Ibid. 5.

God did not spare Jerusalem, so in this verse [2:1] God is said to have forgotten it. For if we handle badly and abuse the things that contribute to the worship of God, if they foster and cover up our vices, God burns with fierce anger. So let us not cast away our readings, meeting together, sacraments, and gospel, but let us value faith and approve the good life. These God cannot despise; what we handle badly God will easily cast aside and let the Turks trample.[1]

After Lamentations Vermigli began an interpretation of the first three books of the Pentateuch. He was still working on Leviticus when, in October 1547, an English party arrived with the request that led to his appointment as regius professor at Christ Church, Oxford. His time in Strasbourg had sharpened Vermigli's vision of a church shorn of medieval encumbrances. Unlike Luther—whose knowledge of Hebrew was limited—Vermigli, following Bucer, allowed no dichotomy of Law and Gospel: the proper relationship between the old and the new covenant was one of continuity. In his lectures on Genesis, delivered in the mid-1540s, Vermigli told his students that the book 'entails instructions about the Law, the Gospel, and the promise of Christ'.[2] According to Emidio Campi, Vermigli 'sees the community of the patriarchs in Genesis as parallel to the church and their faith as the same faith which the church has today. In this sense, the teaching of Moses, as stated in Genesis, is not bound to the Jews of his time, but may be properly extended to believers of all ages as they all worship the same God'.[3] Calvin too 'was convinced that there was one covenant and one people of God in both testaments, and he thought that Luther's distinction did not do justice to the economy of divine self-manifestation'.[4] A corollary of this, detailed by Jerome Friedman, was that 'the OT retained a measure of importance in Reformed circles it did not command in Lutheran Protestant thought'.[5] For Bucer in particular, says Basil Hall, 'all legislation [was] to be derived from Scripture, not least from the Mosaic code of law'; Hall is also of the opinion that 'Bucer's attempt to use the Old Testament for all aspects of society, led him astray from social reality'. Bucer, he claims, was 'more

---

1 Ibid. 71.
2 Quoted in Kirby, Campi, James, 217.
3 Ibid.
4 Ibid. 218.
5 Friedman, 100.

rigid than Calvin, who believed that sixteenth-century states could not be simplistically instructed on all matters by Moses'.[1] It is certainly true that no one strove harder than Bucer, in Strasbourg and in England, to establish a community of love ordered according to the laws and commandments established in Scripture. His last great work, *De Regno Christi* ('On the Kingdom of Christ') was just that: a detailed charter for the assimilation of civil and religious authority, and for securing the observation of God's law in all private and social life. Greschat refers to 'the two supporting columns of [Bucer's] religious thought and activity: first, the law of God, implanted in all creation as the order of all being, but finding its expression above all in the Bible; and secondly the Holy Spirit, who enables human beings both to know and also in particular to assent gladly to this law, and hence to fulfil it'.[2] Here is the dualism that drives the theology of Strasbourg and pervades its mature formulation of the Supper. The material sits with the spiritual, the subjective with the objective, the reality with the sign, the eternal with the created, the allegory with the bald statement.

'The notion of transubstantiation', declares Vermigli, is propagated by 'superstitious sort of folk'. It is 'an absurd device': a 'permanent illusion'.[3] The Lord's Supper is always a meal, never a sacrifice; it is certain then 'that just as the two natures remain whole in Christ, so the substance of the bread must not be removed in the eucharist'.[4] As for the Lutheran position, the Florentine 'cannot allow such a crass connection of the body of Christ with bread so that He is contained in it naturally, corporeally, and really'.[5] He repudiates the notorious *manducatio indignorium* ('the eating of the unworthy') and talk of the ubiquity of Christ's body: 'For whatever the Lord instituted he did for our health; but a carnal and corporeal eating is not healthy for the wicked; therefore Christ instituted no such thing. Whatever the wicked eat corporeally they should not call an eating of Christ's body, unless you wish to attribute the name of the reality to the sign or symbol. Further, we will not agree that the body of Christ is everywhere, or scattered through everything or in many places, since this is against the conditions of human

1　'Martin Bucer in England' (essay) in *Martin Bucer: Reforming Church & Community*, 156.

2　'The relation between church and civil community in Bucer's reforming work' (essay) in *Martin Bucer: Reforming Church and Community*, 18.

3　Quoted in Kirby, Campi, James, 390.

4　Ibid. 199.

5　*The Oxford Treatise & Disputation on the Eucharist* (1549), 121.

nature'.[1] But Vermigli also insists that Christ 'is eaten spiritually, and is truly joined to us'.[2] In a letter of June 1549 he confirms that he 'does not differ at all' from the position adduced by Martin Bucer: 'I acknowledge', writes Vermigli, 'that we truly receive the *res sacramenti*, that is the body and blood of Christ; but I say that it is accomplished by soul and faith, meanwhile granting that the Holy Spirit is effective in the sacraments, by the power of the Spirit and the institution of the Lord'.[3] In another place he says that 'it is certain to the same degree that our souls are nourished by the body and blood of Christ as it is certain for our senses that we eat bread and drink wine'.[4] That bread, that wine, shadows of an absent reality for the Anglo-Zürichers, become, for Vermigli, Calvin and Bucer, efficacious instruments for the salvation of the believer. In his Oxford *Treatise* Vermigli censures the followers of Zwingli for their tendency to (as we might say) over-spiritualize the Christian religion:

[I am] not happy that they mention only rarely a sacramental mutation of the bread and wine, although this is no light matter, and one that the Fathers intend whenever they seem to favour transubstantiation. Scripture does not condemn it, because in his treatment of the sacrament, Paul does not call it simply cup, but cup of the Lord. We see also in the Old Testament that what was offered was called not merely holy, but holy of holies, that is, in the Hebrew phrase, 'the holiest'. Therefore they have no right to say that this change is a little thing, since it is of great moment. But if they pretend that they do this because we should not cling too much to symbols, we reply that a remedy is easily found for this evil through doctrine, by which men are taught that Christ is joined to us by an excellent union when we communicate, so that He dwells in us and we in Him. In the next degree He is also joined to words, through signification. And in the third place He is joined to symbols, also by signification, but less than that which belongs to words. Indeed through the former (of words) the symbols derive their sacramental signification. If these things are taught properly there will be no danger.[5]

---

1 Ibid. 121–122.
2 *The Oxford Treatise & Disputation on the Eucharist* (1549), p. xxxviii.
3 Ibid. p. xxxvi.
4 Quoted in Kirby, Campi, James, 396.
5 *The Oxford Treatise & Disputation on the Eucharist* (1549), 122.

In line with Bucer and Calvin, then, but contrary to the Zürichers, Anglo- and otherwise, Vermigli grants our actual participation in the body and blood of Christ. Because such a synthesis in unfathomable, the language of metaphor is allowable. But this metaphor admits of no dilution of truth; it describes, in fact, a heightened form of reality: the Divine Idea without which nothing can be called anything. Thought of from a slightly different angle, the presence of which we speak is not imagined. What makes it real is faith in the crucified and resurrected Christ. Long after his return to Strasbourg, Vermigli was spelling this out in a letter to Calvin. 'I indeed am entirely convinced', he wrote, 'that whatever sustenance or spiritual food is received by us from the body of Christ is had from His true and natural body, which for our salvation was formerly fastened on the Cross, and is now seated in Heaven, enveloped in utmost glory. For since all sustenance (which is indeed very great) is derived by us through Faith, who will say that it contemplates a fictitious or imaginary Body? Assuredly none will so hold who would maintain the truth and dignity of Faith. For Faith apprehends things as they are. Wherefore, seeing that Christ's Body is not divested of its nature, either formally on the Cross or now in Heaven, it is received by us through Faith a natural body, as it is'.[1] To Bucer, however, Vermigli's *Treatise* was a let-down. To Theobold Niger he wrote that 'since the Zürich people have here many and great followers', Vermigli ('I hardly know how')[2] had been induced to adopt terms—'signification', for example, and 'absence'—that bore the taint of memorialism. More alarming still was the assertion that 'it does not agree with Christ's body, so greatly glorified, to be in many places'.[3] This ran contrary to Bucer's understanding of Christ's spatial location, and how we draw life from Him. It also put Vermigli at odds with Calvin. Bucer and Calvin agreed—both insisted—that Christ's glorified body was in heaven and not, *pace* Luther, capable of occupying two places at once. But the Holy Spirit, said Calvin, 'truly unites things separated by space'.[4] Christ's actual presence at His Father's right hand did not, wrote Bucer to Vermigli in June 1549, preclude His actual presence in the Supper:

For, though we should grant you, that He is circumscribed even in

---

1   Letter in Gorham, 341–342.
2   Ibid, 142.
3   Ibid. 81.
4   Inst. IV. vii. 10.

heaven by a physical place, how is that inconsistent with His being now truly present by faith; even as the sun in whatever part of the world we behold [it], is truly present to us by sight. Certainly all errors which can possibly arise from the name 'presence' may be altogether excluded by such words ... I entreat you to have the kindness to explain to such an one my sentiment more correctly: which is this: that Christ exhibits Himself at the same moment and truly, by the Word and by His sacraments, present to us, although we are existing in many places; but that we see and apprehend Him, present, by faith only, without any idea of place.[1]

Vermigli's failure to underwrite every feature of his mediation theology was enough to plunge Bucer into sullen introspection. 'I am sorry for master Martyr's book as anyone can be', he told the Swabian Johannes Brenz. 'But that disputation took place, and the propositions were agreed upon, before I arrived in England'.[2] What to make of such a reaction? Several things ought to be borne in mind: not least that the *Treatise* is more critical of Zwinglians than of Lutherans. Vermigli affirms that the body of Christ 'becomes present to us by faith, and, by communicating, we are incorporated with Him, and are transformed into that Body'.[3] The bread and wine 'signify, offer and most truly exhibit the body of Christ, although spiritually, that is, to be eaten with the mind, not the bodily mouth'.[4] The sacraments are 'sensible words of God'.[5] Unbelievers *(impii)* only receive the bare sign. In the face of such unqualified support for Bucer, and for his core belief in an exhibitive real spiritual presence of Christ, the impression persists that Bucer's efforts to build bridges between the theologians of Zürich and Wittenberg in the 1530s had left him unwilling—and perhaps unable—to allow differences of emphasis and expression to emerge in England. The background in Europe was one of bitter infighting, signal setbacks, thousands of miles travelled and the drafting and re-drafting of endless statements. The scar tissue was still too fresh. McClelland's judgement, that 'the Bucer-Martyr disagreement concerned terms rather than substance'[6] is surely the right one. Vermigli's

1 Gorham, 90, 92.
2 Quoted in *The Oxford Treatise & Disputation on the Eucharist* (1549), p. xxxvii.
3 Letter in Gorham, 81.
4 Ibid. 124.
5 Ibid. 123.
6 *The Oxford Treatise & Disputation on the Eucharist* (1549), p. xli.

reluctance to make a fetish out of vocabulary shouldn't then be pushed too far. Nor should his accent on Christ in His heavenly glory. His was, after all, a different personality from Bucer's, coming from a different homeland, operating in a different environment, dealing with different opponents, having different conversations.

In arguing for an active communion with Christ, Martin Bucer wanted to foster a view of the church as a community of those 'entering properly and wholeheartedly into covenant with God and obeying Him (which almighty God demands so strictly in His Word)'.[1] The sacraments, he said, 'are precisely what they are said to be since they really confer (*re ipsa exhibent*) what they signify—the covenant of the Lord, the cleansing of sins, communion in Christ'.[2] Bucer was extremely watchful of those who wanted to implant invented, more spiritualistic meanings into the Supper. That kind of approach, especially when allied to allegorical interpretation, risked falling into the kind of subjectivism—where God becomes the hero inside yourself, the mirror of one's own opinions—to which he and Calvin were viscerally resistant. Both bore the scars of their battles with anabaptists: those 'giddy men', who, wrote Calvin, 'make a great display of the superiority of the Spirit, reject all reading of the Scriptures themselves, and deride the simplicity of those who only delight in what they call the dead and deadly letter'.[3] In emphasizing instead the inviolable link between the external sign and the internal significance, the giants of the Reformation were both, in their different ways, placing the role of teaching firmly within the ministry of Christian discipline: 'the yoke of Christ'. Bucer, according to David Wright, 'more lucidly than any Reformer to date, was firmly of the conviction that discipline belonged with the Word and the sacraments as constitutive marks of the church of Christ'.[4] The same theme was taken up by John Bradford. 'If ministers did their duties in catechizing and preaching', he wrote, 'then doubtless to call the sacrament "Christ's body" and to esteem it accordingly, could not give occasion to idolatry, and confirm it. Therefore woe unto them that preach

---

1   Quoted in Martin Greschat, 'The relation between church and civil community in Bucer's reforming work' (essay) in *Martin Bucer: Reforming Church and Community*, 25.

2   Quoted in David Wright, 'Infant Baptism and the Christian community in Bucer' (essay) in *Martin Bucer: Reforming Church and Community*, 100.

3   *Inst.* I. ix. I.

4   Martin Bucer, *Concerning the True Care of Souls*, ed. Wright (Edinburgh, 2009), p. xvi.

[this] not!'[1] For Bucer as well 'it is necessary that nothing other than certain words of God be preached in the churches, words on which reason can rely beyond all doubt'.[2] With regards to the Lord's Supper, those 'certain words' were found in the Gospels of Matthew and John, where 'the Lord Himself is giving instruction there on the true eating and drinking of His flesh and blood, in regard to which only later did He institute the sacrament; in this He also gives the food, Himself, His true flesh and true blood, about which He had spoken and taught in John 6'.[3] Bradford approached the same passages in the same spirit as his mentor:

> But how shall we best know the mind of Christ? Forsooth, as a man's mind is best known by his word, so by Christ's words shall we know His mind. Now His words be manifest and most plain. 'This', saith he, 'is my body': therefore accordingly should we esteem it and take it and receive it. If He had spoken nothing, or if He had spoken doubtfully, then we might have been in some doubt. But in that He speaketh so plainly, saying 'This is my body', who can, may, or dare to be so bold as to doubt of it? He is 'the truth' and cannot lie: he is omnipotent and can do all things: therefore it is His body. This I believe, this I confess, and pray you all heartily to beware of these and such like words, that it is but a sign or a figure of His body; except you will discern betwixt signs which signify only, and signs which also do represent, confirm and seal up, or (as man may say) give with their signification … In the Lord's Supper the bread is called 'a partaking of the Lord's body' and not only a bare sign of the body of the Lord.[4]

In the wake of the Elizabethan Settlement, a memorialist view of the Lord's Supper won new ground and eventually became normative for evangelicals in the English church. In 1554, writing from his cell, his martyrdom only months away, Bradford set down on paper his belief that 'the contempt for the sacrament in the days of king Edward hath caused these plagues upon us presently'.[5] It is a sobering thought that in the desultory processes that have marked our observance of the Supper since the Reformation, we might be

---

1   *Writings*, i. 95.
2   Quoted in Greschat, 82.
3   Quoted in Hazlett (essay) in *Martin Bucer: Reforming Church and Community*, 78.
4   *Writings*, i. 93–93.
5   Ibid. 96.

seeing the plagues of our own inglorious age writ large, including the creation
of a religious culture with no sense or expectation of God's presence in its
midst. God cannot, after all, be depersonalized and remain God. Nor can
faith be treated as an arbitrary part of the human condition.

Patrick Collinson has written that 'for the English reformers, the alignment
of their eucharistic opinions and doctrines in relation to the major schools of
continental thought involves problems of notorious delicacy which remain
controversial'.[1] So: is that where we are, 450-odd years after the death
of Cranmer? Still enmeshed in 'problems of notorious delicacy'? If so, a
measure of responsibility must be laid at the door of Cranmer himself, and
what MacCulloch calls his 'remarkable penchant for temporary adaptions
to circumstances'.[2] Even under Edward VI, the archbishop's lack of clarity
in theology was routinely gossiped over. When challenged by temperaments
more tenacious than his own—said friend and foe alike—Cranmer was likely
to waver. It was joked that he took on the colours of the last guest to stay at
Lambeth Palace. And indeed, at various times, and even at the same time, he
was branded a closet Lutheran, a shameless Zwinglian, a reluctant Buceran, a
convinced Calvinist, a camp follower of Bullinger by way of Laski and a blind
disciple of Oecolampadius. The fact that his was never an original mind, that
he was first and foremost an academic, would explain the imitative nature of
his thought generally. 'His primary impulse', writes G.W. Bromiley—in an
especially telling comment—'was to amass knowledge rather than to state
or discuss it'.[3] Hence his willingness to bend and stretch the explanation of
how God approaches man through Christ. His aim was to mollify his critics:
any critic. It does, however, seem certain that by the end of Edward's reign,
Cranmer had abandoned any idea of the elements of bread and wine being
transformed into Christ's actual body and blood. If the 1549 *Book of Common
Prayer* had reflected a broadly Lutheran understanding, the 1552 liturgy was
suffused with memorialism. As was *A Defence of the True and Catholic Doctrine
of the Sacrament of the Body and Blood of Our Saviour Christ (1550)*. 'Zwingli's
favourite text (John 6:63)', says Brian Gerrish, 'stands like a banner on the

1   *Archbishop Grindal 1519–1583: The Struggle for a Reformed Church* (London, 1979), 42.
2   MacCulloch, 630.
3   *Thomas Cranmer, Theologian* (London, 1956), 3–4, 7. See also Gordon P. Jeanes, *Signs of God's
Promise: Thomas Cranmer's Sacramental Theology and the Book of Common Prayer* (London, 2008), 5.

front page of the *Defence*.[1] In this major work—or stumbling block—of the English Reformation, Cranmer careers off down a spiritualistic path:

> And marvel not, good reader, that Christ at that time spoke in figures, when he did institute that sacrament, seeing that it is in the nature of all sacraments to be figures. And although the Scripture can be full of schemes, tropes and figures, yet specially it uses them when it speaks of sacraments.[2]

He goes on to erect a wall of disparity between spiritual and material realities. The bread is not transformed. In this manner he stands clear of Bucer and his talk of a supernatural synthesis, an apportioning of 'the food of the new internal man, the food of eternal life, the strengthening of faith by which the just man lives, the increase of new life, the life of God in us'.[3] Instead Cranmer offers a meditation on truths felt to be remote. He affirms, says Gordon Jeanes, 'like Zwingli, but unlike Calvin and Bucer, [Christ's] presence by His divinity, not by His humanity in the substance of His flesh'.[4] And where Bucer and Vermigli both argued that the visible elements are connected to the body and blood of Christ in the manner of words to their meanings, Cranmer emphasizes a division as much as a relationship:

> And not to the ethnic and carnal, but to the faithful and spiritual ears, the words of Christ be figurative, and to them the truth of the figures be plainly opened and declared by the fathers: wherein the fathers be worthy of much commendation, because they travailed to open plainly unto us the obscure and figurative speeches of Christ. And yet in their said declarations they taught us, that these words of Christ, concerning the eating of His flesh and drinking of His blood, are not to be understood plainly, as the words properly signify, but by a figurative speech.[5]

It is hopeless trying to reconcile this sort of thing with Buceran (and

---

1   Hillerbrand, ii. 79.

2   *Archbishop Cranmer on the True and Catholic Doctrine...* ed. C.H.H. Wright (London, 1907), 156. See also Alister E. McGrath, *Reformation Thought* (Malden, 1999), 258.

3   Quoted in Ian Hazlett, 'Eucharistic Communion: impulses and directions in Martin Bucer's Thought' (essay) in *Martin Bucer: Reforming Church & Community,* ed. D. F. Wright (Cambridge, 1994), 81.

4   Jeanes, 7.

5   Quoted in Jeanes, 151.

Calvinist) opinion that Christ's words in Matthew 26 are 'manifest and most plain'.[1] Yet as late as 1550/1551 Cranmer could be found clinging to open contradictions within his theology. He defends the instrumentality of the sacraments: 'whereby He worketh, and therefore is said to be present in them'.[2] He speaks of Christ's body being 'exhibited': the hallmark of Bucer's eucharistic doctrine. The Lord, he says, is present 'verily and truly'[3] in the elements of bread and wine. And his punchy endorsement of Calvin's dictum that we become 'flesh of His flesh and bone of His bones'[4] serves, in part, to disable his own case. Such indiscriminate couplings with more secure thinkers, and the confusion that resulted, are expressive of a man of decent instincts more interested in reconciling factions within a theologically divided nation than in responding to revealed truth with integrity and faithfulness. Writes Jeanes: 'Whatever the quality of his liturgical prose, his major theological writings in defence of his eucharistic theology are not only polemical and negative in tone, but obscure and equivocal. They provide infinite difficulties for the sympathetic reader, and innumerable traps for the unwary'.[5]

For Christians of the twenty-first century, revisiting these sixteenth-century debates on the Supper would constitute an important step in defining afresh what it is they believe: and what it is they do not believe. Not to attach themselves to a theological dogma, but to challenge the spiritual, moral and intellectual poverty of our age, and more credibly call fellow Christians to discernment. One thing is certain, if the processes of Reformation are to be re-ignited, those who practice the religion of the Reformed cannot allow themselves to be immobilized by tact. In elaborating the concept of a truly evangelical faith, they will follow the government of the Spirit according to the Word. They will oppose anything that vitiates the purpose of Christ's ministry. With the forces of disintegration all around us, it seems perverse to talk in vague terms about the love of God and suggest that all is excusable in His sight. Only when we can say with Peter Martyr Vermigli that 'It is the prerogative of the Scripture alone to command our faith as that certain rule

---

1   John Bradford, *Writings* (Edinburgh, rep. 1979), i. 93.
2   Quoted by Brian Gerrish in Hillerbrand, ii. 79.
3   Ibid.
4   See Ephesians 5:30.
5   Jeanes, 2.

which prescribes what we must believe'[1] can we begin to reshape church and nation.

---

1 *Life, Letters, Sermons: Peter Martyr Vermigli,* ed. J. P. Donnelly (Kirksville, 1999), 145.

APPENDIX 2

ROBERT BARNES' *A SUPPLICATION* (1531; REVISED AND REPRINTED 1534)

In the course of his remarkably varied career, Robert Barnes entered into a number of schemes for the reformation of the church and of the common life. In *A Supplication* his object was to present a compendium of theological fundamentals. John Fisher, the bishop of Rochester, is brought to book for his assertion that 'faith begins justification in us, but works do perform it and make it better'. How can he, asks a wrathful Barnes, 'thus trifle and play with God's holy Word?'[1] First and last it is 'faith [that] makes me depend on God and His blessed promises made in Christ through His sweet and precious blood, and not to fear death, nor any affliction, nor persecutions, nor tribulation, but to despise all these things, and not only these, but to despise also my own life, for Christ's sake'.[2] Many of Barnes' remarks on justification bear a striking similarity to those of Calvin. Indeed, some commentators have questioned the usefulness of classifying Barnes as a Lutheran at all: for, says Carl Trueman, 'this blanket term hides those areas in which Barnes' emphasis, and even his doctrine, differed from that of Luther'.[3] This amounts to a serious over-egging of the pudding. In nearly all his public statements, including those on the Lord's Supper, Barnes' stance is classically Lutheran. But a couple of differences between Barnes and Luther are worth highlighting. In the 1534 edition of *A Supplication*, Barnes speaks approvingly of the Epistle of James; Luther, famously ('an epistle full of straw') never did. Where Luther read James as a subversion of Paul's message that the just shall live by faith and not by works, Barnes reconciles James to Paul by building up

---

1   *A Critical Edition of Robert Barnes's 'A Supplication'*, ed. Douglas Parker (Toronto, 2008), 235.
2   Ibid. 233.
3   Quoted in Parker, 104.

the role of works as a corollary of justification. An absence of works bespeaks an absence of faith. So while 'The glory and praise of justification belongs only to faith in Christ's blood, and not to works in any way':

> [We] do also laud and praise good works, and do teach [men] diligently to do good works, in as much as God their maker has commanded them, yes, and also to profit their neighbours by their good works. And furthermore, that other men, who blaspheme the truth, might be moved through their virtuous living, and conversation, to the holy religion of Christ. For these causes, and more, I say, do I teach good men to live well, and virtuously. Yes, and we teach that good works shall have a reward of God as Scripture testifies. But not remission of sins, nor yet justification, for their reward.[1]

Some have suggested that Luther himself, by 1534, was rethinking his earlier defamation of James: that what we see in *A Supplication* is simply a pupil belatedly following his master's lead. But Korey Maas has shown that Barnes, in the 1534 edition of his magnum opus, is restating beliefs that predate Luther's grudging admissions by at least four years. 'The two judgements of the apostles Paul and James are not contradictory', writes Barnes in his 1530 *Sentenciae*, 'when one says man is justified by faith without works and the other says faith without works is dead. Because one speaks concerning works which precede faith, the other concerning those which follow faith'. His marginal notes cement his position: 'Thus neither works preceding nor following justify, because they follow righteousness and are the effects, not causes, of righteousness'.[2] Barnes' attitude to the law—as towards the Old Testament in general—seems to have been more positive than Luther's. His emphasis, writes Trueman, 'is not simply upon the law in convicting of sin and revealing a man's impotence, but also upon the link between the law and the practical morality of the believer's life'.[3] Not a hundred miles away, then, from Bucer and Calvin, both of whom looked to the law as their 'guide to life lived in gratitude for the grace of redemption'.[4] This 'third use for the law' *(usus in renatis)* was actually more important, for the two Reformation

---

1 Parker, 240–241.

2 Quoted in Maas, *The Reformation and Robert Barnes* (Woodbridge, 2010), 47–48.

3 *Luther's Legacy* (Oxford, 1994), 183.

4 Ole Peter Grell and A.I.C. Heron in *The Oxford Encyclopedia of the Reformation,* ed. Hillerbrand (New York, 1996), i. 241.

masters, than the functions of convicting us of sin *(usus elenchticus)* and setting standards for civil society *(usus civilis)*. The law exposes our sinfulness; it alerts us to the daily questions of right living. To obey the law, then, becomes an act of faith. Grell and Heron conclude that 'There can be no doubt that this comes closer to the authentic Jewish understanding than an exclusive insistence simply on the opposition between law and gospel; it may also have contributed to the fact that anti-Semitism generally did not flourish on Reformed soil'.[1] It is a sad fact that Luther, in the 1530s, advocated the wrecking of Jewish homes and synagogues and the burning of their books.

Barnes' career—Barnes' life—proclaims an absolute refusal to allow habit and tradition to cage the spirit of one wedded to the Gospel. What animates *A Supplication* isn't, in fact, the wrath of a rebel, but the heroism of a pilgrim. His animadversions against Romanism cut deeply. Now and then they lapse into crudeness. But conventionality is not morality, and Barnes' bitter knowledge had been wrung from experience. He may have been at the heart of the Reformation, but he was also at the heart of his own life. And as a moral agent—as a writer—Barnes was not attracted to cool, immutable gravity. Nor to half measures. His best happiness was the power and the will to be useful in establishing Christ's kingdom. To that end he launches himself at 'the whole rabble of you that call yourself the holy church'.[2] He argues that 'with all your holy ornaments, such as your holy mitres, your holy cross-staves, your holy pillars, your holy red gloves, your holy anointed fingers … all these together cannot make one crumb of holiness in you, nor help you one iota forward toward being in this church'.[3] If such things could aid Christian progress, says Barnes, 'then it would be simple to make an ass of the church of God'.[4] Christ alone is the purchaser of grace: and 'you cannot by all your power and holiness make good wine or ale out of green fruit'.[5] To the elect of God 'the church is nothing else but that congregation that is sanctified in the Spirit, redeemed with Christ's blood, and sticketh fast and

---

1   Ibid.
2   *The Reformation Essays of Dr Robert Barnes,* ed. Neelak Tjernagal (London, 1963), 40.
3   Ibid. 42–43.
4   Ibid. 43.
5   Ibid. 39.

sure only to the promises that are made therein'.[1] He indicts the church of Fisher and More for following the practices of 'that false prophet Balaam':[2]

> Now they sell us, they sell the people, they sell holy orders, they sell church hallowing, there is no better merchandise in Cheapside. Wilt thou know what is the price of a church hallowing? No less than eleven shillings. They sell pardons, and remissions of sins as openly as a cow and an ox is sold, for they never grant them without money. The suffragen of Ely did ask master John Purgold eleven shillings and the offering for hallowing St Edward's in Cambridge: yes, and he would not usually do it so cheap, but only because he had a goddaughter buried in the churchyard. And this may be proved by other answers you know. For bring forth one church in England that you have hallowed without money, or without hope of money, and I will grant my conclusion false.[3]

In passages like these, closely-packed and crackling with invective, we recognize one who 'stamped English-speaking Christianity with ... a concern for morality as the clue to theology and the core of religion'.[4] The pope—variously styled 'an adder' and 'this wretched idol'[5]—is upbraided for making it 'heresy and high treason against the king's grace'[6] for ordinary people to read the Scriptures. How could antichrist be better known, asks Barnes, than by this assault on God's design of grace? Despite having 'no wife, nor ever went about to marry, I thank God of his grace',[7] Barnes also excoriated Rome's celibate ideal. He saw that 'in marriage are many things that doth disturb and distract a man's mind'.[8] He deemed his own chastity a gift from God. But he was alert to the danger of extrapolating too much from his own experience. For Barnes, matrimony was, first and foremost, a God-

1 Parker, 559–560.
2 Parker, 521.
3 Ibid. 522.
4 William Clebsch, quoted in Maas, 10.
5 Parker, 155.
6 Ibid. 613.
7 Ibid. 330.
8 Ibid. 295.

appointed and 'singular medicine for [the] disease'[1] of sexual immorality. Virginity itself, he wrote, was 'no nearer way to heaven than marriage is'.[2]

Elsewhere in *A Supplication* Barnes draws a bead on Cuthbert Tunstall, the bishop of London. Tunstall had berated William Tyndale for disobeying the Constitutions of Oxford, which expressly forbad any attempts to translate the Bible without the approval of the bishops. A later injunction would deem it unlawful to buy or own an English Bible. Beginning in March 1526, three thousand copies of Tyndale's New Testament, printed in the German city of Worms, had arrived as contraband in the docks and warehouses of London. Another edition, printed in Antwerp, appeared in the summer of 1530. Unbound copies could be bought at the house of Simon Fish by the White Friars, or more usually in Honey Lane, near the church of All Hallows. The curate at All Hallows was Thomas Garrett (q.v.), future martyr, former Cambridge student and an ingenious smuggler of every kind of evangelical text.

In every district, in all walks of life, a fierce desire to possess the Holy Scriptures was possessing the citizenry. Through the ministry of the Word, cast in the vernacular, the Holy Spirit was shining in the hearts of cobblers, weavers, bricklayers and servants to give them the light of the knowledge of God. It was nothing less than a sensation. At Paul's Cross, outside the cathedral's west door, bishop Tunstall, convinced of its capacity to 'infect and contaminate the flock committed to us, with the pestilent poison and the deadly disease of heretical depravity',[3] declaimed with sullen ferocity against Tyndale's work. It was strewn with errors, he said, and should be burned. Barnes, for his part, accuses Tunstall of being 'so blinded, and so obstinate against Christ, that you would rather all the world perish than His doctrine be brought to light'.[4] For the English Lutheran, the voice of Christ and the pure text of the Word were indivisible. Any church that looked to the church fathers for its authority was groping after an illusory security. 'I have the Holy Word of God and our master Christ', he said, 'which is elder than our fathers; I also have the practice of the holy apostles who understand these things better than all your councils'.[5]

The church hierarchy was convinced that the availability of the Bible in

1   Ibid. 290.
2   Ibid. 295.
3   Quoted in Brian H. Edwards, *God's Outlaw* (Darlington, 1986), 92.
4   Parker, 614.
5   Quoted in Maas, 84.

WHITHER GOD BRINGS US

English would plunge the nation into anarchy and schism. Such anxiety is easily understood. You cannot, after all, have the beginning of something new without the end of something old. These men had been guided all their lives by the religious, judicial and administrative authority of the Roman church. As such they were slaves to a tradition that saw itself as a source of revelation independent of the Bible. And here was Tyndale translating the Greek word *presbyteros* as 'senior' rather than 'priest'; *ekklesia* as 'congregation' not 'church'; 'charity' became 'love' and 'confess' became 'acknowledge'. This was consistent with the doctrine of the priesthood of all believers, set out by Martin Luther in a publication of 1520. God, declared Luther, is equally accessible to all who come to Him through a living faith. There is no spiritual aristocracy. The priesthood is not qualified to mediate between God and man. This represented a seismic shift: away from the institutions of the church, towards local congregations of believers. Small wonder that for Tunstall, Tyndale's book had about it 'a damnable colour and a deadly reason of the devil';[1] or that Thomas More, Tunstall's great friend, accounted Tyndale one of the 'hell-hounds that the devil has in his kennel'.[2] Both would conspire to have Richard Bayfield (q.v.), James Bainham and John Tewkesbury executed for proclaiming the doctrine revealed to them in Tyndale's text. Barnes, in *A Supplication*, denounces as 'holy hypocrisy' Tunstall's efforts to staunch such obvious outflowings of the Holy Spirit: 'To be ignorant in Scriptures', he opined, 'is to be ignorant of Christ':

> Take away Christ's Word and what remaineth behind of Christ? Nothing at all. I pray to you my lord, to whom was this Word first preached? To whom was it written? Only to priests and not to laymen? Was it not written to all the world? Yes truly. Whereby will you convert a Turk or an infidel? Not by holy Scripture? When they be converted, what will you teach them? What will you give them to read?[3]

Barnes warns his readers that tradition is the word of man as much as Scripture is the Word of God. And in order to establish that the pope is 'not of God' we must 'perfectly know what is Christ. Not only by name, for that the antichrist grants, but we must search out the property, and the

---

1   Parker, 613.
2   Quoted in David Daniell, *Tyndale's New Testament* (New Haven, 1989), p. xxix.
3   Parker, 614.

nature, and the very effect of Christ, and that we shall know Him: In holy Scripture Christ is nothing else but a Saviour, a Redeemer, a Justifier, and a perfect peacemaker between God and man'.[1] Only when human beings accept Christ in each of these offices will they drink supreme felicity from His fountain of light. They will renounce their 'stoney and woody images',[2] their praying to saints, and all forms of works righteousness. As instruments of the Holy Spirit they will tear up 'the pope's licence'[3] and exhibit instead the will and inclination to help their neighbour who is in need. Those fastened to the Father through the Son are liberated from the tyranny of self-interest:

> Wherefore if you will truly honour the image of God we will open that thing unto you that is of truth, so that you must do well unto man the which is made unto the image of God, give him honour and reverence. Give him meat when he is hungry. Give him drink when he is thirsty. Clothe him when he is naked. Serve him when he is sick. Give him lodging when he is a stranger, and when he is in prison minister to him: this is the thing that shall be counted to be given God truly.[4]

And yet, says Barnes, hordes of idolaters spurn this glorious image and 'run to Walsingham and Ipswich with great pomp and pride to honour dead shadows'.[5] Barnes tells them it would be 'better for you to burn these idols and warm the true image of God there'.[6] If they would only lean on the Word of God inscripturated, and apprehend by faith His blessing, 'they should perfectly know that they need no more than this won Christ, and that they should seek no other mediator to obtain anything else to make them worthy'.[7] What was needed was a transformation of society into close-knit communities in which 'the Maker and Lord of all rewards'[8] would reign over everyday life. This raw honesty led him to be viewed with suspicion by Henry VIII. One of the startling aspects of *A Supplication* is the candour with which Barnes addresses his notoriously thin-skinned monarch. For

---

1 Ibid. 531.
2 Ibid. 665.
3 Ibid. 173.
4 Ibid. 665.
5 Ibid.
6 Ibid.
7 Ibid. 656.
8 Ibid. 555.

the English Lutheran, moderation in the Gospel cause was no virtue, just
lack of conviction dressed up in fancy clothes. Having called upon Henry
to 'defend this poor and simple labour of mine from the violence of the
bishops',[1] he doesn't hesitate to remind him of his 'tytylle [of] defender of the
faith'.[2] Nor does he flinch from directing the king's attention to the eternal
consequences of not making the Bible the foundation of all true religion.
'How were your grace able to answer to it', he wrote, 'before the dreadful
throne of Jesus Christ? This present life is short, and soon faileth us. But
if we suffer the godly Word of the everlasting God to be overtrodden and
oppressed by violence, there remains nothing to us but everlasting woe and
damnation, for we are lost forever'.[3]

---

1   Ibid.
2   Ibid.
3   Ibid.

SELECT BIBLIOGRAPHY

Ackroyd, Peter, *The History of England,* (London: Pan Books, 2012)
—*The Life of Thomas More* (London: Chatto & Windus, rep. 1999).

Batley, J.Y., *On a Reformer's Latin Bible, being an Essay on the Adversaria in the Vulgate of Thomas Bilney* (Cambridge: Deighton, Bell & Co., Ltd, 1940).

Bradford, John, *The Writings of John Bradford* (Cambridge: Parker Society, 1848 and 1853; fac. Edinburgh: Banner of Truth Trust, 1979).

Beilin, Elaine, *The Examinations of Anne Askew* (Oxford: OUP, 1996).

Brown, Andrew: *Robert Ferrar: Yorkshire Monk, Reformation Bishop and Martyr in Wales* (London: Inscriptor Imprints, 1997).

Bucer, Martin: *Concerning the True Care of Souls* (Edinburgh: Banner of Truth Trust, rep., 2009).

Burnett, Amy Nelson: *The Yoke of Christ: Martin Bucer and Christian Discipline* (Kirksville: Sixteenth Century Journal Publishers, 1994).

Cattley, Stephen Reed (ed.), *The Acts and Monuments of John Foxe* (London: Seeley & Burnside, 8 vols., 1837–1841).

Coverdale, Miles, *The Letters of the Martyrs* (London:1564; London: J.F. Shaw, rep.,1837).

Crisman, Miriam Usher, *Strasbourg and Reform* (New Haven: Yale University Press, 1967).

Clebsch, William A., *England's Earliest Protestants 1520–1535* (New Haven: Yale University Press, 1964).

Collinson, Patrick, *Archbishop Grindal 1519–1583: The Struggle for a Reformed Church* (London: Jonathan Cape, 1979).

Corrie, George Elwes (ed.), *Sermons by Hugh Latimer* (Cambridge: Parker Society, 1844).

Dickens, A.G., *The English Reformation* (London: English Universities Press, 1964).

Evenden, Elizabeth and Freeman, Thomas, *Religion and the Book in Early Modern England* (Cambridge: CUP, 2011).

Gorham, George Cornelius, *Gleanings of a Few Scattered Ears During the Reformation in England and of Times Immediately Succeeding: 1533 to 1588* (London: Bell & Daldy, 1857).

Greschat, Martin, *Martin Bucer: A Reformer and His Times* (Louisville: Westminster/John Knox Press, 1984).

Hillerbrand, Hans J. (editor-in-chief): *The Oxford Encyclopedia of the Reformation*, four volumes (Oxford University Press: New York, 4 vols., 1996).

Hopf, Constantin, *Martin Bucer and the English Reformation* (Oxford: Basil Blackwell, 1946).

Ives, Eric, *Lady Jane Grey* (Malden: Wiley-Blackwell, 2009).

Jeanes, Gordon P., *Signs of God's Promise: Thomas Cranmer's Sacramental Theology and the Book of Common Prayer* (London: T. & T. Clark, 2008).

Kittelson, James M., *Wolfgang Capito: From Humanist to Reformer* (Leiden: E. J. Brill, 1975).

Knott, John R., *Discourses of Martyrdom in English Literature 1563–1694* (Cambridge: CUP, 1993).

Loane, Marcus, *Masters of the English Reformation* (London: CBR Press, 1954).

MacCulloch, Diarmaid, *Thomas Cranmer* (New Haven & London: Yale University Press, 1996).

Martin, Joseph William, *Religious Radicals in Tudor England* (London: Hambledon Press, 1989).

Marshall, Peter and Ryrie, Alec (eds.), *The Beginnings of English Protestantism* (Cambridge: CUP, 2002).

McLelland, Joseph C., *Peter Martyr Vermigli: The Oxford Treatise and Disputation on the Eucharist, 1549* (Kirksville: Sixteenth Century Essays & Studies, 2000).

McClendon, Muriel, *The Quiet Reformation* (Redwood City, Calif., Stanford University Press, 1999).

McGrath, Alister, *Christianity's Dangerous Idea* (London: SPCK, 2007).

McNair, Philip, *Peter Martyr in Italy* (Oxford: Clarendon Press, 1967).

More, Thomas, *Complete Works of Thomas More* (New Haven & London: Yale, 1979),

Moule, H.C.G. (ed.), *Nicholas Ridley: A Brief Declaration of the Lord's Supper* (London: Seeley & Co., 1895).

Moynahan, Brian, *If God Spare My Life* (London: Little, Brown, 2002).

Mozley, J.F., *John Foxe and His Book* (New York: Octogon Books, rep., 1970).

Parker, Douglas H. (ed.), *A Critical Edition of Robert Barnes's 'A Supplication Unto the Most Gracyous Prince Kynge Henry the VIII, 1534'* (Toronto: University of Toronto Press, 2008).

Pauck, Wilhelm (ed.), *Melanchthon and Bucer* (Louisville: Westminster/John Knox Press, 1969).

Pearse, M.T., *Between Known Men and Visible Saints: A Study in Sixteenth-Century English Dissent* (Madison, NJ.: Fairleigh Dickenson University Press, 1994).

Potter, G.R., *Zwingli* (Cambridge: CUP, 1976).

Rex, Richard, *The Theology of John Fisher* (Cambridge: CUP, 1991).

Rupp E.G., *The Making of the English Protestant Tradition* (Cambridge: CUP, 1966).

Shirley, T.F., *Thomas Thirlby: Tudor Bishop* (London: SPCK, 1964).

Tjernagel, Neelak S. (ed.), *The Reformation Essays of Dr Robert Barnes* (London: Concordia Ltd, 1963).

Strype, John, *Ecclesiastical Memorials,* 3 vols. in 6 (Oxford, 1822).

Trueman, Carl, *Luther's Legacy: Salvation and the English Reformers 1525–1556* (Oxford: Clarendon Press, 1994).

Vander Zee, Leonard J., *Christ, Baptism and the Lord's Supper* (Illinois: IVP, 2004).

Wandell, Lee Palmer, *Images of the Poor in Zwingli's Zürich* (Cambridge: CUP, 1990).

Williams, Glanmor, *The Welsh and their Religion* (Cardiff: University of Wales Press, 1991).

Wright, D.F. (ed.), *Martin Bucer: Reforming Church and Community* (Cambridge: CUP, 1994).

Wright, N.T. (ed.), *The Work of John Frith* (Oxford: Sutton Courtenay Press, 1978).

Wriothesley, Charles, *A Chronicle of England during the Reigns of the Tudors,* ed. W.D. Hamilton, 2 vols., (London: Camden Society, 1875–7).

INDEX OF SCRIPTURE

Index of Names

A

B

C

THE AUTHOR

David Llewellyn Jenkins is the author of *SAUMUR REDUX: Josué de la Place & the Question of Adam's Sin*. He divides his time between Norfolk and Ceredigion.

Lightning Source UK Ltd.
Milton Keynes UK
UKHW01n1218060518
322134UK00002B/26/P